The Healing of a Person with Dissociative Identity Disorder

by
Debra Bruch

2nd Edition

Debra Bruch

Bruwicked Productions • South Range, Michigan, USA

A Bruwicked Productions Original

2nd Edition Copyright © 2016 Debra Bruch

Copyright © 2015 Debra Bruch

ISBN: 978-1530410705

2nd Edition

The cover photo is a 1917 picture of the actual barn at "The Farm."

This printed book is a shortened version of the ebook.

This book is copyright material. Apart from any fair dealing for the purpose of private study, research, teaching, criticism, or review, no part may be copied, reproduced, transferred, distributed, leased, licensed or publically performed or used in any way under which it was purchased without written permission. Any unauthorized distribution, including digital or print, or use of this text may be a direct infringement of the author's and/or Bruwicked Productions' rights and those responsible may be liable in law accordingly.

Names have been changed except for Debra Bruch (her parts), Bruce, and Frances S. Waters. (Bruce and Mrs. Waters not changed with permission.) All writings attributed to Bruce and Mrs. Waters are published with permission. Any resemblance to persons, living or dead, or location is entirely coincidental.

Fractured Mind: the Healing of a Person with Dissociative Identity Disorder chronicles the healing process of a person suffering from DID. The disorder happened due to a long sustained period of traumatic violence during childhood. The book depicts the working of the subconscious and how it reveals itself layer upon layer from the surface of the subconscious to its depth. With hope and the support of amazing people, and at times the teaching and intervention of God, angels, and the Holy Spirit, a reformation of the psyche takes place. This book is a witness of the living Christ. Warning: this book is for adults only due to explanations of sexual and physical violence causing dissociation at an early age.

Dedication

Fractured Mind is dedicated to all children who experience violence.

IT MUST END

Table of Contents

FRACTURED MIND: 1
THE HEALING OF A PERSON WITH DISSOCIATIVE IDENTITY DISORDER
   Dedication 3

TABLE OF CONTENTS 4

FOREWORD 6
FRAN S. WATERS, DCSW, LMSW, LMFT
   Author of Healing the Fractured Child: Diagnosis and Treatment of Youth with Dissociation

FRACTURED MIND 11
   INTRODUCTION 12

SECTION ONE: VIOLENCE 22
   CHAPTER ONE 23
      Subconscious Level 1: The Fab Five
   CHAPTER TWO 77
      Subconscious Level 2: Scott (7) Wakes Up
   CHAPTER THREE: FAB FIVE BLENDING 151

SECTION TWO: EMOTIONAL CONSEQUENCES OF TRAUMA 168
   CHAPTER FOUR 170
      Subconscious Level 3: Lucas (7) and Anna Marie (24) Wake Up
   CHAPTER FIVE 188
      Subconscious Level 4: James (12) Wakes Up

SECTION THREE: RITUAL RAPE 202
   CHAPTER SIX 203
      Subconscious Level 5: Laura (4) Wakes Up
   CHAPTER SEVEN 220
      Subconscious Level 6: John (14 - 20) and Ephrin (14) Wake Up
   CHAPTER EIGHT 247
      Debra/Laura Grows

SECTION FOUR: RELEASING TRAUMA FROM THE BODY 261
   CHAPTER NINE 262
      Subconscious Level 7: Billy (7) Wakes Up
   CHAPTER TEN 286
      Subconscious Level 8: Alexandria (4) and Adama (15) Wake Up; Billy ages from 7 to 10
   CHAPTER ELEVEN 300
      Subconscious Level 9: Angela (8) Wakes Up
      Angela ages 8 to 13 and Billy 10 to 11
   CHAPTER TWELVE 308
      Subconscious Level 10: Joshua (14) Wakes Up

CHAPTER THIRTEEN 316
   Subconscious Level 11: Heather (4) Wakes Up

SECTION FIVE: CHANGING IDENTITY 323
CHAPTER FOURTEEN 324
   Subconscious Level 12: Francis (16) and Joel (8) Wake Up

SECTION SIX: THE MOTHER ISSUE 353
CHAPTER FIFTEEN 354
   Subconscious Level 13: Kate (13), Shaun (10), Cole (8), Joseph (38), David (7), and Baby Lynn (infant) Wake Up

SECTION SEVEN: COVEN AND SATANIC RITES 426
CHAPTER SIXTEEN 427
   Subconscious Level 14: Michael (6), Dawn (14), Baby Heart (infant) and Isaac (6) Wake Up

SECTION EIGHT: NEW FAMILY 457
CHAPTER SEVENTEEN 458
   Patrick (4), Timmy (3), Shannon (13) and Kale (14) Wake Up

EPILOGUE 475

ABOUT THE AUTHOR 477

OTHER BOOKS BY DEBRA BRUCH 479

Foreword

By

Fran S. Waters, DCSW, LMSW, LMFT

Author of *Healing the Fractured Child: Diagnosis and Treatment of Youth with Dissociation*

Dr. Debra Bruch walked into my office about five years ago and began to talk in a quiet, articulate manner about her traumatic past. I listened intently and was amazed at her ability to recount the chronology of her known life at that time that was replete with considerable betrayal by her parents and their ongoing, horrific acts during her childhood. I admired her fortitude, but was perplexed at how well she managed to build a functional life. I wondered what made that possible for her to achieve an illustrious career and to have maintained healthy relationships. I pondered what else might she discover about herself while I suspected more dissociation, given her persistent symptoms. Dr. Bruch had been aware of some dissociative states many years earlier for which she sought treatment. I suspected there were still more hidden parts of herself and more traumas yet to be learned that affected her recurring severe depression, anxiety, and unexplained and intense somatic pain.

This personal story will give the reader a window view of the inner workings of a fractured mind and the courageous healing that occurred in this remarkable woman. Dissociation was Debra's only escape. Dissociation is an instinctive, automatic survival defense mechanism of freezing, immobilization, and numbing when the child has no choice - when fleeing and fighting are simply not an option. The most extreme form of dissociation is separating from the self to survive by developing parts of the self to hold traumatic memories, feelings, thoughts and bodily sensations that were simply impossible for a young child to endure. These parts would take control over Debra's body for which she had no control and awareness. This condition is called Dissociative Identity Disorder.

Dr. Bruch instinctively and unconsciously developed parts of herself as a defense in order for her to remove herself from the horrors of what transpired from an early age until she could escape at seventeen years old. Parts of her took bits and pieces of what simply was intolerable for any human being to endure alone. These memories were securely encapsulated in her unconscious. At seventeen years old, Damon emerged, walked away from her parent's farm, and went out into an unknown world. He was completely void of any earlier training, preparation or knowledge of what to expect or do. The reader will have first hand information - an intimate front seat view of Deb's inner life -

and her healing journey of five years, when the hidden selves became no longer hidden and their secrets were no longer secrets.

This story is not only about her trauma and dissociation, but it is more about Dr. Bruch's incredible healing - her courage and strength to face what was unfathomably done repeatedly to a young, vulnerable child. I have pondered much about how Debra could continuously muster the energy to keep moving forward in her recovery as she faithfully entered my office week after week. I wondered what were the critical elements of her determination and steady voyage to heal. I see several critical elements that played significantly in her recovery, for which she details clearly in her book.

One of the crucial elements is the power of relationships. This is truly a story of one's ability to develop the capacity to form enduring and healthy relationships, in spite of early and ongoing torture and absolute betrayal by her parents and others. Debra's inquisitive and intelligent mind observed and studied other people and how they lived their lives differently from the one that she had experienced. She used this knowledge as a roadmap to live a different life void of abuse. When Dr. Bruch was seventeen years old, unbeknownst to Dr. Bruch, Damon emerged and walked away from her parents' farm not knowing anything about how to provide a livelihood. He lived on the street and began to attend college. Dr. Bruch always had a thirst for knowledge that propelled her as Damon to learn what he/she could about life as if "newly born" in this world.

Early on in her adult life, she sought out and connected with caring people - church mentors and parental figures and therapists that provided the fuel for Dr. Bruch to connect with the unknown parts of herself, to rebuild her identity, and to become an integrated self. It was a slow, arduous journey for Debra to reframe her past image of herself as unworthy and to see that she was worthy to be cared for and loved by others and, most importantly, loved by herself. It is through these healthy attachments that Debra was able to see how other people related to her and each other, and to learn from them. This process was the beginning of reconstructing her identity. It was a careful process, as you will read about, in which trust in others and in herself was a relentless and at times intimidating equation to sort out.

The reader will view this process of Dr. Bruch consolidating her identity particularly through constant emails that focused on how her adopted "dad," Bruce, guides her and all parts of her, as a parent would guide, direct, and nurture his own biological child from infancy to adulthood. Bruce accepted her in totality - meaning acknowledging and parenting each part that emerged over many years, demonstrating amazing insight and, particularly, without judgment. His display of a remarkable and uncanny ability to understand her complicated system of selves and to treat them with respect and caring, while acknowledging their unique needs, gave all parts of Dr. Bruch a chance to grow up - to develop within a nurturing relationship. Debra's selves were truly able to move from their tortuous first life marked by recurring painful traumatic memories and betrayals to the second life in which they were able to recognize the notable difference between the two. The dialogue can inspire others to model such empathy and skill with children and adults who have experienced severe trauma and dissociation.

Dr. Bruch's commitment to heal was notable by her determination to travel two hours each way to my office weekly for five years, even during snow blizzards and slippery roads. I knew that I could depend on Debra to show up in spite of inclement weather. Such a drive literally and figuratively can inspire other survivors to stay in the undoubtedly painful process while still encountering obstacles. Dr. Bruch knew when she entered my office that she was going to face pain, that she was going to explore the origin of her disturbing dreams, the layers of her mind - her selves - and discover the underlying source of the terrifying and painful somatic feelings. We forged a close therapeutic relationship and I had the honor over time to be trusted by her parts as they emerged and engaged with me in their healing. I admired and accepted each of them - even those who initially appeared threatening. I understood that their threats were a protection from harm, and I validated their feelings while negotiating with them to reframe their angry behavior (usually directed at Debra) in a positive role. This respectful approach facilitated them to trust me and engage in treatment with me as they recognized that I appreciated what they had to do to survive.

This truly is a story of each part telling their story from their own perspective that entailed their different ages, different genders, different traumatic experiences and specific traumatic roles that they carried. This is a chronology of often the cold, hard facts of child abuse. This is a story of the heartbreaking realization of how Dr. Bruch's parents can subject a child to such cruelty, and the arduous process of recognizing and reconciling the difference of the first life of abuse from the second life free of its traumatic clutches, as Debra processed in therapy what occurred. There were many mixed moments of fear, pain, tears, humor and laughter that we shared together. I encouraged Dr. Bruch's honesty with me and accepted and listened when she differed with me on an approach. It was truly a team approach between her and her parts and me, as we forged ahead session by session.

This is also an amazing story of faith – the other critical and inspiring essential that propelled her to move forward in her healing - when she felt so unglued. Dr. Bruch's belief in God and her connection with what she entitles the Other Realm, the spirit life beyond this earthly realm, and how the spirit world played an integral role in her healing. It is an astounding story of Debra's spiritual connections - her faith that held her and kept her from slipping forever into an abyss or into a constant state of immobilization and despondency. Through the strength she received from the Other Realm, she was able to repeatedly learn about her emerging parts and experience with them the terrors that were hidden for decades in her unconsciousness, and particularly lodged in her body that suffered perplexing pain, until their source was revealed and resolved. However, there were times that Dr. Bruch felt immobilized. She did not want to go outside, wanted to say in bed, but her faith and relationships with others, including the Other Realm, lifted her up every morning to go to the university and teach, and to engage in social and church activities.

You will enter into this sacred realm and learn how Grandfather, a man in this earthly world who transcended into the Other Realm, had also raised and nurtured her. It was difficult for me to understand this relationship and we had many discussions when I would think it was a part of her - a self-state that she incorporated into her identity, a man she knew and admired in her earthly life. However, Debra was clear that it was not and clearly differentiated Grandfather from her parts. She described how she would enter the Other Realm and saw Grandfather in the spirit world grieving for what she experienced - something he did not know about in this earthly world. He also held and nurtured her little young parts. Dr. Bruch also experienced angels, Mother Mary and God who played specific roles in nurturing and healing her and her parts when Debra recalled horrific abuse. All of these spiritual figures truly anchored her and gave her strength so she could rise every morning to perform her collegial responsibilities. No one at the university had any idea of what was encapsulated within her and what she experienced the previous night or even that morning. I truly admired her capacity and endurance. Dr. Bruch's dissociation - her temporary ability to segment off horrific memories and even parts of herself - actually allowed her to function. However at home and in my office, those memories crept slowly into her consciousness as parts of her emerged and released their once-hidden defenses. One after another part of her appeared, and slowly and methodically worked diligently with me to release their traumatic past and heal.

I would sit in my mauve cushioned rocking chair close to Dr. Bruch, as she would often lie on the couch while a new part emerged to meet me. As our bond and her trust in me grew, Debra needed to have that proximity to me to feel the human connection. I was her anchor, as well, to hold and sustain her during trauma processing. As I sat close to her, I wondered what was the difference between Debra who did not abuse others, and those other survivors who did. While no doubt the capacity to develop healthy attachments and her faith played a significant role later in her life, I queried her about what kept her from hurting others when as a child and young adult. She sat for a pregnant moment in deep thought looking away, then looked at me and in that same steady voice recalled when she was around fourteen years old seeing Holocaust pictures of skeleton men, women and children. She looked at them and recognized the common human suffering that she and they had shared - one with which she was so familiar. At that moment, she drew strength within herself to begin to feel her own hidden pain that began to rise to the surface. Dr. Bruch's ability to feel her own pain appeared to be the safeguard for her not to hurt others. She could empathize with others' sufferings and did not want to incur that on anyone else. Other survivors can gain strength from Debra's endurance to manage her suffering and to recognize a commonality in all human suffering, and be inspired and hopeful to face their own pain and to forge ahead in their own recovery.

The reader will be taken on an astonishing journey of honesty, courage, resilience and faith of an individual who was able to overcome the first seventeen years of a horrendous abusive life, and develop a new life free from the clutches of her traumatic past. This story is truly inspirational for all who have experienced trauma, for clinicians, and for those who want to understand deeply about the inner workings of the mind with different selves, and how healthy relationships and faith can help one to survive from such severe adversities and thrive. It is a remarkable story of healing and fierce determination to truly reclaim one's life free from the grips of the past.

Fractured Mind:
The Healing of a Person with Dissociative Identity Disorder
Debra Bruch

I will never understand why a parent would torture a child. While I can accept the reason why to be mental sickness or a seriously flawed childhood so the parent acts toward a child the way he was acted upon, I think that reasoning is incomplete. I think the implications are far more serious than that. It's a darkness of the soul. For whatever reason, the parent cracks open a chasm into himself, letting something in, something that creeps in and silently corrupts, creating a hunger for the dark. The dark creates an illusion of the self – empowering a separation from humanity resulting in terrible action. But at some point, it was a choice. It was a choice.

I have a mental disorder called Dissociative Identity Disorder. Except for a bout of anti-depressants, I did not and do not take medication. It is not schizophrenia. Schizophrenia is a mental illness marked by the person not being able to perceive reality. DID, that used to be known as Multiple Personality Disorder, is not a mental illness but a mental disorder that happens when a child is seriously traumatized over a long period of time, usually by his or her own parents. DID is the way the child can survive and function in real life, due to a part of a child holding the trauma and the other part of the child cannot remember or know the trauma. By not remembering or knowing, the child can keep perceiving reality accurately enough to successfully function in society. This way, a child who is fractured into parts can live and function in life into adulthood; in other words, DID is a disorder that KEEPS the person mentally healthy.

As a child, I had no real concept of God. I stood at the face of torture, pain, fear, and despair alone. I felt alone, utterly and completely alone. No matter which part of me was out and living daily life, that part always felt alone and afraid. The very core of me connecting to all of me knew little more than despair and loneliness and fear. I felt completely, utterly without worth to be loved. I thought everybody felt alone. I thought that feeling alone and afraid was life as it should be, although watching television and seeing something different caused me to question my living. Every part of me also thought that every child felt as I did, and that I deserved to feel badly. The parts of me who took the pain thought that all parents hurt children and I deserved to be hurt. And so I was. And yet, God WAS there. Did he let it happen? Yes. The why, though, is so profound, so unlike my own sense of justice and love that it hurts to even ponder it.

Sometime during my healing, I recognized that God kept me mentally healthy by way of Dissociative Identity Disorder. And I saw that God was with me all along, not only through my healing, but throughout my entire life. God helped me live and actually thrive and gain an education and a job and live well in society according to my capabilities by allowing my trauma to fracture my mind. The trauma took a toll on me, no doubt about that. But I have been mentally stable. And that's the miracle.

As I write this manuscript, my healing has progressed to the point that I am nearly integrated. I suspect that I will always be DID and not "normal" the way most people are. I will be an integrated DID. A person can't really change life-experiences and I will always know and feel the echoes of my various parts. Time will tell if I'm right or not.

I am neither a therapist nor a psychologist. While at some point during my therapy I read about it, I have no expertise in DID. I simply am DID, and this manuscript reflects my own experiences as a DID. Others having Dissociative Identity Disorder may have similar experiences and some may have different experiences; I am unable to write for anyone else.

This story tells of a journey of healing. It's a story of horror and of hope.

Introduction

A few years prior to the beginning of this healing journey, I became aware that I was a multiple. At that time, the understanding of Dissociative Identity Disorder was in its infancy. I thought that my experiences were that of multiple personalities, mainly because my therapist at that time told me I was a multiple. But calling this phenomenon of the psyche multiple personalities is a misunderstanding. While a "personality" often seems to be a separate person, they are in actuality different parts of one person. Each is a different state of consciousness. Each part responds to his or her world differently (and consequently seem to be different people) because during my formative years each part had different experiences and developed according to those experiences. For instance, one part experienced the beginning of torture but dissociated and another experienced the acute physical pain of the same torture. Furthermore, each part drew upon a particular set of characteristics of the whole person in order to handle the experiences he or she encountered. So whilst each part came from the whole, experiences and the mix of personal characteristics differed. This somewhat explains why each part seems to be different in personality from the others.

Background

Five parts of me woke up a few years prior to this healing process: Philip, Nils, Little Debra, Damon, and The Adult (Deb). The host at that time was The Adult or Deb. The host part is the part in control of the body and lives day by day.

During my chronological childhood, no part knew of the existence of the other parts. Over time during my present healing, each of the other parts came from the subconscious to the surface of my mind and by awakening, all the parts then knew of the existence of the other parts who awakened. Not only did each become aware of the others, but the past experiences of my trauma also became known. When those past experiences came to the surface of my psyche during this healing process, those experiences became a common memory.

Each part of me resided in the subconscious and was stuck in the trauma. That is, my subconscious lived the traumatic experience over and over and had no way to stop. My psyche separated into parts during chronological childhood and became the way for me to survive. When each part came to the surface, then, work had to be done in order for that part to no longer be stuck in the trauma. Also, thinking often needed to change as well as a need to gain a sense of safety.

Several years before my healing process, I experienced a vision explaining my healing. I was too damaged to be healed by therapy alone. My parents had severely traumatized me during my formative years so I had to be reformed. I had to grow up all over again, but this time in love instead of violence. The vision included the image of a dirt road lined on both sides with barbed wire. Beyond the barbed wire were meadows. The vision told me that I am unable to travel past the barbed wire, but as long as I walked down the road, I was okay. My healing allowed me to enter the meadows and live life fully.

Throughout my life except when Damon was host, I knew the broad feelings and memories of growing up, but I did not know the specific actions or the traumatic experiences of my parts until this healing process brought subconscious to conscious. Throughout the years, every time I talked about my past, my body grew very cold. The cold made me shake. I never knew why I turned so very cold, but now I suspect it was due to tendrils of memory touching the trauma.

Bruce

Bruce was and is an important factor in my healing process. He and I had been friends for over ten years and he was my mentor for church ministry. During the healing process, the "dialogue" between each part of me and Bruce were emails over the several years it took for me to heal. The healing process included one or more parts awakening, reliving the trauma, becoming released from the trauma, and integrating into the whole of me. Bruce accepted the responsibility to see me through my healing process.

With the support of his family, Bruce raised me as each child part awakened, with all the problems, wonder, and difficulties of childhood. The healing process was not just to awaken and integrate, but also to be repaired. The foundation of all of me had to be rebuilt. This was Bruce's outrageously awesome generosity because he decided to raise me. That was a difficult aspect of the healing process. He did not know what he was getting himself into. Neither did I. Due to Bruce's influence, each child part experienced a change from fear to trust. Each child part was reformed before each was able to integrate.

Bruce quickly became Dad. His role was to parent the child parts. He continues to be Dad today, but the relationship is appropriately adult to adult.

Before my healing process began, I visited Bruce and his family for a couple of days one summer. He strongly urged me to exercise. My problem was that I had no idea what I was doing, so he took on the responsibility to teach me some life-lessons about how to exercise correctly and eat right. When I began to exercise, my body was moving in such a way that I was feeling a great deal of emotional pain. I did not understand why, but I began to rebel almost immediately. I cussed a lot.

Bruce: How does cussing honor God in your life?

Deb: I don't know how cussing honors God in my life. I don't know how eating honors God either. Not giving you a hard time. I don't.

Bruce: It is called stewardship over body, mind and spirit. What you put in makes a difference as to what comes out, what you eat, what you think, how you pray, what language you use inside and out, whether you are thankful everyday. They are all connected to your holiness, to your ability to express your divinity – the spirit that lives in you that expresses the unconditional love of God as best as you can. Your cussing inhibits that, your poor diet inhibits that, your lack of exercise inhibited that. Proof? Take an inventory about how you feel since you started eating right, exercising. Look at the blessings you have received in the past months. Need more proof???

After a few weeks, the emotional pain stimulated by exercising became very intense. I wanted to quit, but Bruce more than urged me to continue. My inner conflict caused the (then) four parts of me to explode to the surface of my psyche with such swiftness and painful violence that I immediately bled. It was like being a volcano. I could not contain the parts in me any longer. They did not want to come to the surface, but when they did, it was so forceful and fast that suddenly I felt and saw a bright light, my body jerked, and they were at the surface again. It hurt. I very hesitantly told Bruce that I was separated, that is, in parts, and that I'd known about it for several years and that I had thought I was integrated until that time. I also told him their ages. He accepted me, accepted the parts, and began a relationship that changed my life.

Parts

Dissociation means my mind, my psyche, fractured into two or more parts. I prefer the word "parts" instead of "personalities" or "people" because "parts" is more accurate to the disorder. However, parts seemed to me to be people when I lived as a DID. I often write "we" or "they" throughout this manuscript when discussing parts. Naming a part not only helped differentiate one from another, it honored the unique experiences and the mix of personality traits inherent within an individual part.

As mentioned, the host part controlled the body and lived most of daily life. During chronological life, only six parts dissociated to live daily life. The earliest host parts are Laura and Little Debra. I am unable to tell which was host until four years old when Laura went to sleep in the subconscious. At nearly six years old, Little Debra dissociated and went to sleep. Philip then was the host part until my life changed when I left the Amundsons. Philip dissociated, went to sleep, and Damon was the host part until I became older. Damon went to sleep and I became what the others called The Adult.

Being "out" is different than being a host part. The host part lived chronological life; the "out" part controlled the body after parts started to wake up, so there were more than one part living daily life. After the parts started to wake and come to the conscious surface, one part was always "out" to control the body and live daily life. The other parts that had awakened continued to be active in my conscious psyche and often aware of what the "out" part was doing. Very often it felt as if a part was looking over the shoulder of the part that was "out".

First-life - Second-life

I call the second-life to be from the beginning point of my healing process to the present. The first-life happened during my chronological childhood when the trauma happened. But the first-life extends to the beginning of my healing process as well because I lived in a survival mode and also lived the consequences of the trauma. Throughout this document, I speak about the first-life (chronological childhood and life before this healing process) and the second-life (during the healing process to the present).

Relivings

A reliving is a re-experiencing of a past traumatic event. A buried part of a child gets stuck in the trauma, meaning the part of a person does not experience a release of the trauma. But it is as if the part of a person has been continually traumatized, and constantly reliving the trauma over and over in the subconscious. The process of healing triggered various parts of me to come to the surface and relive on the conscious level. We call them relivings because during them on the conscious level we see, hear, feel, taste, and smell the trauma as if it were happening in the moment, even though the traumatic event was not actually happening in the moment. At every reliving, we also re-experienced the fear, pain, sadness, helplessness, and despair that we had during the original trauma. Often in the moment, we could not know that years had gone by between the real event and the reliving. Most of the relivings during this healing process happened when we were alone and at home. We felt safer that way, and also we often screamed. Since nobody could hear, we felt safe doing that. When a part of me writes while experiencing a reliving, I show it in italic font.

Philip, Nils, Damon, and Little Debra knew a portion of their stories of their past trauma at the beginning of our interactions with Bruce. They had their relivings several years prior to the beginning of this journey. However, none of their relivings had been processed completely and their trauma still affected them. Several years before this healing process, a kind man named Ken gave the five parts of me a stable and secure way to handle the relivings and the beginning of the healing. I learnt later that not being able to process completely at the beginning is usual for DID. There seems to be a several year gap between the shock of waking and the ability to finish the healing process. Ken's gift kept me alive and healthy.

Email

As part of healing, the parts of me experienced the relivings by emailing Bruce. Emailing helped pull the images and experiences together, and each part of me was still connected to the trauma when we emailed. Writing to Bruce was much like journaling, but instead of writing to myself, I wrote to Bruce. Emailing helped pull us out of the first-life, out of the trauma, and into the second-life and was a vital component for healing. After the reliving of a part of me had been processed, each part of me integrated.

The emails in this manuscript are real email communications between each part of me and Bruce. They are not reflections after the fact or fabricated dialogue, but copies of email. I edited some spelling errors to be correct, but not all. While they may seem to be face to face dialogue at times, a response took a day, and for some responses, several days or weeks.

Most of my parts are children, boys and girls, but mostly boys. To process relivings and to help heal, nearly all of the parts wrote emails to Bruce. Some of my parts were significantly young, and eventually I noticed a pattern where they could not write, had to "learn" and then they could write. It was like an older part stood over the very young to help them write, not only to physically write on the keyboard but also to help put their words together without telling them what to write. The older parts couldn't do that anyway because they did not know what the child was writing about until the child was actively writing. I always thought that it was God helping me process my healing.

Fran Waters

Throughout the years of my healing process, I was also in deep therapy with Frances S. Waters (DCSW, LMSW, LMFT) who is an internationally known expert in the field of Dissociative Identity Disorder and related trauma. Mrs. Waters specializes in sexual, physical and emotional abuse and dissociation in children and adults. She also conducts forensic evaluations of children suspected to have suffered child abuse. She is an internationally recognized trainer and consultant in the field of childhood trauma, abuse, and dissociation. As an invited presenter, she has conducted extensive training programs nationally and internationally ranging from a day to five days in Europe, Africa, South America, and North America on a variety of related topics.

Fran Waters used her professionalism and techniques to help me draw out a part from my subconscious and process through my trauma to integration. Integration does not happen immediately. Blending happens before integrating. I knew I had blended when I no longer heard or felt a part within me. I could no longer determine a part separate from the rest of me.

Within the manuscript, **Fran's Notes** indicate the notes she took while I was in therapy session. Most of her notes reflect what I say during the session because she knows what she did and her notes help keep track of what I say. I include very little of what I say because the emails between my parts and Bruce cover that.

Fran Waters did not use talk therapy during my sessions with me. Many people associate mental health work with talk therapy. She used EMDR that means Eye Movement Desensitization and Reprocessing Therapy. I held an end of wires in each hand that was connected to a small box that Fran controlled. The end of wires alternated vibrations. It stimulated and connected the synapses of my brain. We called the machine the buzzies. I always got a headache, usually behind the left side of my nose, eye, and forehead. I always thought parts were connecting with each other, but after some research I discovered this technique connected memory to present awareness.

The buzzies did not cause healing by themselves. During the sessions with the buzzies, Fran's positive words toward me helped transform horrific memories to something more positive and broke the cycle of the trauma. When she affirmed me with positive words, the buzzies stimulated both sides of my brain to reorganize where my memories were stored. Once the placement of memories was achieved, I could remember without feeling the trauma. This took a very long time. Unfortunately, my trauma was so severe that it took a great deal of effort from Fran for me to accept the reality of her positive words. She actively developed a bond of trust and, frankly, love for me in order for me to believe her saying anything positive about me. For more information, please see the EMDR Institute Inc. online at http://www.emdr.com

While she worked to help me deal with the trauma, with all its implications, Bruce worked to rebuild by raising the various parts of me who came to the surface over time. The result of both their efforts was a change of how I viewed the world; it changed my understanding, perception, and acceptance of life as well as a change of perception about myself. When the parts healed, they were no longer separate entities but blended. Also, the trauma no longer held any control over the part of me who experienced it, but became an impotent memory of a long-ago past. And those memories became memories of the whole psyche, not just a memory of a part.

Mommy in the Air

The host part of me until nearly six years old was mostly Little Debra. I was born in Alberta, Canada. My mother, Eleena, had a helper named Jeanie to take care of my brother, Jack, and myself. When I was about two or three months old, my biological father lost everything and we moved to the U.S. I never saw Jeanie again during waking life, but that also meant that Eleena had to take care of a newborn and a two year old by herself. Eleena was utterly unprepared to take care of children and was pretty frustrated. Unfortunately, she took that out on me. Eleena divorced my biological father when I was almost four years old, and immediately started to see Walter Amundson who was her high school sweetheart. Walter Amundson made her feel good and important, but with his influence I experienced some pretty horrific events beginning around four years old. Due to these horrific events, I became aware of my Mommy in the Air. At four years old, we lived in an apartment complex. They married and moved quite a lot, mostly onto farms. The longest place we ever lived was on the Missouri farm that Jack and I call The Farm.

I did not know anything about God at the time and did not know who was my Mommy in the Air. But this personage was with me throughout my entire childhood and made me feel better. Sometimes this personage would tell me what to do. Also if I hurt anything or anyone, this personage would tell me that it is wrong to hurt. I never was able to think that it was wrong for people to hurt ME though, but did gain an understanding that it is wrong to hurt other people and creation. One very significant lesson for me was to know that Eleena's ridicule to make people feel badly about themselves was wrong. So I seemed to always have mixed messages in life!!! When Little Debra went to sleep, Philip knew Mommy in the Air.

Near-Death Experience and the Other Realm

By the time I was nearly six, Walter Amundson had chosen a lifestyle to rape and torture me, mostly by tying ropes around my ankles and wrists and lifting me up. He did not stop when Little Debra went to sleep, so Philip (a dissociated part) also experienced the same kind of trauma. He usually did this in whatever barn was there on a farm. The pulleys and rope that he used moved with us from place to place.

But Little Debra told my biological father's second wife, Helga, about the violence she was experiencing and Helga did not believe it. A couple of days later, Walter Amundson wanted to demonstrate how easily he could kill me if I told anybody again. So he filled the bathtub with water and shoved my head, my body, under water. My mother, Eleena, stood and watched. But he went too far and Walter Amundson drowned Little Debra, me. I died.

One of the awesome blessings of having a near-death experience is that since then I've seen the "Other Realm." When he killed Little Debra, she went to the other side, the Other Realm, and saw Jesus. He wanted her to go back but she didn't want to. He told her that he'd make it so she'd be okay and then he took her cord and separated it. Every time I'm in the Other Realm, I see this cord that comes from me, from my belly button, to out someplace. It just fades away into the mist. But Jesus took my cord and made many cords. He told Little Debra that she'll be okay now and she went back. When Little Debra went back, she felt Walter Amundson pound on her back and immediately she was pulled back to the Other Realm and went to sleep. Philip was born at that moment.

I'm aware now that what I see is probably metaphor and other people see God and the Other Realm differently than I do. While I've been told the Other Realm is very pretty, I see it as gray and misty, so I can't see very far. I don't see God or Jesus all the time but I do sometimes. When I see Jesus, he is always surrounded by people. After waking up several years ago, one time in the Other Realm, Little Debra walked to the edge of a cliff and looked down into a valley. There were people all over the place. All of a sudden, she sang to God and they stopped and listened. It was awesome. I am blest with being able to see some people who have passed from this life to the next.

Another blessing of my near death experience is not only being able to connect to the Other Realm but also being able to perceive spirit in creation. Trees and birds and other beings have talked to me and I to them. This gave a great deal of comfort to Philip and the rest of us throughout life.

God

Perceiving God differs as many ways as there are people. Whilst some people do not believe in God, others who do have a relationship with God have an idea of who or what God is according to the needs of the individual person.

I see God as a "he", "father", as that perception met my psychological and emotional needs. So throughout this manuscript, God is "he". Furthermore, God morphs. To me, God is Creator of all and as I see him, he changes at will into any creature. God is a shape-shifter if you will! But to me, God's true self is light, power, spirit, and love.

I do not intend to demand for any other person to believe in God. For those who do, I respect his or her own perceptions, whether God is Creator, or Woman, or Spirit, or any other kind of perception. I reveal God and his wondrous love during my healing process and my life according to my own experiences.

Some people will have the opinion that my perceptions of God, angels, and the Other Realm are figments of a demented and creative mind. I don't really care. I offer my perceptions and my experiences and that is all. But I do strongly think that every person has the ability to know God.

Grandfather

Besides Bruce, Grandfather has also been a parent to the child parts of me during my healing process and continues to be a parent to me today. He is a person who died several years ago. While we knew each other before he died, our relationship was of friendship during his life. I once told a person that I was raised by a couple of men. One is passed now but the other one is alive.

Grandfather lives in the Other Realm. Because of my own sensitivities, I am able to see and hear Grandfather as clearly as I can anyone on earth. In the Other Realm, I also see parts of me as distinct and separate people. I do not know why except for love of me, but Grandfather decided to parent me. Because he resides in the Other Realm, he was with me throughout this healing process. Grandfather has been present with me in waking life. Often in the stage immediately before sleep, I could see Grandfather, parts of me in spirit, and the Other

Realm very clearly. Grandfather supervised all of the children parts of me throughout the healing process.

Age Differences

Sometimes the age when I dissociated during the first-life differs from the age of the part awakening. I do not know why.

*****

Little Debra did not have much contact with Bruce during the second-life. The only reason I can think of is that she just did not need to be raised or helped anymore, that her interactions with Ken healed her. Eventually she integrated.

From the time Little Debra dissociated and went to sleep until about sixteen during my chronological childhood, Philip was the host part. He lived day by day during that time and has the normal kind of memories of growing up. However, he never developed past the age of fourteen years old. During that time, Philip was unaware of any other part coming out, so he was not aware at that time of Nils. At the beginning of the healing he was aware of Nils, Little Debra, Damon, and The Adult because he and the other three had awakened.

Section One: Violence

This manuscript tracks the layers of the subconscious. So the trauma presented here is not in chronological order of my living, but in the order of the degree that a particular trauma affected my psyche, from the surface of my subconscious to the bottom of my subconscious. So the journey of healing was not about tracking what happened to me during my childhood, but a journey into the subconscious, layer by layer.

Subconsciously, my chronological age during the trauma in real life did not and does not matter. Furthermore, because one layer of my subconscious did not know anything residing in the layers below it, my healing journey reflects then-present activities. For instance, the part called Isaac along with his trauma resided in the bottom layer of my subconscious. Yet he was six years old and, like Philip, experienced trauma at the same farm in West Virginia. In real life AND during this healing process, Philip or any other part of me did not know Isaac or his trauma until I came to the depth of my subconscious. As parts and trauma were awakened and revealed, sometimes perceptions were incorrect. At the time, every part thought he or she was the last, the bottom. Every part wanted the journey to end. Sometimes the imagery I experienced also pointed to the end. But it did not end until it ended.

The identification, relivings, and healing of the upper levels of my subconscious seemed to focus on those parts having a clear interaction with the real world during the first-life. Most of these parts lived daily life and experienced day-to-day challenges. They held their own trauma and developed as best they were able. To me, the parts' ability to live in the world, survive the brutality of childhood, attend university, and lead a life appropriate to the demands of society is a testimony of unwavering stubbornness!

Chapter One
Subconscious Level 1: The Fab Five

I begin my story at the beginning of my true healing process. Bruce's involvement and the start of emails mark the beginning of the process of healing. The whole of my life before this point is what we call the first-life. It includes the real time of the trauma. From this point on, we call the second-life.

Five parts of me were awake at this time: Little Debra, Philip, Nils, The Adult, and Damon. Little Debra was five years old, nearly six; Philip was thirteen; Nils eleven; Damon fifteen; and the Adult an Adult. They had originally awakened a few years before my healing process. I realized later, and my therapist agreed, that my adult psyche never developed past the age of fourteen while my emotional maturity did, and my intellect certainly did.

The Adult part tried to control what was going on in the beginning, including if and when the other parts of me emailed Bruce. That lasted about two seconds, and whenever I tried to control, I utterly failed until I gave it up. Philip was the first to make contact with Bruce. At first the interaction was pleasant, but Philip's anger soon came to the surface and relationships became difficult.

Philip: I'll email if I want to.

Bruce: You may not like it now, Philip, but you have great potential!

Philip: yeah yeah yeah   You must be a die-hard flower child. :p You know what :p means? I'm sticking my tongue out at you! Ha!! It sucks to be me.

Bruce: Hey Philip, What is your definition of a "flower child"? I would be interested in hearing about that without you sticking out your tongue. Besides, with your tongue out I can't understand what you are saying!! You can say life sucks or you can look for the good that is in you and others. 13 is a hard age but a great age if you want it to be. It is your choice!

Philip: :p:p:p:p:p:p:p:p:p:p:p:p:p

You know what THAT is? That's a raspberry! hahahahaha!

Flower child: You're old, and I think you're tied to the 1960s. But it's somebody who says love love love all the time and sings a lot. Picks flowers and smells them. Thinks the world is full of roses, at least for other people. Everything's good good good.

I have a really important question for you. And I mean really important. If you and I were in the same room, I mean for real, physically, real. If you and I were in the same room and the monster came after Little Debra, would you protect her? Would you try to stop him from hurting her?

Okay. That's the question. And it's really important.

I know what it's like to make a decision. You know? When the monster drowned Little Debra, she died. I think that's why we can see spirits and dead people and Jesus and God and angels - because she did. Anyway, the monster pushed the water out of me and I woke up. And then I got sick. I was just in bed all the time and Eleena, our mother, would come in and just look at me. She wouldn't say anything or touch me or anything. Just look at me. I didn't eat or drink anything. She looked mad. I was almost six years old. I looked at her and I knew that she was waiting for me to die. She wanted me to die. And I made the decision. I didn't want to die and I didn't want to grow up to be a monster. I felt my Mommy in the Air and I made myself breathe because she told me to. She told me to, and I got up and got me some water and I took off my clothes and found a way to not lie in my pee in the bed and I got up when I had to pee and then drink water every single time my Mommy in the Air told me to and I got well again. It was really hard, but my Mommy in the Air helped me. I think two monsters raised me.

You know that girl on the news? I see that and I'm very sad because she died. But I didn't. I survived. She had a monster in her life, too.

I'm sorry that I don't know what the good is in me or in others. Maybe you can help me with that. Help me see.

Bruce: Philip, Yes I was alive and well in San Francisco during the Hippie era. The streets were relatively safe and friendly. Life was good for some and then some folks got into drugs and gave the whole movement a bad name. There is nothing wrong with taking time to smell the flowers. There are so many gifts that God gives us that we do not take the time to appreciate.

Now to answer the important question. Yes, I would protect Little Debra just as I would protect any child from a monster. I have done that before and I would do it again.

Philip, you are good because you take care of Little Debra. You also have a good mind in that you ask good questions. You have a good curiosity and you seem to know "right" from "wrong". This is a very good start.

Philip: Wow! You're awesome. You'd protect us? You said any child. You'd protect me, too? Does this mean that I don't have to be in charge all the time? I mean you care about me, too? When the monsters come for me, you'd care about me too? Yeah, the Adult thinks that taking time to smell the flowers is good, too. I think that's what we do when we walk in the woods. It's totally cool. I'm not sure I know right from wrong, but you're an adult and I'll take your word for it.

*****

A phenomena of being dissociated means that a part of me always needed to be "in charge." Even though the Adult Deb was capable of living in society, Philip seemed to be in charge, the dominant part, after the five woke several years before the healing process. He was a child, but a very strong part of me.

*****

Bruce: Yes Philip, I would protect you also. You are important and no you don't have to be in charge all the time.

Philip: I don't wanna go to work on Monday. I'm not going, and if I'm not going, then we don't go. People are motherfuckers and I'm scared. I'm in charge. And I don't wanna go. I think we should just quit and stuff.

Bruce: Hi Philip, You are going to work on Monday because you have a responsibility. You know it is the right thing to do. Have courage!! I believe in you and in your strength to do the right things. So go to work and tell me how it goes. I already know it will go well for you!

Philip:
:p:p:p:p:p:p:p:p:p:p:p:p:p:p:p:p:p:p:p:p:p:p:p:p:p:p:p:p:p:p:
p:p:p:p:p (me taking a breath)

:p:p:p:p:p:p:p:p:p:p:p:p:p:p:p:p:p:p:p:p:p:p:p:p:p:p:p:p:p:p:p

Bruce: Nice spelling! But you are still going to work.

Nils: Hi. I'm Nils and I'm 11. Hope I don't freak you out. We're kinda hoping that you'll find all this pretty interesting. Just remember that it's still Deb that you know, just in pieces, and you get to look at Deb in the past even though you're in the present, and you get to look at Deb's insides. (Star Trek music, do, do, dododo dooooo: to go where no man has gone before!! Okay, few men!!!) At least until we merge again. See?

Bruce: No worries Nils. Tell me about yourself. That is if you don't mind talking to an old person.

*****

Nils was not a host part; he did not live day by day during the first-life of chronologically growing up. Philip did. Nils came "out" during the first-life only when my stepfather did a particular action against Philip. The non-host parts would either have a particular function or they came out when Philip or any host part came to a breaking point. During the first-life, the host part was not aware of any other part. So Philip did not know about Nils when he was living the chronological age from day to day, and Nils did not know about Philip.

It's important to me to note that during the first-life Philip came back after a part like Nils took a trauma that Philip could not handle. Philip temporarily went to sleep so all the non-host parts did not become hosts. I think that because Philip was strong enough to sustain his living from nearly age six to sixteen is one reason why I have been emotionally stable throughout life. Through Philip, I retain the memories of day-to-day childhood. I lost them when Philip went to sleep, but I think having that sustained childhood helped me.

Not until well into my healing process did I realize that when a trauma was especially harsh my body did not black out. When Nils was taking a trauma, for instance, Philip was asleep. But during the first-life, Philip always thought his body went into shock and he blacked out. He did not know what happened to him; nor did he know of any other part taking the trauma that emotionally and mentally he could not handle. This is a miracle to me. Philip literally did not know and consequently emotionally and mentally could continue his living. There was an emotional residue however. All of his life, Philip felt fear and knew he was in danger, but did not know the complete reason for those feelings. He knew that his stepfather tortured him and how he tortured him because he was awake when the trauma began. But his fear and feeling of danger went deeper than that.

During my healing process, the part that is out has control of the body and can see, smell, hear, touch, and taste in real life in real time. The other parts that were known at any given time seemed to stand right behind the part that is out. When a part came out, he or she stepped to the front of the pack. Not always, but most of the time the other parts who were not out were aware of what was happening, what was said and the feelings of the part who was out. They often were aware, but because they were not out, the parts not in control of the body did not experience the same as the part that was out. Nevertheless, they did not go to sleep like they did during the first-life.

Although this is incorrect, I can't help but see my parts as separate people. Before they integrated, Philip was one person and Nils was another person. Each part seemed to be different from each other, and yet there were some commonalities amongst all of them. For my healing, I had to face the fact that each part experienced life differently than another and each part drew upon different emotional and mental aspects of the whole of me. Because of this, they seem to have different personalities, but they were really different degrees of consciousness of my psyche. During my healing, I noticed that each part resided in a different place within me, so as I delved deeper into my subconscious, another part came to the surface. Where they resided did not seem to be determined by chronological physical aging, but seemed to be determined by the various traumas and how deeply a trauma affected and consequently resided in my subconscious. I see it as the degree in which the trauma connected to self-identity and how self-identity determines personhood. The trauma itself happened during my formative years and I developed emotionally and psychologically according to my life experiences. I never thought of myself as a person until very late in my healing process.

Nils and Philip did not know each other during the first-life. However, they did know each other and their trauma by the time this healing process began. So some of what Nils writes includes Philip's experiences.

*****

Nils: Okay. I'm Nils and I'm 11 years old. Philip runs up and down from 8 to 13 but I'm pretty much just 11. I was born on the floor of a chicken coop in Ramona, California. I forgot to feed Mike, the dog that lived in the chicken coop. The monster took me out there and Philip thought that he was gonna get beaten up again. But he pulled down my pants and made me go face down on the floor and he laid on top of me and stuck his thing in my butt. It burns. I'm crying now because I'm bleeding down there right now and I hurt there and it feels like every time after he did that to me, but not as bad.

Sometimes he made me bend over a hay bale and sometimes he just made me bend over and he lifted me up. He usually made me take off everything down there. Most of this was in a barn or someplace. We moved a whole lot. After the first time he did it, I fell asleep and Philip came out. On the way back to the trailer he told Philip he'd kill him if he told anybody. He didn't know what Walter Amundson was talking about but he didn't wanna tell anybody anyway. But we went into the trailer and Eleena looked at Philip and said What's going on? He didn't say anything and he told her nothing was going on. Eleena hates us. A lot of times after he would stick his thing up my butt, I got to put my clothes back on. And then he made me put his thing in my mouth. He did it because I cried but I tried not to but I cried. So he choked me and choked me so I wouldn't cry until my nose got all full of stuff. Then he took me to the horse water thing or the pigs water thing and made me drink water. He wouldn't let me spit it out. He did this to Philip too. Philip and I were living at the same time. Little Debra was asleep.

Sometimes he would do this to me when Eleena was away. But most of the time that was when he tortured Philip. I guess because Philip fainted a lot and woke up with his clothes back on and lying in the corner of the barn. Sometimes I fainted too. If I didn't sleep in time, he'd kick me.

He liked doing all of this.

I don't think that I SHOULD be protected because he stuck his thing up my butt and that's just too gross. I'm a freak. I deserve it.

I know I just wanna be held and somebody to tell me stories and tuck me into bed and sit on somebody's lap and somebody to kiss me and care when I'm sick but I just don't deserve that. People don't do that for me. I know I'm just feeling sorry for myself and I'm supposed to just say, okay, that's the way it is. But it doesn't take away how I feel. I'm sad. I'm sorry.

But I like computer games and science fiction and stuff. That's all I can write about me for now. Bye

*****

Nils was born when we lived on a farm at Ramona, California. We lived in a trailer that Eleena hated, and on the farm were rows of old chicken coops with no chickens. Chronologically, I was eleven years old. Walter Amundson and Eleena were angry at each other and he became violently angry when he found out I as Philip had forgotten to feed our dog, Mike, and took Philip to a chicken shed where Mike stayed. In the shed, Walter Amundson threw Philip onto the wooden floor and violently sodomized him. Philip had been sodomized before this time, but Walter Amundson's violence was horrific, so the experience separated me again and formed another part. Afterwards, Nils went to sleep and Philip woke up again. I as Philip was terribly hurt and unable to walk very well and Walter Amundson dragged me back to the trailer. He told me that he'll kill me if I tell but Philip didn't know what he was talking about. It was night. I still smell the dust and feces of the wooden floor of the shed.

During my relivings, re-experiencing the brutality of the trauma often affected my body. In this case, Nils felt the burning and the body bled.

*****

Bruce: Nils, Thank you for sharing with me. I am sure that was not easy for you to do. I am sorry that those things happen to you. They will never happen again! I will protect you from that happening again, OK? The monster is nowhere around and he cannot come to you anymore or do things to you anymore. He made you feel awful and bad but you do not have to feel that way anymore. You are not a freak. You never deserved to be treated that way.

Fractured Mind

You are not a bad person. You deserve love and affection. You deserve to be held and to have stories read to you. What stories do you like? Do you have favorites?

*****

Protecting a child, any child, is critical to their mental, physical, and emotional health, and that is what parents are supposed to do. To a child, parents are perceived as bigger than the child, and this is what Nils and the other child parts of me experienced with Bruce and, later, Fran. But when a parent hurts a child the way mine did to me, that sacred trust of protection is shattered. It did not matter if they were nice to me later from time to time or that they fed, clothed, and sheltered me. The harm of shattering that sacred trust of protection also shattered my self-identity. Once is enough! The child is then unable to feel safe around the very people upon whom he or she depends. Neither can the child get away from parents on his/her own, as a child is dependent on the "bigger" people.

If parents harm a child as a lifestyle, the child must find a way to live with the stress and fear the inevitable harm generates. Sometimes a child releases stress and fear by dissociating, as I did. That is, the child fractures into mental parts and one part does not consciously know the harm inflicted upon a different part. Dissociation releases the stress enough for the child to be able to perceive his or her world accurately enough to live life. A downside is that dissociation is a way to hide, not only from other people but also from the self. So seeking help, if any kind of opportunity of help is available, becomes very difficult. Furthermore, dissociation throws the affects of the trauma into the subconscious. The child is unable to control or change deep feelings of fear or worthlessness as well as his or her harmful behavior. And because the child part living day by day does not know the source of his or her pain, explaining the problem is out of the question.

Therapists knowing and implementing the techniques to help a child tap into the subconscious seems to me to be the only way to truly help a child. Therapists know the techniques to help a child draw trauma from the subconscious. But establishing trust to the point that the child can feel protected is critical for therapy, and, given the court system today, removing the child from further harm.

Because I was not helped as a child, I grew up into adulthood as a dissociated adult. But the child parts within me continued to be stuck in the trauma. When I am able to reach down into my subconscious and a child part awakens, the technique to heal that part is the same as for a child of that chronological age. That is because the parts of me are children. By healing the part of me, the foundation of my psyche is healed and rebuilt. The child parts of me are actually myself as a child.

*****

Nils: You'll protect me. You make so it never ever ever happens again. I'm crying now. Is that okay? Can I cry? Can I have these feelings? I'm scared. I'm awful scared and I feel so bad. I mean I feel bad cause he stuck his thing in me. It makes me feel like I don't count, like I'm not supposed to do anything. You say I'm not supposed to feel that way. How am I supposed to feel? You won't let it happen. Please don't let it happen ever again. I don't know anything any more.

We don't know any stories to be read to me. Nobody read to any of us. I don't know any stories. I'm sorry.

Bruce: No, I said you do not have to feel that way anymore. Because those bad things will not happen anymore. If you are scared, I understand that. If you do not trust people, I understand that too. You can trust me and you can trust the adult.

Nils: I don't see how anybody can love or like somebody that had a thing put up the butt and then cry. It's like total shame. I don't like myself. I think I'm pretty bad and rotten. I think I deserve all the hurt from people. It's like the monster broke me, but didn't break Philip. I hate myself and I hate the body. I don't really wanna die though.

I'm sorry. I know it's wrong.

Sometimes the monster was gone for a couple of weeks and sometimes a couple of months. That was good. But then there was Eleena. So we never knew what it was like to feel good about ourselves.

He beat up Philip once or twice a week. He did either the rape or torture to Philip or the sodomy thing to me about every month or two months. Sometimes he did the torture and the sodomy the same day. This was for over 12 years.

Philip found a way to not die by rebelling and turning off the pain in the body. I didn't. I just couldn't figure out how.

I just wanna be treated like a normal child. Maybe I'll stop hating myself. I hope so. I don't wanna hate myself. Really. I know it's wrong and I'm bad for hating myself.

Bruce: Nils, You are not alone in the shame that you feel. Many people have had that experience over the history of mankind. Soldiers used to do that to kings when they conquered lands. This would shame the king and nobody would follow the leadership of the king anymore. The good news is that you are different. Most people that experience something put up their butt think that they have done something wrong and that it is their fault. That isn't true. It isn't their fault because they didn't make it happen. The monster made it happen and it is the monster's fault and the monster's shame, even

though the monster will not admit it. When children have parents that go through divorce the children feel it is their fault and that isn't true either. So, the first thing that you can say out loud is that "it isn't my fault. I did nothing wrong." And then say, "I accept and love myself for who I am today and others accept me and love me for who I am today also." Say these things many times a day until you begin to believe them. It is OK to cry when you say them.

The monster may have broken you back then but God is building you up into a new person, and will always remain in the days ahead. You are a good person!

Nils: I have the paper in my pocket. Without looking, I can remember the "It isn't my fault." But there's a wall around the other one. I need to explode the wall. Okay, it's "I did nothing wrong." Don't adults punish children? And didn't the monster punish me? So didn't I do something wrong? I don't get the big sentence. I'm sorry.

Bruce: Nils, Adults do not punish children. Parents sometimes discipline their children but they never hurt them over and over again. We don't need to explode the wall, we need to tear it down piece by piece and the more you can find the strength to say out loud "I did nothing wrong" the quicker the wall will come down.

The monster didn't punish you, the monster hurt you, took advantage of you, forced himself on you. People that do those things do not love you because they are only thinking of themselves. So do not think that all adults are like the monster. They are not. There are only a few monsters in the world and I do not think any are around where you live. You are safe.

OK let's forget the big sentence and say a smaller one. Try this, "I am a good person and people like me." Let me know how this one works. By the way, you are a good person and I like you.

Nils: They don't? Adults do not punish children? Gee, that's all we know. No, wait, you said the monster didn't punish me, he hurt me. Huh? Do you discipline me without punishing me? Is that correcting me - the same as disciplining me?

Bruce: Yes, correcting is a good word. Guiding is another good word. Sometimes parents take away privileges from their children when they don't behave. Maybe they will take away some TV time, or an X-Box game or some computer game for a while until the child starts to behave again. But, no hitting, no monster stuff at all – ever! You like computers, right? Well, if you were not behaving yourself I would take the computer away for a day or two depending on what you did. This would be a form of disciplining.

Philip: Can I put my head on your chest?

Bruce: Hi Philip, If you want to put your head on my chest and listen to my heart that would be OK with me.

Nils: And now I feel more secure. There's you who's bigger than me who will discipline me if I don't behave myself. I don't wanna have the computer taken away. But I don't have to do everything right, either. I don't have to be in charge and I can make mistakes. Right?

Bruce: We all make mistakes at times Nils and nobody does everything right all the time. I will discipline you if you don't behave. So, if we all work together and respect each other things will go well. No one will be scared or afraid.

*****

One common psychological characteristic that bridged all parts of me was to live in survival mode. I never experienced living without needing to survive. Despite all the exceptionally good people placed in my path before this second-life, I never stopped feeling the need to survive, diligently survive. I always thought people were going to hurt me, especially people in authority, and the anxiety of living in the survival mode throughout my life took its emotional and physical toll on me.

The motivation for the survival mode was fear. Fear was also a characteristic that bridged all parts of me. Until recently, I never knew life without it.

Despite my chronological age, these parts were real. By them coming to the surface and living, Bruce was actually touching ME at a formative age. He was rebuilding my foundation, because these kid parts WERE me at that age. He saw me at a young age and communicated to me at a young age. (Several young ages.) The older, host, part of me during my healing process had to surrender to it all in order for my "insides" or my younger parts to be rebuilt. For the first time, me as a child had somebody older and bigger to be in charge. It actually took a long time for me to stop being in survival mode, but Bruce's gift was tremendously significant to me.

By this time in the healing process, Bruce had laid down some rules, especially about eating.

*****

Nils: Philip's crying almost all the time now. Last night we went to bed at 10:00 and woke up at 11:30 and Philip cried until 2:30 about and we woke up again at 5:30 and he cried again until 7:00 about and we woke up again at 8:30. Today he's been crying and feels out of control. We

Fractured Mind

went to a movie to see if that will calm him down, refocus, and it did except one time he cried but was able to refocus again. The Adult made meatloaf and he was able to refocus until that task was done. Damon/Adult are doing all they can do to try to get Philip to refocus. Going to the store was the task for Damon/Adult and that worked okay. To refocus, they're trying to push Philip back behind them. Damon/Adult HAVE to work tomorrow and I don't think Philip will make that not happen. The focus of Damon/Adult is to live in society. Philip got candy at the movie. Philip says if I send this, he's gonna hit me. If he hits me can I hit him back?

Bruce: Hi Nils, Hitting does not solve the problem. It only makes it worse. SO, no hitting .... no hitting from Nils and no hitting from Philip.

Philip: That candy-ass motherfucker Nils! It's none of his fucking business about me and I'm gonna beat the shit out of him if he opens his fucking mouth again! Nobody likes a tattle-tale. Goddamn it. I didn't mean to get candy at the movie. I just wasn't thinking. He just wants me to be in trouble the fucking asshole. Yeah, I'm crying. So fucking what? That motherfucker tells on me again and I'm gonna beat the shit out of him!!!!!! And that's a promise!!!!!!

Bruce: Philip, Language!

Philip: okay okay I'm sorry. I'll be good. I don't know how to stop this rebellion thing. I don't wanna be angry and I know it's wrong and I'm so scared all the time. I like it when I'm just a normal kid. I just feel it's too big for me. I mean life and stuff. And me being out is too big for me. I think I'm just a child but I'm not supposed to be but I don't know what I'm supposed to be. I don't know how to be anything else except just a child any more. I don't know why I have to survive right now, I mean rebel to survive. I just want what Nils told you HE wants. You know, to be read to and kissed and sit on somebody's lap and just be a normal child, to just experience things of a normal child. But I think I'm gonna be hurt instead. And I don't think I can keep the others alive any more like I used to and that really scares me, but I'm trying awful hard to.

Bruce: Hi Philip, Fear is a very strong emotion. Anger is a very strong emotion. Neither emotion helps you feel loved or comforted. What scares you the most? Does it scare you that someone may hurt you? Ask the adult how long it has been since someone physically hurt the adult or you. Ask the adult if the person who used to hurt you is still around. For the adult it has been many years since someone physically hurt the adult and the person that hurt the adult is not around anymore. So take a deep breath and look all around you. Do

you see anyone that will hurt you? You are safe. Say it out loud: "I am safe." Any time you feel scared, take a deep breath, take three deep breaths and look all around you. If there is no one there that will hurt you say: "I am safe."

Focus on working with the others. Be nice to Nils and help Damon and the adult get to work, go shopping, fix meals. You are the strong one because it takes strength to rebel. We want to focus that strength on getting better and merging once again when all of you are ready.

You are an important person. I care about you.

Philip: The Adult's a motherfucker. I hate her.

Bruce: Do something constructive like working on your story. Foul language gets privileges taken away!

Philip: It's 12:40 a.m. and I woke up crying again. I wish I could stop. I know that writing my story will help. The Adult is so far behind right now though. She hasn't been able to do anything last week or the week before really cause of everything with us. She worked really hard tonight until bedtime trying to finish so I can write my story. I gotta honor that, you know? I've lived with this pain an awful long time. A little longer won't change anything really. I'd put my head on your chest, but it makes me cry harder, and I'm just a crybaby so I don't think I should put my head on your chest. I don't think you should hold me at all. Do you think I'm really worth anything? I mean, really, for real? Tomorrow I think maybe I can start to write my story.

Bruce: Philip, First, you need to apologize to the adult for your language.

Second, when you put your head on my chest just relax, even if you are crying. Just let it out and breathe deeply, relax and breathe deeply.

Third, you're a gifted person and I care about you and Nils equally – always.

Fourth, help the adult get her work done first. This will lower her stress and then you can work on your story. Maybe after you tell me your story you will not be as angry and maybe you will feel better.

Fifth, when you wake up and are crying remember that I am praying for you and that God is with you – always.

You are going to do great things Philip but we have to get this anger worked out. So, do your best everyday, stop fighting with Nils and

Nils can't make you say anything you do not want to say. So you can't blame Nils for your poor language – even if he triple dares ya!

See Philip, even though you are in pain you are thinking about another person. That is brave and courageous and it takes a strong person to do that. You ARE a good, strong person.

Philip: Nils is a good boy. prissy, stupid, boy. I'm a bad boy. I'm tough. I ride motorcycles. You love Nils more than you love me!! And I don't give a RATS!!!

Bruce: Philip, Nice try but this "you love Nils more than" stuff doesn't work for me OR for you. Don't have a pity party for me. If you want to think of yourself as bad that is an image that you are promoting and no one else. Sorry, that image doesn't work for me or for you either. Why don't you focus on constructive things like your story (when the adult is finished with her work), and work on your language and anger. You are a good person and I am glad to know you.

Philip: Adult, I'm sorry I called you a motherfucker. stupid adult

Bruce: That's the idea except for the "stupid" part. By putting the "stupid" in your comment means that you were not sincere about the first part. Gotcha!! I really like you Philip!!

Philip: You didn't say I had to be SINCERE about it!! Gotcha!! I like you too! I'm at a good part in my story. I guess I wanna tell you about the good stuff too. Okay?

Bruce: That's good!! Put in the good stuff also. An apology that is authentic (meaningful) is sincere – always. Gotcha!!

Philip: My dearest Adult: I'm so very very sorry I called you a motherfucker. I doubt that I'll call you a motherfucker again, unless it slips out and I accidently say motherfucker to you. In that case, as is true in this case, you're not really a motherfucker and once again I apologize for calling you a motherfucker.

Bruce: No sarcasm there Philip!!

Philip: You said that we have to get this anger worked out. Why can't children be angry at their parents?

Bruce: Philip, Children get angry at their parents all the time when they are disciplined, when they don't get what they want all the time. But, they don't stay angry and neither do the parents stay angry because they love each other and want what is best for each other. Just like you not coming "out" so the adult can get her work done. You are terrific!

Philip: I started it, writing I mean. I'm trying to push it back, to not feel this. I'm awful scared. I gotta tell you though that I promise I won't touch the body. I started writing and I got a taste of what I'm going through. What I HAVE to go through. I promise I won't touch the body. I used to burn myself or cut myself or hit myself but I promise I won't do that unless I hit Nils cause he deserves it. I'm not sick any more. I'm just not well.

So this is what it feels like and what it looks like. But I'm not touching the body and you don't have to worry about that. Honest honest honest.

It feels and looks like I got a knife and I'm cutting myself open from the top down. I've started doing that, and this shit is in me and when I open me up, the shit comes out. And I have to reach in and pull it out too. I cut a little bit open and pulled a little of it out already and kinda fainted. The computer is in the bedroom upstairs and I feel myself begin to black out and I get up and get on the bed and I sleep. (This is real, the body does this part, to get up, get on the bed and sleep.) I wake up just a little later and I feel my head on your chest. I'm not crying now. I feel kinda shocked, you know? So I got up and wrote some more. I think it's gonna be like that until I'm finished. So it's gonna be pretty slow I guess. I don't know.

Are you here?

I gotta get the shit out. Are you supposed to put good stuff in me afterwards? Will you put good stuff in me? Please?

I gotta get the shit out. And now I'm crying again.

Are you here? I'm awful scared.

*****

While I did not know it at the time, fainting, falling asleep when healing, or blacking out related to a trauma is an indication of another part of me coming to the surface. During life at the time of the trauma, the parts of me did not know the others existed. At this point in my healing, I thought I had blacked out during the real, chronological age trauma, and I thought that Philip's fainting or falling asleep when writing his story was just that: fainting. It wasn't. As is typical with DID, none of me knew that there were other parts buried in my subconscious. The reason for that is when the trauma happened during real life, a part would either take a part of a trauma or a different trauma. Some parts, though, carried the emotional and psychological pain without anything done to them specifically. The parts did not know each other so that the part of me living at the time could function and still be mentally stable. It took a while, but Philip's processing here is actually pulling other parts to the surface, although nobody knew it at the time.

*****

Bruce: Philip, I am here. I will be here. Take your time and take care of yourself as you go through this. I am trying to put good stuff in you now. And good stuff will just appear and be there after you are emptied out. OK? Put your head on my chest anytime you are scared. I am there for you. You are a good person underneath all the anger. God loves you so deeply and He wants you to be free of your anger. He is with you right now and he is with you while you write your story.

*****

Around this time, Bruce found Fran Waters and she took us on as a patient. So we started seeing her. It was a little rocky at first, mainly because of my trust issues, but her knowledge, experience, technique, and caring changed all that.

*****

Fran's Notes: Diagnosis: Dissociative Identity Disorder.

Philip: My Life in Vivid Technicolor Detail

I don't know why the monster did all these things to me. I don't know what I did wrong. I know you told Nils that he did nothing wrong and I think I'm supposed to say the same about me. But I don't know why my life was the way it was.

I think the world is really scary. I'm always afraid that a monster will come around the corner and kill me and the rest of us. You say there's not too many though. Sometimes I think that everybody's a monster. You're not though.

I never hated anything until I was 14 years old, the body was. I was just lookin' at books in the library at school during study hall and I ran across a book about the Jewish thing and Hitler and everything. And I saw pictures. And I knew it was all true. Because that's what people do to other people when they can. Because there's monsters. And for the first time in my life I hated because those people were hurt so bad.

I didn't know any other life. I didn't know about anything else. I thought that life was like this. You know?

The monster and Eleena made me kiss them every night. I wanted to do that cause I secretly hoped that somebody would hug me but they didn't. I hugged Eleena once and she got mad. Now she wants to hug all the time when we're in public. I don't get it.

I kept hoping they would be different and I tried really hard to work for him good but I could never do things right. The thing is, I didn't do things wrong but he just pretended that I did stuff wrong. When I was sick, they were mad, especially Eleena. I'm not doing this in order, you know, historic order. I hope that's okay. I worked for him good, especially after I grew physically. I know I did. I wanted to cause I secretly hoped that maybe he would stop hurting me and like me. But he didn't.

Besides, I really liked working. The smell of the earth and of cut grass and the wind and sky was healing to me, you know? After we moved to Missouri on the Missouri farm, I'd sneak outside in the middle of the night and run into the woods. I'd lie on the ground just to feel as close to the earth as I possibly could. It was like I hugged the earth and the earth hugged me back. They never, ever, caught me. But the sky is special to me. In Missouri we lived on top of a hill and I could see these great big clouds come in with rain and lightning and I just loved it. There was something bigger than the monster. And the monster and Eleena never knew how I felt about it and they still don't. Cause they didn't know, they could never take it away from me. After we moved here where I live now, the earth told me that I belonged to the earth, and no matter where I go I will always belong to the earth.

I can hear the spirit voices of trees and animals. I guess because Little Debra died and I had Mommy in the Air. In California someplace, I think the body was 9, I slept on a porch. And I had bugs in my bed that bit me. But then I talked to the bugs, and they agreed and they slept on one side of my bed and I slept on the other side and they didn't bite me anymore. I had to write something for school and I wrote about that. Next thing I knew Eleena was at school and met with my teacher. When Eleena walked out she was really mad. The teacher said to me that she was sorry and the teacher looked really scared. Eleena beat me with a belt that night. I didn't see my bug friends anymore and I was sad about that. I was bad. I just don't know what I did. But that was my life. Not knowing what I did. I figured I just wasn't supposed to be here, you know, living, and I was a MAJOR inconvenience all the time.

Beating me didn't hurt. I know it hurt the body, but I didn't feel it. And it drove them NUTS! Especially Eleena. She'd make me lie on the bed face down and she'd take a belt and beat me and beat me and I'd just lie there looking at her mean-like and sometimes I'd smile and she'd beat me some more until she just gave up. I was pretty happy about it cause every time they beat me they got TOTALLY frustrated!!! I knew I was rebelling big time.

Well, to be honest, at the actual time of the beating, it didn't hurt. But afterwards I felt it and it hurt to move. The good news is that the monster and Eleena weren't around me when I could feel my body hurt.

I never, ever, knew what I did wrong. Not ever. Not really. I know I rebelled and that made them mad. But all the other times I never knew.

A snake spanked me once. The instant it happened it felt just exactly like the other day with you!! You know, about the cleaning up my language NOW. I saw a great big black snake trying to get somewhere and I took a stick and I kept putting the stick right in the way of the snake so the snake had to go around it. I'd just walk next to the snake as he moved along and kept putting the stick in front of him. Finally, the snake reared back and bit the stick and at that moment said to me, "You WILL respect me!!" And I felt disciplined. You know? I never did it again.

I once had go over at the same place with bees. Out in the field. There was this old rusted disc leaning up against a tree that had a hive in it. The monster stood back and made me go on and get the disc. But the bees and I talked and so I was able to just do what he wanted, right in the middle of a swarm of bees, right by the hive. I walked out and gave him the disc. I smiled. The monster was pretty disgusted. I think I was rebelling then, too. I haven't been able to do that since without getting stung.

One day I discovered that I could tell the monster what to do. Jack and the monster found a great big king snake in the shed. They were about to kill it when I screamed at them NO!! They both stopped, pretty surprised. And I told them that king snakes eat mice and they're good to have around in a barn. They won't hurt the horses or them or anything. And they believed me. Boy, I was REALLY surprised at that. And I watched that king snake go. He lived because of me and I felt pretty good about that. The monster didn't succeed that day.

I've said HI to a flock of birds and they said HI back to me. This doesn't happen all the time, you know. Just when I can hear.

I worked for the monster all the time. I'd come home from school and work for him. Then when we came inside, he got to rest while Eleena made me work then for her, too. I really resented that. I was tired all the time. I tried really really hard to make bad enough grades to have to go to summer school. I didn't care that he beat me for that. But most of the time I just couldn't get bad enough grades. I never did my homework cause I was working for him all the time. So when the teachers complained, he just beat me up but still didn't let me do my homework.

He wouldn't let me drink water or anything when I was working for him. I'd sneak off the tractor though and drink out of the pond or the horse thing whenever I could. In the summers it was hot and he wouldn't let me drink anything. Sometimes he'd catch me with this rebellion and he'd beat me. Most of the time he didn't catch me though.

If I didn't work good enough for him, he wouldn't let me eat either. So I snuck off to the shed and ate the horses' food, oats. They never caught me at that. Almost, but not quite.

I was 11 years old, the body was, and I had to clean up a house that burnt down. The monster's sister came to visit and saw me do that and she made me blow my nose. She taught me how to blow my nose. Black stuff came out cause of the burnt house. She was mad at them.

I didn't feel it when he beat me. You know, like I said. He didn't hit me much in the face. The only time he and Eleena got scared was when he broke both my eardrums. I couldn't hear a thing for a time. Then he told me he'd kill me. He had to yell it and got pretty frustrated. I coulda heard him well enough but it was fun watching him get frustrated.

Sometimes when he beat me up though I'd faint, even though I didn't feel it. I'd wake up alone. He did this lots out by the edge of a field. So I'd wake up on the ground. It felt good to be on the ground and I'd look up at the sky and I wondered why I was here.

He used his hands, his fists, a belt, or a horses lead or reign. He beat my older brother Jack worse than me. He sometimes used the buckle of the belt or the metal part of the horse's lead on me. But he did that a lot to Jack. He'd kick Jack, too. The monster would reach right across the table and knock Jack to the floor. That's cause Jack stutters really bad. He's a photographer now. He's two years older than us.

Right when we separated this time, Jack needed to talk and we didn't call him back. Then when we did, Jack started to complain that we didn't call him back. The Adult said, "I'm sorry. You're right. I should have called you back." Then he started to complain some more and the Adult said, "Yes, I should be more attentive to your needs, and I will from now on." That shut up Jack right then and there and he was happy again. That made us feel good. Nobody can expect Jack to know our world and he doesn't. But he hurts too, you know? And he doesn't HAVE anybody else to talk to except us about his past. Maybe his ex-wife who's his really good friend, but she wouldn't understand really like we do and he knows that. I think I'm awful blessed. You know?

David, my younger brother, once accidently got hurt when he was really really young. And they ran around worried and took him to the hospital. And I stood there pretty dumbfounded and wondered by nobody cared about me. I guess I'm just selfish.

I was born when Little Debra died. Sometimes I think I'm a monster.

Unlike the beatings, I could feel the torture.

I don't know why he gave me a rabbit and put it in a cage. I thought it was a terrible life for a rabbit. I didn't have any idea how to take care of that rabbit. I just didn't know. The rabbit died and the monster told me I killed it. I think he's right, I did. He made me bury it and I did and I was really sad and all I could say was I'm sorry. I still think about how I killed a rabbit sometimes.

He said I couldn't read. So I rebelled and read everything I could. He hardly ever caught me either, I was so good sneaking around. I read *The Yearling*, and *20,000 Leagues Under the Sea*, and just about everything I could get my hands on. I'd do this at night when I was supposed to be asleep. I was happy reading. I supposed I should have been doing my homework instead but I didn't think about that.

To be fair, though, when the monster beat me he hit me only once or twice or three times most of the time. When I fainted, that was more. When I knew it was coming, I'd stand there and yell, "Go ahead motherfucker! Hit me. Hit me!" And he did. I figured why not stand up to him? He was gonna hit me anyway. This was my way to rebel.

Eleena, though, would beat me until she tired out. Usually with me on the bed with a belt. I didn't work too good for her and often didn't do what she told me to do. I did it on purpose cause I then got to watch her get so frustrated beating me. I know I'm a bad person for provoking her. I liked it when she tried and tried and got so frustrated.

If I was to give one word to Eleena, it would be ridicule. She ridiculed me and other people, strangers you know? She still does. Once when we were living here and Damon was out, we visited and had dinner with Eleena and David. Our waiter was pretty gay, and the two of them made fun of him, just loud enough for him to hear. Damon saw that the waiter was hurt by that. So Damon said to them, loudly, "You know, what you're saying right now tells me a whole lot more about you than it does about him." That shut them right up and they looked all embarrassed and the waiter smiled at us. Such motherfuckers, David and Eleena.

My Mommy in the Air taught me that doing that was wrong. I know it hurt me, so I really do know it's wrong. I saw it and see it all the time with Eleena though.

I once had a butterfly that was wild. A great big monarch purple butterfly. I was 10. I'd sing to her and she'd fly down and land on my head. I put her on my nose. I petted her wings, but I was really gentle at that and nothing came off on my fingers. Eleena took a picture of the butterfly once. I don't know if I have that picture or not. I stole a bunch of pictures not once but twice from her once we were living here. The butterfly was my friend.

I got a puppy once. We were living in town. His name was Joey and he was brown. But he was sick. He lived in my bedroom. I didn't know how to take care of a puppy. He pooped on my bed and on the floor and everywhere else. After he died, they came into my bedroom and cleaned it up. They had to throw away the carpet. They were really mad at me. But I think he died because he was sick, not like the rabbit. I was really sad that Joey died.

When we moved to the farm in Missouri, I was 13 or 14 years old, the body was. He wanted to build a house and when I lived there, there was only the basement. My bedroom was concrete on the floor and the outside wall. The other walls were not finished, just the studs with the wall on the other side, so I had a whole bunch of little shelves. There wasn't any heat. In the wintertime, I'd wake up and the whole outside wall was covered with frost. I thought it was beautiful. I slept between two mattresses.

They gave Jack a new coat. What he had was an old army coat. But my coat was worse, so I took his old coat. They complained that I stole Jack's coat. They were just gonna throw it away, so why couldn't I have that coat? I never could figure these people out. For some reason, they let me keep it.

I think the monster really liked to control me. I think it's wrong to try to control other people. Sometimes I try though and I know I'm bad.

I'm running out of the good stuff. I guess I'll have to face the bad stuff.

Bruce: Greetings Philip, I am proud of you. You are a brave person. You are a strong person. God has blessed you with a gift of strength because it takes strength to be defiant when a monster is attacking you, torturing you, mistreating you. It takes strength to rebel and to say I am not going to take this anymore. It takes strength to leave home and find a better life. It takes strength to stay strong when you feel that nobody cares. It takes strength to pursue an education and become someone great, someone that is helpful, someone who is compassionate, someone who cares for others. It takes strength.

I admire your appreciation for nature, your relationship with the earth, the sky, the animals and the bugs. You have reverence for God's creation. Having reverence is a fine quality in a person and you have that quality. Hang on to it for the rest of your life. You have a special relationship with God. God, the one who loves you deeply (a lot), God who desires for you to be whole and healthy, God who has been present with you through all of your life and the same God who will face Walter Amundson and see him suffer for all that he has done.

You have been wonderful. You write very well, you were very matter of fact about things with no bad words except when you told me what you said to the Monster and that was OK. You are smart,

intelligent, and strong. You will continue to grow and be successful, I know this. You are safe now. No more monsters – ever. And if there ever would be, you could take care of them, they would not hurt you because you would not let them. You are strong, smart and you know a lot because you have experienced a lot, you have studied a lot and you are wise.

God always sends his angels to people to say to them "fear not" and that is God's message to Philip this day: "fear not." For God is with you and loves you. Continue to take care of the adult and Nils. I have to go to work now. I will write a little more later.

Philip: Well, this is the easy part compared to what I did today. Everybody has some kind of pain in their life, you know.

I guess I just wanna list the monster's favorite ways he liked to do to torture me.

Eleena would take Jack and David and go into town to do shopping. When the monster let her do that, she'd take all day. Jack never wanted to go. I begged her to let me go. She just said that she needed to take a break from me. After she left, I knew what was coming for me.

I felt the torture. He really liked doing this.

For much of this, I blacked out and woke up in the corner of the barn, hidden. If I didn't wake up in time, he'd kick me and I'd wake up with him kicking me.

If I cried, he'd make me put my clothes back on if they were off and then he'd put his thing in my mouth and choke me until my nose filled up. He wouldn't let me spit it out, but he'd take me to the horses' trough or the pigs' trough and make me drink. I usually didn't cry.

He'd take off all my clothes. He had two pulleys rigged in the barn. He'd string ropes through them and tie the ropes to my ankles. Then he'd hoist me up, and I'd be upside down with my legs apart. He'd tell me to pee and I had a hard time peeing.

In this position, sometimes he would simply explore me, my insides.

In this position, sometimes he would take his cigar ashes, open me up, and try to see if he could drop the ashes inside of me.

In this position, sometimes he would swing me back and forth.

In this position, sometimes he would have a knife in his hand, swing me back and forth toward the knife and tell me how easy he could kill me.

In this position, sometimes he would put honey or something on me and in me and just leave me there.

In this position is the only time he took my clothes off. Everything else, clothes were on.

He'd tickle me and it hurt.

He'd string me up by my wrists and leave me there. This only happened during the summer.

In California, the farm was full of rocks just lying on top of the ground. He'd have me fill a wheelbarrow full of rocks. Then when Eleena was away, he'd make me lie down and he'd dump the rocks on top of me.

He got the idea to use bricks and cinder blocks. He'd make me lie down on the ground and put bricks or cider blocks on my chest.

He'd put a bag over my head and tie me to a post and leave me there.

In the winter, he'd take off my coat, tie me to a post and leave me there.

He'd put my hands in a vise.

That's it.

I never could figure out how to rebel with this.

Nils: Boy, he knew he wasn't supposed to, but Philip had candy at the movies.

*****

Philip hit Nils in the face. Of course, it was the body's face, and the attack was so sudden I thought I had broken the keyboard. It took a while to realize it, but Nils tended to "bait" Philip. Philip did not communicate for a while.

*****

Fran's Notes: Debra can't concentrate at all. There is a lot of time with the personalities. Damon figured out a schedule for all of them and maybe they won't get into any trouble. Philip hit Nils and had to go to his room. I have been learning a lot about her personalities.

Philip: Okay. I'll quit hiding. I'm sorry. I knew it was forbidden to hit. I'm awful awful awful awful scared and have been since yesterday. I just wanna get whatever I get and sit next to you and put my head on your chest and cry.

Bruce: Philip, Obviously you know that hitting Nils was wrong. So let me ask you a question? Do you want to become like Walter Amundson and hurt people? Because to a degree you are headed that way unless you can control your anger. People that cannot manage their anger end up in trouble a lot. Being violent is worse than poor language. Neither one is acceptable and for your act of

violence you cannot "come out" for 3 days. No e-mails, nothing. If you hit again I will lengthen the time that you cannot "come out." If you curse at me or anyone else in your next e-mail I will lengthen the time. When Thursday comes you will apologize to Nils without a ":p" expression. If you do put a ":p" expression in your e-mail it will cost you another day.

Hitting someone over them telling someone you had candy is very poor, very poor.

*****

When I first started to wake up, we were given rooms, our own room for each of us, in the Other Realm. Sometimes we spent a lot of time there, but each room was a place to go and sleep when we were there. So we had a bed and Little Debra also had toys. There was (still is) a person there who decided to take care of us while we were in the Other Realm. Her name is Jeanie, and we discovered that she is the same person who took care of me right when I was born. Her face is the first face I looked at when I was newborn.

(At this moment, I am not yet integrated. I try to maintain my "offer and explain" mode, but I find working on this book to be difficult. Whenever I am overwhelmed with grief, I fall asleep. I also become ill with nausea and headache. By now I know that's a pretty good indication of something in my subconscious coming to the surface. This healing process has not been fun. But I do think I am called to write this book, even though I feel terribly vulnerable. I honestly don't know why I'm writing this book.)

Bruce discovered that he could discipline any one of us by sending us to our room. It was a time out and pretty effective. If I did not surrender to Bruce and to this process of healing, I'd get in trouble with God. Not good. I think that the trouble these kids get into is a testament to just how healthy these child parts of me really are!

*****

Nils: Hi. It's me. Nils. I don't wanna hit Philip any more even though he hit me. I was so mad and I got worried cause I thought he'd busted the keyboard cause I reacted and I had to pry up the shift key. But I'm not mad at Philip any more.

I think I'm the easy one for you. Maybe that's cause Philip lived all the life except the sodomy thing. And at the time, we didn't know each other at all.

I don't know if Philip will tell you this. This isn't Philip talking through me at all and he's not mad that I'm telling you this, just scared of you about it.

But last night God took Philip. And God talked to Philip, but Philip couldn't hear too good. But God said that he had to obey you. God talked some more and told Philip that he did not have to rebel, you know, on a deep level, any more and said to Philip about the rebellion and his need to rebel you know so he won't die: "It's over, Philip. Be at peace." And that's when Philip really cried and every time he remembers that part, he cries again.

I like what you say to me and stuff, especially the praising part. But I don't understand a lot of it. It's like you're talking to the adult through me, but she doesn't get it either cause I don't get it and, besides, it's not HER experience. Strange, I know. Are you afraid to kiss me and cuddle me with your words, or do you just not want to?

Anyway, me and Philip are just children. I know I try to be an adult sometimes cause I think I'm not SUPPOSED to be a child, but boy it sure doesn't work any.

Anyway, we're gonna go to a movie today. We usually do once on Saturday and once on Sunday.

*****

I had no conscience throughout life. I had a system of morality, but not a conscience. During the early part of my healing, it was formed, mainly through discipline, but I guess God knew what he was doing because it was successful. I now have a conscience that I find to be pretty pesky.

*****

Bruce: Greetings Damon, Nils, Adult and Philip (when you come out on Thursday),

You have to pull together as a group for the sake of merging again. Each one of you has talents and gifts that make up the group. You have to work together to make the adult successful, which in turn makes you successful and happier. Families that fight, argue, tell on each other, are common. Families that pull together, in spite of the fighting, arguing, etc. are exceptional. Sorry, but you fall under the exceptional category because you are bright, perceptive, intelligent and you have a unique relationship with God. So, let's not blow this opportunity with pettiness and smallness. If Damon likes to exercise then Damon is in charge of exercising and the rest of you will cooperate – why? Because it is good for the whole. Philip is the mover and shaker, so put your energy into making the adult successful and responsible - both at work and at home with the chores. Philip – make good choices, spend wisely, eat well. Nils, you are the creative one, the information officer, who observes everyone

else and explains things to me. If you all work together there will be less stress, more fun, more success, less fighting and anger. Get it?!

NOW, another important part: Forgive each other, every day, twice a day, three times a day if necessary. Love each other, do daily acts of kindness to each other. This is what God wants from you and for you. So, practice and discipline yourselves, work together. Make this a good day and make everyday a good day – attitude!

Fran's Notes: Philip feels vulnerable with me and that I'll hurt him and won't care. Philip was beaten and tortured as well as sexual abuse that occurred. It was so constant.

Debra has a hard time relating to women. She has a best friend who is a woman.

Philip: You said I can come out of my room today, so I'm OUT.

From now on if I have to go to my room again, I'm gonna play with my friends!!! I still won't be OUT anyway, so I'm gonna!! Screw you!!

Here's the big important apology:

Nils, I'm sorry I hit you.

There. I said it. But I don't think he should tell on me all the time. He's just a stupid blabbermouth little twerp.

And screw everything and I think I can do anything I WANT!!

I didn't stick my tongue out and I didn't do any cursing so you can't discipline me.

Bruce: Good morning Philip, Good to hear from you. Your comments show no remorse at all but only a defiant attitude. So go back to your room and think it over for two more days. We will see where your attitude is Saturday. If it hasn't changed we will repeat the order to go back to your room. And the longer you are defiant the longer it will be before you earn some privileges. In other words you will have to demonstrate good behavior for a period of time in order to enjoy any privileges. So think it over long and hard!

Nils: We're all pretty scared that when you let Philip out of his room, that he's gonna just take over and wreck stuff and do whatever he wants. The Adult's a wreck, but I'm not supposed to tell you about her.

I know that *I* just wanna be treated like any normal child and kissed and cuddled and stuff. You said that I could put my head on your chest and that was the first time you reached out to me like that really. I didn't have to ask! And, gee, yeah, I wanna put my head on your chest! Of course I do! I want and need what children want and need. See?

Bruce: Greetings Nils, One of the things that you should learn is that you should always tell the truth. Honesty is important. Sometimes it is not easy to be honest or when you do something wrong admit that you did it. Some kids will lie about what they have done to keep from being punished. But if you want to grow up to be a responsible person you have to be honest about what you do or have done. Most people will respect you for your honesty. When my son was growing up he wasn't always honest about his actions and I would catch him in a lie. I would tell him that by not telling the truth or by lying he made it difficult for me to trust him. If you do not trust your son or daughter then you will not let them do things or have as many privileges.

Always do your best work. Work hard. You have great ideas. Your language is at a higher level than an eleven year old so that's great. If you accept a responsibility work hard to fulfill the responsibility and do your best work.

If you have trouble I will be here for you as much as I can be. Like I wrote to you before, I have not thrown you away, nor do I intend to throw you away. The same is for Philip.

So what would you like to do if you had free time when you are out?

Nils: Hi. It's really Thursday night but I can't really go to bed yet. On a weekend, I wanna go to a movie that I like and be out without Philip being out instead of me. I wanna make decisions on if we take the dogs someplace and stuff. I know I can't drive or anything and at my time I wanna be out. If you say I gotta do the chores that the Adult would do in the morning, then that'll be okay. Like dishes and laundry.

Um, okay, um on the way home today God talked to me. And um he said that I gotta tell you about me, too. Tell you stuff that I do that's poor, too. And and he said that um he was gonna enforce me too, just like he does Philip.

And then I read what YOU said to me today and I just couldn't BELIEVE it! You know? It's like you and God talk to each other about stuff, you know? And between you and God I'm just doomed. Just doomed.

Well, what I did today, well, let me preface it by saying that usually I'm pretty good, you know? And it's the first time I didn't tell you stuff about me. And it's not much really. Just a little wrong, you know? And nothing came of it or anything.

Um, what the little thing I did today was that when Philip blew, you know, after he found out that he had to go to his room. Well, what I did was I um I double-dared him to call you a motherfucker. I knew it was forbidden for him to say that to you and stuff but I double-dared him anyway.

Fractured Mind

Oh please Daddy, please. I don't wanna be disciplined. Please. I'll be really honest next time. Really. I don't lie. Not really. I just didn't tell you, you know? And I won't double dare Philip to say that again. And I'll tell you everything next time and from now on. Daddy! Please?

Bruce: Nils, You know that daring Philip is wrong. You know that and still you did it anyway because deep down inside you want to see him get in trouble. Philip may be hard to live with and you may resent his behavior towards you but we all have to work together for the sake of all. You have responsibilities to the adult, to Damon, to Philip and to Little Debra. All of them have responsibilities to you. All of you have responsibilities to each other to be kind, to be helpful, to be trustworthy, to be loyal. What you did is wrong and this isn't the first time you have dared Philip. So, you cannot be out today and if you do this again I will make it two days. Understood? If God hadn't talked to you, you probably wouldn't have come forth with your confession. When you behave like this it erodes my trust in you.

When you come out tomorrow you will be nice to Philip regardless of how nasty he may be. If he is nasty I will deal with him strongly and so will God. When you come out tomorrow you will do chores – dishes and laundry with a good attitude.

If all goes well we will talk about you making a decision on the movie and on taking the dogs somewhere next week.

Fran's Notes: Philip has transference issues with me given that I asked some questions before and it triggered feelings of neglect from his mom.

Debra and I talked about nurturing Philip but she doesn't know how. Her anxiety level is so high. She had no nurturing by anyone and there was a lot of neglect. She is beginning to build self worth.

Damon: Peace at last! Peace at last! Thank God Almighty, there's peace at last!!!

Hi Dad. Two kids crying in their rooms. A bit difficult to concentrate with all THAT din going on, but we'll manage JUST fine!!

God talked to the Adult on the way home yesterday, too. He told her that Philip/Nils are now who she would have been without the terror. She replied with, "Gee, I sure do get in trouble a lot." And God said, "Yes, you do." The Adult doesn't understand anything, you know. Not really what's happening, she doesn't understand any of it. Maybe because she's never been who she should have been as a kid, never had this experience that the kids are having now. I don't know.

Bruce: Greetings Damon, If Nils and Philip mature and have new understandings perhaps the adult will have a new consciousness about the whole thing when you all merge again.

Enjoy the peace, I can't say the quiet but maybe they will stop crying at some point. Tomorrow ought to be fun with both of them coming out.

Damon: Thanks, Dad. Have a good weekend. Maybe after that Tasmanian Devil comes out again, eh?

By the way, we're wondering if Nils isn't changing into a girl. I know you have no way of knowing that. But sometimes, not always but sometimes, we're thinking "she" instead of "he" and we're pretty surprised at that. Pretty strange on this end!!

Bruce: Strange indeed! But we will work with whoever shows up - male or female. You have a good weekend also – Tasmanian Devil and all :>)

Damon: Oh Dad, God's a pretty good therapist, you know? I asked if I should tell you this, and he said yes, that you already kinda know, but yes.

God told us to go upstairs and get a bath. Sometimes we hear God really well in water. So we did. So we found ourselves standing before God. All of us. God said to the Adult, "Who are you?" She said, "I don't know. I thought I did. But then, I was just shoving all this aside so I can live. But I don't know anymore."

We all stepped back except for Philip. God said, "Who do you want to be, child?" And Philip said, "I don't know. I don't know." Then God talked about you. He said, "I've placed you in the most capable hands in the world, Philip. Now what do you want?"

"I don't know."

"What do you want?"

"I don't know."

"What do you want?"

"He won't hit me. He won't even throw me away and I don't know why not."

"What do you want?"

"I want him to kill me."

And when that secret came out Philip cried. And I mean the kind of cry that feels like vomit. The body sweat profusely.

The only thing that Philip can see is his life that was, you know? And when he cried, that's what he saw, and he felt the fear he knew nearly every day of his life. Philip said that he wanted to die really, and he always wanted to die but he just couldn't and he just didn't want to live like this anymore. But then God talked to him. He told him that it isn't that way any more and that God needs to help Philip know a different way. He said, "The fear will end, Philip. It'll take some time, but it'll end. You must obey Bruce. And I must enforce that to help him help you through all of this. It will be the most difficult thing you've ever done in your life. It will be very very hard, Philip. We must be very hard. But Bruce is here and I am here. You must obey, and the fear will end, not quickly, but it will end."

"But what about merging?"

"I don't want you to think about merging. That will happen by itself when it's time. Right now, you must be yourself and obey Bruce."

"But if I'm myself, then I'm gonna just screw everything up."

"You're my child, Philip. You're mine. Just be yourself. The fear will end."

And that's it.

Who knew that a little exercise and a couple of vegetables would lead to this? Sorry, lame humor here. It's Friday night now. Bye.

Bruce: Damon, The road to wholeness comes a layer at a time, a consciousness at a time. Each time something comes to the surface it provides an opportunity to deal with it. I don't have all the answers but I know killing someone isn't the answer but it does tell us how much suffering Philip has been through. It will take time to build him back up so that he feels secure enough to explore who he wants to be and have hope that it can happen. Thanks for sharing with me and watch out for the exercise and vegetables!!

Fran's Notes: *She can't believe how much Eleena hates her. Manipulation. Eleena always wants her to be a child again. Her mom sounds like a child and is a nasty person.*

Philip: This isn't me trying to get out of anything. It isn't cause God talked to me and it isn't cause I think I know what's in store for me. It's because I don't wanna be this way. I don't know what I'm fighting against. I don't know why I say the things I say. What you said about honesty isn't crap. It's nothing but truth stuff, real stuff. I feel like I'm fighting the biggest dragon in the world, and that dragon is within me.

I wanna be a prince. And that means I gotta try harder to obey you. You talk about honesty and loyalty and stuff and that's prince stuff, you know? To be honest with you, I'm not sure that I can NOT be angry. But I know that you don't deserve me being angry and nasty. And I sure don't know why on earth you don't just throw me away. I really AM trash, you know.

I know you don't believe me right now. Shoot, *I* wouldn't believe me either. And I know that trust is earned. And I honestly don't know if I can NOT be angry and nasty and NOT say foul language stuff. But I want you to be proud of me and I think that's gonna take some time.

I feel like I'm just a nothing person, empty, you know? And to be honest, it really scares me that you WON'T throw me away. Cause then I gotta try and I really don't know even HOW to try. I do know that I need you to be really really big. Really big and really hard so I can listen. Cause I don't listen too good. And I don't respect at all. I need you to be bigger than the dragon and stronger than the dragon and harder than the dragon. Will you forgive me please? I'm sorry Daddy.

*****

Philip and the rest of the parts did not know it at the time, but the "dragon" was a consequence of a layer of the subconscious moving toward the conscious.

*****

Bruce: Hi Philip, I am proud of you for this e-mail. This e-mail that you sent was honest, open and humble. There was no anger and there was remorse. I am very proud of you and this is the first step in slaying the dragon. Stay strong today and know that I care for you very much. I will not throw you away. So, talk to me about books and things that interest you. I understand that you like sci-fi.

Also, Philip I want you to put your head on my chest and breathe deeply and listen to my heartbeat. When you start to feel angry stop! Put your head on my chest, breathe deeply and listen to my heart. Try this technique and see if it helps. Now if you can't stop your anger just go to your room and sit a while. If you can do this on your own I will be very proud. So the general rule is to stay in your room until you are no longer angry. When you think you can be out of your room and be nice and use good language and help others – that is when you can come out of your room.

Philip: I'm doomed to eternity then. :(

Bruce: Philip, The Little Engine that could is a story of a small train engine that didn't think he could pull a load up a hill but he kept saying "I think I can, I think I can." So Philip, adjust your attitude from "doomed" to "I think I can." After all, you have had a great day as far as I can see. And on a computer, you can't see far :>) Write me tomorrow and tell me about your attitude!!

Philip: The Little Engine that Could is for babies, Dad. Geez.

Damon: My Story. I don't have the pain that Philip does and Nils did, no worries there. And I'll make it as quick as I can.

I came out after Philip left the Amundson's. I did not know my past at all, didn't know Philip or Nils or Little Debra or anything that happened. Somebody would ask where I was from and I didn't know, so I'd tell them where I was born. I did know about my parents, but they didn't have an affect on me, except I was scared of them. I just knew that I must stay away from them and that I didn't like them and I was afraid of them.

But I didn't know anything else, either. They didn't teach Philip anything at all. I didn't know about where to go to buy anything, about money, jobs, cooking, nothing. I had to figure that out on my own. I stole things first until I figured it out. I didn't know how to talk to people either. I was pretty shy.

The ONLY thing I knew I had was my intelligence, my mind. So while I was part of the drug scene, I didn't do it. And I didn't drink either. I knew that if I ever needed help, there was nobody to help me.

I went to university because I didn't know what else to do and I liked learning things. The Amundson's found me and went to the university and tried to get me kicked out of school. I figure he wanted his farm hand back. But all of a sudden, I was REQUIRED to go to counseling. And the chair of my department started to take an interest to the point that I was in trouble all the time with him. I had to answer to him about grades and everything else. He gave me my first job in theatre. Semester by semester all the way through doctorate, I wondered if I'd be able to go back financially. Somehow, I always managed.

I kept on through uni because I didn't know what else to do. I tried to get into the Army, but couldn't because I'm Canadian. (Got my U.S. citizenship in 1979.)

I had no conscience. I had no sense of right or wrong. I had no guide. I ran across an old essay called *Desiderata*. I copied it down and carried it with me and thought it was a good way for me to be. So that was my first sense of values.

There was absolutely nobody who cared about me or loved me. And I don't mean this the way it is now. This was a reality; nobody did. In filling out the forms, "In case of emergency please notify ..." I had nobody to notify. Sometimes I would live on the streets. I was doing that when Ian Bruch picked me up hitchhiking. I was a good thief and never got caught.

I felt utterly alone and completely unloved, and I just thought that I deserved it.

Once as an undergraduate, a man tried to rape me and I beat the shit out of him and he didn't succeed. But I got cut up pretty good and was covered in my blood when I went back to the dorm, where I was living at that time. I made the terrible mistake of calling up Walter Amundson and I wanted somebody to care. He didn't. He told the police that I just made it up for attention. The police told me that it was very obvious by evidence at the scene that I didn't make it up.

I saw other people have families and do Christmas and Thanksgiving and all that and wondered why not me. I still do, frankly, although I handle it better now.

I was utterly, completely alone. And I was utterly, completely lonely.

I saw your wife and daughter text each other and man, I STILL wonder why I'm so alone and why my life has been the way it's been but I hide that pretty good.

Anyway, the real reason I'm telling you this is that I had to create my own values and my own understanding about that. The church helped a lot once I got into that.

You see, Little Debra, Philip, and Nils have no sense of values except from when they came out with Ken and now you. Everything the Adult and I are, or have been, when it comes to understanding life has come from other people like 10 years of you, through me and the Adult, not from any childhood teaching or caring. As you know by now, we got some, and maybe a lot, of it wrong.

What's happening, in part of course, is that transference is happening between you and Philip/Nils. Philip/Nils have very little values or understanding; that's come from me and the Adult, see? But there's been very very little that was formed in our childhood.

So when you teach THEM (and you've been teaching us for 10 years now), but when you teach THEM, it's at the foundational level. The no-hitting is one. And your essay on honesty is another. What you say ABOUT them, doesn't connect yet because they haven't been able to believe it yet. Except for Nils, he's accepting better and easier than Philip.

So this is why we want you to teach Philip/Nils too. Like the honesty essay. Values. Beliefs about life. Understandings about life. So Philip/Nils can build a system, a good system this time, and it'll be on our foundational level. So transference can take place.

Whew! And THIS is short!! Thanks! Have a good one!!

*****

Damon was born when we left the Amundson's and was a host part. We had been living at The Farm near Maryville, Missouri. My brother and I call this place The Farm because it was the longest place we lived to date during the first-life, and also Walter Amundson was around all the time, unlike the other places we lived. At this time, Philip went to sleep, which means he was no longer out and living but buried in the subconscious. Nils also went to sleep at this time. Little Debra went to sleep when Philip was born. Damon was not born during the first-life due to trauma from the Amundson's. When I left The Farm, I did not know anything. I did not know how to get a towel! By this time, dissociation was the way I handled fear. I only knew the world to be a fearful and lonely place. Damon was out and living, but he did not know of any other part. Neither did he have memories of a past. When somebody asked him where he was from, he did not know. It felt like the answer was "on the tip of my tongue" but it would not come. During the second-life, he is fifteen years old.

When not attending university, during summers, and sometimes when I was living in the dorm and was required to leave during Thanksgiving, Christmas, and winter breaks I as Damon would live on the streets. I did not like the cities very much so tended to hitchhike. I managed to graduate with a Bachelor's Degree, but I continued to be lost. I lived on the streets all the time after I graduated. I was hitching north of Kansas City on I-35 one summer and Ian Bruch picked me up. He asked me where I was going and I said, "Nowhere man." He then told me that he was going to a church reunion and did I want to go. I said, "Hell no." He said that I would have a bed and food for a week for free so I went. During that week he bugged me quite a lot and I figured it was how I was paying for the week. But he eventually got through and wanted me to settle down. He said he was moving to Lamoni but I could not find work there so I asked him where he was from and he said Independence, Missouri, so I promised I'd go there. He also told me he did not want me to steal anymore and I just laughed at him. He insisted and I told him fine, but if I needed money he was going to give it to me. He agreed and later on a few times I needed $20 and he sent it to me.

He never let go of me. I do not know why he took an interest in me. He told me once that he immediately saw my potential, saw that I was socially inept, and because God asked him to. He taught me about God and I eventually embraced it all. What he did was God's grace in action.

I also do not know why I responded to Ian Bruch. It took me a year before I could trust him. I thought he wanted to have sex but he never did. I did what he wanted and settled down in Independence. It took me ten months before I could keep a job and later learnt that street people often took ten to twelve months before they could trust the system enough and know expectations enough to keep a job.

I had no conscience but I had a system. Fran Waters, my therapist, says that a person who is a sociopath, psychopath, or pedophile do not have empathy toward other people. I did two things to help me not turn: I created a system of living and I bottled up my severe anger. During the Philip, Nils, and Damon phase of my healing, I gained a conscience and had to give up my system. All this raising me a second time helped me gain a conscience. So during my second-life formative years with Philip, Nils, and Damon, I gained a conscience.

*****

Bruce: Damon, Thank you for another piece of the puzzle. Your explanation is very helpful and I shall continue to be prayerful about the appropriate foundational pieces to fill in for Nils and Philip. By the way, you have a wonderful sense of humor. Blessings to you, Friend Damon.

Fran's Notes: Philip hasn't worked through the trauma. Philip goes to Bruce and puts his head on his shoulder and listens to his heart. Nils also has that permission too, but he doesn't need it as much.

Nils: Hi Daddy -- Um, we had a pretty good day I think. We went to a movie that Philip wanted to see, about vampires. He thought it was cool and I didn't MIND it. But it was kinda stupid. When you think of it, we get two for the price of one. Anyway, I'm finishing the laundry now.

But I'm caught in this honesty thing, you know, cause you're not right here to see for yourself and stuff. And, um, well, let me preface this by saying that me and Philip didn't get mad at each other exactly. And I think it's just children stuff anyway, and I don't think I should be disciplined cause it's children stuff is all. And it's all pretty minor.

But if I don't tell you, then it's a lie, and Philip can't cause he's had his email for the day, which in my opinion just sucks.

Okay. We went to the movie. Philip got a lemonade and popcorn. We started watching the movie. I double-dared Philip to get candy. I wanted him to be in trouble. He finally said, fuck it, and got candy. Then HE figured that if I told on him, then I'd have to tell you about ME wanting him to get into trouble, so he got the candy so I COULD get in trouble. Besides you never said that candy was forbidden, but he did remember that before we separated again you said no to that.

I did remember the discipline last time and what you said and everything, but, alas, the temptation was just too great and I ignored it all.

So *I'm* thinking that since we didn't actually get mad at each other or nasty with each other, that all this was okay after all.

Bruce: Wrong again my little friend, Your mistake in the matter was the "double-dare". Philip's mistake was getting the candy so you would get in trouble. So, you are both doing things for the wrong reasons - getting each other in trouble. So, both of you will spend the afternoon in your rooms. You can come out at dinnertime. Let me also say that I am proud of both of you for not getting angry at each other. So there is some good things in this scenario and some things we still need to work on.

*****

Philip and Nils went into the Other Realm and into their rooms, but not after Philip became angry and said some pretty nasty things. For some reason, God literally shoved him OUT.

*****

Philip: Oh FUCK!!! I'd just as soon stay in my room but I just can't do ANYTHING I wanna do any more!! God just shoved me OUT!!

Okay. I'm sorry, Daddy.

Well, what the hell is remorse anyway? And how am I supposed to feel it? The only thing I know is that I feel bad for calling you a big dumb fuck. Cause you haven't hurt ME. And I feel kinda ashamed that I called you a big dumb fuck. I didn't mean it. Not really. I figure that people will hurt me as soon as they can. So fuck them. But you didn't. I really HATE this discipline thing but that's my lot in life I guess. I don't get WHY I can't do whatever I wanna do!! I mean, who gives a rats ass anyway?

And I'll tell ya, I'll beat the shit out of that Nils cause I really hate it when that pansy ass motherfucker tells on

oh, shiiiiitttt

I just blew it, didn't I? I shoulda just stayed in my room. I shoulda shut up right after "I'm sorry Daddy." And this no-deleting rule just kills me. I guess that's connected to that honesty crap you talked about, huh.

I just wanna be held and cuddled and kissed and maybe for SOMEBODY to love me, but that's just not in the cards I guess. And I really do want you to trust me and stuff.

yeah, yeah, yeah, I know the drill. Back to my room. How long THIS time?

Oh, sweet freedom, how you elude me so!!!

(Braveheart)
FFRRRREEEEEEDDDDOOOOOOOOOOOOMMMM!!
Fuck. I'm going. FUCK.

And unlike pansy ass Nils who trembles and fears as he walks to his room, *I'll* have courage and whatever dignity I can muster up as I walk to my room and toward MY doom. Okay. Maybe I'm not THAT tough, but I sure wish I was.

Fuck everything! Fuck everybody! FUCK THE WORLD!!

I'm going. fuck

Bruce: Philip, Remorse is feeling bad after you have done something wrong. Usually, feeling bad is a strong indicator that you did something wrong. Once you realize this you need to figure out how to make it right. When I tell you to apologize to Nils that is making it right or reconciling. If you want people to stop telling on you, stop doing things that you are not suppose to do. It is that simple!!

Damon: I swear you and God talk to each other!! The kids just don't have a chance to get away with anything! Last night, God called Nils to him. God asked Nils what he did wrong. And Nils told him that he tried to get Philip into trouble and he ignored the warnings that were going on within him at the time. Then God told Nils that he had no remorse at all. Nils replied that he's gonna feel remorse pretty soon. God said, no, that's not remorse, that's self-pity, that's getting caught and being sorry about getting caught, and there's a difference. And God told him that remorse happens when a person loves another person as much as himself. That didn't quite compute with Nils because we all know that we don't love ourselves at all. But then God sent him to bed. Between that and what you said to Philip today puts it all together and is really freaky on this end. None of us can understand any of this. And what's really amazing is that NONE of us can predict either you or God in any of this. All I know is that what you say and what God says is sticking, even though we don't understand. So I guess we just don't need to know, and maybe it'll compute as we progress. Meantime, we have like NO control over ANYTHING!!!!

And yet strangely all of it, and I mean ALL of it, feels like security. Don't ask me why!!

I do know that Philip felt really badly that he said that what you said about honesty was crap. And he just didn't feel good about it at all and felt that he might have hurt you by saying that and he found that he cared about whether or not he hurt you. And that's how he found himself talking to you. And he understands better about that because of what you told him today.

When Philip was living on the Missouri farm, from 13 to late 16 years old, he was downright suicidal. He cried to sleep nearly every night and learned to cry silently. When they caught him crying, they'd become angry or beat him so that he'd "have something to cry about". But then Eleena had an encounter with the Holy Spirit. She told Philip that she was praying to God saying "Help me. Please help me." over and over again. She felt God speak to her and say "You're praying for the wrong person." She felt really good and important that God touched her. And she thought that the other person she was supposed to pray about was Walter Amundson. But Philip knew that it was him. And that saw him through.

When Philip was 14 years old, Jack left. Jack just up and left the day after he graduated from high school and nobody expected it. A year ago, Jack and I (merged) went to see David supposedly for the last time, as David was dying. Both Jack and David smoke, so when Jack and I left, I felt pretty sick. It was a four hour drive back to Kansas City where Eleena was and I lay in the back seat, sick. Jack told us that during those four hours of driving, he turned off the radio and thought about his past. He said that he went all the way through his past and he had no memory of me at all in it. None. He couldn't remember anything about me at all.

My humor is a combination of genetics and rebellion against life. Same as Philip's really. But Jack and I have the same sense of humor and wit. And that's the genetics. David doesn't have it at all, but he has a different biological father. The rest of it is a result of our life really. It's a way to look at life and deal with it by mocking it instead of letting it get you down.

And I'll MAYBE shut up now. Take care, friend Dad!

Bruce: Friend Damon, So, do you think with these interactions with God and myself that there may be the beginnings of a trust level developing with Philip and Nils?

The mysteries of God are wonderful. I am just trying to pay attention to the Holy Spirit when I answer the e-mails. I do not know how all this works either but I know it does work in part because God loves all of us and wants us to be whole, healthy, happy with the ability to love others.

Friend, Dad, Bruce

Damon: Um, the trust level between you and BOTH Philip and Nils is right now very very high. Me too. We don't see that changing.

What God has given us is a spirituality that has connected all of us to him. It began at our baby life with Mommy in the Air. We can feel you, your spirit. Whether it's delayed or not, we don't know. But Philip knew how you felt when you first read his email when God shoved him out and you weren't happy about it. And that alone got him thinking about not wanting really to hurt you and he felt remorse.

Philip can feel you when he puts his head on your chest. All this takes spiritual concentration, but God helps.

And the kids' trust level is high with God, too. Neither one of you hurts their insides, and they know that. The trust level with you is much, much higher than any we've experienced before. We've seen it, you've talked about it, and we know that you have a high, mature, healthy, relationship with your wife to the point that we, none of us, have to worry about anything at all. We just don't have to worry about it with you. Period. You're a different father to us. One that WILL NOT do these things.

One of the things you taught us was that we can't fix it for other people. That it's their choice. Well, sometimes a person can't really MAKE a choice. And, guess what, you're hip deep in fixing!!! But I think that takes a real relationship with God, too, and a trust in God, and even a dependence on God to help someone on this kind of level.

Bruce: There is a subtle difference between fixing and teaching. Fixing can be short term and a remedy without much thought for the individual. "Let's just get it done or fixed" attitude. Teaching values a person and generally has a longer vision of the goal that is being worked on. Teaching is optimistic in nature believing in the giftedness of the individual. The teacher may not quite have a handle on the details of the giftedness nor the depth of the giftedness at first but the exploration with the student will bring those gifts to the surface. It is a combination of discipline with expectations, even when the student may not have any, pastoral care for the wholeness of the learner and tenacity to see it through even when the learner whines – kinda like the adult!! Just kidding :>)

Nils: Yesterday when I was thinking about double-daring Philip, all sorts of things went off in me. I remembered what you said about what would happen if I did it again. I remembered the discipline you gave me. Is that a conscience? Am I like developing a conscience about stuff? Sure, I ignored it all, but is that a conscience? Philip hasn't experienced this, but I did yesterday.

Bruce: Nils, Sounds like you are developing a conscience. When you are able to think about the right and wrong of things prior to doing them or reflecting on the right or wrong of what you have done that is being conscience of your actions.

Philip: Daddy, last night when we went to bed, God came and got me out of my room. And I had to stand before God and eventually he said, "Philip, it's wrong to hurt anybody. It's wrong to hurt any of my creation. You were meant to heal."

And then all of a sudden God was gone. And something else was there. It sure looked like God but it didn't feel like God. And I looked around and I saw black demons here, and they were in my bedroom too. And I said, "You're not God." And then all of a sudden it changed into something scary and I bolted. I mean I just ran.

And I ran right to you, Daddy. I ran right to you and I grabbed hold of you and you held me too and I put my head on your chest and I heard your heart and I breathed deep. And I went to sleep. I mean the body went right to sleep. It's in the middle of the night now cause I woke up, but I promise I'll go right back to bed. Can I stay with you today? Please?

Bruce: Yes, Philip you can stay with me today and I will hold your hand. And you can put your head on my chest. Hey, I am proud of your response to the demons and I am glad I was there for you. Good job, Philip!

*****

Through the course of several weeks, Bruce taught me some life lessons. Both Nils and Philip had their own allowance and could buy something only from their own money. He also taught me how to live in more healthy ways like brushing my teeth and washing my bed sheets once a week, to throw away any rusted pans and utensils, and to clean up the kitchen every day. The kids had weekend chores that I still do today. Dad says that adults take care of every day things and then do other things once the living activities were finished.

When I was about fourteen years old, I started to beat up my classmates at school. I wanted to know why my stepfather liked hurting me so much. But I did not like hurting other people. Nevertheless, I kept trying, and found myself required to go to a mental health institution.

*****

Damon: The Adult told the therapist about the high school counseling after Philip started to beat people up. When going to high school, Philip started to beat up other kids and then had to go to the outpatient clinic of the mental health institute at St. Joseph. That was the first time we saw a therapist. That guy was good, I think, because like by the second or third visit, he brought in his wife. And they demonstrated what two married people are supposed to be with each other. We'd never before seen such a thing, you know? They touched and laughed and hugged and kissed in front of us.

This was in Philip's first-life, so I didn't remember that happening, but what it did for me was that I saw people. I observed relationships, you know? And I tried to learn that way. I think I did pretty good really, but I didn't know the insides of things you know. And not only between married people, but I observed parents and kids, too, but I don't know the insides of that, either, until now. We didn't know, cause what we know comes from movies and TV and books. And now we're finding out that that's not correct. It's really hard to know that what you think is right turns out it isn't. Kinda blows me apart a little and I'm not too sure of things anymore. I don't think I'm supposed to be sure of things of what I figured out before.

It's like people give us books to read and expect us to learn. But because we're so friggin' smart, nobody can believe that we don't know how to read so nobody's taught us how to read and we can't learn that on our own. But the expectation's there anyway. I think maybe you're teaching us how to read.

Nils: Something's wrong with Philip. He's like been in his room, like withdrawn stuff since yesterday. I know that he heard you about chores and stuff and after you explained, he thought that was okay then. I don't know. I'm trying to figure it out. I know he's got this first-life in his face and he doesn't know why the monster hurt him so bad. I don't know. He's scared.

Gee, it'll take me two more movies before I can get popcorn too. Can our allowance go up to $12???!! Please?

Bruce: **Nils, Let's see how Philip does in the next couple of days. Be really nice to him because he is probably feeling vulnerable (sad). Remind him that he can put his head on my chest or hold my hand if that will help.**

Sorry, no pay raise on the allowance. Go to a movie every other week and get the movie, a drink and popcorn. Think it through and live within the money you receive. It is a discipline that will pay off later as well.

Philip: I don't really wanna be out this weekend. I wanna just stay with you and hold your hand and when you're not walking around put my head on your chest and stuff. I'll do chores if you want me to and maybe go to a movie, but mostly I just wanna stay with you this weekend. Okay?

Bruce: **Philip, That is fine with me. I'll be glad to have you around as my buddy this weekend.**

*****

Fractured Mind

Nils tells Bruce about pain in my ribs in the right side of my chest. To this day, the pain is still there.

*****

Nils: It was really cool to be out by myself for such a long time at once. Cause it was trash day, I had to clean up the turkey pots and stuff from last Saturday and it was really gross and I had to get all the meat off of the bones so all that stuff would go into the trash. So I did that. The only thing I really really didn't like about it is that my ribs hurt me. After a while being out, I felt that old pain. I think that Philip and the Adult can block the pain, but I can't. It's the right side of my ribs. And only one spot. Doctors know, but they can't do anything about it now.

Philip remembers this happening really really clearly when he was on the Missouri farm. Out by the edge of the field, the monster would beat him pretty bad. And if Philip fell down, he'd kick him. Thing is, Philip always fell down when it happened that bad. And the monster wore these big farming cowboy boots and he kicked Philip in the ribs. After the beating and after Philip woke up and he could feel his body again, those ribs were wrong and hurt too much. He made the big mistake of telling them cause he hoped they'd help him, maybe Eleena might, but he was wrong. Once the monster knew of THAT spot, he'd hit it. Just touching it even now, it hurts. The others have learned to live with it except the times it flares up, but not me. They can ignore it, but not me.

So that was the ONLY bummer about yesterday, and I'd do it again in a minute! Thanks, Daddy, for letting me be out like that!! Totally cool!!

Bruce: Nils, Glad you had a good day, a good weekend. You were very busy, productive and responsible. I will expect you to improve on your eating habits. Cereal for dinner is not acceptable. Having that many dishes to clean up at the end of a week is not a good practice either. I will speak to the adult about this.

Little Debra: Hi Daddy! I'm 6 and I can see animal spirits and stuff. God taught me how to see animal spirits. They don't relly die, you know. They go back into the earth, but I can see them run around when I see a dead animal by the road. Sometimes Michel brings a spirit animal to my room and say hi. Philip can see them too and he can talk to trees and stuff and they talk back and teach him stuff. Once he hugged a grandpa tree and it broke a little cause Philip was to excited cause the grandpa tree taught him important stuff. The tree told him to not do that again!!! But he's seen a tree ripped up and the tree was hurting and that was wrong for people to rip up a tree. But once Philip saw a tree die and he was really sad, but the tree said what's the big deal? The tree just went back to the earth and didn't die. Jesus says I gotta come back to my room now and play with my friends. Bye Daddy!

*****

    I don't know why Little Debra came out to talk to Bruce. Years prior, whenever we would pass road kill, she got very very upset. God gave her a gift to be able to see the spirit of the animal immediately and gradually she became calm. In the Other Realm, an archangel named Michel befriended her and brought her the spirit of animals to pet for a little while, and visited her during this time also. During this healing process, she stayed there in the Other Realm playing with other kids there until she integrated. Jeanie took care of her.

*****

Damon: I asked God this morning why my survival mode is a wrong now when it wasn't in my first-life. He told me that back then I was living on the streets, and my survival mode was necessary in order to not let some people hurt me when I was in that situation. But now, it's a wrong because it's either directed at people who won't hurt me or we have a different set of skills and different avenues now to deal with people who will hurt us. And it's too easy for me to hurt people with my survival mode, and hurting people is wrong. I just can't realize any of this by myself, Dad. If you hadn't said your truth-talk, I just don't think that either I would have made the connection that it's wrong that then led to God or that God would have made the connection for me when he took me.

God explained more about the first and third cussing wrongs. The first wrong is that cussing disrespects God. We didn't understand everything, but people see God in us and when we cuss, we trivialize God in us and put up an illusion about God. We don't understand this yet. The second wrong is that cussing hurts people and hurting people is wrong.

But the third wrong about cussing is that it disrespects you. God said that it's one of his basic laws to honor our parent. And for the first time in our life, we have to do that law. And you're our parent and we have to honor you. I think that not just no-cussing, but to honor you means to obey you and learn from you and for us to honor you by making right choices. Philip asked God what about Eleena? God told him that we need to leave Eleena to him, to God. God told us that only the Adult can have any kind of relationship with Eleena. That the rest of us MAY NOT have any kind of relationship with Eleena. And that this needs to be law to us even after we merge.

Bruce: Damon, I thought God's explanation about cussing was excellent – and of course it should be it is from God. All of us are made in God's image, we come from spirit that is created by God each of us in the flesh have been created by God. So, God's spirit resides in us and we have the potential to reflect God's spirit to others. Cussing

violates our potential to represent God's love or reflect God's spirit to the world.

You are learning a lot. All of you are learning a lot. Transformation can be overwhelming at times but you are never alone in transformation. God is right there with each of you. Hang in there because it will get easier as you go. Just keep your focus on the lessons God is teaching you and on the lessons I am presenting to you.

*****

Our first reliving during this healing process came from The Adult and was tied to mother, Eleena. The actual reliving is in italic font. Afterwards, I colored the font when the reliving was focused on The Adult's words instead of Eleena's. Writing while reliving was highly painful, but it was a critical part of our healing. Because it was the first and not connected to a single actual past event, I did not know what it was or understood why it happened. It was what I was periodically told throughout my chronological childhood. Bruce did not know what it was either, and his response is incorrect. (Later, he did understand.) This particular reliving is long-term emotional trauma. My mother continues to find ways to hurt me and I am in process of breaking from her now. A reliving an event or a compilation of events or attitudes in my subconscious waking up and coming to the surface, and because it's a reliving, the degree of emotion associated with it is the same now as it was then.

I need to edit the "n" word. I'm sorry, but I just can't pass that on. It is not a matter of being politically correct; it is a matter of not reflecting my story onto somebody else as an act of violence. Walter Amundson's favorite saying to me was, "You're as worthless as a n----r." This reliving reflects that.

(Re-reading the reliving below has made me very ill. Either a part of me is holding the emotions or there's another part within my subconscious that I do not know about that is holding the emotions. If it was me holding the emotions (the part that is out and working on the book that is the Deb people know), I would be emotional but not ill. I am quite ill.)

*****

The Adult: I had a terrible nightmare. The dream: Okay. I was at the therapist and she gave me a book with pictures in it. It was a copy of a book she already had. And I looked at the book but couldn't understand it. And she gave me a bunch of cutouts, little cutout pictures of meerkats.

Then I saw her working with a boy who was sad. He didn't look like Philip. But she was showing him another copy of the same book I had.

And he was sad. And I thought that maybe I could make the boy feel better. So I took the cutouts and some scotch tape and in one page in the front of the book she gave me I taped a bunch of meerkats playing together. And then in another page in the back of the book, I wanted to tape two meerkats kissing. But I only could tape one meerkat there and it was really hard for me to do that. I couldn't tape the other one in there to kiss the first one. And then I gave the therapist the book hoping that she'd give the book to the boy. I thought it was my gift to the boy. So I gave her the book.

And she got really really mad because it was her book and I ruined her book. And I tried to find the two pages to take the tape off and the pictures out so that the book wouldn't be ruined. And all the time she was mad at me for wrecking her book. But I searched and searched and I couldn't find the two pages. And I said that I was sorry for my two mistakes, my two wrongs, but she was just so mad because I ruined her book. And then she used what I told her about myself against me. She said that she's given up her time for me and tried her best with me, but I repay her by ruining her book. And she won't take a paper check any more. And I told her I was sorry about the two wrongs, and what did she mean she won't take a paper check any more?

And that's when I woke up, but it didn't end there. All of a sudden I had Eleena, mostly Eleena in my head, and me, all jumbled around in my head, and this is it and I can write it because it's still going on in my head now.

Oh dear God, I'm so tired, so tired. Oh God, please don't make me do this. Please. Okay. Mostly Eleena, me. Mostly Eleena, then me. It's all jumbled up. Please don't make me.

..... okay. here it is Oh dear God please here it is

you're selfish you're selfish you're selfish you're selfish you're selfish you're selfish you're selfish you're selfish you're selfish you're just selfish you're just selfish you're nothing but selfish you only think about yourself you only think about yourself i'm selfish i'm selfish i'm selfish I don't care that you hurt I don't care that you hurt this is family family family nobody's business just family's business i'm not supposed to care about me I'm not supposed to care about me i'm selfish just selfish I don't care I don't care about you I never wanted you in the first place You don't belong here just let it roll off your back you're too sensitive you're too sensitive Just let it roll off your back no doctor no doctor I wish I had a real daughter I wish I had a real daughter you're a homo you're a homo you're a whore I don't want you here you don't belong here why can't you be like a daughter to me this is family only family family family family family this is family family family family family family family family family I don't want you I don't want you you can take the trash out of the trailer but you can't take the trailer out of the trash i'm trash i'm trash i'm supposed to hurt i'm not supposed to care don't care don't care don't care i'm as worthless as a n----r i'll always be worthless as a n-----r i'm a whore you're a whore i know you're a whore i'm a whore no touching no touching no touching i'm a whore you don't deserve anybody i don't deserve anybody i'm just worthless i'm trash

Bruce, throw me away! Please! Just throw me away! I'm just trash. Don't you know that? Can't you see that? Please, just throw me away! YOU'RE SUPPOSED TO THROW ME AWAY!!

Bruce: RELAX, BREATHE IN BREATHE OUT, RELAX, BREATHE IN, BREATHE OUT, BE STILL AND KNOW THAT I AM GOD, BE STILL, BE STILL, BREATHE IN, BREATHE OUT

This is an illusion and sounds like a sabotage of your progress. First you have to admit that this is an illusion. Next you have to tell yourself that you will proceed in your quest for wholeness. One step at a time. Tell yourself you will proceed and then let go of the illusion. Let go. Breathe, let go. Breathe and let go.

You are fine, you're OK. Focus on the day and let go of the night. FOCUS. This may qualify as an anxiety attack. IT is over. RELAX.

Nils: Whew! Finally I'm on and I can write you now. Me and Damon had to go to our room. We're forbidden to do anything Eleena. That's the Adult, and that's the vomit that came out last night and all day today.

The therapist talked about Eleena and wanted the Adult to focus on Eleena. Boy, the Adult sure didn't know that it was gonna come in that dream and then it wouldn't quit. And every time the Adult rested, it came again. The Adult saw your caring. But God said to obey you, you know? So the Adult kept going back to what you said and knew that it was God in you. What you wrote was God in you, God talking through you, the important parts. So she obeyed.

Right now the Adult's in her room and is having a dream again. She's facing a wall. She looks around her and it's all gray and dead and decay stuff. But over the wall is light and healthy stuff, not decayed. It's really pretty over the wall. She knows she has to break down the wall. And right now she's saying over and over again, It's not my fault. I did nothing wrong. She has to let Eleena go cause Eleena's the wall.

I've almost broken down MY wall, Daddy! I can almost say it myself without climbing my wall. Boy, we never knew that therapy by email would work. And I'm really really amazed at you, Daddy. We know that all you have to be is yourself, and you did and you have been with me and the Adult. And Damon and Philip. And you're helping us heal. It's like you said, when we know of something, then we can deal with it.

All of that what the Adult wrote right after the dream was what Eleena told her, what Eleena's taught her. For real, Daddy. The therapist told us yesterday that emotional abuse is worse than physical abuse. I think she was right. The vomit that came out of the Adult was pretty awful bad.

We even know what the dream means, too. The therapist turned into Eleena, although she didn't look like Eleena. But Eleena just cares about Eleena and about her stuff, you know. And the two wrongs was having friends. They always took away our friends. And the other wrong was love. We still can't but maybe it's happening. The therapist wanted the Adult to nurture Philip but she can't. And now we know the real problem is cause we're not supposed to love ourselves, and that's what you call the illusion. One of the illusions and that's monster Eleena. And you're right. We're figuring out that the first-life is gray and decay and illusion. The second-life is pretty and real. We gotta knock down our walls, Daddy. When we know what they are, then we gotta knock them down. Cool, huh?

Bruce: Cool Nils, Keep working on the walls. The good news is that you can see on the other side of the wall and it is pretty and beautiful. It won't be long. Take care of the adult this weekend. She has been working hard!! You are a good person Nils, a good person.

Keep after the idea to eat on a regular basis. As hard as it may seem, you need to eat regular meals even when you going through difficult things. Eat smaller meals if you must but eat regularly – and tell the adult to drink water!! Lots of water. Not only is she vomiting out junk but she needs to flush her system at the same time. So drink some water every hour.

Philip: FRRREEEEEEDDDDOOOOOOOOMMMMMM! I'm out I'm out I'm out I'm out.

Do I still have to do dishes? We all remember you saying "this discipline will always be required of you." Does that mean I have to do dishes for the REST OF MY LIFE??? I can't just pile them up? You said that's an unhealthy practice. I guess I think you're gonna say yes, I gotta do dishes now for the rest of my life. So if you say that, then I'm gonna say I wanna be the chef too. I wanna cook, too, so I control what dishes we use and how to handle them. I wanna be the chef. Besides, turns out I'm kinda interested in it. I wanna handle the food as long as I gotta do the dishes anyway. If you say I DON'T have to do the dishes any more, then forget about the chef stuff. Okay?

Okay, I've been thinking about this for a really long time, but I've been in detention so much that I haven't been able to do it. I wanna get drunk. I gotta know what it's really like to get pissing drunk. I was gonna tell you AFTER the fact, but God said absolutely no to that. I told God I just

Fractured Mind

gotta, and he said "I know, child, but you won't like it." I wanna smoke too, cause that's cool, at least try it, but right now it's a really huge drive for me to get drunk. Nils knew about me wanting to get drunk and he didn't tell you cause he wants to get drunk too. uh-oh. It just occurred to Nils that that's deception and according to our system, that's a wrong. And he thinks that might be a real wrong. And now he's scared.

Anyway, enough about Nils. According to Damon's system, drinking is wrong, but *I* don't know that's it's wrong. Cause Damon got that from the church, you know. But I see it in movies and TV all the time and it doesn't seem like a wrong to me. So I thought I'd get some vodka cause I heard once that it doesn't taste too bad. And if I drink it real fast, I'll get drunk real fast and I'll do it here at home so it won't hurt the Adult or anything.

I didn't wanna tell YOU until AFTER I did it cause I think you'll say no cause you're so strict. And for some reason, I gotta honor ... gee, HEY DADDY! I GOT A CONSCIENCE NOW!!! Cool! Okay. I just was gonna think about honoring my parent and that's a big God commandment. But I don't really GET this honoring thing, Daddy.

I asked God once when I was in my room, if this honoring the parent stuff is kinda like you mentoring the Adult. God said yes, except that just a mentor doesn't raise the children in the Adult, that it goes deeper than that. God says there's building roots going on. And we all need to honor you for your compassion and your actions. And God just now told me that we're now carrying a part of you around in us. And, God now says, gee, this is hard, he says it's that we have a part of you in us that makes you our parent, our earthly spirit father, and what that is of you in us IS our roots. And we need to honor thy parent.

But *I* don't know that it's wrong to drink. I don't know. I DO know I got this really really big and serious drive to find out, and I don't know if I can NOT try it. I don't know if I can wait. I think I'll get some vodka anyway in case I'm wrong, um, incorrect, about everything. And I got this drive, you know. But now I gotta honor you. Daddy, can I please get drunk, just to see what it's like?

Bruce: Greetings Philip, On the subject of dishes - Yes, you will have to do dishes for the rest of your life. I am still doing dishes every day. If you eat you have to wash. Get ready to be a chef. Wash your hands with soap and water prior to handling the food. IF you are going to be a chef you will need to plan a menu for the week for the dinners so the adult can shop for the appropriate food.

Tell the adult that you can pack your treats/snacks ahead of time and take them with you. This takes some planning but it insures that you will have good snacks and not junk food.

The answer to your "Getting drunk" question and "smoking" question are the same – NO! If you were to drink vodka very fast you could die. Vodka has no taste really and so you get fooled into thinking it has not effect on you but it does. Getting drunk is no fun either. Most people act differently, mostly in bad ways. Many people end up vomiting most of the night after they drink enough to get drunk and feel bad all the next day. Smoking, like alcohol is addictive and bad for your health. If you want to see what smoking can do for you go to a cancer clinic and look at the patients. It isn't pretty.

To honor your parents, mother and father, you would respect them and obey them; in the case of having "monster" parents that does not apply. You honor parents that love you and respect you and want the best for you. I am glad you are out.

Nils, Why would you keep something from me that could be very harmful? Getting drunk is NOT FUN! It may look fun on TV but it is not fun when you are vomiting.

Nils: Hi Daddy. Yeah, I knew Philip was thinking about getting drunk and I didn't tell you that he was thinking about it. Cause I wanted to do it too if HE was gonna do it, so Philip and me was gonna get drunk together and have some fun. It wasn't MY idea to get drunk. Philip did it. I didn't think that me not telling you was like deception stuff. I didn't think about it at all. I just think it'll be fun to get drunk. And if you'll say yes to it, then I'd appreciate it.

And I think I just dug my grave a whole lot deeper. :(

(Later ....)

I guess I'm wondering if I'm not a good person any more. That I'm a bad person really. Or maybe it's just that I'm a kid and I'm really really hoping that these are kid mistakes instead of me being a bad person.

Bruce: Nils, You are not a bad person. Remember God wants you to behave in appropriate ways.

Nils: I won't keep anything from you again. I'm sorry. I didn't KNOW it could be harmful. We see people do it in real life and they have fun or it LOOKS like they have fun and we see all sorts of stuff on TV and we've always wondered about it. I'm glad I'm not a bad person. Thank you Daddy.

Bruce: Nils, Do not ever believe that you are a bad person. Sometimes we make bad choices, like getting drunk or cussing, but that doesn't mean we are a bad person, just a person who made a bad choice.

Fractured Mind

Philip: Would you tell God to lighten up a little Daddy? Please? Geez. With a physical parent like you, I can do it behind his back, but I can't do that with God and it's just not fair.

I've been thinking. I know, you're saying "uh-oh". But I've been thinking cause yesterday Nils started crying right when God said, "Come here, Nils." And Nils doesn't even really KNOW what he did wrong! Not really! He thinks it was deception, but was it? Geez! And he cried and cried and cried. And you know what? Nils cried mostly cause he didn't want you to think bad about him, to be disappointed in him. He cried cause maybe you won't like him any more or trust him any more. Geez, everything just cuts him to the quick. He has a pretty strong tie to you, Daddy. And I think of all of us, his tie to you is as close and as real as any real son's tie to his real father. He really looks up to you. I do too, but he REALLY looks up to you.

And I was thinking about what Eleena said all the time, that we're too sensitive. And I think most if not all of that sensitivity went right into Nils. And I know I've called him pansy-ass but I think I was bad to do that. I know you've been telling me that that's poor behavior, but I guess I don't think he's a pansy-ass anymore. I think he's sensitive. And I don't EVER wanna be like Eleena, so I think maybe being sensitive is a good thing for a person to be. I know that Nils and I are opposites.

I think EVERYBODY ought get disciplined by God at least once in their lives. Cause then they'd REALLY know God! Talk about a close encounter! Did you ever get in trouble with God? Is there ANY way I can get into trouble with God and NOT get disciplined?

I know, I know. Suck it up. It just isn't fair if nobody else gets disciplined by God.

Bruce: I have been in trouble with God. When I was in my early 20's I cussed up a storm, I smoked cigarettes but I did not drink. For smoking I had to quit cold-turkey. I quit smoking because I watched my mother die of cancer when she was 53 years old. I quit cussing because I have a better vocabulary than cuss words and I wanted to communicate better with people. Cussing is offensive to people and places a shadow of sorts over you and what you represent as a person. And if you represent Jesus to others, you will find that Jesus didn't swear.

Philip: I've been obeying you, Daddy, but I haven't respected you much. And I'm sorry about that. Really sir. This isn't any kind of an excuse, it's just that I get so mixed up between the first-life and this second-life. I'm not used to ANYBODY to love me and want the best for me, you know?

Do I have to be a perfect person? I mean I'm pretty scared that I'll do stuff wrong and you'll get mad at me again. I mean, I feel like I'll just

BREATHE, and BAM back to my room. I'm not too secure about anything about me any more. This second-life with you is an awful lot like an alien world!! I don't know much how to live in it yet.

Okay, I get to learn to be a chef. We never do wash our hands before touching the food. So I gotta start doing that. We don't plan anything either, and I'll tell ya, I'm pretty sick of going to the grocery store and THEN figuring out what we want. I take it I'm not supposed to cuddle the dogs any when I'm doing food? We do that, too. But maybe that's okay cause the dogs are clean. Except my roots are saying that you'll say no. Man, this is so new to me!!

I, we, don't know what good treats and snacks are, Daddy. To take with us when we travel.

Bruce: First, nobody is perfect. Second, do not touch the dogs while you are preparing food. If you do touch the dogs wash your hands with soap again before you touch the food again. Third, take bottles of water with you to drink, cheese, crackers, carrots, celery, peanut butter sandwiches, or anything else that is HEALTHY. :>) Fourth, you are doing great Philip, just great. Keep it up!

Philip: Carrots are SNACKS?? Are you out of your mind????

Bruce: The angels said to the shepherds in the fields, "Fear not." I have administered to each of you this early afternoon so "fear not." Everything will be fine and as this passes I can say with enthusiasm "GOOD ON YA!!" I can also give Philip a "GOOD ON YA" for fixing the lunches and doing the dishes. A big "GOOD ON YA!!" goes out to Nils for being honest. And a hearty "GOOD ON YA MATE!!" goes out to Damon for snow blowing. You see how when we all work together things get done and each one of you are being responsible. Can you see how wonderful you all are, how gifted, how caring, how compassionate??? I am proud!

Damon: It's really really nice when you're proud of us. And your administration today gave us, especially the Adult, hope that we can do what we need to do.

*****

My healing process and my life changed at this point. A man I used to know in life decided to be a part of the healing process. He's in the Other Realm, but being there meant he could be here with me. He became another parent besides Bruce and I call him Grandfather. He supplemented Bruce's efforts in raising me and I think consequently a lot of stress lifted off of Bruce. He supervised all of me day by day, so I had parental supervision through the healing process. I had to obey

Fractured Mind

Grandfather the same as I had to obey Bruce, but I had pretty much surrendered by then. Being in the Other Realm, Grandfather could see the parts as separate people, I mean literally see them, and interact with them individually.

*****

The Adult: Do you remember Greg? He's dead now, but he came to us last night and is staying with us. He told people several times during life that there's a special bond between him and me, although he doesn't know why. I always saw him as grandfather and he'd kiss me a lot whenever I'd come to visit. He's an American Indian and I always saw him as a holy man. He's in that same place as God. And he'll be helping us.

Bruce: Say Hi to Greg for me. Tell him he is one of my favorite Evangelists. Wow, Deb, look at all the help you are getting. WOW!!

Fran's Notes: There is a dragon part of her discovered. It was connected to Philip who started to cry. Memories were coming back in his face, reliving torture all over again.

*****

    At this point, the parts of me became aware of a deeper part coming to the surface of the subconscious. None of me had experienced it before like this, especially during this second-life healing so I got it wrong when I thought it was so dangerous. But in a way I wasn't wrong, because within the subconscious, the part was full of rage and I thought it was angry. The Adult tried to explain to Bruce what was coming so he could be prepared.

    I don't know how I knew the part's connection to Philip and it's role during the trauma of the first-life.

    I do know that I did not make it happen or will it to happen. Fran Waters, my therapist, did not place any kind of idea within me that there were more parts within me. This came as a surprise (they all did later on) and I had a difficult time accepting it and dealing with it. By this time I was able to trust my therapist and try hard to accept the new part coming to the conscious. The more the part rose to the conscious, the more I knew the connection to Philip and torture.

*****

The Adult: Don't freak out! This is not a demon in me. This is not a devil in me. This is a spirit, a soul, that is so damaged that It is capable of killing another person, having no conscience (sound familiar?), and having no remorse and no compassion. This is a spirit of a child and It's connected to Philip. It ISN'T Philip, but It's connected to Philip. It holds my own self-loathing. This is a damaged child, a severely damaged spirit, part of our spirit. The goal is to not "throw It out" but to embrace It. Heal It. And only God can heal It. There is utter rage here and the capability and drive to maim and kill. But I also know that It doesn't want to do any of that.

Why is It connected to Philip? It's the torture. The years of torture. Philip blacked out during the most painful parts, and this thing came out and experienced the brunt of these tortures and beatings. It's just like Nils taking the sodomy and Philip and Nils didn't know about each other at the time. Philip didn't know about this thing, either. But, unlike Philip, this thing ONLY experienced the worst of the torture. The monster didn't put our clothes back on, It did and then hid in the corner of the barn until Philip came back. It also took the worst of the beating, when Philip blacked out.

I also think that we might have to be in water. I was quite alarmed yesterday when I took a shower and just THAT water began to draw this thing out. I don't take a shower every day, so it didn't happen today.

What's really strange is that me, Nils, and Damon are scared to death. Philip, on the other hand, says, "Bring it on." He also wants to know if it'll be okay to cuss during this. I'll never understand this kid. Oh, wait, maybe I WILL someday, since this kid is me. Cheech!

Anyway, that's what's coming down.

Grandfather says hi and that he's always thought highly of you, too.

Bruce: I am not freaked **outttttttttttttttttttttttttttttttttttttttttttttttttttttttttt.**

Philip: We've having nightmares again. Tornado nightmares. And nightmares of the other thing of me coming out and killing us or trying to really hard. I'm kinda afraid that you won't help us and I'm scared to have it come out without you. I don't mean to say you GOTTA help us. I just think it might kill me, for real, you know, it'll kill us physically, if I don't have enough help. But I'm willing to take my chances if you don't think it's good for you to help me. I get all confused and stuff when I get scared. Funny how I don't seem to rebel now though. How come you didn't punish me cause I forgot to wash my hands?

Daddy, why is God wanting us to change so much? Why do we feel more secure than we've ever ever felt cause you're our Daddy? I mean, it's really weird. Cause half the time I think the hammer's coming down and I'm scared of that, but at the same time, I feel really really secure. And not just about you, but about me and living and life and everything.

How come we don't get stuff?

Okay, I'll shut up now. Bye!

Bruce: Philip, No one is going to kill you, no one! I am here to help I am still figuring out how. The adult sent me some information and I am thinking about it and talking to God about it. So, do not worry. Parents do not punish for everything. You needed to be reminded about washing your hands, so I reminded you. IF it happens again I may punish you because you have had enough time to learn and establish the good habit. When you make a poor choice and do not have a consequence, then you will probably be tempted to make that choice again. So, for right now God and I have to be very strict. You are doing very well compared to where we started. I am glad you feel secure. There is nothing to fear, not even the dragon. We will get through this together.

Nils: Here's what happened on our end. You see, we're home now. So just as soon as we knew you were praying, and I think it was right after you sent it. We turned off the lights and laid on the bed. It was different this time. You were at the same place God is and Philip faced you. You took him and held him. Pretty soon, Philip started crying. I mean the crying that's really really deep. But you wouldn't let go. Gee, I think he cried like that for a really long time. And you just held him all the time. The body sweat an awful lot.

And then the dragon came out and Philip's crying turned into screaming. Every single breath was a scream. And you and Grandfather held him and the body tried to move cause the thing was gonna kill us. All the time screaming. But you and Grandfather wouldn't let the body up from the bed.

Philip felt the torture, the worst part of it, but you and Grandfather kept him. And then the rage and hate came out. Boy, this lasted a long time with Philip just screaming and screaming. And finally the monster wasn't here any more. And the dragon became weak. And Philip then cried some more. And he settled down and stuff. The bed's pretty wet right now. So's our clothes. We didn't expect this to happen now, but it did. And I think the danger stuff is over. Thank you, Daddy. We hadn't even eaten breakfast yet and I think we'll go do that. I think that's good cause I think we would have vomited for real.

Anyway, that's what really happened.

Bruce: OK, good. Now have a prayer of thanksgiving to God for His blessings and presence with you. The rest of the day I want you to drink lots of water so you can cleanse the body, take a long, hot shower and relax, rest and have a feeling of letting go of all your fears. You are safe. How special it is for all of you to have a close relationship with God. Very few people have that kind of relationship. This means that you have been chosen by God for special attention and healing. This is why it is important for you to make the right choices so you can be in a position to be the servants of God that you have been called to be. Many people are called but not everyone has the discipline to make the right choices.

*****

Philip did not scream as Nils describes it, but Scott did. When he came out for the first time, he was not only frightened out of his mind, he was enraged with physical pain. We then pushed that part of me down back into my subconscious. We told Fran about the incident and she helped us process it. This was the first time another entity or part came to the surface that we did not already know about.

It took a couple of weeks before "the dragon" we later named Scott come out of Philip again, out of the subconscious, to wake up completely. When he woke up, it was on a Saturday morning and he woke up screaming. He was, as Fran would say, stuck in his trauma. He screamed and screamed. Grandfather took him by the body and tried to calm him down. He held him. Once Scott was not "out" but in the Other Realm, which is where we go when some other part is controlling the body, he ran away from everybody he saw, including Grandfather. If somebody tried to come close to him, he'd scream and run away.

After he woke up without Philip, we saw the therapist. She encouraged us to name him. I talked to Bruce over the phone and said we should name him Bruce! We named him Scott because that would have been my name in real life had I been born a boy.

*****

Philip: Daddy, he's out! The dragon, Scott. He can come out and he can talk. Is he gonna kill me? I'm really scared!!!!

Bruce: Philip, Stay calm. He will not kill you.

Fran's Notes: I worked with the Dragon and developed an internal anger room to work out rage and a comfort room with tv, movies, and food. I worked with Debra on understanding the dynamics of this one and how this part formed to only know rage. The part was willing to use appropriate safe anger discharge and learn how to relax and feel joy. At some point, I'll work with Philip on processing his traumatic memories.

Chapter Two
Subconscious Level 2: Scott (7) Wakes Up

There really is no such thing as a person with multiple personalities. Multiplicity, yes – multiple personalities, no. Despite the differences of the "people" presented here and how much they seem to have their own characteristics, what is really going on are different states of consciousness of the same person. It's like looking at me as a child from different angles. I am not a whole person, not until I completely integrate, but I have separate states of consciousness that endured horrific, life-threatening trauma.

Many people have difficulty accepting multiplicity or parts of the self because of the abundance of misinformation, confusion, and misunderstanding of what sustained, horrific trauma does to a vulnerable child's psyche. For people to accept dissociation means they must face the horrors of what happens to some children in society, and that is overwhelmingly painful. Many people are simply unable to comprehend these kinds of acts upon other people, much less children. But even if a person is unable to comprehend, it is important to accept it in order to combat violence against children and be compassionate toward those who have dissociation.

To me, the important word in Dissociative Identity Disorder is the word Identity. I have never in my life had a sense of self-identity. I don't know who I am and I never have known. Nearly all of my life I have not even seen myself as a person. I certainly don't know what a woman is, and I feel badly about that. I can track the activities of my living and know what I have done, but even though I know what I have done and my various roles in life, I don't know who I am.

Of course, the words Dissociative Identity go together and it means my psyche separated into parts due to sustained serious trauma, those parts formed my subconscious, and the parts became stuck in the trauma. Each part has its own role or experiences of life, and those experiences were dependent on whatever trauma was being inflicted on me. The mind is so complex! Each part developed his or her own identity. But, to me, that alone meant I had no sense of self-identity because self-identity within non-traumatized people encompasses the whole of the psyche along with a known history of life experiences; self-identity is holistic and I have been separated without a known history of life experiences. (Remember, one part did not know about other parts until they passed from subconscious to conscious.) And so it seems as if each part of me (through dissociation) is his or her own person with a separate identity. However, look closely and there are some similar patterns, concerns, and ways of thinking common amongst nearly all the parts.

And that is because the parts are different states of consciousness of the same person.

A common trait amongst the parts were their ability to write. If a part woke up as a very young child, that part would have to grow some to be able to write – the age of four seems to be the common age to being able to write. During my chronological age of four I was playing at writing because I was so fascinated by it and I was able to read. But during my healing, once a part woke up, the other parts told that part what was going on (not that every part was able to listen at first) and taught that part how to write on the computer. Often, an older part would help the young part write, but because the older part did not know what the younger part would say next, that help was in physically typing, spelling and some grammar. For instance, when Scott was out and writing, the actual words were only his; another part may have helped with spelling. Each part quickly caught on. I believe that sometimes the parts of me would "leak" into each other when writing, but that phenomenon was due to healthy changes in perception when healing was taking place. "Leaking" did not happen when a part was reliving.

After Ian Bruch taught me (as Damon and later The Adult as host parts) about Christ and the expectations of church (and that felt good to me), I grabbed hold of the mindset of service and letting God use me for the greater good. In this way I was able to live my life appropriately and with some purpose. But I could not see me. As long as I was able to focus outside myself onto other people in service, I was okay. I was unwilling to focus onto myself because every time I did I experienced overwhelming emotional pain. Healing meant experiencing and confronting the pain by looking at myself. I'm not writing about self-assessment; that is different. I'm writing about coming to accept and understand the horror and loneliness and despair of my life so I will be able to perceive and experience the wonder of my life. This healing process requires me to focus onto myself, and now is and has been the time to do that.

Scott's language when he first came out was fear expressed as anger. My therapist consistently treated each part of me with respect and caring. Bruce did too. Fran taught me that I (and others) need to honor the different parts of me and to accept and honor and know what each part of me did to keep me alive and mentally stable. The result was a different life experience from the very beginning of my healing that affected each part and helped each part rather quickly know that life was different than the trauma. Sometimes, knowing that the second-life is different than the first took time. After experiencing this second-life, Scott was able to reveal himself.

A consistent characteristic of me either in parts or the whole is that I respond to kindness. I am drawn to kindness like a moth to flame. It has been such an alien experience to me. Even today I can't understand

Fractured Mind

kindness toward me but I am drawn to it. Kindness is a wondrous thing. I think that kindness heals.

Scott said that he is twelve or thirteen years old, but he was really only seven. He thought that if he said he was older he could control Bruce. He was wrong!

*****

Scott: Hello motherfucker.

I'll hurt you before you hurt me motherfucker.

I'm the dragon, motherfucker.

You wanna enter my world? The pain surrounds me like air, as thick as brick, and hard as steel. I survived. Will you, motherfucker?

Fran's Notes: Debra has barely been able to function. She feels totally vulnerable and doesn't know who she is. Scott has a comfort room. Scott let out a lot of his anger on Bruce.

Bruce: Hi Scott, I won't hurt you because I am in the present and not the past. Your anger is about the past. I am not the past. I am not going to compete with you and I will not punish you because you need to heal. You cannot hurt me and your title as "dragon" does not intimidate me even a little. So talk to me and tell me your story and I will listen.

I cannot enter your world because I have not lived your life. All I can do at this point is listen. I know you do not trust me and I understand that but if we keep communicating maybe you will learn to trust me and I will learn to trust you. I am glad you survived and now you have an opportunity to learn that life can be better than what you experienced in the past.

How old are you Scott?

Scott: I think I'm 13 but I might be 12. What's it to you?

Bruce: It just helps me know who I am talking to. Anything else you want to share about yourself?

Scott: I'm smarter than any of these idiots here. I'm smarter than you I bet, motherfucker. I won't kill anybody cause okay I don't know why. I write poetry.

Bruce: I am not competing with you and I will not compare you to anyone else. I will tell you that a smart person would not address anyone with the name "motherf-----." The name "motherf-----" is

79

an angry term, a demeaning term and I have done nothing to you. My name is Bruce. Show me how bright you are and use my name. IF you do I will listen more closely to you.

I will also confirm for you that you will not kill anyone because you are better than that. You have much to offer to others through your poetry and others will learn from your poetry. Some of poetry will be filled with pain but some of your poetry will be filled with beauty and wisdom.

Scott: You're bigger than the monster, Bruce. But I'm a monster, Bruce. Are you bigger than me, Bruce?

*****

Bruce found himself dealing with all the different parts of me at once. Nils and the others tried to be helpful, but it must have been a zoo for Bruce at this time!

*****

Nils: Wow, Scott's now a little scared of YOU!!

Bruce: Like I said I am not competing with you (bigger/smaller; smarter). I am a person. You are a person. You are not a monster. You may feel like a monster because of what has happened to you in the past but that monster is not here anymore. A poet is a person of feelings, a person of sensitivity, a person who is able to express himself through phrases, words, rhythms. A poet is a smart person. Being a poet makes you an interesting person.

Philip, I will be gone Monday-Thursday. I will write to you if I can find an internet connection. If you need to come and stay with me you can.

Greeting Nils, I will drive carefully. We will all work with Scott when he allows us to. He is important and courageous. The therapist is good for all of you as well. We are on the way to being whole. :>)

Scott: No, I didn't mean you were competing. I meant you're bigger than the monster. I've never met anybody bigger than the monster.

You got rules you just put on me. I wasn't gonna follow your stupid rules, but, um I think you're bigger than me.

Bruce: Our friendship is beginning. You respect me and I respect you. Yes, I have rules, rules that help people learn things, rules that will help people achieve become lighter with happiness and less heavy with darkness. Like I said, you are smart, you are a poet, you are a quick learner you have some real good qualities. Anything else you want to share?

Scott: There's a person here. He says he's my grandfather. He says I gotta treat you with respect cause you're some kind of parent. He says he's gonna be next to me all the time. What the hell is wrong with me? I come out and the world is different and I don't get it. Why is grandfather here? Who are you? What the hell is going on?

Bruce: Scott, First you need to know that you have come out to people who care about you and will not hurt you. You have a lot of catching up to do but you are a smart and quick learner so I have confidence in your abilities. There is NOTHING wrong with you and if you are patient you will understand in time and you will trust in time. Welcome to the second-life, the good life, the life that cares for you and will not harm you.

Scott: I don't know. I don't know what to do. Your rules scare me cause I don't know what to do. I wanna hurt people cause maybe they won't hurt me then. Everything hurts. Everything hurts. Who are you?

Fran's Notes: There is a dead guy who has been with Scott ever since he came out. This guy would kiss Debra. Scott came out and said, "I'll hurt you before you hurt me."

*****

Scott was experiencing physical pain during this time besides emotional pain. His anxiety level was very high. It took me a very long time to understand this, but the body holds trauma as very small crystals within tissue. When Scott came out, the body started to release the crystals. This connection among body and trauma and a part like Scott continued throughout the rest of my healing process. Sometimes the pain was acute and sometimes merely uncomfortable.

*****

Bruce: I am a parent of Nils, Philip, Damon and the Adult. I help them and I give them rules that help them. They, too, were afraid at first and didn't know what to do with the rules. But they are not afraid anymore and they feel secure because they have some rules and I am watching out for them along with a minister named Grandfather and God. We are here to help you.

If you want to tell me about how everything hurts you can. I will not hurt you ever but I will listen. You are going to have to trust me, probably a little at a time. So, if you want you can tell me a little bit of your story and see how I do. IF you feel comfortable afterwards,

then you can tell me a little more. But if you are really uncomfortable you do not have to tell me anything. It is up to you.

Scott: A parent is bad. A parent hurts too much. Philip says there's a difference between what I went through and you as parent, but I don't know. God is a motherfucker. He lets big people hurt children. And that's what makes him a motherfucker. He doesn't care. If I call you a motherfucker again, are you going to discipline or punish me?

Damon: Gee, Dad, the dragon Scott was gonna kill us and now he's not! You took out his fire! Man, we were all pretty scared. But, geez, Grandfather is right next to him all the time.

Bruce: Scott, Your experience with a "Parent in the past" was bad. But not all parents are like him. Most are different in good ways. You can judge for yourself over time if you think I am the same as the "parent from the past." But you will need to give me a chance.

God does care and you will find out how much in a short period of time. People have choices to make. God created people that way. Your "Parent of the past" made some very bad choices and he will have to answer to God for his actions. It won't be pretty.

You do not need to call me a motherf----- anymore. I have not called you names, In fact I have been nice to you, I have encouraged you, I have noted your giftedness and your pain. I do not think I fit the definition of a "motherf-----" but if you persist in calling me that word I will discipline you. I will not allow you to be out.

Scott: I'll cut the body to ease the pain. I'll cut the body enough to ease the pain. I'll not kill the body but I'll cut the body. This person next to me is very stern. He says nothing. Get him away from me! He's a motherfucker! Tell him to go away from me!

Bruce: Cutting the body will not ease your pain.

Scott: What do you know? I think it will. This man next to me, get him AWAY FROM ME!!!! He says he's my grandfather. He says I have to obey you. Fuck that! GET AWAY FROM ME GET AWAY FROM ME NOW!!! Leave me alone. Leave me alone, you motherfucker!! GET HIM AWAY FROM ME!!!!

OKAY! OKAY! I WON'T CUT THE STUPID BODY! FUCK! GET HIM AWAY FROM ME!!!

It don't matter anyway. The body's got a stupid fever. cold cold cold

Fuck you. Yeah, right, you've been nice and everything, but is it real? You playin' me? How do I know you won't hurt me? What am I supposed to do? They say you're gonna be gone. Good. I can do whatever I want then. Right? What the fuck am I asking you for? Aw shit. I can't I can't what the hell is going on? What's making me ask you stuff?

Bruce: Scott, Right now you are going to your room until Monday. When you come out of your room on Monday you will stop cussing. If you do not stop cussing you will go back to your room until you decide not to cussing. Got it?

Scott: I'm not gonna cry. I'm not gonna cry!! FUCK YOU!! FUCK YOU FUCK YOU FU

The Adult: Oh hey! Grandfather grabbed him, he tried to bolt, he screamed and screamed. Grandfather got him and lifted him up with one arm around his waist and carried Scott away and Scott screaming. I'm assuming Grandfather took him to his room. I can't go there. Thanks. He was out too much for me!!

Scott: See, I can come out. I don't have to obey you. I can sneak past that big Indian.

Everybody says you're my parent except you. I know stuff now. I know what's been going on now. Parents are monsters but you say you're not one. You gotta be buddies first, huh? Gotta be my buddy? Oh yeah, this is some kind a adoption agency ain't it? Well, nobody's gonna wanna be my parent cause I'm the UNLOVABLE. I'm not all squishy like Nils is. Nobody wants ME I can tell ya. Your so-called religion says to accept people for who they are, but I ain't good enough. SO THERE!! So come on down off your self-righteous pedestal and walk among people who can't choose, you self-righteous prick.

You're a coward. I know you're a coward. You let God be the bad guy and that's what's easy for you. I know what's been going on. You think you're better than God cause you got better standards. You like standing on your pedestal and saying that you're better than God cause you let God just be the bad guy all the time.

Don't you know it's balance, you idiot? Don't you know that heaven's gotta match earth, you idiot? Heaven's here, right here, trying to match up with earth. Whether it's a person or a tree, if heaven and earth match up, then things are whole, are in balance, are all lined up. And that's Zion. But you're an idiot. AW FUCK!!!!!

*****

Grandfather pulled him back.

*****

Bruce: Nobody is angry except you. Nobody is saying you're unlovable except you. Nobody is calling people names except you. Nobody is cussing except you. Like I said before, you do not intimidate me and you do not bother me with your anger and your cussing and your name calling. You are the only one who is suffering and when you decide to change you won't suffer anymore. But first you have to trust and that is difficult and it takes courage. Grandfather is with you because he cares for you and wants to help you. You will see that in time. I will be glad to communicate with you when you are settled down.

Scott: Do I still gotta stay in my room until Monday?

Bruce: yes

The Adult: Hi. When you have time, I'd like to know what's really important. I live in a world where your worth depends on your accomplishments. I don't like it. It makes me feel bad really, because people always seem to compete and say that someone is better than somebody else. Any kind of evaluation seems to depend on what you've been successful at without any recognition of the process, just the end.

I find that how I feel about myself depends on all of this and I don't want to feel this way any more. I know I don't have much of any kind of self-esteem and it seems like I'm just trying to validate myself this way because of this work world I live in. I do know that I'm happier and feel better about myself when I focus off of myself and onto trying to meet other people's needs. Val taught me to say in the morning to God: "What have you got on today that I can be a part of?" And that makes me feel right. It seems to me that what's really important is listening to God and trying to reach out to people and to God's creation. But that doesn't seem to have any worth in society. How do you deal with this?

Bruce: This is where our faith journey separates us from the world. Our validation of our worth comes from God and no one else. This is an internal knowledge that isn't underscored by accomplishment or education. The exercise of gratitude to God helps us stay in touch with this validation. When we buy into the ladder climbing, title holding competitive world that sets us up for external validation that is really a false sense of worth because it can come and go in a heartbeat. The One who validates your worth is the One who never has thrown you away.

Philip: Hi Daddy. We're washing hands after bathroom almost every time. It feels funny if we don't now. I'll try better before food.

Daddy, what happened is that I couldn't keep from feeling the bad beatings and the torture and stuff and I just left and let Scott take it all. And then when the hurt went less, I came back. I'm just a coward, Daddy. I let Scott take it cause I'm just a big fraud and a coward. I feel really really bad that I just let Scott take it when it got really bad. And I think that really DOES mean that I'm bad. I know it's a rule and stuff and I know I'm bad cause I ran away when the pain got really intense and I let somebody else take it instead of me.

*****

When Scott came from the subconscious to the conscious, Philip became aware that Scott "came out of him", that there was a tie between him and Scott. In the first-life, Walter Amundson took Philip or called Philip to come to him and prepared him to be tortured, like taking off his clothes and wrapping ropes around his ankles or wrists. Philip also experienced being lifted and swinging back and forth. But there came a time during the torture when Philip's terror and pain became too much for his psyche to handle, and until Scott awakened during this healing process, Philip thought he blacked out. For the first time, Philip knew that he did not black out during the torture, but that Scott came out and experienced the worst part of it. Then when Scott felt safe enough after Walter Amundson left, he went back to sleep and Philip came out to continue to live life. When Philip woke up, he was dressed. Until now, Philip always thought Walter Amundson put his clothes back on, but Scott did that.

*****

Bruce: Philip, Everyone deals with torture differently. Some have the tolerance to deal with it and some can deal with some torture and others cannot deal with any. They are all good people with different levels of tolerance. Tolerance is only one of many gifts that God has given people. You can tell Scott that you are sorry.

Scott: It's Monday and I know I gotta say it's Monday. It's barely Monday but somebody called and talked on the phone until the TV was over.

Um, okay, um grandfather says I gotta say stuff to you. Um, um, okay, I lied to you before about how old I am. I'm almost 8. I'm the same age as when I was born. I know I lied to you but I wanted you to think I was older so maybe you won't hurt me. I don't think you'll hurt me now. I hope.

I snuck out of my room on Sunday and grandfather took me and said I had to obey you. Grandfather's been wanting to kiss me and hold me and stuff but I don't want him to. I hurt when people touch me. So I'm scared about that. I know that grandfather's touched me and it didn't really burn me or anything but I'm really too scared.

And, okay, after the monster left. Well, you call that the first-life and now I'm in a second-life. But the first-life is really noisy right now. But, okay, after the monster left, I put my clothes back on and I tried to hide cause I didn't want monsters to come after me and find me again. And I'd find a place to hide and curl up and suck my thumb until I went to sleep. So, yeah, I'm not too big at all really and yeah I suck my thumb and I know I'm bad cause I suck my thumb and stuff. I'm not a big boy but I wanna be cause maybe people won't hurt me then but nothing works for me. So I'm really almost 8.

Yeah, okay, grandfather says, okay, I'm supposed to say I'm sorry for cussing and I'll be a good boy. And, um, I'm sorry I called you names and tried to be old.

When I was in my room, I'd go to sleep and wake up and grandfather was right near me but I screamed and screamed cause I thought he was the monster. But he said he was grandfather and he was.

Okay, and they say that children don't choose their parent and they didn't choose you but you're their parent. And they said that you're really really strict but you're a good parent and not like the other one at all and I know you talked to me about that too. And, um, I know I'm bad and I've been bad with you. But can I have a parent too? Will you be my parent too? Can I belong to somebody? I don't know what the difference is between you and the monster except that you said nice things to me when I didn't I know that. I guess I don't think you'll want anybody like me but I thought I'd ask and grandfather talked to me about stuff. But I don't think you'll want me and I figure that's okay and I know I don't deserve anything. So maybe I shouldn't have asked. I'm sorry.

*****

When I was chronologically a child, I was defiant for as long as I can remember. What I got was beatings and my response to that was, ultimately, defiance.

My need to be cared about when I was chronologically a child was very acute. My fear of people and of death at any moment was also in the forefront of my life experience. Even when my first-life parents were nice to me, that fear, stress, and extreme loneliness never went away. I always grabbed a hold of the times when my first-life parents were nice to me; I always wanted them to love me. But they were not able to.

All these pieces of me seem different because they all had different experiences in the first-life and no piece knew of the other piece. A huge portion of the healing process was that whatever was happening in this second-life all the pieces who had awakened at any given time knew about it. All the pieces did not always experience what another was experiencing at the time, but they all knew what was going on.

Fractured Mind

As strange as it sounds, these pieces are real children when they're out. Bruce re-raised me because the pieces of the child in me were real. And because he couldn't see the physical me, he was able to discern each piece as a separate child and consequently deal with the individual issues. Bruce is extremely gifted with children, but dealing with this many at once was a challenge. Because these were real children, or pieces of me as a child, Bruce, God, and Grandfather were able to reform or remake my foundation.

*****

Bruce: Hi Scott, I am the parent to Nils, Philip, Damon and the Adult and since you are part of them I will be your parent also. And you are not bad. You have had bad things done to you but you are not bad. God cares for you, Grandfather cares for you, Nils, Philip, Damon, the Adult and I care for you. No more lying about age or anything else. You will feel better and more trusting with all of us in time.

Scott: Okay. No more lying. Grandfather says that trying to make illusion is lying too. you know, that I'm older.

Are you Daddy? I think the monster was daddy too.

How come I have to obey you? How come I gotta do the rules? Is it cause you're everybody's daddy and mine too? What if I don't wanna? Oh, grandfather says I gotta behave. Why do I gotta behave anyway?

God's a motherfucker.

The Adult says I can't tell you my story stuff except while the body's at home. I can at home, but no place else. I touched on it once and my mind exploded and she said that she and the rest of them exploded too and I got really really scared when my mind exploded and shut it off right away. But I can't do anything like that except at home. Um, she tells me to explain that exploded means that I live in the first-life again and for me it's pain and she says for me to tell you that it's a reliving and I see and feel everything now that I did then. And it's so intense suddenly, she says, the visual images and the pain, that it feels like an explosion when I touch it. Like I'm living right now and I don't feel pain right now but when I remember, then the pain explodes into me. And I guess everybody here feels and sees the same thing I do.

I know I'm supposed to go back there. I know I'm supposed to do that.

The Adult: Well, I've failed on my end here because Philip broke tonight, in the early morning hours. He simply broke. I've never known him to cry like this. Look, I've been trying to tell them, all of them, that children just aren't kissed and cuddled and things, and they don't have fun with a parent. Despite what they see in the movies and what the stupid therapist says, children just aren't and they don't and that's it. I've told them that children are disciplined and the rules are to help them and to be grateful for your wonderful gift. And they need to be thankful that we have a parent who will NOT beat them, rape them, sodomize them, or torture them. That we have a parent who is a disciplinarian and to be thankful for that because it's far better than what we've ever known. But children just aren't hugged and kissed and to just accept the gift you give.

BUT, I never could control anything here. And Philip broke and they're depressed, all of them. I don't get it. It's MY job to accept whatever you think is best. But I don't get it. I don't understand why they can't see the difference between the first-life and the second-life and I don't understand why they can't just accept the discipline for the gift that it is.

I'm really sorry.

Bruce: Philip, When you get out of your room tomorrow you can spend time with me. I will give you hug if you hug me back. I will hold your hand. You are a strong person and a responsible person. You are a gifted person and the family relies on you to get them through each day. That is a lot of responsibility for someone so young but you do a good job. I am counting on you and you can count on me not only for guidance but for hugs and kisses. How is that?

Philip: Daddy, I'll ALWAYS hug you back!! ALWAYS!!! And I'll ALWAYS kiss you too back and stuff. I just thought this life was like the first-life about all that. Thank you Daddy. Thank you.

I'm going now sir.

Nils: Gee Daddy, I heard that some parents just can't show affection and stuff and kiss and hug and stuff but just did the discipline stuff and I thought that you were just a person who just couldn't with us, you know? I do know you love me and stuff but you just didn't wanna do that with us. And I figured it was because I wasn't your real son, you know? I know I've been grateful for you and teaching me and everything. I know we all have. But I just don't know what love is – I mean to actually FEEL it, you know? I do know that our biological father said that he couldn't love us. So I thought that since you are raising us and you don't kiss and cuddle that you just couldn't as a person. That I wasn't the right person mostly is what I thought.

Philip knows how to work. He doesn't have any idea at all how to have fun.

He doesn't know what he likes.

Bruce: I will hug and kiss you as well Nils. Remember when Jesus said "suffer the little children to come unto me" the first thing he did was

hug them and he probably kissed them as well because he wanted them to know they were loved and they were important. Just like you - loved and important.

Nils: Boy, I sure am crying a lot after reading what you just wrote, Daddy. I just didn't think that I was supposed to want to be kissed and hugged and stuff. I really am trying to be good, Daddy. Thanks!

***Fran's Notes:** I continue to work with Scott. We worked on the trauma of being hurt.*

Scott: I think you're mad at me cause I lied and cause I ask too many questions and cause I'm awake now and I'm not supposed to be alive and cause I don't understand much and cause I asked you if I can call you daddy too and cause I don't know why I gotta obey you and cause I asked about that too and cause I said that God was a motherfucker. I know I'm a bad boy.

Bruce: No, I am not mad at you. Grandfather and I are trying to help you understand about the second-life and that will take some time but nothing bad is going to happen to you anymore. You may get disciplined from time to time and you may get sent to your room for poor behavior from time to time but that is it.

You are not a bad boy. You are a wonderful boy that is waking up to a new life. And this new life is strange to you with some new people in it. None of these people are monsters, none. So, it is normal that you have a lot of questions and you are seeking answers to those questions. Keep asking the questions and we will try to answer them.

I am your Daddy if you want me to be. I will give you hugs if that is OK. I will hold your hand, if that is OK. I care about you. You have to obey me because I am in charge of all of you in good ways. Just talk to Damon, Philip, Nils or the adult. They will tell you I am strict but good.

Now that you know it is wrong to lie and that it is wrong to cuss you will be held accountable for those behaviors. If you cuss or if you lie there will be consequences. Have a great day, Scott.

The Adult: Humm, Earlier when nearly asleep I went to Grandfather. He told me to hang in there, and, yeah, it's nice to be kissed!! Anyway, there was Scott and he stepped behind Grandfather when I came and then asked me who I was so I told him. Then Grandfather picked him up and the kid clinged to him. No more fear about Grandfather from Scott now!!!

Bruce: Progress is being made here.

Nils: Um, Daddy, are hugs like a reward for being good? So if we're good, we get a hug and if we're bad we don't? Are kisses and hugs privileges that you'll take away when we're bad like allowance? I know that Pippin first felt loved when we gave him a rubdown all over. He was standing up at the time and he didn't lie down or anything but boy he sure did like it! So we cuddle the dogs a lot and they'll come up to us for a cuddle and we give it to them. Then they're happy and go and do their own thing again. We never got touched unless it was to hurt us. Actually, we hardly ever get touched now. We don't want people to hurt us, you know. So maybe it's a good thing that you can't physically hug and kiss now in case it would hurt us.

Bruce: Hugs and kisses are expressions of caring or loving someone. If a person gets mad at another person sometimes he/she will not feel like hugging or kissing in the moment. But later on the hugging and kissing will resume.

Scott: So it's bad to say that God is a motherfucker? Cause motherfucker is a cuss word? But the thing is, is that I think that God IS a motherfucker. So why can't I say what I think? Is that why you got mad at me for calling you the name motherfucker? But why can't I say what I think? It's okay if your my daddy. Are you my mommy too? Is having a daddy special? Grandfather says you won't hurt me. Do most daddy's hurt children? I think they do, but they say you don't. What's a hug? Have you hugged me yet? What's a kiss? Is that like what grandfather does to me on my face? Is that a kiss? Does this stuff hurt? Have you kissed me? Do you wanna hug me and kiss me? If you do, how come? Is consequence what happens if I'm bad? And you're in charge of consequence? How come your in charge of me? Why can't I be in charge of myself? Why is grandfather here by me all the time? Can I go out and see the world by myself now?

Bruce: How many times do you think you can write "motherf-----" in a paragraph. IT is an unacceptable word, an inappropriate word, a bad word. Do not write that word to me again. If you do not like God you are intelligent enough to choose another, less offense word. If you cannot think of a less offense word then write a paragraph about why you do not like God and leave out any cuss words.

Talk to Damon about my role as Daddy and mommy. He can explain this to you. I will not hurt you and most dads do not hurt their children. Some dads discipline their children when they do not follow directions or rules.

Kiss is what grandfather is doing I think. When someone's lips touch your cheek. Hug is when someone puts their arms around you and holds you for a moment. IT doesn't hurt.

A consequence is something that happens when you do not follow the rules or a direction from someone that is in charge. Your consequences are going to your room.

The reason you cannot live on your own is because you are connected to other people: Damon, Philip, Nils and the adult. What you do impacts them and what they do impacts you. So, you need rules to live by for the sake of all.

I am in charge for now. I have taken on the role of Dad. Grandfather is there to help you and to bring you some understandings. He brings you security that resides in someone that cares about you.

Philip: (Braveheart)   FREEEEEDDDDDOOOOOOOMMMMMMM   Hi Daddy. It's Wednesday and Wednesdays seem like big crazy days for you and you're busy. I'll be good. Aaaaannnddd, I'll do this first so you'll know that I'll ALWAYS return them, even when I'm mad at you!

*** hug ***   *** kiss ***

*****

I had no real concept of God until Ian Bruch taught me and I understood my sensitivity toward spirits in nature to be connected to God. I did have a false awareness of "God" that my first-life parents taught me. It did not matter if I was being hurt or not when Walter Amundson told me that God wants me to be good and wants me to be punished because I'm bad. He told me that God wanted him to hurt me, and God could stop it if he wanted to. But I deserved to be hurt.

I thought my mother to be deeply religious. She often took a hold of my arm and forced me onto my knees with her. She prayed, asking God to help her. I hated it.

*****

Scott: Dear Daddy --

Why I don't like God, An Essay:

Every time I waked up, I hurt a lot. My body hurt and my mind hurt too. So everything hurt. And a man was there that I knew was my daddy cause he said so. And he told me that I was bad and he was gonna straighten me out. He said he was gonna do stuff to me cause I deserved it cause I was bad bad bad.

But God was there, too. I think it was God. And sometimes my ankles hurt and my legs hurt and I was cold and my chest hurt when he did the blocks too and my arms hurt. And then he said he was gonna do more stuff to me. And he put his hand inside of me and sometimes a stick and he smokes cigars and open me up and stick that in there too. And more stuff like when I hanged upside down he'd lift me, the ropes a little, and then take out his thing and rub his thing all over me and put it in my mouth and choke me until my nose filled up. And sometimes with me hanging he'd put his thing in me down there, he'd lift me up and swing me a little and stand there holding my chest and it burns and burns and burns. And sometimes he'd lick me and bite me. And sometimes when I was hanging he'd take a belt and hit me and talk about the red marks he made on me. I was naked. He'd say that I was bad and that he had to hit me because of something I did bad. And he had to do these things to me because I was bad.

And all the time God was there cause he said so and I was scared, really really scared all the time and hurt all the time. And I asked God to stop him, to stop him and I begged God to stop him. But God didn't. He didn't stop anything. So I think that God thinks I'm bad too and that I deserve it cause he didn't stop it. And I think maybe God liked watching him hurt me cause he didn't stop it. And I think I'm really bad too, like God does.

And that's why I don't like God.

End of essay

Bruce: Scott,

> **I can not answer as to why God let that happen to you. God created people with the ability to choose. God does not usually intervene when people are making poor choices. Children suffer all over the world because of adult decisions, adults suffer all over the world because of adult decisions and God is present. People also have the ability to make good choices and to help each other. God wants people to value each other and to help each other. There are many people in the world that choose to respect others and to help others.**
>
> **Now God has worked with the adult and helped her get better one step at a time. God will respond to people's requests at times. So, hopefully some day you can ask God yourself why HE did what He did when you were suffering.**
>
> **You can talk to the others about being thrown away. Being thrown away is an interesting term that leads to the word "bad" and then to the word "trash." And what do we do with trash? We throw it away. Ask the others if I have thrown anyone away. Ask the adult if I have thrown her away. You can talk with each other and reason together. You seem to feed each other's fears. You might try reflecting together about what surrounds you now.**
>
> **To me, you are not bad. I cannot throw you away unless that is how you choose to feel. Your feelings are your own and my feelings are my own. We have to own our feelings and this is a difficult lesson to**

live. It is much easier to blame others for our feelings. If you feel scared I understand but I ask you and the others to look around and tell me who has hurt you recently? Who has told you that you are "bad?" It is hard to erase the past memories but those memories can be diminished if we work at it.

Scott: It was really hard for me to tell you my story but I'm glad I did. Grandfather says that pretty soon I gotta go and visit God.

Bruce: Listen to Grandfather. He has wisdom and he cares for you greatly.

Damon: Oh, man, thanks Dad. I don't get this parent thing either! When I exercise, I feel like I'm gonna die. Nils the drama queen insists he's gonna die. Heh.

Report:

1. Started exercising, noted screws needed tightening.
2. Went to bathroom, no hot water, frozen pipe.
3. Went downstairs, tried to see about frozen pipe, took care of dogs, called plumber, had breakfast.
4. Pondered, then got dressed.
5. Started to exercise, but forgot to get clean glass for water and started downstairs real quick.
6. Nils walked into bedroom instead.
7. Nils gets in trouble and acts like it's the end of the world as we know it.
8. Nils writes you again.
9. Plummer comes.
10. Dealing with plumber (pipe did not burst!)
11. Plummer leaves after $80, get the friggin' glass, and upstairs again.
12. Downstairs, got screwdriver.
13. Upstairs, took apart bowflex, tightened, and put it back together again.
14. Backed up and did the stretching all over again and then exercised. 8 reps, 2 sets, all types.
15. Now it's past time for lunch.

One of those days, Dad!!   :-)

*** hug ***

Bruce: Damon, Grandfather wants you to be healthy, happy, and confident in yourselves. He also wants you to be well, whole, healed. Discipline is the pathway to sustain all of these qualities. You will appreciate it in the long run and you will desire to be disciplined once these areas - eating, exercise, work habits - are honed.

All of this happens out of love. Parents are constantly molding their children through discipline in the hope that the children will grow into young adults and be successful. It is hard work with lots of reminders. You are fortunate to have Grandfather. In most normal family scenarios there are grandparents who are wise, patient and loving. You have been blessed with Grandfather. You are fortunate.

Stick with the light workout until you do not feel like you are dying and then step it up a notch.

Let's be careful not to label the other children (drama queen). Labels can always backfire on us and then start an unnecessary conflict.

hugs

*****

Throughout this healing process, I have had special support from special people. I am amazed that these people accepted me and the complexity of my disorder during this time, and is a witness of just how much God works through people to heal others.

*****

Jack: *Hi Deb. The need for prayers is life-long, just sometimes they need to be more intense than others.

PATIENCE DEB!!!!!!!!!!!!!!!!!

While God has rolled up his selves and started the project of rebuilding my friend Deb Bruch, she needs to help Him and not get in the way. She needs to be silent and hear His words as He speaks. Deb, your God-ear works better than mine. You need to hear what He says and respond accordingly.

Rebuilding the weak is much easier for God than rebuilding the strong. You have not survived being weak!!!!

Close your eyes and hear the voice that echo's across the eons of time and yet speaks anew today in your place. "Be still and know that I am God."

Prayer

Holy Father, I come humbly to Your Throne on behalf of my sister Deb. I bring her with great expectation because of the many times we have been here before and Your grace has been poured out upon us.

Those times are in the past and we seek a new blessing for Your handmaiden. She carries her cross boldly in the face of opposition. Those who would strike her down and laugh in her face. We ask not for revenge but that those who oppress might feel the power and love in Your grace. They need Your presence in their life more than they know.

Today Father please rain blessings into her life, suited to her immediate and future needs. May she always be found in the Glory of the shadow of the Cross and gain the strength she needs in the moment. I will not lay out her needs before You, because You are aware of those needs better than I.

Please hold her close enough for her to feel Your heart that will beat and break with hers. May she be blessed in this life's new beginning and see the opportunities that will come forth to continue to testify of the goodness of Your watch-care. I have been privileged to see the single set of footprints as You have protected her and carried her across the sand to a safe haven. Please, Father, continue to do so, in the name of our Savior Jesus. Amen!!!!

Deb as you can probably tell this prayer took on it's own life and I just typed it.

In Marion each Sunday morning they share names on a Prayer Board and then they sing a song that touches my heart. The words are as follows:

When you pray, will you pray for me, for I need His love and His Care, When you pray will you whisper my name in your prayer.

When I pray I will pray for you, for you need his Love and His care, when I pray I will whisper your name in my prayer.

I Love You Deb.

Love and Blessings

(*copied with permission)

- The Adult: I'm sorry, but Nils just cracks me up. He is SO dramatic! And he's just so totally devastated that Grandfather's paying attention to the day-by-day thoughts that you can't and is doing something about it. Of course, WE can't tell you because we have no judgment about things. So I guess that we've entered a more subtle area of behavioral modification and conscience/parent building, although I know that things aren't letting up with you.

- Scott: Daddy, some of the vomit came out tonight and now God wants me to tell you about it. Okay? Is it okay that I tell you about it and when it happens too? Cause it's just the first time tonight.

I came out tonight though I didn't want to. I cried and cried cause I didn't wanna relive the vomit, the torture. Grandfather was here but I had a hard time seeing him. I wanted to call you on the phone Daddy, but I know it's forbidden at night. I know it's forbidden to call. I just didn't wanna be alone, you know? Then there was God and he told me to take a bath and I was scared cause I knew it would come out. But I did cause Grandfather took me. And I threw up a little and then got into the bath. I was so cold. So cold, Daddy. And in the bath I felt my legs and ankles hurt and then I felt the monster hurt me down there. He put something in me down there and it hurt and hurt and I just screamed and screamed tonight. Grandfather was here and I could feel him, too. Then God came in real quick and said that was enough for now. That was enough. And Grandfather lifted me up and dried me off and dressed me and I'm so tired. And God said to tell you about it cause it will help calm me down.

God isn't a motherfucker, Daddy.

He wasn't the same God as who was with the monster, Daddy. Yeah, I'm calm now and gotta go to sleep. But I still wanna throw up. It isn't over, Daddy. There's lots more. Can I tell you like this when it happens? Can I please? Can I put my head on your chest too? Okay. Grandfather wants me to go to bed now.

*****

For Scott to recognize that God was not the meanness surrounding him during his first-life was a significant hallmark of healing. I do not know what I saw as Scott. Perhaps because the body was in so much pain, coupled with the mindset that I deserved being hurt, it merely seemed that someone or some thing was happy in my despair. Was it Satan? I don't know. The only thing I do know is that the experience itself was evil, and that evil surrounded me like a thick fog of vomit.

I'm not even sure that Walter Amundson was really born an evil man, but he chose to be evil. It seems to me that he corrupted himself, and when he chose violence, he actually opened a way for evil to enter the world. I am far from the most hurt, far from the most hurt. Every person who ever lived has experienced hurt and mine is neither greater nor less than any other person's experiences. The bottom line is that violence corrupts, all sorts of degrees of violence corrupts. And we have the ability to discern those various degrees of violence a person chooses just by looking in his or her eyes, be it a deliberate debasement, a striving for power at somebody's expense, a lie, to murder. God loves every aspect of His creation, all people, all creation. We were not made to be evil, but we do seem to have the ability to open ways for evil to enter the world. We do seem to have the ability to become evil. Violence begets violence by way of corruption.

We also seem to have the ability to open ways for Light to enter the world. While I have not always succeeded, my hope is for violence to end with me. Kindness heals. Little acts of kindness heal. Kindness is Love in motion. And people who have corrupted themselves also need to be healed.

*****

Bruce: Hi Scott, I know this is a rough period for you. You can stay with me and I will hold your hand. You can sit on my lap and put your head on my chest. But listen to Grandfather and get as much rest as you can.

hugs ***kiss***

The Adult: :-)

Okay, so, I'm being raised by God who I belong to, by a father who is a long-distance parent, and a grandfather who is a dead person. And it is, indeed, the dead person who can and does control my body sometimes.

There is no way, NO WAY I'm telling the therapist!!!

Seriously though, I think I'm amazingly blessed. I can't tell you just how right the combination feels, just how real it is. I know I haven't been able to do some things or understand some things that are just now beginning to take shape in my understanding. And I can't forget that God told me some time ago that these kids in me ARE who I would have been without the monsters. I just hope that I can and always will honor myself, God, you my parent, and Grandfather and all the people God put in my life so I can live.

But Philip will always come out of his room by saying FREEEEDDDOOOOOMMMMM.

Hey, that's what's really happening I reckon!!

Bruce: Deb,

Freeeeeeeeeedom!!

It is difficult but you are doing well and are making progress. Just look at Scott today vs. Scott two weeks ago.

Scott: I'm better today. I know I gotta experience the torture again until it's out completely. But boy, it sure is scary. There's different experiences of the torture that I gotta have now cause that's the way it was in the first-life, and that's why just once isn't enough. Is it okay if I email you after that stuff happens? Cause I went to sleep after Grandfather told me to go to bed and I didn't have any nightmares for a change.

I give the body a headache when I'm awake but not out, and that's cause of the stuff in me that's gotta come out. Grandfather says I need to sleep, not the body, me. So I can be strong when the stuff comes out.

Damon: Hi Dad -- Boy, things have changed around here with Grandfather in charge of day-to-day stuff. We knew that he said we had to be in bed, lights out by 10:00. But last night we asked him if we could stay up until 11:00 because of that Jesse Stone movie on TV. He said yes, but if I didn't get up in time (6:15 a.m.) this morning, then the TV will be off for a week. For everybody. Well, that made everybody pretty interested in me getting up on time! Man oh man! I don't suppose you'd tell Nils-the-drama-queen that in this country 6:13 is actually on time?

Grandfather says I have to start watching my time, too. I guess I fool around too much. He wants the exercising done by 7:00 and washed and dressed by 7:30.

We woke up at 4:00 a.m., as usual. Went to go pee. We haven't washed hands in the dead of night, but last night Grandfather just said "room" and Nils turned around and washed hands. We also started talking to each other and Grandfather told us to be quiet and go back to sleep. We know to do that by concentrating on breathing.

Dad, why is Grandfather making us do all this?

Bruce: Damon, Grandfather is refining the discipline in real good ways. Children/youth need constant reminders to learn the disciplines they need to succeed in life. You are most fortunate to have the loving presence of Grandfather. By doing well, you honor Grandfather, God and me. Keep working at it Damon.

hugs

*****

My younger brother, David, died during this time of my healing. David was Walter Amundson and Eleena's son, so he was my half-brother. I left when he was eight years old so I don't know what he went through. But knowing the lifestyle of Walter Amundson, he was probably hurt. David responded in life with a great deal of anger, drugs, and a dangerous lifestyle. I met him when I was The Adult and he frightened me to the point that I thought he could injure or kill me. So he was not a part of my life.

Jack and I went down to Wichita when we knew he was dying. All of a sudden during this time in my healing, I was in touch with Walter Amundson. I had not talked to him for many many years.

*****

Fractured Mind

The Adult: Hi. Again. The hospital called and said that David won't last much longer. Aaaannnddd, I just talked to Walter Amundson on the friggin' phone. I needed to know if I needed to take care of things. Scott's asleep, but Nils and Philip beat it to their rooms so fast you'd call them Flash!

Geez, the monster's as dumb as a post. I told him to make sure he goes and sees David probably for the last time, so he'll be doing that either today or early tomorrow. It's an 8 hour drive for him. I told him to do what's best for David, and sometimes that means letting him go. I told him that he'll need to sign papers if and when David passes. And to have him cremated and I made sure that he's expecting to pay for that. So he might need to deal with a funeral home for that. And I told him to not pay for a fancy urn but tell them to put David's remains (which will be in a plastic bag) in a box and then his anxiety level will be lessened, as then he'll have possession of David's remains. And I told him to wait until May to deal with his remains as people want his remains to be buried near our grandmother.

And I have no idea what the heck I'm talking about. I've not gone through this before either!!

Talking to the monster was interesting, interesting indeed. Timing couldn't be worse for me!!!

Life is interesting. Strange just how utterly stupid the man is.

:-)

Bruce: All of this is interesting – especially the timing. I am sure Walter Amundson will have to go through a funeral home for the cremation.

The Adult: Eleena just told me that she'll pay for Jack's travel, but not for mine. Man, the crap with these people just never ends. I'm now trying to follow the discipline of choosing how I feel, to let this worthlessness pass. I think it's working though!

All this is connected to the first-life. And the first-life doesn't matter because I'm living in a second-life where I have a good parent who actually loves me and a grandfather who's here and does too. Right? Right!

Bruce: Deb, It doesn't matter who Eleena pays for and who she doesn't pay for. That is her game and you do not have to play; stay detached from all of this and remember you are a grown woman, a self sustained grown woman who does not need Eleena's money nor approval. Go if you want but on your own terms, not theirs. Go out there on your own motivation and not out of Eleena's expectation

and if you need to - declare your independence from them. You have nothing to fear because they have no hold on you. Not anymore!!

The Adult: Okay. I don't need to pay for anything. So I'm not going there now. I said goodbye to David over a year ago, and that's sufficient for a person who has been so violent toward me. If they wait to "bury" David until May, then perhaps I'll go then, but I'm not going to cater to Eleena any more. I don't need her approval or her money and that she'll die hating me is and always has been her choice. It is and always has been her choice how she regards me and how she treats me, and that's not my problem. I won't make it my problem any more. She can continue to treat me like crap and that's her choice too, and it's my choice to not be affected by it anymore. God has wanted me to separate myself from Eleena for years now. It's been difficult.

Um, the grown woman part is, well, hard for me to see for rather obvious reasons at the moment!!!

Thank you.

Bruce: We are working on the grown woman part. First, you need to have a vision of it that is within you.

The Adult: Vision? I have no idea in the world what the difference is between a woman and a person. I have no idea what it is to be a woman. I never have. I'm not sure I'll ever be able to, Bruce. And if I can't, then that's okay, and I've been okay with that really.

Or is this one of your expectation thing that I can't comprehend yet? :)

Bruce: Deb, Let's start with the basics: you are human. How long will it last? I do not know but you are closer than you have ever been before. What you are going through is difficult, more difficult than the average child/person. You are as good as other people. Every person is different from another and every person has his/her stuff to deal with. Yours is more complex by far and demands more of you but you are doing well. People find it hard to have gratitude for the struggles they go through. If you can look at this as a gift (I know that's a big stretch) so that you can learn from it and help others, that can make a difference in your attitude. Hang in there.

Scott: *It was a beating tonight. He hit me and hit me. Mostly with a horse lead. And I'm on the ground and he kicked me over and over again. He told me I was bad. I'm just scared all the time.*

I didn't resist it this time Daddy. I hurt too much to cry. I kept looking at his legs and his boots, you know? I was on the ground and I hurt too much to cry. I screamed though. He was right here.

My chest hurts Daddy. It still hurts. I'm crying now but I hurt too much to cry when he beat me this time.

I'm nobody. I don't deserve anything. I don't understand why I gotta see it and feel it all over again. I just wanna end it, you know? What did I do wrong? Why am I being hurt again? I think it's just me, that I'm not supposed to live. I don't wanna live anymore Daddy. My chest still hurts a lot. Do you think I can die now? Can I go and die now? I don't think I'm supposed to be here in the first place. Nobody wants me and I don't think I'm supposed to be wanted and stuff. I don't deserve anything at all and I know I'm not a person. I'm just bad. I'm scared all the time. Can I die now? Please? Will you let me die?

Bruce: Scott, You are somebody, Scott, and the person that has taken your value away is not around you anymore. Instead there are people who value you, who think you are somebody and who want you around. The people that are around you now will not hurt you. I do not want you to die. I want you to live.

*****

Despair is surrounded by fear, but it is beyond fear. It wasn't courage that caused Philip to walk up to the monster and stand there silently and quietly while he tied ropes to his wrists. It wasn't fear. It was raw despair. It's like being surrounded by a heavy mist that you have no control over. It presses on you hard to the point that you can't see, but you know that fear is just beyond the mist waiting to consume you. You can't go forward. You can't go back. It just is, and nothing is meant to be different. Through despair you look at death and pain in the face and it doesn't matter. You long for death, not for death's sake, but to make life go away, because there just isn't anything else.

Despair fractured Philip's mind; he went to sleep and Scott woke within the despair. Scott lived a life of despair; that was all he knew. So Scott hoped to die. But Scott didn't die. As much as he wanted to, he didn't die. So life didn't change for me as Scott during the first-life. It took people during this second-life who knew, accepted, and understood. It took people who opened the door to a different experience, and they did it by consistent acts of kindness, the kindness that heals. And once Scott experienced kindness, he completely embraced it.

*****

Damon: Grandfather came and he held me and I just got up and got on the bed in that second bedroom and I just cried, Dad. I know I'm just a baby but I cried.

Then I couldn't tell who I was. Scott, Philip, Nils, me, I couldn't tell. And I could see everything. The monster, the grass, the ground, the sky, his boots. And the monster did something we didn't know happened with the beatings, Dad. He was so angry. He was really really angry. I just couldn't do things good enough for him.

He beat me. We were out in the field, and he took off his belt and he beat me. And he made me lean over the tire and beat me some more on my bottom and my back and my legs. It was like he just couldn't get enough of it. And then he lifted me up and threw me. He was crazy mad. I tried to get away but he kicked me. He kicked me a lot and I couldn't see stuff, things were just black. Then he made me take off my shoes and my pants and my underwear and he just got madder and madder and hit me and kicked me because I couldn't move fast enough. Then he lifted me up by the waist and stuck his penis into my rectum and I screamed and screamed until he finished. Oh God it burned so bad and I felt like I was gonna go to the bathroom. But he finished. That's when he let me lie down on the ground. And he found my clothes and threw them on me and told me to get up and get dressed. I did that. And he told me to get back to work. I couldn't move too good. He said if I didn't get back to work in fifteen minutes, he'll come back and show me what discipline's all about.

This happened this morning, Dad.

(later)

I'm okay now. God just told me that Scott needed help and I helped him this morning. I helped Scott with his reliving. Scott just couldn't do it. Scott just couldn't do it alone and God had me be out when it happened. To help Scott.

Wow, Dad. I didn't know that God thought I was strong enough to do this. I'll try to help Scott out more, Dad, if that's what God wants me to do.

Bruce: Damon, I am proud of you for stepping up!

Damon: Truth talk:

I know we don't respond all the time like other people seem to. I know you've been affirming all of us, and you have since day one. And it occurred to me that if a parent can take away worth, another parent can put it back. And that's what you've been doing. Thank you, Dad. Especially since it's awkward for you. Thank you.

soooo ***great big hug*** ***and maybe a little kiss from me***

Bruce: Whew!!! A kiss from Damon :>) Right back at ya ***kiss***

The reality is that your worth does not really come from anywhere except inside you, your God center. God created you in love. No one can change that. You will always be loved by God and by others. No one can change that either. Never assign your worth based on one

person's opinion, especially if it is negative. You must consider the source. Of course a child is not equipped to do that so others around the child need to step up. You are the oldest of the children and you have stepped up to the big brother role. Keep watch for the others, including the adult.

A big ****hug*** to you.

Scott: Daddy, when is this gonna end? Do you love me? Do you care about me? Cause I got tied up this morning to a post and the monster put a bag over my head. It doesn't seem to me like there's people here now who value me much. I know that Grandfather does. But not people here. Why don't you want me to die, Daddy, why can't I die?

Okay. About 5:30 this morning I woke up and started crying. I'm so alone, Daddy, and nobody cares about me at all, and I'm so scared all the time, you know?

The monster came this morning and tied my hands around a post and he put a bag over my head. He said that if I'm gonna be useless I'll be useless here. I was in the barn and I could hear stuff like horses. I could stand or lie down today but the ground was cold. I heard him come back and I cried and he asked me if I was crying and I said no and he said I was lying to him and he kicked me. Daddy, sometimes when he kicked me I messed my pants and I did that this morning. I mean, not for real this morning, but in the first-life, and in the reliving this time I messed my pants. And sometimes I'd just have to pee when I was tied to a post and sometimes I'd have to mess myself too without him kicking me. But in this reliving, I messed myself when he kicked me. And this morning he made me stand up and he took off his belt and beat me some cause I'm so useless.

When he walked away, I tried to sleep some cause I knew the sounds was the wind or the horses. I just knew that nobody cared about me and I think that's the way it's supposed to be.

This morning he came back and he pulled down my pants. But he saw that I messed myself and he took my pants and underwear off and he took straw and cleaned my bottom a little. Then he made me bend over and he kicked me lots cause I messed my pants and that made him mad. And I was supposed to hug the post and not fall down or anything when he kicked me.

He said he didn't know why he feeds me any cause I'm so useless and not worth dirt. But he left and I had to stay the rest of the day with my pants off and I couldn't get them back on. I was awful cold.

I cried a lot this morning. I always do. I just feel lonely all the time and I don't know why I'm living. You say he took away my worth, but I don't know what worth I have. I don't know. And Nils and Philip and Damon and the Adult don't know what worth they have either. It seems like if he took it away, then he took it away forever. Cause I don't know why I'm living and I really really wish he had killed me in the first-life.

Bruce: Scott, I can not imagine what you feel even though you are telling me. I can not imagine having to be treated like that. Thank you for sharing, for your honesty, for risking. Reliving these experiences makes you want to die again, but I can tell you these experiences won't last much longer and when it is over you will want to live. Why? Because you will experience life anew and it will not be close to what it was in the first-life. IT will be way better: no monster, no torture, no suffering, no fence posts, no body kicking you and telling you, you are worthless.

Scott, I care about you and I want you to live. I care about you and I want you to get through this and be well and be happy. I care about you and I want you to get through this so that you can enjoy sleeping, resting, movies, food and learning. God loves you, Grandfather loves you, Damon, Philip, Nils and the adult care for you. You are surrounded by love. Hang in there.

*****

Through David's death, I met people associated with the first-life. I learnt that David eventually confronted his father. Walter Amundson also kicked him enough for David to mess his pants. David asked him why a father would do such a thing to his son. Walter Amundson did not reply.

Damon says that he's letting the Adult in with him. I did not know it at the time, but for one part to leak into another part is a sign of the parts beginning to blend.

*****

Damon: I know I'm letting the Adult in here with me: David's in hospice now. He's bleeding internally and the hospital has given up. He can't swallow and they can't fix him. His intestine is bleeding. But Walter Amundson is there, so that's good. David's gone through about 20 pints of blood, and they're not giving him any more. I guess that means he'll just bleed out and go to sleep and die. But I don't know, Dad.

Eleena called and said that he's still lucid and talking. We don't really believe her much cause she said that they just gave him morphine. But she gave the Adult David's phone number at the hospital so the Adult can call him before he dies. She also told her that she's been crying all day, which is okay, and that Jack's been crying too.

So the Adult called Jack. Here's the conversation: Jack, "Hello." "Hi Jack." Jack, "I'm not calling him." The Adult thought that was great cause she doesn't wanna call him either. But they talked about paying a price with Eleena if we don't. Jack agreed, but he doesn't want to call. The Adult said that yeah, we said goodbye a year ago and that was the proper way to do it. And that's what we want to remember. The Adult wants to know if she's a terrible person because she doesn't want to call David right before he dies.

Turns out Jack hasn't been crying either. The Adult figures that Eleena was just trying to make her feel bad cause Eleena knew that the Adult wasn't crying. And if she and Jack were, then the Adult is heartless. Typical. I figure David will die today or tomorrow if he hasn't passed already. We'll have the cell phone with us, so we'll know.

Well, Dad, enough of that!

Bruce: Damon, Tell the adult to stay detached about David and not to get sucked into Eleena's web. The one thing you all can do is pray for David's transition and for his soul when he meets God. Keep that in mind.

Scott: Hi Daddy! I feel better. I read what you wrote to me and I know you mean it and it makes me feel better about stuff. I know it's not all out yet and the worst is coming. I think that's why the Adult needs the physical administration, that it's really for me so I can get the worst out.

But there was no reliving today or last night. God's told me that it won't happen while we're traveling so don't worry about it.

Daddy, in the first-life I thought that who I saw was God. And I asked him to stop it and he didn't. I do know he smiled a little. I don't think it was God, Daddy. Was he Satan or somebody like that? If he was Satan, can I say that Satan's a motherfucker? But I'm thinking that he was there for the monster and not for me.

Anyway, thank you for your help Daddy. And letting me tell you about it. And for caring, you know. I know you don't want me to die although I really wanna sometimes. And I'm sorry I first came out lying and calling you bad bad names. I thought you were just gonna hurt me and I was trying to get you to go away. But I'm sorry Daddy. And I'm really glad you're my Daddy now. And I hope you're okay that I'm your son. You CAN throw me away, you know, and I'd understand and stuff.

Grandfather's here and he's coming with us. Wish I wasn't going though. Am I gonna have responsibility and get disciplines and into my room again one of these days? I figure maybe that's all normal what the others are going through and I wanna be normal too some day. Will I be normal Daddy?

Bruce: Hi Scott, Yes, you will be normal. You can't call anyone a motherf----- because it is a bad word. The person smiling at you was probably the devil or one if his friends. God would not smile at your torture, He would weep. Yes, you will have some responsibilities pretty soon. Yeah!!

Damon: Everybody says hi. Yeah, I think we know that Grandfather is a huge blessing for us. The parent in us isn't fully developed yet and it gives us a lot of security to know that we're not alone. Supervision isn't a bad thing, considering just how much we get into trouble when we ARE supervised!!! Everybody had a grand time at the Fields Natural History Museum yesterday.

We landed in Evart at the Super 8 here. The movie is quite a ways away and since we're pretty tired of driving, we'll just stick around and watch TV. So, no movie today. Rats. But the body really is tired. I guess the clocks switch tonight, so getting up even earlier is a pain. But if we can find the church, we plan to go to church tomorrow. It's still daylight here, so before we get into the room, we'll go and try to find it. I'm pretty sure that Jack and Ruth go to this church, which is why we landed here. I don't know if they'll be at church tomorrow here, but we want to go anyway. Anyway, we don't plan to call them until tomorrow afternoon anyway.

David is still alive. Apparently, Walter Amundson has realized that his son is dying. According to Jack, he's a wreck. Geez, considering he sodomized and beat and kicked David, it really surprises me just how much he seems to be grieving. Eleena's still doing her thing. Jack is freaking out, but the Adult is trying to help out there. David had a so-called friend named Valery. Walter Amundson is freaking out about dealing with David's things when he passes. He can't have much. But Walter asked Valery to help him with David's things, and she said she'd do it for $1500. Boy, some friend. So Jack now plans to go and help him after David dies. Jack's freaking out about it though, to have to work with him. Eleena's really laying it on Jack about just how much she's proud of him and he's her rock, and she says he is the only child of hers who cares, etc. etc. etc. But we're (the Adult really) isn't buying into it.

Dad, when we were driving down to Chicago, God gave the Adult permission to have her spirit visit David's spirit. They had a conversation. David's afraid of dying and the Adult told him that God knows him better than everyone else, and he knows what he went through. David said that he didn't do anything wrong because he couldn't help it and the Adult said that he did make a lot of wrong choices. That he chose to let his anger out on his own body with drugs, alcohol, and sodomy and he let his anger out on other people through violence and swindling people out of money. And God gave his a precious gift of being able to build things, a carpenter, and a deck designer, but he chose

Fractured Mind

to misuse that. And that he'll have to answer for that. David knows that he's dying now because of what he did to himself. But the Adult also told him that passing means that he'll be healed of things and that God understands and that things will be okay. God told him that he won't go to hell, and reminded him that she told him that a year ago, but that God loves him and wants to heal him. His spirit went to sleep after that, Dad. His body is still alive, but his spirit's asleep. We've taken your guidance to heart and have concentrated on helping David transition. David is still bleeding and they're not giving him any blood any more. Any food he eats can't get past his stomach. He's on morphine now just about all the time.

Jack said that he was involved with the 7th Day Adventists and Walter Amundson wants a memorial service in May and then we'll go and bury his ashes in Kansas by his/our grandmother. Eleena's mother.

Scott tries to sleep as much as he can. The reliving is right on the surface. Man, this sure isn't too much fun.

Well, I'll sign off, Dad. I know this is a long email, but we've dedicated to not have EVERYBODY email as usual while we're on the road. I mean, I'm surprised that we got access to email as it is. BUT we also remember that you're entering some hard-core ministry and you need to turn your spirit onto them. And we think that's TOTALLY cool! And we'll pray for you to sustain that and help them. Philip's hoping that you'll forget about the cake incident and he says he's sorry and that he won't do it again. But we know by now that nothing gets by you and nothing will get you to do anything other than what you'll do. None of us can figure out much of anything. So maybe we're SUPPOSED to just experience getting raised. Okay, I'll sign off now, Dad.

And from all of us:

*** hugs ***   *** kisses ***

Bruce: Greetings Damon, Philip, Nils, Scott and Adult,

Glad things are going well and that your trip has been safe. I am also glad that you are over your homesickness. I have talked with Jack and he is making preparation for the administration. My sense is that you should go into this with good expectation. Good on ya Damon for exercising. Good on ya Grandfather for "No McDonalds." Each of you are real fortunate to have Grandfather for a spiritual companion. He is a huge blessing for you. Have fun, eat well, drink water and get rest, along with enjoying the movie.

Philip: FREEEEEDDDOOOOOOMMMMMM!

Hi Daddy. Hope things are going okay with you.

Boy, I'll think again before I ignore this parent thing in me. Grandfather says that eventually the parent thing will affirm us too - tell us that we've done good. It doesn't yet.

We just got home. Nils is in his room. Gee, Dad, that's a hard one to remember. It doesn't feel like a rule and it's just hard to remember. I'm not making an excuse, honest, I'm just saying it's more hard than most of the stuff.

Daddy, do children get into as much trouble as we do? Or is it cause it's accelerated stuff? The Adult always figured that if she had a regular childhood, she'd be this ideal child. Boy, was she wrong about that!! It's really hard for me to not have my own mind about stuff and to do what I think is okay. It's like I'm trying to unlearn as well as learn as well as do what kids do I think. Pretty strange.

I'm okay. I've been good. Really. I think. Humph. I just asked Grandfather, and he says I've been delightful. Whatever THAT means!! :)

David is still alive, but his spirit is asleep and he isn't responding to anything. The monster got pneumonia and is back at his house in Colorado. He made arrangements for David to be cremated and he paid for it. Jack said he's going there in two weeks and get the monster's truck and deal with David's things himself. The monster says that David has an oriental rug and a Japanese thing that's his that he wants back. I guess the monster said that he may or may not help if he's well by then. Jack's expecting to pick up David's remains then too. So that's the latest. We think that David is dead, but his body is still going on auto. I guess we'll be going to the memorial and then bury David in early May.

Scott's been asleep too. Grandfather's with him and us. And that's the scoop.

*** hug ***   *** kiss ***

bye Daddy!

Bruce: I am sick and after I finish with the retreat at noon tomorrow I am going home to bed for a couple of days.

Scott: If I can't die, can I then go to sleep forever and not wake up? That way, the others can live, but I can just sleep and not relive anymore and not be bad anymore.

Okay. I cried a lot in this second-life today and I relived. Please Daddy make it stop please make it stop.

Okay. I relived when he hunged me. There were two pulleys and ropes on the pulleys and he tied the ropes around my wrists. And the two pulleys were far apart and when I woke up I was up in the air really high and he said, *You gotta be like Jesus. Your mother says you're bad and she wants you to be like Jesus. So you gotta be like Jesus.*

My back is on fire and my chest and my arms and my wrists hurt on fire on fire. And I was high up like Jesus and I couldn't breathe too good and I was on fire. He left me up there for a long time. And then I got really cold and I didn't care any more. He let me down and I could breathe and I just wanted to go into the ground. Maybe he wouldn't see me in the ground. But I didn't care any more and I was so cold. I knew I wet myself and he took his belt and hit me. He lifted me up again and told me to stand up on my toes and he hit me with the belt. Then he lifted me high again and I'm just cold and I didn't care and he poked me with a stick and told me to be like Jesus. And I couldn't breathe and everything was on fire and I thought that maybe I could die now. But I didn't. Then he let me down and put his thing in my rear but I didn't care and I felt it but I just didn't care. Then he let me down and left me there. I put my clothes on and hid in a corner so I could maybe go to sleep. I sucked my thumb though.

*****

Throughout Scott's reliving, each part lived his or her own life, but they did try to help Scott despite the continuing emails to Bruce. The Adult found herself overwhelmed by grief, and this very strong feeling has lasted throughout this healing process.

*****

The Adult: Okay. Man oh man! I hope you get better soon. This cold/flu is going around and it's nasty, if that's what you have. Anyway, you take care of yourself. Scott just had a reliving. I'm sorry he sent it to you at this time. Get well, and we'll all talk to God about your needs. In other words, we'll pray for you. We care.

Damon: Hi Dad -- Man, I hope you feel better soon! Being sick is awful. Life has been upside down so much lately, but it'll get back on track next week. And I'll get back on track too, Dad.

Scott cries whenever he comes out now, Dad. And he cries hard. He sleeps a lot, but Grandfather thinks that he needs to start being out so he can know the difference between the first-life and the second-life. Right now because of his reliving, the first-life is all he really can know and experience. I know that there's another reliving for him. I don't know if there's more. But Grandfather says after this next reliving, he needs to be out and go ahead and cry and experience the second-life better. Right now, there doesn't seem to be anything anybody can do that makes him feel human. He only feels exactly how he felt in the first-life. We plan to ask the therapist today to help him.

Anyway, I hope you get better soon, Dad.

Scott: Hi Daddy -- I heard you're sick. Boy, I hope you're getting better now.

Daddy, I'm not crying all the time while I'm out. We went to the therapist and Grandfather wanted me OUT, and I mean OUT to her. And Grandfather like SHOVED me OUT!! The therapist was happy about that.

She put me through a technique of hers that connects both sides of the brain so that stuff can get loose and come out. It felt like when I have a reliving. But she didn't stop there and I went from the monster kicking me to him not kicking me to him leaving. And she didn't stop there either and I went from event to event like. Finally, I told her I could smell the earth but I couldn't go on. She asked if I'd go to sleep then and I said yes and that's when Philip came out and continued the journey. He went as far as the worthy-wall. That's there's a wall that separates us from us feeling worth anything. It looks like the Eleena wall that the Adult had.

I said that my sense of worth is at 0 and at the end Philip said it was at 4. But I think it's back down to 2, but that's better than 0. And I don't feel like crying right now, which is a real big change for me.

I know that I have another reliving to go. I honestly don't know if there's any more than that. I sure hope not.

Well, I'd better go. I think that Philip's gonna write you his part. Bye Daddy. GET WELL SOON!

*** hug ***   *** kiss ***

Bruce: Scott, It sounds like the session was very good for you and that the therapist really helped you. I am sure that was hard work and it was the type of work that made you feel tired afterward. That is how the people feel after I work with them when we get into the hardest part of our retreat.

I am feeling better. I do not have all of my energy back but it will come in a couple of days. Get some rest.

hugs   ***kiss***

Nils: Hi Daddy. We're home now and I got into trouble just as soon as we got in the door. Daddy, I don't know HOW to be disciplined! I really really don't!! Okay, here's what happened.

A couple of nights ago, we went back to David and his spirit was awake. He really doesn't wanna die cause he's so scared. And we saw around the foot of his spirit that demon spirits had embedded into him. We got some of them out, but the deepest ones we couldn't. We were aware that he did it, let them be a part of his spirit, a long time ago.

So last night, we went back to see if we could help David some more. But a couple of real angels were there with David. They told us it would be better now if we didn't come around David. The Adult said, "Oh, I'm sorry."

But they said that was fine. Everybody left except me and Philip. An angel turned to us and said, "Go on, now, all of you. Scoot." And Philip left.

I didn't. I've never seen an angel before Daddy. Around Jesus there's people all over the place. And Michel is an archangel. But I've never seen real angels before. Nobody seems to be around God when he calls us to him.

They're big and really full of light and stuff. But the angel said to me, "Nils, scoot." And I said, "You know my name?" And he said, "Of course I know your name. Scoot. Now." So I walked backwards as long as I could so I could see them until I couldn't any more.

This was about 2:30 a.m. And I couldn't quit talking about it, you know? I woke up Grandfather. I didn't think he slept but he said that a person's spirit needs to rest as much as the body does, and I better start letting the body get back to sleep. But I just couldn't, Daddy. Grandfather told me to stop talking. I think I finally settled down around 5:30 a.m. to let the body sleep. But I just couldn't shut up, Daddy. I don't know how to discipline myself. Honest I don't.

So I think I did this not thinking of others again and thinking only about myself again. And you said no repeat and I think I did a repeat. But I just couldn't shut up, Daddy cause I was so excited and stuff. I couldn't be disciplined stuff.

I'm sorry.

Bruce: Nils, When you talk is a choice - your choice - no one else's choice. You are held responsible for your choices. When they are good choices you receive praise and rewards, when you make bad choices you receive consequences. DO NOT TELL ME YOU DO NOT KNOW HOW TO BE DISCIPLINED.

You know perfectly well what you are doing and that you are at the center of your world. Get use to being a part of a whole and not the center or you will make a lot of people grumpy – AT YOU!! So go to your room until Tuesday morning and think about your choices. Again, learn from this lesson and do not repeat or you could be put in your room for several days.

Bruce/Daddy

Nils: Okay Daddy. Yes sir. But Daddy I really couldn't stop!! Really!

Okay. I'm going now.

*****

To this day, I don't blame Nils for being awestruck the first time he saw an angel. He got into trouble because he didn't leave with the others once he knew he interrupted something that was none of his business and then did not let the body rest. But angels are truly awesome!

There seems to be different types of angels in the Other Realm. The Michel I know is an archangel and they are very very powerful. They also seem to have a specific role there, like Michel takes care of animals and helps their spirits become comforted and happy and normal creatures again after death and as their spirits go back into the earth. From what I understand, the spirit of the animal returns to the earth and yet retains it's individual spirit. Later, the animal is born again and lives again. Sometimes when I wander in the woods I see the spirits of animals, and sometimes they are all over the place!! I do not know what happens to animals who cannot return because their species is extinct, but I have a feeling that God takes care of such things.

But animals also have choices. They can return as themselves, and some find their companions, even human companions. They can also choose to wait in the Other Realm until their companions can join them there. To this day, when I see a dead animal and I'm upset by the senselessness of the death, I am blessed to see the spirit of that animal running around and happy. I do eat animal flesh, and it is comforting to me to know that the animal is actually safe and will return. I have a great deal of gratitude for their sacrifice so I can live. But it's also nature's way. It's just that there's more to nature than meets the eye.

Archangels were the only angels I saw who had wings. I get the feeling that they used to be people, though, not solely angels. I also think that Archangel is a priesthood office that is only in the Other Realm. But I don't really know.

Then there are smaller angels that talked to me. These seem to be the angels who comfort people in need and that is who Nils saw.

And THEN there are the angels that were very large, like ten feet tall who were the most powerful beings. They did not talk to me and I asked once about that. The angel touched my mind to tell me that even their voice would hurt me.

All the angels are full of light, bright light. So is God. Everybody has a different perception of God if they have one at all. The God I see morphs constantly, and once God played with Philip. When I was Philip, I wanted to see God for who he is, and God morphed into a mouse. I, as Philip, said no that's not it, so God morphed into a rabbit. God had fun and laughed throughout all this. I said gee whiz and God asked me if I really want to see him as he is and I said yes please. The next thing I knew was that I was out in space and God changed into a huge pillar of light that went up out of sight and down out of sight. It was power beyond words and comprehension! It hurt!! In a couple of seconds, the Philip part of me said, "um, okay, had enough." I was then back in the Other Realm and God just laughed at me, morphed into human form, and hugged me. I suspect that if he had revealed all of himself, even my spirit would have fried.

*****

Damon: Hi Dad

The therapist had Scott hold two things, one in each hand. It vibrates one hand, then the other, and back and forth. She says it's a technique to connect both sides of the brain. She'd tell him to think about a bad thing the monster did, then she turned on the power. He did, and the images were pretty clear, but it was a memory, not a reliving. But his emotions went up. Then she'd stop the power and ask Scott to tell her what he saw. He did. But unlike the reliving, she didn't stop there. So she'd say go with that and start the power up again. We call those times events. So with Scott, the monster stopped kicking him, another was when the boots went away, and so on. Finally, he could smell the earth and see the sky. But he couldn't go on from there. She asked if that's when Philip came back, and Scott said yes. So she continued with Philip.

When Philip came out, we felt the old pain in the side of our chest, but the therapist seemed to think it wasn't real, but a connection to the first-life. Philip eventually came upon a wall that he calls the worthy wall. Like Eleena's wall, it had writing of bad words on it, bad words about us. It came to be, Dad, that you're giving us the tools to tear down the wall ourselves. And that's the discipline stuff. Boy, I sure don't know how it works.

All I really know is that Scott hasn't been crying whenever he's out or not asleep anymore. He hasn't been doing that since the therapy session. It's like she starts with the torture and then helps us get beyond the torture. Very strange.

Scott has one more reliving that we know of. He feels pretty strong right now. And that's good.

The Adult told the therapist that she thinks she sees a pattern with the torture and thinks that the monster got sexually aroused by torturing. It turns out that he mostly sodomized Scott but sometimes raped. And that seemed to be his climax with the torture. The Adult is furious. She thinks this is really why he did it. The therapist is appalled that the Adult is talking to the monster NOW, after 40 years of not speaking to him.

Jack is flying to KC two weeks from yesterday (Friday). The monster will meet him in Wichita and take care of David's things. It turns out that the landlord had to take out some of David's furniture so he can clean the apartment of David's blood, and that the couch is totally ruined. David is still alive.

Anyway, that's what's going on here.

Glad you're feeling better, Dad. Hope you're not overdoing it too soon.

*** hug ***

Scott: This reliving is hard for me to get over, Daddy. I'm still having trouble breathing. I threw up a little though just now. And I still wanna throw up. I think this one is the worst. I don't know. It won't stop, Daddy. I'm sitting here and trying to tell you so maybe it will go away like the others did.

I woke up with my hands tied and the rope tied to a post. I woke up lying on the ground on my back with my hands above my head. My pants are off and he's putting something inside of me. I think a handle of something. My feet are apart and he put bricks on my feet and legs and he's sticking something inside of me. He left it there.

He says he's building character. There's a pile of bricks. I'm in the barn. He picks up a brick and says You have to know what it's like for me. You're just a burden to me and you have to know what it's like to be a burden. He says the brick is me and this brick is useless. And I have to repeat whatever he says. Yeah, I'm useless. I know that. Another brick. Yeah, I'm worthless. Another brick. Nobody wants me. Another brick. I don't belong here. Another brick. I'm useless. Another, I'll never be loved. Another, nobody likes me. Another, I'm bad. I'm bad. Another, I deserve this. Another, I'm not worth dirt. Another, if I think anybody cares about me, I've got another thing coming. Another, I deserve to die. Another, I'm not worth the food on my plate. And over and over and over again until he's got a pile of bricks on top of me and I can't breathe too good. And I'm awful scared cause I think I'm gonna die now. I'm a heavy burden, it's awful heavy.

Then he takes them off one by one and I gotta remember what the bricks mean, what part of me they are. So I say, I deserve to be hurt. Another one, I'm worthless. Another one, I don't do anything right. He says I gotta really really mean it. And I do. I do mean it. I know he's right. I know I gotta be punished this way or I won't grow up any good. But he says I'm not good anyway. I'm trash. I'm not worth any food he gives me. I'm just trash. I know I'm just trash. He says I'm trash. He says he'll just kill me and throw me away with the rest of the trash. He says he'll get more bricks and kill me and throw me away cause I'm just trash. I'm trash. He says nobody wants me. I know that. I really really know that. Nobody wants me. Nobody wants me. Cause I'm just trash and I don't deserve anybody to care about me.

So he takes off the bricks and I feel invisible. I know that nobody will care. Nobody will ever ever care cause I'm not worth caring about. He says that's right, that's right. Nobody cares about me cause I'm worthless. And the only reason I'm still alive is cause he believes I mean it cause if I didn't mean it, he'd kill me.

And I tell him. I tell him he's right. He's right. That I deserve everything, just everything bad. That I know I'm a bad person. He says I'm not a person, and I say he's right. I'm not a person. He says I'm not human. And I say he's right, he's right. I'm not human. I'm not human at all and nobody cares and nobody will ever care about me cause I don't deserve anything like that. I really really don't. And I tell him he's right, that I'm worthless and I'm just trash and I promise I'll never forget it. Never ever. And if I ever want anybody to care about me, that I'll get thrown out with the trash, cause I'm trash. He says he'll do this over and over so I'll remember what's true. I tell him. I do. I know it's true.

And he's really happy now. I made him really happy. He takes the stick out of me. And he unties the rope from the post and he lifts me up and he makes me bend over a hay bale and he puts his thing up my rear and it burns me and he's happy now. And then after, he tells me that I must never ever forget that I'm just trash and he'll just throw me away with the rest of the trash anytime he wants. And the only reason he doesn't throw me away is cause he don't want to right now. But just as soon as he gets tired of me, he'll throw me away. And if he throws me away, I'll die for sure then. And I know it's true.

Oh gee, I'm so scared, Daddy. I know I don't belong anywhere and I know I'm bad and I know I'm just trash and deserve to be thrown away. I'm sorry I'm a burden. No, no, this is the second-life, isn't it? I'm so mixed up. Okay, Grandfather's here. Gee, Daddy, Grandfather's crying. Why is Grandfather crying, Daddy? I'm so mixed up. I don't know what to think or what's real. I'm sorry. I wish you'd let me die cause I don't belong here, you know. No, this is the second-life. I'm just so mixed up, Daddy.

Okay, I'm trying to settle down. Grandfather wants me to go to bed now, and he's gonna sleep with me in my bed tonight. I don't feel too good, Daddy. I feel invisible. Bye. Grandfather wants me to go now. Bye.

****

Daddy, it's 3:30 a.m. and I just relived it again! The bricks! This time he didn't stick the thing in me and my clothes were on except when he did his sodomy stuff.

I know I'm not worth anything. I tell him that so he'll stop and maybe he won't kill me. I know it's true, Daddy. I know I'm trash and useless and a big big burden to him and everything. Daddy, it was all over again!

I think I might have a demon in me Daddy. Embedded in me like I saw in David. We told Jack and Susan there wasn't any demon but maybe there is, Daddy.

He says he can throw me away any time and the only thing that's keeping him from it is he doesn't want to right now. But any time he could and I have to build my character he says. And if he throws me away, then I'll die for sure. And I deserve to be thrown away. I know that. I know that.

Why do I have to relive again? Help me, Daddy. Please help me. My chest and my stomach still hurts and my arms and legs. Just everything won't stop hurting.

Okay, Grandfather wants me to go back to bed now. I think the headache's a demon, Daddy. Please help me. I know I'm bad. I think I'm evil. I must be evil. Okay. Grandfather says NOW. I gotta go now, Daddy. Grandfather will hold me again he says. Okay.

****

Gee, Daddy, I woke up again around 4:30 and had another reliving. Grandfather didn't want me to get up and tell you about it then, but now it's okay.

This was the first time he did this to me. I mean before the bricks and stuff. I woke up with rocks on top of me. Philip says that he and Jack had to pick up rocks off the ground and put them in a wheelbarrow. This was in California, out in the field. But we were too slow so we got it full and the monster came and kicked Jack and told him to go back to the house. So it was just Philip. And he told Philip to lie down on the ground and he dumped the rocks on top of him.

I woke up and I couldn't move. He told me to get up, but I couldn't move. I told him it was too heavy and I could hardly breathe. And he got really happy and he picked up a rock and said that this is what I feel like to him. I'm a burden. And with each rock he took off he said that I'm worthless. I'm useless. I'm bad. I'm just trash. And I cried cause of what he said to me. And he got really happy and made me repeat what he said to me and I did. And even when I could get up, he didn't let me, but picked up a rock and said that I didn't belong here. And that nobody loved me. And nobody will ever love me. And I deserve it. And he could throw me away any time he wanted to. And if he did, then I'd die for sure. And I cried and cried and had to repeat it.

He didn't do the sodomy stuff. He just let me get up and put the rest of the rocks into the wheelbarrow and he left.

I had another one not too long ago, but Grandfather wants me to write it separate. Okay.

*****

My chest and body hurts all the time, Daddy.

This was in the barn and he tied my hands together and then the rope to the post. I had my clothes on though. And I'm on my back again.

He did the same thing with cement blocks. They hurt me more, but he couldn't put on too many. He told me how easy it was to kill me. And he did the same thing as with the bricks. And I repeated like he said. And I believed it cause if I didn't, he'd kill me.

I coulda quit breathing, Daddy. Why didn't I just quit breathing? Why didn't I die then, Daddy? I wanted to, but I didn't quit breathing.

I just wanna die, Daddy. I wish I'd died back then but now I just wanna die. I woke up and had this other reliving not too long ago and I don't think there's any hope for me. If there's a demon in me, then there's no hope at all. Cause I don't wanna relive anything anymore. I don't think there's any more of this kind of torture but I don't know. I think I'm just a broken thing and I don't know why I'm here. I feel awful alone.

Okay, Grandfather says enough and wants me to come back to him. I know the Adult's gotta go to work and stuff. But Grandfather says he wants me back so he can hold me again. Okay. Bye.

Fran's Notes: *Continue to work with Scott.*

*****

Of all the torture Walter Amundson inflicted on me, the bricks and rocks and cement blocks were significantly harmful to me emotionally. It was one of his favorite acts of violence to me and he did it often throughout the years. I grew to truly believe what I was required to say. It was, indeed, how I grew up to know myself – as trash – as unlovable – and absolutely nothing more. As I write this, I have not yet healed enough to comprehend a sense of self-worth. I am unable to feel love from another person or to feel love toward another person, and I feel badly about that. In an attempt to be accepted by people, I try to do something for them. That does no good, of course, as I have never felt that I belong to a community.

One way I counter the feeling of not belonging has been to find a role for myself. For instance, I take care of the canteen during reunion and I can then have a reason to be a part of the group. Having a role has been very helpful, even critical, for me to be a part of a community. Even so, I have never in my life known a sense of belonging with people – with the earth, yes – people, no. I have always felt as if I were standing on the outside looking in. I just knew that I had no worth, and even though people said they loved me, I have not been able to comprehend it. I do have gratitude, a great deal of gratitude, for people who tell me they love me. It has always given me hope.

Whilst I am unable to experience a person's love toward me, I have been very fortunate to be able to experience compassion toward others and toward creation. As painful as compassion is, I think it has kept me healthy. At one point, Little Debra said that she would rather die instead of a deer. Immediately, God took her and talked to her. I don't remember what God said to me as Little Debra, probably because I could not comprehend it. But I do know that I am supposed to think of myself as having more worth than a deer.

*****

Bruce: Scott, You do not have a demon in you. Repeat this - "I do not have a demon in me"

The monster is the demon. Repeat this - "The monster is the demon."

Repeat this - "The monster is not here and I am safe."

Now, look around you. What do you see?

No barn, no rocks, no blocks, no bricks.

This is the second-life.

Look around you and who do you see? Philip, Damon, Nils, the adult, Grandfather, the dogs. No one here will hurt you, they only care for you, love you and want you to be happy, not scared, well and not sick. They want you to breathe deeply with a smile because you are worth a great deal.

Second-life, second-life, the place where life can be good and people are happy.

Make sure you tell the therapist about all that has come out of you.

This is hard, but good. You are healing, you are getting better.

Listen to Grandfather.

hugs   ***kiss***

Bruce/Daddy

*****

It turned out that because our growing was accelerated, it seemed as if we were in trouble all the time. But we weren't really. The living of each part could not be normal, but in time it all seemed normal perhaps because all of these interactions were healing the parts. It took a while to figure out acceptable behavior but as I delved deeper into the subconscious, things seem to have straightened out. Here Grandfather told Philip to focus on having dinner at the same time every night and

Fractured Mind

true to form, Philip was flippant in his response. Whenever I would complain to a support person named Susan, she'd say, "And how's that working out for you?" I got no sympathy!! :-) The Adult periodically asked Bruce if these parts were really children and he said yes, and they most definitely behave as normal kids. This is amazing to me!!

*****

Nils: You wanna know what's up with me?

YOU DON'T LOVE ME ANYMORE!!

*** me stomping back to my room and slamming the door really really hard ***

Bruce: Keep it up Nils and we won't be seeing much of you for a while. Let's see, you will stay in your room until Saturday afternoon for coming out of your room, stomping your way back to your room and slamming the door. You can come out for the therapist and after the therapist session is over you are back in your room. IF you come out of your room again I will extend your time more.

I hope you can express to me after Saturday what is bothering you. You seem angry, you seem spoiled, and neither behavior is going to get you anywhere except in your room.

I used to say to my father "You don't love me anymore" and he would answer "I don't love you any less either." Think it over.

Bruce/Daddy

Nils: Yeah, well I wouldn't get disciplined if I was your REAL son in a first-life!!!

(Later)

I'm sorry Daddy. I'm sorry I'm sorry I'm sorry I'm sorry.

*** me going back to my room and quietly closing the door ***

Bruce: See you on Sunday, not Saturday Nils. Anger gets you into more trouble Nils. Learning to control your anger is very important for anyone's success. You need to learn this lesson and quickly. No allowance this week, Nils and if I get one more outburst from you there will be no allowance next week either.

Nils: Daddy, if I promise to be good, can I come out of my room now? Please? I'll be good. Honest.

Bruce: Add another day Nils - you can come out Monday, now. Your credibility with me is lacking since you are the one who has thrown

the tantrums, slammed doors, stomped your feet. This is just a ploy to get what YOU want with "the promise" and all. Here is the rule – you do the crime – you do the time. In other words, you keep misbehaving (coming out of your room) and I keep increasing your time. It is pretty simple.

Scott: I wrote down what you said on a piece of paper so I can look at it and remember. Gee, thank you Daddy.

I don't know why, but I'm having tornado nightmares. The Adult says that that's typical of people like us until we're healed and we've had the nightmare all our life. I still have the headache and I give it to the others. I broke through something this morning and heard a dog bark in my head. But it closed right up. I don't think this is a reliving though. But I don't know. It feels like I'm supposed to walk through hell and face the monster.

I don't think this is the second-life for me. I guess it's a hallway to the second-life. Bye Daddy.

*** hug ***   *** kiss ***

Bruce: Hi Scott, Hang in there and it will become clear to you over time. This is very difficult for you, for all of you but you will be OK.

Hug   ***kiss***

Bruce/Daddy

Fran's Notes: We did body work in which Scott pushed bricks off of him. After the session, Scott did not cry like he did before the session. She made significant improvement. We'll continue.

Scott: Hi Daddy. I read some last night. Somebody started reading a book called *Sarum* and I like it. It's a historical novel about just one place in England and it starts before the English Channel was formed, in caveman days. I'm at right when Rome fell not too long ago and the Saxons invaded England and finished that chapter that finished with the legend of Arthur.

Every time I come out, I give everybody a headache. I'm not crying all the time though, Daddy. But I don't feel too good. I know I gotta tell the therapist today.

Daddy, I don't think I'll EVER be normal until I really get into trouble like the others have. And I wanna be normal. But I don't know how. I know I could get into trouble if I say that bad word again. But then I'd just be like Philip was and I don't wanna do that.

I overheard God say to Nils that he's testing boundaries, isn't he, and Nils said yes. But he's angry too cause Grandfather tells him what to do and he feels you've abandoned him. I didn't mean to listen in, Daddy, but it's hard not to sometimes when God's around cause I haven't exactly met God you know.

I just wanna be a normal kid. But that's really hard to do when all of my first-life was only being hurt. So I don't know what life really is like. I gotta sleep a lot so it's hard for me to be normal. I just don't know what to do.

Okay, I better go now. Bye.

*** hug ***   *** kiss ***

Bruce: Scott, Be patient and everything will be OK. Keep reading and remember this, everyone is different, no two people are the same. To be normal doesn't mean you have to get into trouble. Safe travels today.

hugs   ***kiss***

Bruce/Daddy

Fran's Notes: "There is a demon in me cause there's a black spot. Big. HOT. Surrounded by something squeezing and then its cold. Band of cold. A thick membrane that's around, black. It's not a demon. I'm not evil. It's got to be busted; open it and let it drain." He wanted to use a knife on his chest but I told him he could hurt himself and the body. I suggested he draw a picture of it and open it up.

Scott: Gee, a lot happened yesterday and last night. I'll tell you in two stages. Okay?

I told the therapist like you told me to about the bricks and stuff. She put a couple of pillows on me to pretend they were the bricks and had me shove them off but it didn't do any good cause there was something else in me that I couldn't get to.

She tuned into that really quick and had me try to describe it. It wasn't another reliving, Daddy. It's like this black thing inside of me. It's black and round and in the middle of my chest.

She asked me how to get to it and get it out and I told her that it had to be cut open. I told her it had to be with a knife and stuff and I thought I should go ahead and use a knife. She said that I could die though and I told her that would be okay. She didn't think that was okay and I remembered you didn't want me to die either. She tried to get me to say that Grandfather could do something else, but it had to be cut, Daddy. I could tell she got worried.

So she thought and got out paper and coloring stuff and I drew it. And then I used a sharp pencil to cut it. And then she had me draw it again with it cut open and I did. And then she had me draw it again with it fading away and I did. And then she had me draw what it would be if it were normal. That's cause I told her I wanted to be a normal kid. And I just couldn't be perfect cause that wouldn't be normal so I HAD to get into trouble like I see the others be in, you know. But it couldn't be fake or anything, but just me, you know. She said there's a little impish in us and told me I was cute. Geez, Daddy....

Anyway, I did that, and the body kept throwing up a little in my mouth and I had to swallow it back down. She told me that was normal cause the body's been holding all of this that the monster did and it releasing it when I throw up a little. She said that everything's stored in the body.

I asked her if there was a demon in me and she said no, that I was hurt very very badly.

She had all of the pictures together with the normal on top and showed it to us. The Adult pointed out that we could see the fading one right underneath it and the pictures lined up perfectly on the papers. Very strange.

Anyway, she was really happy with what I did, Daddy.

****

But it wasn't over, and I knew it. I knew that I did something really good with her, Daddy, but it wasn't over. And this is the second half of it all.

I got to read pretty late and we went to bed for me to read my book. But I was really really tired and turned off the light about 9:30. I went to sleep, but woke up.

I had to walk into the middle of what I broke open, Daddy. That black thing in the middle of my chest was all of my pain, Daddy. Grandfather took one hand and Damon took my other hand and together we walked into the heart of my pain. It was like hell, Daddy. It was really dark, black like soot. And stuff was on fire. And there WERE demons all over the place!!! But I knew that the demons weren't in ME but in the body. So there wasn't any demons in me, but they were throughout the body.

Something called Philip and Nils and Little Debra into the pain too and they came. Grandfather said that this was their pain too. They all came to us, to Grandfather. But unlike me, they didn't stay very long. And something took them out again. Right before, the Adult came cause she was called too, and something took her out again too.

The body literally felt ALL of the pain that it got throughout all those years. I couldn't hardly take it. Really. But Grandfather and Damon were there. But the body relived all of the pain all at once after we got in there. And it really really hurt, Daddy. And it didn't just go away. So the body was just screaming, but I didn't scream, Daddy. And I didn't cry much at all.

Grandfather said that I was going to be administered to now. It turns out that Damon's an Elder, Daddy. He anointed my head and said a little prayer, and then Grandfather put his hands on my head and started to pray. He then told me to turn on the light and read my patriarchal blessing. We have a copy right in the drawer by the bed, so I did that. What popped out was that God loved me and has all the days of my life. And in his way, he'll give me what I've desperately needed. And to use my influence for good. And he said that I was given lots of gifts and he'll give us more and more gifts throughout life and stuff. And he said that I was by adoption a member of the House of Israel.

And then some angels came into me, Daddy. Right in the middle of my pain while the body's just screaming pain. And I mean every inch of the body where the monster hurt us felt the pain.

The angels worked to clean up. They're getting the demons out of the body and they're doing other stuff too, but I don't get it really. Me and Grandfather and Damon had to stay and we're still there, Daddy. Grandfather had us lie down in the hell of my pain and go back to sleep. So he lied down with me on one side and Damon on the other side of him and he put his arms around both of us and we snuggled up against him and he told us both to calm down and sleep.

We slept for a while, but then I woke up and so did Damon and the pain in the body was gone. But the body's really really sore and tired. Grandfather told us to go back to sleep and we did. The angels were still there working.

So Grandfather told us to go back to sleep and we both did. Me and Damon and Grandfather were still there and we're still there now. The angels are still in here with us too doing stuff but I sure don't know what. I got to leave to tell you all of this, but I gotta go back. Right now, it's lots better. I don't see any demons any more and it's not black any more and there's no fire any more. I don't know how long we gotta stay here. But I think we're gonna go home as soon as we can. The body's really tired and we think we gotta finish this. But Grandfather's with me and Damon's with me.

The angels are really cool, Daddy. They're not saying anything to us. But they sure are doing something!

Okay, I gotta go now.

Thank you Daddy. Thank you for being my parent!!

Bruce: Dear Scott, It sounds like you have made big progress with the

therapist and then with the experience after. God is with you through all of this and the angels are doing what they do to make you better, to heal the pain and to continue your journey to health. My prayers are with all of you.

Get a lot of rest this weekend. Tell Damon that it is only light workouts but to continue to drink lots of fluids.

hug ***kiss***

Bruce/Daddy

Fran's Notes: Scott told me about his experience in the center of his pain. Debra came out and said her body feels like it's been hit by a truck. She doesn't know who she is and is breaking down. Some talk about boundaries. Debra thought it meant her standing on the outside looking inside. I told her that boundaries means expectation of appropriate behavior.

*****

I learned later that trauma resides in the body as well as the mind. In the body, the trauma is within tissue as minute crystals. I think the angels were making it possible for my body to release the crystals, to make it so the physical pain of that happening would be manageable. Also, it turned out that there was a part of me who suppressed pain in the mind during the first-life, and perhaps the angels were also preparing for that part of me to be able to wake from the subconscious to the conscious. When that part woke up, the pain in the body was constantly acute, but I think the angels made it manageable. When my body began to release the crystals, toxins flooded my body and I was sick quite a lot through that. Releasing the crystals and dealing with the toxins took a couple of years.

*****

Philip: Hi Daddy! When me and Nils and Little Debra went into the center of all the pain last night, there was something surrounding us so we didn't feel it like the others did. I think Damon and Grandfather really took a whole LOT of the pain, Daddy, so Scott didn't have to. And I think Damon took more than Grandfather. I did recognize my pain, I mean the pain the monster did to me and the body when I was in the first-life. So did Nils. Little Debra too.

An angel came to Little Debra and told her that she is honored cause she was the first, the very first to survive by totally separating. If she hadn't done what she did, then we would not be alive, and God really wants us alive.

Everybody says for you to drive carefully! We wish we were there to hear you teach and then preach! And it just occurred to the Adult that you might be traveling today, so if you don't get her message and our messages, to not worry please. You're cool.

Scott, Damon, and Grandfather are still inside the pain center.

Gee, Daddy, the spirit world and how it connects to the physical really IS a mystery!!

love ya.

*** hug ***   *** kiss ***

Bruce: Philip, A mystery it is but also confirmation of how much God loves you and conformation of all the ways he is with you. How many people can say that the angels came to take on the evil in their lives and to take on the pain that was caused by the evil behavior of the monster. Take care of yourself this weekend.

hugs ***   ***kiss

Bruce/Daddy

Damon: I don't remember if you know or not, but Scott can't have anybody touch him without it hurting him. A touch burns. The therapist knows. He's wondering if that's changed now though.

Scott: Me, Damon, and Grandfather went out of the pain place, Daddy. When we left, the angels had gone and there was no more black and no more fire stuff and no more demons around. There wasn't anything that hurt me any more. The opening was really cool light and stuff and we went out that way.

I met God, Daddy. He laughed a lot. He said I didn't HAVE to get into trouble to be normal. He said I might once in a while, but I didn't HAVE to in order to be normal.

He picked me up and sat me on his lap and stuff and held my face and told me that I was hidden in pain way too long and he wanted me to live and know the second-life. He said that the first-life won't hurt me any more and that you'd make sure the second-life wouldn't hurt me either. And I can touch people cause most people won't hurt me, even though in the news and on TV it sure does seem like everybody does. He said that I belonged to him and that you were my parent so I can feel really really secure and stuff and I don't have to be afraid any more.

I asked him why the monster did this to me, and he said that I don't have to worry about that. He said I don't have to be afraid, even if I see him again. When I do, I'll see that he's just a little man inside and Damon won't let him touch me.

He said that he wanted me to be happy and stuff, but I told him I didn't know how. He told me that he'd help me learn how and that there's people that will help me learn how too.

He told me that he's loved me all the days of my life. But I told him it sure didn't feel like it. But he said that he protected me from letting the demons into my soul and he protected me as much as he could, and that I'm the way I am now cause God protected me. I don't understand that too good, Daddy. But God said that I don't have to worry about trying to survive any more and that he's given me a bunch of gifts that make my life special and that it's a big adventure just finding out what those gifts are and how to use them good.

I told him I was sorry I called him that bad word and thought that he was a demon and stuff. He told me not to worry about that, but that I had to obey you and not say that word or any word like it any more.

He said that I'm gonna merge with the others, but I'll never lose myself. And even when we're merged, I can separate out whenever I want, but I might not want to. But then I'll go back in the merge. He said that I have a special place with him. I told him that we've seen your spirit from a distance and that it's full of light, and will mine be too, and he said yes, but it already is.

I told him that I feel a big loss cause of my life in the first-life, and he told me that all of that is gonna be made up now. So now it's okay to feel a loss, for all of us to, but that it's not gonna last cause God is gonna make up our lost life and it's a big adventure. He said that sometimes people will disappoint me, but that's normal stuff and I gotta remember to honor him and you and Grandfather with all that I do. And it's okay to be disappointed, but to always forgive.

Then he told me to go on back with Grandfather and to be a good boy. He said it was okay to make mistakes, that making mistakes doesn't make me a bad boy. So he told me to be good and go with Grandfather. So he lifted me off of his lap and I took Grandfather's hand and came back.

God's pretty cool, Daddy.

Damon: The body feels like it was hit by a train. I know I'm not exactly sick. Gee, the angels were in the body, what, 3 days? Maybe 4. It really was amazing, Dad. I know that what I experienced was the combination of mind, body, and spirit, but where I was I knew was spirit and mind. I know that the Adult didn't know what she was afraid of concerning breaking the mind, but it was that. All I knew was that there was no way I was going to let Scott and Grandfather walk in there alone. When we walked in, it looked like a cave made out of muscle, but the ground was firm. The muscle cave was black, but not as a natural color black, but dirty, filthy sooty black. I could see black things moving in and out of the

Fractured Mind

muscle cave and felt them move throughout the body. I do think they were demons. And little fires were all over the place. It was hot and I really thought that I had entered hell.

After we entered, the pain hit and hit harder than I could ever have imagined. I could feel all of the body like I'm out now, and every place the monster hurt was on fire. I knew that this is what Scott experienced during the torture, but not all at once. I felt my mind bend, Dad. And I was determined to not have it break. When the others were called in, they were protected or buffered, but not us. I can only think that it was important that we be the connection to the mind while the others did not need to be.

I asked Grandfather if he felt the pain and he said that he was aware of it, but he didn't. He really knew what to do, though, and gave great comfort to Scott and to me.

When the angels came in, they ignored us but went right to work. The black things got angry and made the pain more intense, but the angels did things to either destroy them or send them away. After a while, Grandfather had us lie down, one on each side of him, and he cuddled us and told us to sleep. Through the grace of God, we did.

When we woke up, the pain had diminished and the cave was cleaner, and it got easier and easier for us. And this continued until all the fires were out, the demons gone, and the cave was clean. It looked like healthy muscle. When we woke up the last time in the cave, the angels had gone.

The angels had form, but it was difficult to see. They were full of light.

We could still be out during the day, but when we weren't out, we found ourselves right back in the cave. It never occurred to us to try to flee any of this experience.

I really do think we experienced hell, Dad. What hell really is.

It amazes me that Grandfather helped the way he did. He didn't have to, you know. I think that's love. And he's still here.

Well, I'd better go now. Have a great day!

*** hug ***

Bruce: Again, I say what a blessing Grandfather has been for all of you and continues to be. Part of his responsibility as an Evangelist is to be a Spiritual Companion and he has fulfilled that calling to you over and over.

Be patient with the body and it will respond well. Give the body plenty of rest, good food, lots of fluids, some exercise and the body will be assured that it is being taken care of. As the body recovers

the connection of mind, body, spirit will continue to grow. Again, when you feel the body is ready increase the number of sets from two to three.

You have learned more about angels, pain, healing and spiritual companioning than most people. Use your knowledge with wisdom to help others.

hug

Scott: There was one more reliving that I did but it was really really short and I was still all worried about the brick stuff and everything. And it happened right before the therapy stuff last Thursday. But I can't get it out of my head though so I gotta tell you this last reliving stuff so I can release it. Right now, though, it's just a memory cause I already did the reliving and it doesn't bother me any.

This happened only once and it didn't take long at all. *We were living in Florida and not on a farm. The monster made me lie down on the ground on top of a nest of fire ants. He told me I had to stay there and not to make a sound. But I couldn't help it and I started to scream.*

The monster got all scared cause we had neighbors and he got me off of there but I was still screaming and in the back yard he took all of my clothes off to get the fire ants off of me and out of my clothes. He didn't do anything to me cause he was scared. And he didn't beat me or anything like that later cause I screamed cause he was scared.

And that's it.

The Adult: Oh wow! I just reread Scott's very first email to you! He said, "The pain surrounds me like air, as thick as brick, and hard as steel." The brick reference was there from the very beginning!!

Anyway, I'm fine. As strange as this sounds, I'm having a hard time giving up MY first-life. I guess I didn't recognize it as a first-life until recently. Well, it'll come.

Scott: Hi Daddy. I'm glad your back. I don't think there's any more reliving any more. Can I be normal now? God says I don't have to get into trouble to be normal. That's good cause I don't wanna go through what Philip and Nils went through and stuff.

I read more and the Anglo Saxons are now living in England.

Bruce: Hi Scott, Now you can focus on the big adventure and you won't have to worry about the past anymore. You won't forget the past I am sure but you will not have to be scared anymore.

You had a good session with God and He is near you always. What

he said about forgiveness is very important to remember and practice.

Have a good day. Enjoy your reading.

hug ***kiss***

Bruce/Daddy

Philip: Boy, I really had to hustle to make lights out by 10:00 but I made it. Then about 10 minutes later the phone rang. I was still out and I answered it. It was the monster! And I just about had a heart attack! The Adult fumbled on out and me and Scott beat it to our room really really fast! The Adult says that as long as he doesn't ask about her, how she's doing and stuff, she'll be okay. So far so good. He's talked about his past just once and that hurt her, but maybe not anymore since Scott's through his stuff.

The good news is that we didn't have any nightmares or any memories pop out last night or anything. Boy, THAT's a big change!

Bruce: Hi Philip, Don't be afraid of the monster. He cannot hurt you anymore. The adult has to take charge without fear.

I am resting today and tomorrow. I am very tired from the trip and the past couple of weeks.

Have a good day.

hug

Bruce/Daddy

Nils: I didn't do anything yesterday. I've been remembering to brush teeth and wash hands and stuff. I'm trying to be good but I don't think anybody cares about me any more. I just feel ignored. I just wanna go to sleep.

Bruce: Nils, Are you feeling sorry for yourself? Be patient and wait your turn to do your stuff. I am glad you have been remembering to brush your teeth and wash your hands.

Bruce/Daddy

Scott: Yesterday I started to cry and the Adult said, What's the matter honey? (Geez, Daddy, she called me HONEY. Give me a break.) But I didn't know why I was crying and stuff. But I feel all this gratitude and stuff and the pain is gone and I don't know anything about who I am or the world or anything cause all I ever knew was hurt.

I read my book some more and the bad Vikings came and they killed a little boy, Daddy. I know it's not real, but I know that's what people do. So I have a really important question to ask you Daddy. Okay?

What's wrong with a person's spirit that they hurt other people? I know you'll say that people have choices and stuff, but what's wrong with them, their spirit, that they would hurt?

I saw on the TV about a father who taught his son to kill deer. And before we changed the channel, the boy killed a deer and it showed it and we knew that the deer was in pain and really really scared like I was. But the boy was really happy about it. Daddy, I think there's something wrong when people kill to make themselves happy but it's not wrong when people have to kill in order to eat cause that's what other animals do and that's the nature way. But why do people kill and be happy about it?

Can I come and stay with you today and hold your hand and when you're sitting down I can sit on your lap and put my head on your chest? Can I please?

Bruce: Scott, There are a variety of reasons people are mean to other people: for some it is the way the were brought up, for some it is issues of anger, for others it is emotional wounds.

You can spend the day with me.

Bruce/Daddy

Scott: Hi Daddy. Thanks for letting me stay with you yesterday. Whenever I was out, I could feel your presence and it was really nice. You feel different than Grandfather. Daddy, is your chest crooked?

Can I be in charge of something now? Damon said lotion a long time ago. Can I do that? I know I'm only almost 8, but can I do that too? Even if it's not that, can I do something, or is reading what I'm supposed to do? Can I have an allowance too?

So I just started the next chapter and that's in 1100 something AD. The body's a little sick, Daddy. I still give headaches and tense stuff and now we got diarrhea. I'm sorry I made the body sick, Daddy. I'm sorry.

Bye!

*** hug ***   *** kiss ***

Bruce: Scott, You are in charge of lotion. I want you to start with the feet, especially the soles of the feet. Apply lotion and rub them just before bedtime. Work the foot from the heel towards the toes.

Yes, you can have an allowance. And don't worry about the body. It will recover just fine.

Fractured Mind

hug   ***kiss***

Bruce/Daddy

Scott: I did the lotion last night! All by myself! Is that my chore? I did the bottom of the feet and stuff and I didn't put too much on it cause Damon's tried that before and the feet and legs got all sticky. So I did it right, cause the stuff went into my foot I think cause it didn't get all sticky.

I just started another chapter and I think it's political problems. Gee, Daddy, why do people DO all that? Oh, I guess people just wanna control other people. Not us. The Adult's got a system so she doesn't do that.

Bruce: Scott, Yep, that is your chore. Good job. Every night you need to do this.

hug   ***kiss***

Bruce/Daddy

Scott: I still give the body headaches. They say it might be Little Debra, but it happens when I'm awake.

Report: Did chore, no sticky feet

I'm going to my FIRST movie today, Daddy!! Monsters vs. Aliens!!! And I'm gonna pay for it, too, right out of my allowance!!

Bye Daddy!

*** hug ***   *** kiss ***

*****

Nobody knew this at the time, but here marks the beginning of true integration of the six parts into one. It took a while, but the parts slowly came closer together. I don't know if David's death and dying had anything to do with the timing of beginning integration or not.

*****

Little Debra: Hi Daddy! Boy, I saw Grandfather talk with Jesus for the longest time. Then he came over to me. I was playing on the ground. And he took my hand, but I broke away and ran to Jeanie and told her that I gotta go and stuff and if she'll be okay without me. She said yes she'll be fine and that she'll see me later. So I went back to Grandfather and he picked me up and carried me.

So I went to where Grandfather is and I saw the others and I said hi to Scott and he said hi. Grandfather told me that whenever I was out, that this is what he'll be doing and me too. So I'm sitting on Grandfather's lap with my back against his chest and he has his arms around me and holding me. Cause I'm out now and this is what he says it'll be like for me all the time I'm out.

And when I'm not out, he'll be holding my hand or carrying me or I can put my arms around his leg and hug it or I'll sit on his lap. And when I sleep, he'll be sleeping with me and cuddling me.

I asked him why and he said it was my chore.

Bruce: Hi Little Debra, Grandfather will take good care of you. It is nice that you are out.

Bruce/Daddy

Fran's Notes: She said, "Little Debra is drowning and we need to work on this trauma." She doesn't like drinking water due to this trauma. Philip was prohibited from drinking water.

The Adult: Went to Wal-Mart and took my blood pressure. It's up to 129/91. It's usually 110/80. That might explain the nose bleeds, but I'll still get a doctor's appointment.

David's still hanging on. The monster says that his eyes are open and his mouth is open and he'll take a few breaths, then quit for a few seconds, then start up again. He's completely non-responsive and they're not giving him food or water.

Last night was the first time the monster spoke like a real person. As long as I continue to be a pastor to him, I'm just fine. But, then, it's all been long distance so far. I have no intention of continuing a relationship with him after all of this.

Jack tells me that he's a wimp and won't confront anybody. And that just blows Jack away. You know, that explains why, in part anyway, he took his anger out on me. A bully/coward in the very worst way.

Because of the weather, Jack was not able to get there to help deal with David's stuff. The monster expects me and Jack to help him with it right after the memorial. So I'll be around him more than I expected. I don't think I can't do it as long as Jack has to as it would wreck my relationship with Jack. Looks like the memorial will be May 8th.

I gave Eleena an update and she acted like I was telling her the weather.

I used to feed David in his high chair. It's the baby I'll miss. I find I'm very sad that David is dying.

Eleena told me that she's been giving Jack money for years, so I'll no longer have any inheritance. (She got thousands and thousands of dollars from her mother.) I'm trying not to care. She could be lying to me.

Is it okay that I think my biological family sucks? :)

I'm not depressed. I just have some serious challenges ahead of me that I believe that God will take advantage of to help me grow and heal.

*****

I learnt later that Eleena was lying to me about giving Jack a lot of money and my inheritance. I think it was a manipulation to tell me she does not care about me. I wish I had been able to just walk away from my mother, as some people can do. But I never stopped wanting her to care about me, but she just could not do that.

*****

Bruce: Deb, I would talk over your family issues with the therapist in preparation for May 8 and the aftermath.

Trying not to care is hard work. IT is OK to care but not get sucked into the emotional web.

You can continue to counsel with the monster but the image of a Pastor does not fit and I wouldn't suggest you not continue to try to fill that image.

The Adult: Hey! Hope you're okay. I'll be around both monsters in early May. I'll be helping her move, and I'm happy for her because maybe she'll be happier in an independent living complex. I just hope she can make friends to play bridge with. I seriously doubt she'll go to the memorial. I'm expecting her to hurt herself again as an excuse to not go. Of course, all she really has to do is say so, but she hasn't done that the other times she had an opportunity to go see David before he died.

And I'll help Jack and the monster with David's stuff. As long as I don't dish out any money except for my hotel, food, and gas, that'll be okay. The kids will either be with you or in their room throughout all of this.

Okay about the no-pastor thing. I need to stay detached, and me having that mentality has helped me to do that. So I'll just focus on them and their needs.

I've been to David for the past few nights. God said it was okay now. I don't see any demons in his spirit anymore. He's terribly frightened about dying, mainly because he knows what his life has been, what he's done, and he thinks he'll go to hell. I'm telling him that he won't go to hell, because God told me to tell him that. His spirit has beat up my spirit every night. Fortunately, the spirit doesn't feel like the body does. You won't believe the horrible things he said to me. But he's scared. So I've been talking to him, but the only person who can break his connection to his body is either his body or his spirit. But last night when I came back here, he called to me and wanted me to stay with him.

I told him he couldn't beat me up anymore though and so I sat down next to him and am holding his hand. Best thing I can do for him, I think. Until his body lets go.

Well, you said to pray for his transition. I'm doing that, but I'm also taking action, since I have that ability or gift.

Yes, I've been telling the therapist about early May. She's not happy about any of it.

And you have a good day!!

Bruce: Why do you invest yourself in the dysfunctional behavior of the family? By your presence and your help you are still playing their game. You are still setting yourself up for pain and uncomfortable encounters. I question the wisdom of going at all. The experience may not just impact you but may impact the kids as well, even though you say they will be with me or in their rooms they will sense what is happening. How does this attendance contribute to your healing process? Just some things to think about.

The Adult: It's the only family I've got. I'm not a member of your family. I'm not a member of the Bruch family. It's the only family I've got.

Nils: I've been good. Nobody's paying me any attention anyway, so I'm getting used to not being the center of anything and just being nothing.

Bruce: It is Ok not to be the center of attention but it is an adjustment. Relax and enjoy life as much as you can. You have been good and that is enough.

Have a good day today.

hugs   ***kiss***

Bruce/Daddy

Little Debra: I'm supposed to be out to the therapist tomorrow. I'm kinda scared.

Bruce: The therapist is very nice and there is nothing to be afraid of. You will be fine, besides, you have Philip, Damon, Nils, Scott and the adult all with you.

Bruce/Daddy

The Adult: Hi. Hope you're well and working well.

David died yesterday evening about 8:00.

I went to David and helped him know that his body had died. He hauled off and hit me square in the face and knocked me down. Once he knew, a couple of people came to escort him away. I told him that it'll be okay. He replied with "Fuck you." This is not exactly the last memory I wanted from David, but he really is frightened. I suspect that by now, he knows he doesn't need to be. But he's truly gone. And I feel pretty privileged that I helped him transition. Grandfather seems to be proud of me.

Talk about frightened, I am. I know that I'm supposed to lose myself and while it seems to be a step backward, it isn't. Apparently, it's necessary. I feel like I'm just flailing though. The kids really believe now that if and when they're naughty or disobey or make wrong choices, you'll punish them, and there's this weird sense of security there. But I feel that if I do that, you won't punish me. You'll throw me away. So I'm pretty scared of you. Since I don't seem to have any rules, I'm pretty scared to even say the wrong thing. I just feel like I'm just hanging out there flapping in the wind with no guide and nobody cares but I'm supposed to no longer just do what I want any more. So all of my security is gone, as not doing what I want is hugely secure for me in this state. And all I want to do is go back to doing what I want in order to have a sense of security back. But I know God doesn't want me to do that.

I also know that I go in and out of this state, but I'm in it longer and longer. I thought it would stop with Scott's reliving over and the angels and all, but nope, that was wrong.

What you said to Damon about a parent pushes the young adult so that he/she would grow and that's what you were really doing with me was comforting to me, but I don't know for sure if you were talking about Damon or about me. I know that God punishes me in a way that has helped break me down. But I feel that you won't punish me, but rather the consequence would be that you would throw me away. It's like I'm supposed to need different things, but I can't for the life of me figure out what they are. And the rules are different for me than for the kids, and I think it may be the age difference, but I haven't been raised so I don't have any background. Oh, heck, I just don't know what I'm doing or who I am. I don't feel like a person anymore. I really really really want to go back to doing what I want, but really really really recognize that as being scared and really really really needing a sense of security that I would regain if I want back to doing what I want.

Bruce: Greetings, You are labeled the adult but you are part of the clan of personalities that are you. So, look at the components of the personalities and you may find part of yourself in that. Nils the computer wiz, Philip the cook, organizer, household keeper, Damon the Elder, protector, inquirer, thinker, the one who cares for the body, Scott the vulnerable and yearning to be responsible and normal, the one who is learning the gentle touch of the hands. These

are components of you. You are not very good at remembering to reflect and to look at what is in front of you. Maybe you have some resistance to owning these components that make up Debra Bruch.

What I said to Damon is about parenting in general. It was not aimed at any individual.

Don't start with the "throwing away" business you know that doesn't fly with me. Punishment - you learn from your experiences because you are an adult and you get punished by others from time to time. But take a look around you and start counting the number of times any of you have been punished lately compared to two months ago. Don't you see something worth celebrating? Look around, do an inventory, think it through. Do you really, really, really want discipline in your life? Most of the discipline is apparent in the kids. Maybe it is time for the adult to set her sights on something.

I am saddened for your loss of David. Going back and being administered to was a great idea and a blessing.

Fran's Notes: Her brother died. She'll go to the memorial service where the perp will be there. We discussed how she can manage that with her alters.

Scott: Oh gee, last night was just too strange and I forgot to do my chore. Oh gee. I haven't been reading lately either, Daddy. We've been sick, and when I try to read, I put the body to sleep. But I'll try again today. We've been taking my book to the therapist and reading in the waiting room and we'll do that again today.

No movie for me this week! I got to see Monsters vs. Aliens last weekend but I didn't have enough money for popcorn. I can't have candy, right? Cause I'd sure like to have candy, Daddy. This weekend, there isn't any *I* wanna see. Nils wants to see I Love You Man and Philip wants to see Fast and Furious. Daddy, Philip wants to see a horror film, but I don't want him to cause I don't wanna get scared.

Bruce: Scott, The lotion is very important for the body. It helps relax the body and gets it ready to sleep. Last night there were other things going on so you are OK. If reading puts the body to sleep that is OK. That means the body is relaxed and ready for sleep. So, Scott, you relax the body in two different ways. Good for you!!!!

Little Debra: Hi Daddy - We gotta leave pretty soon to therapist stuff. AND Grandfather's with me, too!! Gee, he won't let me go. Bye Daddy!

*** hug ***   *** kiss ***

Bruce: Grandfather is taking good care of you. Have a safe trip today.

hug **kiss**

Little Debra: Boy, the therapist stuff was really really hard, Daddy, but Grandfather was there. And he talked to me while I was there cause I had lots of questions.

And I had a headache and I have one now too.

I don't think it's over or anything. I think I had too many questions.

I haven't relived anything. The Adult says my drowning is the hardest cause it was what separated me in the first place.

When the monster first put his thing in me and it really really burned and hurt and stuff, he told me that this is love. And I'm supposed to love him like this. The therapist said that was a lie. What is love, Daddy? Is what you're doing for me love? And what Grandfather is doing love? I think it is, but I'm just not sure cause it's not IN me, you know? I mean the feeling of love isn't in my insides. I know that God loves me and stuff but I just don't know about people.

The first time he put his thing in me, he had me on his lap. The monster told me not to tell, that it was our secret. But then I told my first Daddy's new wife and my Grandmother came in and said that I was lying. And I just knew that nobody was gonna help me and I was really really right. I just knew that I was all alone and nobody cared and stuff. And that nobody would ever care about me or love me or anything and I wasn't supposed to be taken care of and stuff cause my mommy never did either. And my mommy was really really mad at me on the way home and I was really really scared.

And the monster put his thing in me again, but this time he was really really mad and it hurt awful and I cried and cried. And he was on top of me. And he was mad and jerked me into the bathroom and I watched as he put water in the bathtub. And all the time he told me over and over that if I ever told, he'd kill me. He told me I was supposed to love him like that, but if I told anybody he'd kill me. And then the put me in the water and told me that it's really really easy for him to kill me and I gotta learn to not tell. So I'm making him show me how easy it is to kill me. So he shoved me all the way under the water and I was scared. He let me up and he was really really mad. But the last time I breathed in the water.

I saw a light Daddy. And then I was with Jesus and for the first time I saw Jesus and where he was and all the people around him and stuff. Jesus said that he wanted me to go back but I didn't want to. Jesus said that he wants me to do stuff for him, so I gotta go back. But I was too scared to go back, Daddy. So Jesus said that I gotta go back but that he'll bring me right back to here and he'll make it so that I can live. And I saw my cord to my body separate, Daddy, into two cords, and Jesus said that I'll be able to live now and still come back. So he said I could come back right away. So I went back to the monster and I was out of the water and he was hitting my back but just as soon as I knew what was going on, somebody came and took me right back to Jesus.

And Jesus was there and he showed me where my room was and there were a lot of rooms. And he told me to go to my room and sleep. So I went to sleep and I slept until the body was really old. And I woke up again.

That's my story, Daddy. I like you.

Bye Daddy!

*** hug ***   *** kiss ***

Fran's Notes: Debra continued to process the intensive session with Little Debra on the drowning incident. She is processing it and working through the headache and body memories. A couple of days later, Little Debra relived the trauma of the drowning. Bruce was expressing loving care. Everybody is doing well. After the reliving, they aren't afraid of the monster any more.

The Adult: Nobody's afraid of the monster any more. Facing him and seeing just how really small and a coward he is ought to put a lid on it. I'm in charge of the burial of David's ashes, so that will be good for me, too. I doubt that I'll be doing a whole lot with Eleena concerning her moving, as she'll play her game and think it'll hurt me to make it so I don't help much. I'll be staying with the Bruch's during all of that too. So I'll be with the Bruch's before Jack and I go on down to Wichita. Once down there, we will also help with David's stuff with the monster. Then it's back to Kansas City to help Eleena and I'll be staying with the Bruch's then again.

Oh geez. We merged for a little while last night. I was almost asleep when Jesus called me, called all of us. He said that the reliving of the drowning was something we all had to relive, not just Little Debra. Each of our spirits has a cord to the body, and we saw Jesus take the cords and fuse them together. Then our spirits came together.

The first thing I noticed was that I couldn't tell anybody apart. The second thing was that my own self-image changed. I've always seen myself as a fat person, and that literally changed to seeing myself as a thinner person. That has stayed with me. Then I knew I wasn't an adult and I understood the things I told you above.

We then came back here and relived the drowning. We saw, felt, and heard the monster shove us under the water several times and then we breathed in the water and we just panicked for a little and then we stopped breathing. But there was an angel with us this time, and he helped us begin to breathe again. It was frightening, but not traumatic. We didn't die. We did go back to Jesus afterwards. He didn't separate us. I think it just happened naturally. But I know I don't feel quite the same as before.

I saw Grandfather talking to Jesus again for a long time. I suspect it was about this next stage. You gonna throw us away?

Bruce: I will be around. No throw aways here.

Scott: Hi Daddy! Boy, I saw Jesus and he spoke to me just to me and everything. He said he didn't want me to die. He said he wanted me to live for him. Cool, huh?

I didn't do my chore yesterday, Daddy. Jesus said he wanted me to do that and anything else I'm supposed to do, I guess whatever you and Grandfather say. And he said that I gotta read as part of my chores, too.

Cool, huh?

I wasn't afraid any when I merged. I wasn't afraid when I drowned. It didn't hurt the body any, Daddy. Just anxious stuff.

Bye Daddy!

*** hug *** *** kiss ***

Philip: Boy, we merged!! All I really knew was that I seemed bigger inside. I was me, but not me. But, gee, I saw the world outside of me different.

Nils: Boy, Daddy, when I merged I could do even MORE stuff!! Cool, huh? Jesus told me to always always always look outside myself. And when I merged, I did, and everything was different!

I had to drown, though, and I sure didn't like it. I was kinda scared, but an angel was there and told us not to worry. So I didn't. And I lived and we separated again. I don't know for how long.

I love you, Daddy!

*** hug *** *** kiss ***

Little Debra: Gee, Daddy, I sure was different when I merged. Jesus said that we all had to be merged to relive the drowning cause none of us had separated yet in the first-life. And cause he separated us, he was to connect us again. I think we're still connected, but not completely. It's really really strange. I'm not scared though. Grandfather is here. Boy, I saw Grandfather talk a lot to Jesus when it happened last night.

Jesus said that we'll be living a true second-life when we merge. But really really fast.

Bye Daddy!

*** hug ***   *** kiss ***

Fran's Notes: Philip came out on his own. He said he can't find Debra and Damon. Since the last appointment they felt shattered. They would be different ages and only pieces of them. Philip thinks they are merging but said seeing Eleena and Walter Amundson may also be triggering this.

Little Debra: Hi Daddy! I'm okay. I asked Jesus if I wasn't gonna be able to see spirits and stuff anymore after we merged. He said that none of us are gonna lose anything at all. So I'll still be able to see spirits and stuff.

The Adult was worried that merging like we did was a backward step, but Jesus said that none of us were gonna lose anything we've been taught in this second-life. And it's the final thing to do. I'm kinda scared to not have the Adult around, but Grandfather said that he isn't going anywhere. And I remember you said you weren't going anywhere. So I guess it'll be okay.

Bye Daddy!

*** hug ***   *** kiss ***

Bruce: Hi Little Debra, Nothing to worry about although it does feel a little different I would imagine. Merging is a big step in the process and Jesus is overseeing that so, as Damon would say - "no worries"

hug   ***kiss***

Philip: Daddy, I just figured out about merging, and I'm not gonna do it. The others can merge, but not me. There's NO WAY I'm gonna be some kind of pansy ass girl, Daddy. No way!! Girls are stupid. Girls are just evil, Daddy.

Tell God to put a penis on me, Daddy, and then I'll merge. God can do anything, you know, so I think I gotta have a penis for real. I AIN'T GONNA MERGE INTO A PANSY ASS GIRL!!!!

Bruce: Relax Philip, you will have an understanding of what it will be like before you merge. Do not be scared, and do not start name calling or labeling. You haven't been disciplined for a while, let's not start now.

Philip: WELL I WON'T PLAY WITH ANY STUPID DOLLS!!! Gee whiz.

Nils: Daddy, Eleena now wants the Adult to haul up some furniture to keep. The Adult said that she wasn't really prepared for the expense, so now there's like conflict stuff a little. Eleena's putting the pressure to keep the furniture in the family and I think the Adult would like to do that, but she'll have to pay for it. Maybe Eleena will cave in and pay for something for her for a change. Even Jack's telling the Adult what to do about that and is mad. How come the Adult's always the bad guy, Daddy?

Bruce: The adult will have to make some decisions that she is comfortable with about the furniture.

Have a good afternoon!

hugs   ***kiss***

Bruce/Daddy

Little Debra: Hi Daddy! I'm okay. You okay?

*** hug ***   *** kiss kiss kiss ***

Bruce: Little Debra, I'm OK if your OK!! :>)

hug   ***kiss***

Bruce/Daddy

The Adult: I just can't believe that my mother would use David's obituary to try to hurt me! EVERYBODY knows that I do NOT use the name Debbie, EVER. I truly hate it. So she did. And I am embarrassed. I need to live my life as a healthy person. I can no longer allow anyone to treat me as if it were poison to me. I will help her move, and that's it. I will not take home furniture, nor will I pay for storage. If she wants to store it, that's fine. Then after she passes, Jack and I can deal with it then if that's necessary. If she calls me, I'll be civil to her. But I've had it.

God talked to us today, which really helped. Once I get over my anger, Damon will tell you what happened. It's really very cool.

Bruce: Deb, What did your mother call you as a child?

The Adult: Debbie.

Jack says she didn't write it and then lectured me. I told him it would be best if he didn't do that, and that this just shows just how close I am to the brink. I told him that there are boundaries. I asserted myself as an adult. Wow. Well, THAT won't last long although I'll regain it, but Damon will tell you.

And YEP, to the therapist tomorrow (Thursday). I didn't BELIEVE what

God told us today, but Damon wants to tell you!

Damon: God called all of us to talk to all of us. This is pretty much what he told us, Dad, as best as I can do.

He said that he'll block people from seeing, but not everybody, as he will put people in our path who will help us sometimes. Anyway, God will not separate us again, but to simply make it so we can do things, but ONLY during the times that needs to happen. He told us for us to NOT make any assumptions about who we are or who we will be because of the times he facilitates; that it will not be us. And when that isn't going on and it's private, to live, and during those times he will remove the ability so we can grow into who we are.

He told Philip that he isn't going to stick a penis on him because the body is female and that's just the way it is. He DID say, however, that there won't be anything pansy ass about us. He told Philip to think of our female heroes: Golda Meier and Margaret Mead, and remember that they were also strong people. He said that everybody has male and female aspects in them.

He told Scott to never forget the pain in his life and to know that others have pain also and to be on the lookout for that. And that pain is more than abuse from a parent, but it happens through life experiences to everybody.

He told Nils to focus outward and that he will be given the gift of discernment. God told us that he wanted us to grow up as a minister and that means to no longer care so much about how people treat us, but rather discern the underneath of how people treat us, to focus off of us and how we feel, and on to them and discover whether or not it's from malice or if it's due to pain and sickness. He said that we don't have to accept how people treat us, but to engage in what you've been teaching the Adult about choosing to feel bad or not. And to know that a person's pain is not an excuse, but our discernment of that will help us help them.

God told Little Debra that she has a gift of seeing beyond this world and to always trust in that and to use it wisely. He told her that none of our gifts make us superior to anybody else. He told me that we are not entitled to anything because of our first-life or our gifts and abilities.

He told me to protect not only the self, but also others who are experiencing pain due to others. And when I can't protect them, help them deal with it. God also told me to accept that people love us, just because. And that the acceptance of love is my main task.

He told the Adult to have faith and to live a disciplined life. He told the Adult to forgive, but that doesn't mean that she needs to allow anybody to poison or hurt her again.

Fractured Mind

God told us to be careful of the people we choose to be friends with. He told us that nobody is going anywhere, like you or Grandfather. And that he'll be around as well.

God told us that we will face the monster as a child. By early May, we will be a child and we'll face the monster as a child, and this is a good thing for us to do. He said again that he'll facilitate our ability to seem older and nobody will know. He told us that along with that time period, that we'll also face Eleena as a child. I asked him if he meant an adolescent and he said no, but Scott's age.

He told us that he wants us to grow up as a minister. He expects us to continue to learn from you and to learn the lessons. He expects us to live a disciplined life. He said that our conscience will continue to develop. He expects us to honor God, our parent, and Grandfather. Period.

He said that when we teach the class at reunion, we'll be around 14. God said that that is good because it will help us develop the self-esteem we need to be able to be in front of adults. But people will be there to help. Again, he will facilitate us seeming to be older.

God told us to not be afraid. It will be different than what we've ever experienced before. He said that he will be there, and we can count on you and Grandfather to help facilitate our development.

Whew! That's it.

Have a great day, Dad!

*** hug ***

Bruce: Sounds like a plan is made and you have the best possible guide in God. Grandfather and I also will have an active role. So, sit back and relax and let it happen.

hug

Bruce/Dad

*****

The parts of me began to integrate. All but Scott have been awake for about twenty years, and for these parts to actually integrate was pretty significant. The process seemed to be for a part of me to wake up, but that part was stuck in the trauma. So that part had to be healed enough, and I think raised enough, to be healthy. A lot of surrendering had to happen, and as difficult as that was, it seemed to be a key to my healing.

From this experience with God, I thought that once these parts of me merged, then I'll be healed. But what it did was to open the door of my psyche for other parts to wake up and be healed enough to merge. It seems to me that my interpretation of this kind of experience with God is consistently incorrect, I think because I wanted to be healthy and for this to be over so very much.

I think, though, that the experience with God did help us know what integrating will be like once the process is complete. That the integrated self will be greater than the sum of my parts.

The part that is me now did wake up as a baby and I grew up in this second-life.

It turns out that these parts were actually surface parts of my psyche. As I delved deeper and deeper into my subconscious, the process became more and more difficult for me. It wasn't finished at this point.

*****

Philip: Gee whiz. Okay, Daddy, I won't label so I won't say stupid or evil and stuff. But gee, I really really want a penis and not be a girl and I won't play with dolls. I just won't. I don't know any girl or big woman or anything that taught me anything or cared about me or anything without making me feel bad. So I think girls are self-centered and just mean. Little Debra asked the therapist last Thursday if she'd find out what it's like to be against a woman, you know, to hold us like we've heard that mommies do. She said she knew she wasn't her mommy or anything. The therapist did that and told us that she's done that many many times before to little people in big bodies. It was just too strange to us, Daddy, and we didn't really like it.

I guess I'm gonna merge pretty soon whether I like it or not though.

Bye Daddy.

Bruce: Philip, Relax - you really do not know what this is going to be like. You are only thinking about the negative stuff. Let go of it and wait and see. It is going to happen anyway and more positive you are the better the experience will be.

Bruce/Daddy

Philip: Okay Daddy. No more negative stuff. Boy, it's really hard to just let it happen. None of us knows what it means to grow up as a minister or how we're supposed to make that happen.

Bruce: You leave that up to God. He will take care of that.

Bruce/Daddy

Fran's Notes: Philip was the dominant one before they separated again. It has never been Debra. Debra knows she has to work on her anger and she has a plan to paint and hit the punching bag. I advised her to do nurturing of herself throughout the process. She is claiming her own power.

Nils: I get the gift of discernment. Totally cool!

    Bye Daddy!

    *** hug *** *** kiss ***

Bruce: Nils, Discernment is a lot of responsibility. I know you will take it seriously and be very good at it. Remember, true discernment is a spiritual gift from God through the Holy Spirit.

hug ***kiss***

Everybody: Thank you Daddy! Thank you Dad!!

    *** a bunch of hugs *** *** lots of kisses ***

    -- Deb, Damon, Nils, Philip, Scott, Little Debra

Bruce: You are most welcome!

Bruce/Dad/Daddy

The Adult: Hi! Last night *I* went to Jesus in deep prayer and saw him and asked him if this merging and growth was real. He said yes. I asked him how on earth I was going to control anything and he said I wasn't. He told me that I will no longer have my system. He then said that I had to lose myself to gain myself.

This morning, though, there's demons here again. They told Damon to not exercise and then tell you he did. Damon's reply was, "Lie to my Dad? Are you nuts? I haven't lied to him yet, I'm not gonna start now!" We were all made aware that these demons want us to grow up as liars.

They scare us a little but not too much. How do you get rid of them? I know you told us, but I don't remember. I'm fairly alarmed that with me not having any control, that the demons will influence the process and I'll grow up a bad person. If I don't have my system, then what am I to do?

Do you have any idea what God meant by saying he wants us to grow up as a minister? I know you told Philip that God will take care of that. But do YOU know what to do?

Am I supposed to just let go? I guess maybe God told us when he did so we can work through some anxieties. I feel like I'm waiting to die.

Can I please have just a LITTLE bit of sympathy? Please? Please? Please? :-)

Gee, see what a little exercise and good food can do? :-)

Bruce: Do not focus on the demons. Focus on choice, your choice, everyday to do the right thing, to do the chore, to do the exercise, to pray etc. As long as you are disciplined the demons cannot influence you. What they offer is a lie, an illusion of something more enjoyable etc.

Keep your integrity. If you give in to the temptations you will lose your integrity, you will lose your self worth and you will be back into your system, only in rougher shape.

Being a minister is allowing God to guide you each day and allowing God to unfold in your daily life. Being a minister is a sacred lifestyle and you can do it but it takes – discipline! (fancy that)

No sympathy today, sorry (not really), just high expectations and a high level of confidence in all of you. You will be fine and you will do well, probably more weller than a lot of people!!

Damon: Cheech! Did those stupid demons really expect me to lie? Idiots. Grandfather got rid of them. I was in awe!!

Philip: I thought about the girl heroes and I think they're pretty cool, Dad. We have boy heroes, too (besides YOU of course) and they're Mattmy Carter, Nelson Mandela, and Martin Luther King Jr. So as long as I don't turn into some kind of wimp, I'll be okay.

Love ya!

*** hug *** *** kiss ***

Bruce: Believe me Philip, there is nothing wimpy about you! Have a great day!

hug ***kiss***

Nils: Gee, you're my ONLY hero! Hahaha Philip just said "Suck up." But we're just playing, Daddy.

Scott: I was scared that the demons were gonna get back into me, but Grandfather got mad and they ran away. Wow.

Bruce: The demons will not get inside of you anymore for two good reasons: Grandfather will not let them and neither will you by the choices you make everyday. Stay disciplined and you will not have any problems with the demons.

hug ***kiss***

*****

We did not know it at the time, but the "demons" were more parts stuck in their trauma. They were deeper in my subconscious. I wish that somebody had told me that they were parts, but perhaps I was not supposed to know. I suspect that if I knew, the process would not have happened the way it did.

*****

Little Debra: I'm not scared. People and spirits and God and Jesus and Grandfather have been taking care of me so far. Gee! Grandfather was totally cool, Daddy! The demons got scared!!! We dreamed about being merged and growing last night.

Bruce: Sounds like a beautiful dream. Have a good day Little One.

hugs ***kiss***

Bruce/Daddy

The Adult: I still thinking no to all of this. I don't think I have a choice. Sometimes I get into this mindset that I'm an evil person and making all of this up and have hurt you terribly. I question the reality of it. It's just too incredible. But once again, Jesus told me it was real.

And you've said to relax and let it happen. I'll get there.

Have a great Easter!!

Bruce: Positive self-affirmations may help. One affirmation that I use is "I love and approve of myself. I see myself and what I do with eyes of love. I am safe."

Trust - trust - trust.

HAPPY EASTER

By the way, this is an Easter experience for all of you. The old is passing away and the new is emerging in a resurrected state, in the goodness of the creation instead of the despair. HAPPY EASTER!

Philip: Daddy, we're having trouble remembering who we are!!! I mean, we just had to look at who sent what and had a hard time remembering me. So I think we started to merge NOW!!!

I don't feel bad though. I mean, *I* couldn't remember either!!!

Wow!

Have a great day, Dad!

*** hug *** *** kiss ***

Bruce: Great Philip, Sometimes I can't remember who I am either and there is only one of me

:>)

Have a good day and HAPPY EASTER!

hug ***kiss***

*****

Then, suddenly it seems like, the parts blended as Debra Lynn. I do not think Debra Lynn was a part of the first-life but a blending of the six. After a roller coaster ride of different ages, she settled down as the six grew closer and closer to each other.

Most of the Adult was lost at this point. So was Damon. From what I understand, that is because they were too much of the consequences of the first-life and God needed to rebuild because of the severity of the trauma in the first-life. God kept all the good stuff in them though, all that was supposed to be there.

For the six to blend together and all at once seems to me to be pretty significant. Five out of the six parts had been awake and walking around for several years. I can't tell you exactly what happened or how I was healed enough for the parts to blend. Perhaps that's for the professionals to figure out. The blending slowly changed to integration, but none of the six parts were distinct or out as separate parts again.

I had moved on down further into my subconscious. To me, the subconscious is like an onion, layer after layer. As one layer is healed, a lower layer moves up toward the conscious. So while my healing does not follow a linear chronological age, it does follow a linear path into the subconscious. That path is determined by how much the different trauma hurt me psychologically and emotionally – from living it to being affected by it. My trauma happened during my formative years, so its affects are deeply entrenched.

Debra Lynn describes the waking up of another part of me in the therapist's office. Until now, we thought that working on the anger meant letting the anger out the way people usually do, like hitting a punching bag. We had no idea that a part of me kept the anger throughout life. Somehow in my subconscious, I literally bottled up my anger so I could live a decent life and survive.

Debra Lynn is not a dissociated part, but a name for the current blending of the six parts. Later, the name Debra Lynn was dropped for Deb.

When the others blended as Debra Lynn, another part of me came to the surface of the conscious. I was disappointed that the initial blending was not the end of my healing process. But neither was I surprised, perhaps because I felt the part coming out.

*****

Fractured Mind

Debra Lynn: Hi Dad! We don't know who we are!!!

Boy, the anger coming out was awesome! He was like in this sack, you know? And I had to get a knife to cut open the sack and finally when I did, he came out along with placenta stuff, like he got born except he was Philip's age and stuff. And when he was in the sack, he was rage, but when he came out, he saw the world different. And really really fast, he said that he wanted to be happy and I think some of me got into him cause he transformed from anger and rage and stuff to strength. And then he went into me and into the body and it felt like tentacles. And now he's strength.

I'm trying to listen to Jesus and listen to God and listen to Grandfather and I know I'll listen to you and to the therapist. I'm older and then I'm younger and I think I gotta just let it happen. The Adult is pretty much in pieces now and so is Damon, but they both stick a piece of themselves into me, and then go back. So I can drive, but at that time some of the Adult stuck to me, but now she's not. I think I'm getting younger and it sure is weird.

And, boy, it's easier to do stuff. It was today. Like I know I gotta exercise and it was easier to get to doing it. So I did today. And I know I gotta do the other discipline stuff too, but it feels more natural to do that stuff. I know it's only been one day, but I sure do feel different. I really wanna ride my bike and hope it'll get warmer really really soon.

Hope you're okay and having a good time!!

Bye Daddy!

*** hug ***   *** kiss ***

Fran's Notes: Debra Lynn came and was sick. She knows there is somebody older who is running around in pieces. I did an age progression with her from 6 – 9 to 13 years old. When I said her body is changing at 13 years old, her head hurt and she cried. We worked on her accepting her body.

*****

I don't know how the subconscious works or why the subconscious unfolds the way it did with me. Blending is not integration, and some of the six parts later separated out but seemed to be blurred, meaning none of the six parts could be out as a separate entity as before. The anger part that Debra Lynn describes is the part we call James, but for some reason he returned to the subconscious until a little later. Cutting open the sack released another layer of my subconscious and allowed my progression to wake more parts needing to be healed.

Much of my imagery seems to be metaphor. The imagery that emerged during the healing process was not something I consciously created, but spontaneously came from my subconscious, much like dreaming whilst asleep. All of the metaphor has been deeply meaningful to me, and since metaphor is highly symbolic, it represents thought processes and states of being beyond its symbol. My imagery is also highly visual instead of aural, but I think that is due to my particular tendency to better perceive visually. It has been the metaphor, not the imagery, that contributed to my healing. One of the tasks of my therapist has been to help me change the imagery and consequently the metaphor, but even that change has had to come from the subconscious. My goal when this happens has been to just let it happen, to not allow it to be imagination, but to trust in my therapist enough to relax and let it happen. I was highly vulnerable.

The relivings, however, are not metaphor although imagery is involved. Relivings are acute memories stuck in the trauma and involve not only sight and sound, but touch, smell, and taste. They are a re-creation of an event that happened in real life years ago, but the mind is living that event in the present. Relivings come from the subconscious, connects to a particular part of me, and is the first step to dissolving that particular trauma.

Chapter Three: Fab Five Blending

Bit by bit I seem to be healing. While it may seem as if I am sharing or revealing the violence I experienced as a child, what you are really reading are the consequences of the violence I experienced as a child. Dissociation is a consequence. The relivings are the stepping stones toward balance and beauty. As horrific as the relivings are, that these fragments of my psyche can come to the surface, pass through their pain, and discover a different life is a testament to the complexity and urgency toward healing by the human mind and body.

The healing of the real consequences, of course, are deeper than waking up, going through pain, and integrating. Deep in the depths of my subconscious are lasting consequences of violence: a fear of being thrown away by people I need to have care about me, an unending sense of worthlessness, a desire to die that is really a belief that I'm not supposed to be alive and I don't belong here, even a fear that people think I'm a whore or at least as a person who wants something at somebody's expense, a desperate need to be cared about, loneliness, a deep lack of trust, and a great deal of confusion. Currently, I am at the point that at least I know what these consequences are and to an extent I need to doggedly say no to these negative urges and thinking.

The gratitude that I feel seems to me to be as deep as the consequences. Because I had a near-death experience, I have been able to connect to a different consciousness, a different perception. While other cultures perceive a different reality, our culture is reluctant to accept a different perception. But I do and I have been able to perceive the "Other Realm" for as long as I can remember.

Furthermore, during my chronological childhood, everything was alive to me during my waking hours. Everything still is alive to me. Spirit resides within all things and one moment I would be hurt and the next moment I would find refuge and solace with everything except people. After the violence, I would lie on the floor of the barn or on the earth in the pasture and suckle the spirit willing and wanting to nourish me. I knew that I was in danger, always in danger, even if I did not know the specifics due to dissociation. The spirit within everything gave me respite from my sense of danger and it was immensely comforting. Even the smell of horse excrement comforted me. My perceptions balanced how I felt. There came a point in my living after childhood that the earth told me that I belong to her and will for the rest of my living. I belong to the earth and I find that to be significantly meaningful to me.

My perception of the Other Realm, though, is veiled. I know that I'm not seeing everything and sometimes I'm not really seeing accurately. But I can hear accurately. For a man who I knew when he was walking the earth to die and then decide to take me and raise me as his is immeasurably wonderful. It is also immeasurably strange. Just the other day I was unhappy and a little rebellious. I sensed Grandfather standing in front of me and say, "You are my daughter and there's nothing you can do about it." It stopped me cold and I felt as if I was facing a real reality that I can't accurately describe. Who says that to me? Nobody. Nobody has ever said that to me in my life! How can I not have gratitude?

During this time, the parts of me awakened to date were blending, then integrating. Also, the body began to release trauma toxins that lasted about three years. Jumping up and down in age drove me nuts, but by now I felt that God was in control. *I* certainly wasn't!

*****

Debra Lynn: Dadddyyyyyyyyy!!

I had a nightmare last night and I'm really sad cause it was about Pippin but I know it was really about me. Somebody was building a house with bricks and I came with Pippin and asked Pippin to break his face so it can be part of the house. And Pippin tried to break his face but he couldn't do it by himself. So the man broke his face and Pippin didn't cry or anything but he blacked out. I asked the man if he was gonna kill Pippin and the man said that he didn't have to cause the shock will probably kill Pippin by itself. And I saw that Pippin was still breathing and stuff but blacked out. And I knew that Pippin was me cause everything that happens with the therapist is right above my nose and it feels like it's coming out my nose.

Boy, just about everybody's in pieces now and I'm getting younger all the time. I got a real sore throat and I think I haven't drunk enough water. But the good news is that I sound lots and lots older than what I am when I talk!!! I think that as soon as I get my chores done, um, what Philip was supposed to do, then I might go all the way today and I hope I start growing forwards instead of backwards then. But you'd be proud of me, Daddy, cause I'm responsible too like Philip is. Not perfect though.

Grandfather's here and an angel is here with him too. The angel doesn't talk to me but that's okay. He's here. Except I think he's a girl, but I can't tell for sure.

I don't know what's going on though, Dad.

*****

David's death threw me into new and strange circumstances. He suffered the same childhood life and parents as I did, but he responded with violence. He was fifty-one years old when he died.

I planned to drive down to Missouri and stay with Ian Bruch overnight, then meet with Jack and Eleena, and we'd travel to Wichita and attend a memorial service for him. Then the next day drive out to

Fractured Mind

Kansas and bury him next to our Grandparents. Several people were at the memorial service, but only Jack, Eleena, Walter Amundson, and I were at the burial.

*****

Debra Lynn: Hi Daddy. I'm still awful awful sick, Daddy. Boy, the Adult just couldn't break into pieces without a fight even though she tried and my body sure is hurt. I lost a lot of hair and what's under the color is all white now. I think though that God is using me being sick though cause it helps me sound lots older.

I guess I'm kinda depressed. I'm steady, though, and not jumping around all sorts of ages, and that's helped. But I have to be really really careful cause I got skills, but I'm having trouble with the body. And I focus really good on what I'm doing, but I don't remember other stuff too good when I do. The angel still has his hands on my head.

Eleena's playing her games and stuff and trying really hard to make me feel bad, but, frankly, I'm just too sick to care.

Gee, Daddy, I was like 4 years old at first and now I'm about 6. So I've been good for two whole years!! hahahahahaha

Bye Daddy!

*** hug ***   *** kiss ***

Bruce: Debra Lynn, I will pray for you off and on all day. A six year old does not belong out on the highway traveling to a different state. Especially a sick 6 year old. NO travel until you are older and well.

Debra Lynn: Right now, the monster's just too big and powerful in me. God says that when I see him, I'll know just how small he is and he can't hurt my insides anymore and I won't be afraid anymore and I can live this second-life for real without the monster in me.

I dropped the Debra Lynn. That was only to help you know I've changed anyway. But don't confuse the name Deb with the Adult, okay?

I finally found that nose irrigation kit. It was by far the grossest thing I've done in a long time. So here I am with my head in the sink and this thick rope of nose crap tying my face to the sink. Tried to blow it all the way out, but of course THAT didn't work. I had to grab hold of the snot rope and pull and clean up my face that way. Ugh.

I'm still coughing up crap but I have more energy. Humm, I must be feeling better. I'm feeling rebellious.

I'm not totally merged, you know. Well, I borrowed some money out of what we saved when I was separated for a present for you. It's in cash at home here. The Philip pieces of me got together and complained about it. I ended up putting it back yesterday too. But I was surprised to hear this echo of Philip, especially since Philip's in me too (just not ALL the pieces of Philip). I guess when the emotions are strong enough, that's gonna happen. Is this part of this conscience too? I haven't heard him since though.

*** hug ***   *** kiss ***

Bruce: Deb, The antibiotics should eventually take care of your ears. Do not try to do too much or you will inhibit the healing process. Rest and drink lots of fluids. The antibiotics work better when you ret, eat well and drink water.

In terms of reminding you about stuff – make a list, sit for a few moments and reflect on what needs to be done.

Sounds like Philip is going to be part of your conscious, ethics and boundary keeper.

Have a great day. The retreat is going well.

Hug   ***kiss***

Bruce/Dad

Fran's Notes: We continued to work on her acceptance and knowledge of her body. Debra Lynn is 13 years old now. She aged progressed to 16 years old. We discussed her visit with her mom and abuser and how to handle it.

Deb: Hi Dad!!! I'm slowly getting better, but I'm getting better. I've been BENDING younger, especially in the evening. Feels different than when I was jumping around ages. Dad, this is so strange to live it!! I think this is happening mainly because of being sick. I really just wanna be cuddled I think because it's been a long time not feeling good.

I'm not leaving until Monday.

In Debra Bruch years, I've known you all my life now and you've been my parent all my life now. Grandfather's been my grandfather all my life now. I'll see you as your own kid does and I think I already do. I won't be able to see you any other way except as my parent. I'm not able to see you any other way now, and I'm assuming that the older me will know you as parent/friend, whatever is normal. So relax, trust in God, trust in yourself, and fear not. Let it evolve in Christ.

Bye Daddy!

*** hug ***   *** kiss ***

Bruce: Now just wait a minute, who is giving who advice now :>)

I am glad you are not leaving until Monday. I think you do need the extra time to get better and I think you will need all your strength for your journey and your encounter. Hopefully you will be pleasantly surprised as to how little effect Walter Amundson will have on you in terms of fear and that you will be able to look at him and Eleena and dismiss them in your own private way. My prayers are with you for the journey. Is Grandfather going? Remember he doesn't have a driver's license so don't let him drive. :>)

Remember to eat well, drink a lot of water and take your antibiotics (do I sound like a parent?)

hugs ***Kiss***

Love, Dad

Deb: hahahaha you're great! Grandfather says that I may be 16, but I'm a young 16 and he's not going anywhere. He kisses me a lot. Kinda annoying sometimes, but suffering is my lot in life I guess. :)

I think I got the burial service down okay, but I'll have Ian Bruch take a look. I read the Priesthood Manual to help a little. I'm not doing the memorial service, but I am at the illegal burial site. They plan to dig a hole at Grandmother's grave and pour David in.

Have a great day, Dad! I'll be good.

*** hug *** *** kiss ***

Bruce: Deb, You sound like a teenager thinking you got it all together and curious about doing things you are told not to but doing them anyway. But overall it sounds like you are doing the chore thing very well and are moving towards the journey to Missouri.

Reflection is stopping, sitting and pondering about a topic – like gratitude or what have I learned from the last 24 hours, where has God been present in my life or where have I turned away from God? You pose a question and think about it.

Had a great weekend retreat with some healing and renewal for the Canadians.

Have a good and safe trip. Keep your boundaries, remember who you have become not what you have been. Look them in the eye with no fear and dismiss them. Reflect and write about your experience as part of your processing.

hug ***kiss***

Bruce/Dad

*****

I arrived in Kansas City and met with Jack and Eleena. I then spent the night with Ian Bruch. I could relax enough to use his computer to write. I was not a part of the memorial, but they did want me to organize the burial with a short, private, service.

*****

Deb: Hi Dad - It was a long and difficult day here, but I made it through with flying colors!! It's really Wednesday night and we didn't get back here until 11:30 p.m. central time. Bummer. We go to Wichita tomorrow.

Jack and I are supposed to move Eleena after Wichita, but there's just so much stuff and nothing's really been done. I don't think we can do it in a day after we get back from Wichita. I considered staying, but I don't really want to. But I sure don't know how she's planning to move everything or put it into storage.

Anyway, I'm just fine. Didn't interact much with Eleena or anybody. Just pretty quiet.

Hope I don't have nightmares tonight!!

Have a great day, Dad!! Thanks for your blessings and your support. It has REALLY helped me along!

*** hug *** *** kiss ***

Bruce: Deb, You sound really grounded and that is really good. I am glad you are with the Bruch's. Extend my greetings to Walter. You sound very mature, like the adult is kicking in and you sound "very matter of fact" which is excellent. I do not sense any fear just the reality of being overwhelmed by the idea of trying to move someone who is not prepared.

MY prayers continue for you - make sure you are drinking fluids and finishing your antibiotic. You don't need any more fever on this trip.

I have 66 people coming in tomorrow for a retreat. IT is a lot bigger than I would like but I have my classes all prepared and have a sense of great expectation for good things to happen. Busy, busy!!

Hug ***kiss***

Love, Bruce/Dad

*****

To my surprise, Jack and Eleena did not want me to ride with them to the memorial service at Wichita. That was good for me. I knew that Walter Amundson would be there. I hadn't seen him for many, many years, and was scared out of my mind.

We all had hotel rooms in Wichita, including Walter Amundson. We met at the hotel.

*****

Deb: Jack and Eleena are going in one car and I'm going in another car. Thanks for the burial kudos. Man, this is hard!! But I'm doing just fine!! I AM trying to prepare to see the monster.

Deb: The monster's coming in about an hour. We're in Wichita. I'm scared scared scared scared scared!!

Really, Daddy, I'm scared!! Maybe it won't be so bad when I see him. I don't think I'll have much access to a computer over the weekend. I know you're busy anyway. I'm sorry I'm emailing you when you're busy, Daddy. I'm hoping it will buck me up. Cause I'm pretty scared right now. Grandfather's here and the angel still has his hands on my head. I wanna be with you and stuff and put my head on your chest while I'm doing this though. I know I gotta be strong. But all I wanna do is cry. Okay, I'll buck up now.

love you, Daddy!

*** hug ***   *** kiss ***

*****

Walter Amundson came and I saw him for the first time. I shook his hand and my arm broke out in hives. I went back to my room at the hotel and lay on the bed. Through this, I felt my mind bend and I also bent backwards in age. Laying on the bed, I grounded myself on what Fran had taught me so my mind would not break. It bent back and I was okay. My mind bending hurt quite a lot.

I can't really describe all the emotions I felt when I met him. This good-looking man now looked like a clown to me. He spoke with his Missouri drawl as usual, but he seemed to be stupid. It turns out that acting stupid was a mask. We went to the memorial and then out to dinner. His sister, who I like a lot, sat next to me and talked to me about him. That was difficult but interesting.

The next day, we drove to the middle of Kansas to bury David. The ground was wet. Jack tried to dig a little grave but he just couldn't do it. So I got down on my knees and dug the grave, put David's ashes into the earth, then stood, read some scripture and gave a short talk.

At the burial site, I looked at my first-life parents and all I could think about was that we are burying their son. I did not want to forget that and I didn't. Despite what they did to me in the past, at that moment the time was for them and about them. I did the best I could and with God's grace, it was good.

*****

Deb: Hi Dad - I'm okay. As you know, I bent backwards in age quite a bit, but I didn't break, Dad. I didn't break. I'm back where I'm supposed to be in my process. The burial was great for me. I ended up doing everything, from digging to putting David into the earth, to reading what I had wrote. I was on my knees, getting wet, getting dirty, mud caked on my hands while holding the scriptures. I tried very very hard to be considerate of everybody while doing it, just everybody. I was totally immersed in my priesthood, Dad. It was great. It was who I am!

love ya!

*** hug ***   *** kiss ***

*****

After the burial, we drove back to Wichita and to the hotel. Jack talked quite a lot to Walter Amundson. Jack then told me that if he didn't know what Walter Amundson was like when he raised us, he'd like him now and they'd be friends. Jack tried to convince me that Walter Amundson didn't remember what he was like. My encounter with the monster in the middle of the night was a God factor!

*****

Deb: Hi Dad!

Hope your session with the people went well these past few days! I bet it did! I'm finally back in Independence with Ian Bruch now.

I'm okay. Jack almost had me convinced that the monster didn't remember anything. But we had a final encounter. His door at the hotel was opposite of mine, and late at night, we both stepped out at the same time by accident. I had to get some bottled water. He looked at me and he was afraid and I knew that he did remember. He said something really retarded and that was it. I knew he was afraid of me and his stupidity was his way to defend himself. Felt pretty good.

God keeps telling me to leave the monster to God, and to leave Eleena to God too. I've wanted to, but I don't think I really need to forgive him, Daddy. I don't think I can since he has no remorse. His family tried to tell me that he's changed and he was mean but he's nice now, but they don't know what he did to me. They want me to have a relationship with him, especially his sister who's a member of our church. But they don't know. They just don't know, Dad.

I think I can let Eleena go, too, Dad. I know that God has wanted me to separate myself from Eleena for years now and I just haven't been able to. Today she told me that she paid everything for Jack. Of course there's nothing for me. So she made sure that I knew that she didn't care much for me. There's just too much poison around that's connected to the first-life.

But I've been pretty considerate toward everybody. I know it's forbidden to hurt people and I haven't done any of that. Eleena's acted hurt, but it wasn't me, Dad, even though she said it was. Grandfather says I've honored you, God, and him just fine.

So I have a few more days to go here with Eleena and Jack. And then that's it.

Bye Dad!

*** hug *** *** kiss ***

Bruce: Greetings Deb,

I think for your own health you will have to work on forgiveness for Walter Amundson and Eleena. Whether or not they are remorseful doesn't influence your ability to forgive. Forgiveness is an important step for your healing and for your ability to let go. Think about it.

How are you feeling physically?

hug ***kiss***

*****

After the encounter with Walter Amundson, I drove back to Kansas City and stayed with Ian Bruch again. Jack and I packed up Eleena's belongings to move her into an independent living complex. It was very difficult but we got it done. Down in the basement, I looked up and hanging on the wall near the ceiling was one of the pulleys he used to torture me. I nearly fainted.

*****

Deb: Hi Dad -

Yesterday when I got here I found Jack crying. I could not leave him here to finish by himself. So I stayed and we got it all done and I am waiting for the movers to come, then I will take Eleena to her new place and leave. Seeing a 60 year old man cry was not good. I put my arm around him, told him it was okay to cry and listened. Eleena has really misused Jack and me too, but I have just recognized it.

Both God and Grandfather have been pretty lenient toward me through all of this. Grandfather kisses and hugs me a lot.

Homework: woke up with a whole lot of gratitude! Thought about it a lot. Maybe I am at the stage of my process that I change quickly. Really,

Dad, I woke up thankful and found myself listing the good stuff. Even the hard stuff I am thankful about. I am pretty excited about that!

Thank you, Dad!

*** hug ***. *** kiss ***

*****

After moving Eleena, I drove north to spend some time with friends. Near Maryville was The Farm. I mustered enough courage to find The Farm after my visit. The barn was no longer there. It was built in the early 1900s and was there while I lived there. I have pictures of it in 1917. I've decided that the cover of this book will be a 1917 picture of the barn.

*****

Deb: Hi Daddy! Oh man! I finally got home!! Well, I drove up in the storm, as you know, to Maryville, where the last farm I lived on with the monster was. I knew it was on highway 71. As soon as I turned off into only 71, my nose bled. Boy, that was fun! This whole adventure was fun! (sarcasm)

My friends live in Maryville and have known me since high school. I didn't expect to feel love from them and I realized that they've cared about me since the beginning. I just couldn't feel it or know it until now.

I went to the farm, and the man there was very nice. He has healed the land, Daddy. Everything looks different, looks healed, looks very nice. It's like the farm went through a second-life like I am. There's no more feeling of evil there. His kids had friends over and they were happy and their dog was happy. Boy, it's so very changed. Seeing it helped me with closure a lot, especially knowing he had healed the land, Dad.

Jack and I supported each other through this and I supported Jack especially through Eleena's move. He has no malice in him, Daddy.

I stopped to sleep some yesterday on my way back and laid down in the back seat and cried a lot. God took me to him, and Grandfather was there, too. God reminded me that none of this is my fault and none of this is my doing. But I need help with some things and the task is to help me with my need to control and to rebel. God said that the foundation of that is fear. I'm not able to choose about that, and God is going to help me feel secure. I still have no sense of self-worth at all.

But Grandfather hugs and kisses me a lot. And I mean a lot. I see him talking with God or with Jesus sometimes. I feel I have no control over anything at all any more. (Um, I'm not supposed to have control, Grandfather just said!)

I know I'm supposed to live a disciplined life and stuff. And my homework is to work on anger. God said that my homework is also to really really concentrate on my body. To heal my body. And to focus on my body. So I have a whole lot of homework to do.

I actually talked to the therapist last night. I was supposed to call her during the past ordeal, but didn't remember to enter her phone number into my cell phone. So called her last night and she happened to be in the office and answered. I told her what I did to help myself after meeting the monster, when I was so bent backwards. Which was to lie on the bed and concentrate on being in her office and going through the getting older routine. It worked. She was happy I did that.

Anyway, I'm home and I'm okay.

Bye Dad!

*** hug *** *** kiss ***

Bruce: Deb,

I am glad you made it home OK. It sounds like a healing experience to go to the farm and see the transformation.

What gives a person a sense of self-worth?

Set your goals, make your choices and move forward.

hug ***kiss***

Bruce/Dad

Fran's Notes: She is very angry toward Eleena and Walter Amundson. She recognizes she needs time to work it through. She got rid of shame and is claiming herself. We talked about the gains of the last two weeks. She and her brother Jack got closer. She discovered that she's a decent person.

Deb: Hi Dad --

Man, I can't BELIEVE how rebellious and angry I feel! I think I'm gonna get hammered a lot until I can control all that.

Have a good day, Dad.

*** hug *** *** kiss ***

Bruce: Greetings Deb, How long does it take for you to understand that rebellion doesn't work and that most people want to do whatever they want but choose not to, just like you need to choose not to. Typical teenage stuff, rebellion, think you know everything so you don't pay attention to what you have been taught, and you do not

reflect or practice gratitude consistently. HELLO – this isn't rocket science – these are fundamentals. Work out the anger and the rebellious attitude should diminish – so do your homework on anger.

hug ***kiss***

Bruce/Dad

Deb: Geez, I AM a teenager! And people go through this for YEARS?! How do we go through it and end up okay? I HATE that I'm surly and rebellious all the time. Okay, do my homework.

Fran's Notes: She's not doing well. She broke this weekend. She went backwards. She's more Scott than ever. She wants to be alone.

Deb: Last night when I did the foot rub (no sticky feet, Daddy!) it felt good for the first time. Before, it was just rubbing the feet cause you told me to. I think maybe I'm connecting to my body. I'm so friggin' inconsistent in age. But just going with the flow.

When I let go trying to control (and rebel), it's pretty scary. But I find I'm more calm when I do it. I'll work on the anger homework today.

*** hug *** *** kiss ***

-- Deb

Bruce: Deb, The anger will work itself in steps I would think. So, keep after it through the various methods you are utilizing.

I hope you find time and good weather to walk in the woods this weekend.

hug* ***kiss***

Bruce/Dad

Deb/Scott: Hi Daddy -

I'm still one person, Deb, but I'm more Scott than anybody, so that's why the name Scott.

I broke last weekend. So I'm around 7. There was a mix up on the days for the therapist too, so we talked on the phone today (Wednesday) and I'm supposed to go there tomorrow (Thursday) morning. So I will. It was half her fault and half my fault, so I figure they cancel each other and it just happened.

There's this really bad hurt in me that I've had for as long as I can remember. I've managed to squish it down, bury it, all my life, but I don't think I should do that anymore, as much as it hurts. It came up really raw when I broke and went younger. I don't wanna tell you about it. But I do know that God has addressed it, but I don't know really what God means. So I think that I should quit the therapist for a while and go on walkabout and concentrate on God cause I think that God will help me know what he means, that he'll have me experience what he means, and take this bad hurt away so I can heal and everything.

Yeah, the therapist said no no no, but I think that adults don't listen too good and they don't understand really. But God and Grandfather do and they know I'm in bad despair and stuff so I'm not in trouble or anything. And I wanna do something about it, so that's what I think. Grandfather just holds me all the time and I cry all the time, but I'm okay.

Bruce: Hi Scott, I do not think that quitting the therapist is a great idea at this point. Especially if you have a bad hurt inside. And if you are crying all the time how can you say "I am all right?" Obviously you don't feel heard because you wrote that adults don't listen.

Daddy/Bruce

Deb/Scott: Hi Dad! I had a huge talk with God with Grandfather there. God says I gotta choose. He wants me to be happy for people who have good families. But I need to see him and Grandfather the same way. He also told me that people need to belong to families, but that isn't eternal, while what he gave me is.

He told me that most people don't have the close relationship to him and to the spirit world that I have. I asked him to take that away from me for a little while so I can know what most people experience. He said he would, but not now, and not when I expect it.

He told me that I have a really good gift of helping people experience things, including experiencing him. Mostly through my writing. I then had a dream that let me know that people are ready, and I can write really complex things now to help people experience God.

On the news, there was an old woman who waited in the emergency room at a hospital for 24 hours. She fell to the floor and died. What I saw were two people there who just looked at her and didn't do anything. I was pretty upset about it. God told me that the old woman was in his hands, but people like the others need to know him a lot better and I can help with that.

My despair is easing. God said that when I'm in that, to remember about him and Grandfather as my family and the more I do that, the less despair I'll feel. That's pretty cool.

Right now, it's like there's pieces of the others floating around. When that happened, I lost for a while a lot of the feelings I had when you raised me. I've noticed that as I grow, the others' pieces stick and those feelings and teachings when being raised by you and Grandfather are coming back, along with a feeling of being loved. I lost that when I became one person, but I'll get it back so I found out. I didn't even know I'd lost it until the pieces started to stick in me! Boy, Nils really really loves you and I'm gaining that back as Nils sticks to me.

Even the Scott in me lost it. It's like I got wiped when I became one and now as the pieces come back, I'm rebooting and reinstalling software.

I have no idea how old I am now or who, what name, I am. I'm still mostly Scott I guess but Nils is coming pretty strong and his feelings are pretty powerful. But I'm a lot older than 7.

I'm eating right most of the time, and I got hammered Saturday night by Grandfather, so I have to do better again. It isn't rebellion, but it's forgetfulness (like I forget to eat lunch) and getting off the routine so I want and take too much sherbet. Last week, I got home Tuesday evening. I didn't exercise Wednesday, but did for the rest of the week. I have a hard time remembering to brush my teeth after breakfast, but remember when I come upstairs to go to the bathroom. I don't know what you think, but I'm doing the best I can do with everything and I really don't do a whole lot wrong. It's just that I'm telling you the stuff I do wrong, so you get that and not the right stuff so it SEEMS like I do everything wrong maybe. And Grandfather's pretty strict like you are, so I get shoved back on the path pretty quick the very few times I stray.

Bye Daddy!

*** hug ***   *** kiss ***

Bruce: Greetings Deb/Scott, Sounds like you have some clarity from God as to what you are to be focusing on. Quite an assignment and one that you have grown in and will continue to grow into. I am excited for you as the great adventure continues.

I like the terms "rebooting" and "reinstalling software". The metaphor seems to fit your experience.

Keep up the disciplines but also keep in mind that nobody is perfect all the time. But it is the discipline that pays dividends that benefit you in the long run.

Take care.

hug   ***kiss***

Daddy/Bruce

Scott/Nils: Hi Daddy! I call this despair The Big Empty. I have for years. Got it again when a piece of Scott came into me with the rib hurt. I got so tired of hurting, Daddy, and just wanted you to take it away. But I thought about you as my parent and God and Grandfather as my family and I'm okay again.

I talked to Jack yesterday. Walter Amundson is in his face, too, and he told me that he doesn't understand why he wasn't loved any by both parents. We've never talked like this before, and it's a good thing I think.

Talking to Jack made me almost late last night. I begged Grandfather to let me go through MacDonald's and he finally let me (and got a stomach ache last night too!). But he said that the next time this happens, he's gonna discipline me. Gee whiz, Daddy, why can't Grandfather understand that there's circumstances? I kinda resent it a little. I think I'm too old now. But gee, Daddy, I don't think that Grandfather really understands.

Can I call about 3:00?

*** hug ***   *** kiss ***

Bruce: Scott/Nils/Deb,

McDonalds will always teach you a lesson through the art of giving you a stomachache. Grandfather always has your best interest at heart. If you are too old to be disciplined then you must be old enough to make the right choices; one balances out the other. As always the choice is up to you.

You are doing a nice thing for Jack. Maybe part of your journey will be to help Jack's understandings from time to time.

I will be in my office so go ahead and call when you are finished with the therapist.

hug   ***kiss***

Daddy/Bruce

Scott/Nils: Hi Daddy!

Well, God said that I can tell you this, so I will. Okay?

I woke up this morning and went to God. I asked him if I can see him and talk to him whenever I want and he said yes. God laughs at me a lot, Daddy! Then he laughed and told me to come to him.

I asked God why people have to go through stuff and he just said that there's lots of reasons. And for me to look at me, and how magnificent I am and I got all embarrassed, and it's cause I went through stuff.

I cried pretty hard, Daddy, but I asked God why he didn't help me when I went through my stuff. And why he let the monster hurt me so bad. He said that the Scott part of me got to be very very strong just going through the torture and beatings and rape and sodomy. But I need to know that God was there. He was there and God said that he made sure that my body wasn't maimed, had permanent damage done to it during those times. And God made sure that the monster didn't kill me. So while it was happening, I was in the middle of a miracle even then cause my organs weren't damaged and stuff and my bones and cartilage and muscles and skin healed just fine, except maybe the right side of my chest but I don't know. God said that if he wasn't there, my body would be hurt too much for the rest of my life, and sometimes I would have died.

I said that my mind hurt, though, and he said yes, but he helped with that, too. He said that it was him that enclosed the anger and hate so that I could grow into the person I am now. And now I'm healing in my mind, too.

I asked him why nobody wants me and he told me that I need to let go of that lie. And he'll help me let go of it cause I can't do it by myself. He told me that he wants me to go outside and let the earth let me know just how much the earth wants me. I said, what about people? He said that me being with the earth will put that right within me too. He said he wants the child in me to know this relationship with the earth that will also help me about people. He said it will justify what people did to me, to make right or reconcile or put in balance, not to make excuses or give reasons.

God said that he was really pleased with me. He said that I didn't do what many many people do who's been hurt. And he said that I took the responsibility to develop some really good gifts and he's really happy about that. And now I have the real ability to do some really good things.

All this took about an hour and a half, Daddy. God told me to go back to sleep, but I told him that I wanted to watch Sunday Morning. He told me I could, but to go to sleep for a little. I tried, but every five minutes I opened my eyes and I asked if I could get up yet cause, gee, it was like 20 minutes before Sunday Morning when this happened. Finally, God just grabbed me and said that I just don't have any discipline at all, do I!! I said, well, I stayed in bed anyway. He laughed and let me get up to watch TV. I asked God if I had to take a shower, and he said that my parent wants me to shower every day. I take that as a yes.

Anyway, that's my day, and it's only 11:00 right now and I gotta take a shower now. :)

*** hug *** *** kiss ***

Scott/Nils: Hi Daddy!

When doing the before-bedtime-brush-teeth, I was aware that there was a demon in my bedroom. I knew I had to face him, and went in and I saw

Fractured Mind

him and his two yellow eyes. He's fat and lazy and really really strong. And he smiles all the time cause he likes me to be miserable. I don't know how or why, Daddy, but he went right into me! And that's when I knew that he was everything that makes me sick. He's right in my gut, Dad.

I panicked and went to God. Except he wasn't God cause demons like to fool people about that, but I knew quick enough. That always scares me, Dad. I went to Grandfather, and the demon can't duplicate Grandfather and he's real and I'm with him now. And all this time I'm asking how to do get this demon out of me.

Daddy, I feel that old fear about despair and the Big Empty and everything and the demon's trying to make himself integrate with me again. And I am so sick and tired of feeling bad, Dad. I'm really sick of it. It's got to end and I want it to end NOW. When I felt that way, I turned from Grandfather and into myself to fight that demon, Daddy, and my own spirit burst into light! My spirit's light, Daddy! I've seen yours as light, but this is the first for me. I asked Grandfather if he can handle my spirit as light, and he said oh yes.

I can't get that demon out by myself, though, Dad. I don't know why God doesn't just make me older, but he just doesn't. Finally, I could hear God through the demon, and he said for me to go to the earth. But it's been like 45 degrees and raining and I just can't right now, Dad. I think I can this weekend though cause it'll be in the 60s and no rain. But I'm strong enough to keep that demon and all the bad and sick stuff in me separate, even though I feel it pretty bad. It's like I'm detached from that demon and from those bad feelings. Wow! I gotta stay that way. I'm sticking to Grandfather until I can get that demon out of me and it's gotta be forever, Dad and I mean forever. I gotta live life with the normal ups and downs and no more of this constant sickness.

I see the therapist today. I don't know if she understands all this spiritual stuff but I'll tell her. Hey, maybe since I've isolated it, she can treat this demon like it's another one of me but instead of helping it integrate, she can help me get it out forever! I'll ask.

Have a good day, Dad! Keep well, rest, lots of fluids you know. (Somebody taught me about that!) :)

*** hug *** *** kiss ***

Section Two: Emotional Consequences of Trauma

The complexity of the mind staggers the imagination. It would be very nice if my dissociation meant that I would have one part live day by day, then when it got too rough another part would come to take the physical pain, and yet another to take the emotional pain. But dissociation is about as varied as is the violence people can think to do to others, and organized dissociation when parts are completely separate, independent, and simple does not exist. I know dissociated people who have hundreds of parts. I am fortunate.

I do not understand how the mind works or why. I have no expertise. This section of my subconscious seemed to focus on the emotional consequences of the parts above it. The parts in this section seem to clearly connect to living daily life as did those in the section above. But while the others experienced the physical, these parts did not. The physical experiences of early life generated an emotional trauma so severe the surface parts could not handle it. For a part to "come out of" or "come from" another part indicates that the other part dissociated.

For Lucas to hold the emotional reactions of Scott's torture tells me that if I had not separated out another part, the emotional trauma of Scott's torture would have either killed me or broken my mind. Besides physical pain, Scott also felt emotional pain. There came a point when Scott could not hold both his physical trauma and his emotional trauma. Philip and Nils also felt the emotional trauma of violence and the Lucas part helped them as well, but he seemed to be fully formed when Scott was tortured. Lucas was "born" in the first-life before Nils and after Philip. So I dissociated and Lucas carried what Scott and the others could not. And because no part knew of another part, each could live without the mind being broken.

Besides taking part of the emotional trauma related to the others, Lucas was deeply affected by Eleena's response to our living. He was the uppermost surface part relating to Eleena, my mother. This indicates that Eleena's betrayal and ridicule was actually more damaging to my psyche than the torture, rape, sodomy, and beating my stepfather inflicted on me.

Lucas resided in the mind as an active entity. He did not "come out" during the violence or at any time. Yet his response to trauma affected my beliefs about life and relationships and my worldview, as all the parts did.

An unfortunate aspect of dissociation is that Lucas, being a dissociated part, was stuck in the trauma as much as any other part. He could not "let it go" without professional therapy. Being stuck in the trauma means he lived the emotional trauma over and over and the overall person (the whole of me and all the parts) always felt his emotions and could not change that. Furthermore, even though the parts felt the emotions, none could do anything about it. This phenomenon is consistent with all parts being stuck in their experiences of violence until each part is brought to the surface, known to other parts already identified, and become free of his or her trauma.

How deeply violence affects a child's psyche does not depend on the violence but on the child's psychological response to the violence. To judge trauma according to the severity of the violence could lead to misunderstanding dissociation as well as a misinterpretation of a child's needs and pathway to healing. Indeed, to judge any trauma by the severity of violence could diminish a person's sense of worth. All people experience trauma of some kind, including a loss of a loved one, loss of limb, or being bullied. A person's psychologically complex response determines the affect of trauma. Scott's response to violence landed near the surface of my subconscious. The deeper the trauma resides in the subconscious, the more severe the affects of the violence had to my psyche.

Chapter Four
Subconscious Level 3: Lucas (7) and Anna Marie (24) Wake Up

Deb/Deb/Scott/Nils: Hi Daddy. I don't know how to tell you this except to just tell you. You know that awful voice when the despair and stuff comes out? The recurring themes? That's another person, Dad. He's a he.

I read what I wrote to you today to the therapist. She said it's not unusual for a piece (person) to be revealed as a demon. I still did my job, Daddy. I know I did. I don't know exactly what happened in the therapist's office, but it's another person, Daddy. I'm sorry. The therapist said that this is why we're stuck at me, my age. He's a mirror of me, Daddy, who took all of the emotional abuse, the emotional stuff from everybody. I'm sorry.

Bruce: Deb/Scott/Nils Why are you sorry? The therapist said that this is not unusual so you will deal with it just like we have dealt with the other personalities. I have never had an experience with a demon personality before. But let's see how this unfolds. No apology necessary.

Hang in there.

Daddy/Bruce

*****

All my life I've thought there were demons in me affecting my thoughts, words, and actions. I never thought that Satan or evil was me, but something outside affecting me. I did not think I was evil at all, just everything else negative under the sun! The demons always seemed to be separate from me. They were frightening, but as long as I did not focus on myself, all seemed to be alright.

*****

Deb/Scott/Nils: I know what he looked and felt like last night, but she said he's not a demon personality, Daddy. The therapist reminded me about how the others thought of ME when I first came out, you know, as the dragon and Grandfather sitting on me so I wouldn't hurt the body, and then Grandfather taking over my body and washing me in the shower while I was wailing and wanting him to get away from me and cussing and everything.

He's like a mirror to me. And he's 7 years old like I was. And he took all the emotional crap while I took the hard physical torture. You've heard him lots of times as he does the recurring themes, the recurring themes come from him affecting all of us, until now. I asked the therapist if he was integrated in all of us and she said no. It seemed like that. We're talking deep subconscious kid coming up. The therapist says he's a very very hurt little boy who's got all the despair and anger in him from everything, including work. And it's made him think and feel certain ways that you've said aren't today's reality. He held the emotional baggage and we all need to help him and honor him for what he's done for the rest of us.

I wondered why I still have headaches. Now I know. Daddy, I felt bad cause I thought it was pretty much over and it isn't. And you've gone through a whole lot already.

He wants to be called Blood after the movie, *A Boy and His Dog*, and the dog's name is Blood. But we've told him that the therapist won't like that name at all. She's a girl, you know.

(Philip: Hiya Dad!!! Let's see ... demon personality ... hey, I know the perfect name for him! Bruce!!! hahahahahahahaha!)

Oh, okay, and there's Philip!! Anyway, maybe Lucas would be a good name.

There's a lot of despair in him. He feels utterly unloved, trash, you know. And he affects the rest of us. He thinks you don't like him and you don't want him and he doesn't belong anywhere.

In a way, I'm really unhappy about all of this. I was just beginning to feel good about myself, Dad. And now we have to have the really really sick and bad feelings in our face. But I know it has to happen for us to be happy and whole and everything. And I don't really blame Lucas! Gee, he actually took all that emotional crap. People who want to keep us under like Eleena and the monster.

He's connected to me, Scott, Daddy. Do you remember the bricks? I think he was born then, and took Eleena's ridicule and being ignored and everything too. And that's why he's 7.

He's pretty scared to face you. He thinks he's gonna get punished right off the bat, but I told him that he won't until he knows the rules. But he's pretty danged confused right now. And scared.

*** hug *** *** kiss ***

Fran's Notes: I did an intervention with EMDR on this one's trauma. Death is the primary feeling. There isn't anything new. He carries all of the emotional trauma from Walter Amundson and Eleena. This state talked to me with his eyes closed. This one seems to have split off from Scott and will work toward integration.

Lucas: Hi. I hope I'm not in trouble and I hope you won't be mean to me and everything. The others told me to write and taught me to write and stuff. And they named me Lucas and I guess that's okay.

The others say that you're Daddy and that you love us and want us and we belong to you in a really special way. But I don't know. I don't know what any of that feels like. I don't know what feeling good feels like and I get all confused and everything.

I didn't mean to affect the others so much, but my feelings are really really strong and it's the way I gotta see the world. I think that people are mean to me. Just mean.

I don't know what you expect from me or anything. Except I know about the email rule and stuff. I'm pretty scared. I'm not a demon or anything. Honest. I just feel sick inside, like I'm poisoned and stuff. And I know I'm pretty angry. I'm pretty scared of you.

I don't think that I can be good cause how I feel affects the others. I don't think I'm supposed to be alive though. I think we got hurt cause I was alive. That's a secret.

Bye.

Bruce: Lucas, You are not in trouble. You are expected to treat every person with respect and kindness and you have the right to expect each person to do the same for you. No one around here is going to harm you. So you will have to learn how to trust. The adult has been through this routine many times now and she should be able to help you some.

If you have strong feelings tell me about them but do not act out your strong feelings towards others. IF you act out THEN you will be in trouble.

Daddy/Bruce

Lucas: Hi. The Adult couldn't really change her bad feelings when she had them cause they came from me. When I feel really really bad I affect the others. So when I feel like I'm just trash and it's a strong feeling cause of what's going on, the others feel the same way. Is doing that acting out my feelings toward the others? Am I gonna get into trouble for doing that? Or am I supposed to learn how to tell you first? I don't want the others to feel like me. Honest. But I took all the emotional crap and I'm tied to them. So I can't help affecting them when I feel so bad.

I didn't think about acting out my feelings last night, but I think maybe I did. I broke your rule about sherbet and had a bunch. I got a tummy ache, but I often have tummy aches, so that's okay.

I just HAVE to be fat and ugly. Eleena says I'm a whore and it's cause I had sex with her husband and he was a married man. He made me and it hurt lots both in the front and in the back and I don't wanna hurt again so I don't wanna have sex with a married man and be a whore. Eleena says I'm fat and ugly too and I think if I'm fat and ugly then I won't have sex with a married man and be a whore cause men won't want to do that as long as I'm fat and ugly, but since I'm a whore, then if I'm not fat and ugly then I'll have sex with a married man. And I don't want to. But that's why I broke your rule and that's why I gotta try to keep the others from exercising and eating right and riding bicycle and everything. Because I'm a whore and I don't wanna have sex with a married man. But Eleena says and Eleena's my mother and she says that mothers are always right and she's bigger than me and I deserve everything I get. Gee. Seems like everything I get feels bad. But it's what I deserve.

Besides, Eleena likes me better when I'm fat and ugly. When I'm not, then she's lots meaner to me. I want Eleena to like me, but no matter what I do, she sure doesn't. But at least she likes me better when I'm fat and ugly.

Boy, being out is lots different than being inside! The whole world looks different! I sure don't know why I'm 7 except that's when I was born but I think I should be older. But I'm not. Gee, I want hugs and kisses too but I know I don't deserve any of that. The monster says I don't belong on this earth and I think I'm not supposed to be alive and stuff.

I'm awful confused. But you told me to tell you my feelings and I just did. And you're lots lots bigger than me. Are you bigger than Eleena? Am I supposed to believe you more than Eleena? Is that why you're Daddy? Cause you'll tell me what's real and what's right and guide me and stuff and you'll punish without making me hurt inside and feel bad inside? Is you as Daddy mean I gotta listen to you cause are you louder than Eleena? Do you care about me more than Eleena does? I guess I think that you're just gonna quit and throw me away cause I'm just a lost cause anyway. Eleena says I don't deserve anything different and she's bigger than me.

Bruce: Lucas, Yes, I care about you more than Eleena. I will never call you names like - whore, fat, ugly etc. Eleena is not with you now. She is only a memory, the monster is only a memory. You will need to be out for a while in order to feel safe. But in order to be out you will need to follow the rules.

So, you were aware of the rule about sherbet and you choose to eat it anyway. So, when that happens you can not be out for a day. If you intentionally hurt others you will not be out. This is pretty simple stuff. SO, to start out with you cannot be out tomorrow at all. When you come out on Saturday you will have to obey the rules or you will not be out then either. You will need to talk to the others and

apologize for making the stomach ache and you need to talk to them about their experience of coming out.

I am big but I will not hurt you. IF you obey the rules and learn how to act better you will be happier. When you go to therapy next time you should talk with Fran. That is it for now.

Deb/Scott/Nils: Boy, in one fell swoop, you shattered Lucas' world! Being out at all affected how he saw the world. But he really didn't expect to be punished. He had no idea that he belonged, but, boy, he sure knows now. He's in his room. And totally confused. And being confused now is cause what he's experiencing now clashes with what he's always known. He's pretty scared. He now knows he doesn't know what's real. Thank you, Daddy! Thank you!!

And I have to face facts too -- As a kid, I get in trouble a lot!! Out - BOOM - hammered!! :)

*** hug *** *** kiss ***

Bruce: Lucas will learn and be OK.

Daddy/Bruce

Lucas: Hi Daddy. I stayed in my room and everything and it was hard. I apologized to the others and stuff. I'll be good.

Daddy, do you think maybe God will forgive me cause I had sex with the monster and I thought I was supposed to and I thought it was love? Will YOU forgive me for that? Eleena never will. I feel awful bad about that and now I told you how I feel and I didn't act anything against the others or anybody honest.

Well, I took a knife and I WAS gonna cut my wrist so I don't have to feel bad anymore, but I didn't even break the skin. I think maybe I wanna live. But I don't wanna feel bad and afraid any more. But I feel bad all the time.

Say, Daddy, do you think that maybe if I stayed in my room for a month or something for what I did, that I can say it's over and then maybe I can have hugs and kisses and I can grow and then stand on my own and be happy?

Bruce: You do not have to hurt yourself. You did nothing wrong. Hang in there Lucas.

HUG ***KISS***

Lucas: Hi Daddy - Thank you.

Fractured Mind

The others told me to go to Grandfather so I did. Grandfather says that Eleena is to blame too besides the monster because she blamed me and she still blames me. But Grandfather says that my parent (and that's you), him, and God love me more than Eleena loves me. And Eleena doesn't love at all really and she's really unhappy and stuff. But Grandfather says I'm supposed to just leave her alone and leave her to God so maybe God can help her and stuff. And I'm supposed to leave her alone so I don't get poisoned and stuff cause she blames me and hurts me cause of that and makes me poisoned.

Oh gee! Grandfather just picked me up and I'm being held for the first time in my whole life!! I feel safe and stuff!

Thank you for the hugs and kiss, Daddy. Can I do that to you too like the others do?

(I wrote this Saturday after I read what you wrote, Daddy. But this goes off today, Sunday. It's Sunday now.)

Boy, I was out yesterday when we mowed the grass. And we hung up the hammock and I laid in it and looked up at the apple trees and saw the apple blossoms and felt the wind and it was totally cool. Totally awesome!

Last night I met Jesus and God, Daddy! Wow Daddy! Just totally wow!

Have a good day!

Scott/Nils/Philip: Hi Dad!

Dad, do I really have to wear a stupid helmet when I ride my bicycle? Nothing's gonna happen to me. And I didn't wear one in the first-life.

Sunday is my birthday. And here's the scenario with Eleena. She'll either (1) not call or send me anything at all, then she'll call and say she's sorry she forgot, or (2) she'll call a day or two before and wish me happy birthday in case she forgets, then she won't call on my birthday, then she'll call a couple of days later and say she's sorry she forgot. Games.

One year she talked me into coming down to celebrate my birthday, so I did. Then on the day, she had me go to one of her friend's birthday party, she gave her two presents, and didn't say anything to me, but looked at me and smiled. Silly me, I actually thought she forgot, so I didn't say anything. Then going into her apartment, she "remembered" and said sorry and now it's too late. That's when I knew she didn't forget at all. Games.

I just HAVE to accept that I just don't get what I see other people have, Dad. I just have to. Eleena just doesn't like me. Actually, Lucas is changing, and I can feel me change along with that, too. So I think I'll be okay. But birthday, Thanksgiving, and Christmas are hard.

Well, gotta go.

*** hug *** *** kiss ***

Bruce: Scott/Nils/Philip, If you do not wear a helmet you shouldn't ride the bike or a motorcycle. I know a couple of people who have had serious accidents with head injuries. You say, it won't happen to you. I say don't be foolish.

I hope you get the garden in. I planted flowers yesterday.

hug ***kiss***

Daddy/Bruce

Lucas: Hi Daddy!

Hey, I'm growing! I least I think I am. I know you want me to.

Can I give you a hug and kiss too like the others?

God talked to me again. I'm trying to control the future. He told me that I won't be afraid if I live in the present, and not worry about the future, and to not worry about the future and to not be afraid I gotta live in the present.

He told me that thinking about the future is good in terms of a task I gotta do, like the reunion class. But the preparation for that is in the present. But don't think about the future or try to rehearse in my mind what something will be. But to live in him the way it's supposed to be and let the future just happen. He said that I'll be prepared then and not be afraid. And that I can control only what I'm doing in the present. And that control is making right choices.

God told me that I use a lot of time trying to control the future and thinking about what I'll do or say when somebody hurts me. He wants me to live in the present. And he wants me to live in him all the time and to feel secure, cause I will when I live in him.

I know how to live in the present, Daddy. So I can do this. Are you mad at me cause I'm going to God about my stuff instead of you?

I'm connected to the others, I know that. The others sure don't know why my stuff couldn't be completely straightened out with them and neither do I. I guess it just couldn't.

Bye Daddy!

Bruce: Lucas, Yes, you can give me a hug and a kiss like the others.

I am not mad that you are talking to God. God is the best person to talk to anyway. So keep talking. Living in the present and not worrying about the future is excellent.

hug ***kiss

Daddy/Bruce

Lucas: *** hugs *** *** kisses ***

(YAY!)

Boy, yesterday we got 10 bags of manure and put it on the garden and I tilled it in and everything. And boy I'm really strong Daddy! I can toss a 40 lb bag and lift it with one hand and everything. I think that's cause we've been exercising.

I didn't do too good living in the present when exercising today though Daddy. I'm scared about what somebody thinks and so I "rehearsed" what I'd say. And God said that that's all in the future and I don't need to do that cause I don't know if it'll happen or not. So I think it's kinda a habit that I gotta quit. So I tried to quit it this morning.

I got really tired when I tilled and I laid on the grass and that felt really good. It's good up here instead of at Missouri cause we don't have cockroaches. And I can lay on the grass and not get chiggers. And when the black flies and mosquitoes bother me, that Off works for me. So I'm pretty lucky. But I had to take a shower and didn't eat good in the evening. No time.

Daddy, is it okay that I don't feel like a whore anymore cause of what you said? Cause I don't feel like a whore any more. But, gee, I don't know how to feel now. I don't feel anything about myself. I mean, if I'm not a whore, then who am I? I don't even know if I like myself or not, and I think maybe not. Do you like me, Daddy?

Okay. I'll go. We're gonna plant the garden today. It's all ready now.

Bye Daddy!

*** hug *** *** kiss ***

Bruce: Lucas,

Learning to live in the present takes time and practice - keep trying and you will get there. Sounds like you worked hard in the garden. Gardening is a lot of fun and a lot of work. See, exercise has paid off for you in developing your strength. So, don't forget to get up in the morning and exercise.

It is OK to not feel like a whore? How do you feel now? Better or worse? Better in what way? Worse in what way? Are you happy now?

Yes, I like you. I usually don't hug and kiss people I don't like. As to who you are - take a look at the others. You are a part of them - Little Debra, Nils, Scott, Philip, Damon and the adult.

hug ***kiss***

Daddy/Bruce

*****

    All of the parts of me truly wanted to feel better about myself. I think that I wanted it so much that I would try to "make" myself feel better. I'll admit that sometimes I wanted to change and be healed because I thought other people expected me to change. I thought that if I did not, then they would eventually tire of their support and throw me away. I realize now that this was incorrect thinking, but guilt seemed to hover.

    How I felt about myself did not diminish as the parts of me healed. I continued to think of myself as a whore, worthless, deserving of nothing, and I thought that my parents inflicting their violence upon me was the right thing to do. That Lucas thought he was no longer a whore was real. But while the negative feelings throughout the whole of me did not diminish, I noticed much later that when each part was healed, the seeds of doubt grew. Each time a part of me healed, the doubt that the negative image of myself was accurate grew stronger. It did not matter what people said to me about my worth. Because of the depth of the trauma in my subconscious, I could not comprehend anything else except the negative images of myself. Healing truly had to come from within instead of by people's expressions of love and concern; that is, coming from the outside.

    As I write this, the negative and the doubt seem to me to be even. I find myself believing the negative and then not believing it. I am terribly confused, but, oh well.

*****

Lucas: Hi Daddy!

    No, I don't feel like a whore anymore. But I don't feel anything about myself. So I don't feel worse. I feel better cause that's off of me now, you know? But I sure don't know how to feel about myself. I don't know who I am. I know you don't believe me, but you don't listen sometimes, but that doesn't change anything. No, I'm not happy.

Bruce: What are you thankful for? How do you know I don't believe you? That is an assumption on your part and I don't think I ever said to you in your short appearance in life that I don't believe you.

SO you feel better – is that something to be thankful for? DO you eat everyday? IS that something to be thankful for? Sometimes you need to start with the basics to develop some kind of foundation.

You can say that I do not understand your situation – for that would be true and you can say that I cannot fix your situation – and that would be true. The best I can do for you is support your efforts and communicate with you.

Lucas: Gee, I'm sorry Daddy. I think the book says that emotions come from perceptions and if the perception is wacko, then the emotions are wrong. That's what I learnt today from you too and I'm thankful for that!

Well, I've done a whole whole lot since I came out and you've helped a whole whole lot! I feel that my time being separated is coming to a close.

I have the feeling that getting to know who I really am will take some time, and I don't have to do that by myself and we can do that merged even.

I asked Grandfather if he was going to go away (not thrown away) even when we're merged, and he said no. He told me that there will always be a child inside who will need a Grandfather to kiss and hug and guide and discipline sometimes. But he said that everybody has a child inside and that's okay. He said that the child inside will mostly be me who held the emotion ripples of the terror and once in a while I'll feel the echoes of everything and he's gotta make sure that I'll be okay. And he'll be making sure I stay on the right path. He said that he asked God if he could do that.

You know what? I feel secure for the first time in my whole life! I know you won't throw me away and I can be on my own. And when we merge and grow up, we'll be friends. Although you'll ALWAYS be older and wiser you know! Isn't that normal when people grow up though? I mean, the parent becomes a friend and a mentor and doesn't send me to my room? I guess I don't really know!!

I don't know how long it will be before I'm merged. So I don't know if this is my last email. I don't even know if there's anything more I'm supposed to work on!!

Thank you Daddy! Thank you!

*** big hug *** *** lots of kisses ***

*****

The book Lucas refers to is *Coping with Trauma-Related Dissociation: Skills Training for Patients and Therapists* by Suzette Boon, Kathy Steele and Onno van der Hart (Mar 28, 2011). A few years into my therapy, my therapist suggested I read it. I was amazed how much I read about me! However, when I began to integrate, I no longer identified with what I read. It was a very strange feeling!

*****

Lucas: Hi Daddy - I got questions. Well, there's stuff I don't understand. In the first-life, the monsters would be mad at me and beat or, you know, but they never got unmad at me. Ever.

But you and Grandfather get mad or disappointed or stern, I don't know what you'd call it. But then it goes away and Grandfather kisses and hugs. And you do too. So it doesn't last forever.

Well, I just don't understand what goes on, Daddy. I get punished and then after just a little while and I straighten up, you and Grandfather go back to not being stern and stuff. I don't understand what happens. And I get hugs and kisses again and Grandfather smiles at me and everything.

I don't understand why you don't stay mad at me, Daddy. Or why Grandfather doesn't. I don't understand why you change back. And I sure don't understand why I'm not afraid of you or Grandfather and at the same time I know I'll get punished when I'm naughty.

I used to be afraid of you being mad at me cause then you'd just throw me away. But now I feel different, but it's still there. Am I right in thinking that a parent and a Grandfather get stern and punish, but they don't throw away even when they're frustrated cause of me?

I mean, gee, I can't for the life of me figure out why Grandfather would be so stern and discipline me one day and grab hold of me with hugs and kisses the next. Seems to me that cause I'm naughty then I shouldn't have anything good ever.

*** hug *** *** kiss ***

Scott etc: Hi Dad -

Hope you had a great time! Are you taking today and tomorrow off? I bet you did great!

Lucas asked you some pretty important questions, important to us anyway.

Yesterday was my birthday. The body just gets older and older I guess.

take care,

*** hug *** *** kiss ***

Bruce: HAPPY BIRTHDAY TO YOU HAPPY BIRTHDAY TO YOU HAPPY BIRTHDAY DEAR EVERYONE HAPPY BIRTHDAY TO YOU

In terms of the questions by Lucas, you should be able to answer them out of your own experience. So, reflect and see what you come up with.

Dad/Bruce

Lucas: Gee, Daddy, I gotta take a test!!?? I keep looking at Grandfather and he's got his stone face on and his arms crossed. I said "How" and he smiled though.

Okay, so here's my essay....

In the first-life, Eleena and Walter Amundson liked seeing me be hurt. They got either pleasure or satisfaction out of it. So they were thinking only about themselves. And cause they couldn't break out of that, they were always mad at me. And that's why I thought that I wasn't supposed to exist cause I couldn't figure out what I did wrong really and being alive was the only thing I could think of that I did wrong.

But you and Grandfather don't WANT to punish me. And it's different anyway and doesn't hurt my insides, although I get pretty anxious sometimes that you'd throw me away. But you and Grandfather are thinking about me and you punish cause you want me back on the right track that you, Grandfather, and God put me on. So once you see that I'm back on the right track, you don't have to punish any more and that makes you happy. So you give hugs and kisses.

Um, well, I think maybe you and Grandfather aren't really mad at me when you punish me in the first place. You're disappointed that I goofed up and you're disappointed that you have to punish me. And maybe you're disappointed that I don't do stuff good all the time.

And I think maybe you and Grandfather (and God) punish me cause you love me and you want me to grow up right and you give hugs and kisses cause you love me and that also helps me grow up right. But in the first-life, I got punished cause they didn't love me and I never got hugs and kisses anyway so I don't know about that.

Okay, that's it. Did I do okay Daddy? You gonna give me a grade?

*** hug *** *** kiss ***

Bruce: Lucas, You did very well. Parents do not live to punish their children. Most parents would prefer not to have to punish their children but children have to learn what is right and what is wrong, what is good and what is not so good so that they can grow up to be good, responsible people who will do the same for their children. And so it goes from generation to generation.

hug ***kiss***

Dad/Bruce

Lucas: The stuff in the garden is growing! I really really like watching things grow, Dad!!! I think I'm watching a real miracle, you know? Makes me feel all squishy inside.

Gotta go eat breakfast. Bye Daddy! Have a good day!

*** hug *** *** kiss ***

Bruce: Lucas, Watching the garden grow is a lot of fun and awesome. Who would think that a plant would spring up from a tiny seed.

I won't be in the office today. I am running a fever and am resting at home. I am leaving for Dayton Ohio tomorrow and will not be back until Tuesday, late. I will not have e-mail for those days.

Lucas: Okay Daddy. I wish you weren't sick and I hope you feel better by tomorrow! Get lots of rest and drink lots of fluids. (!) Drive carefully.

You're a miracle too, you know!!!

*** hug *** *** kiss ***

Scott etc.: Hi Dad. Hope you're feeling much better now.

Therapy's pretty intense. She says it's peeling away layers. There's Eleena in me, Dad, and it's not pretty. I'd even say it was the dark side of Debra Bruch. She's an adult, nasty, a bully and the best word we can come up with about her is "unacceptable"; the second best word is "poison."

I got scared right off. I immediately started to bleed out my vagina, not much, but enough to scare me. I felt pretty nauseous. I also discovered why I often fall asleep at the wheel, which in turn makes me want a mountain dew to stay awake. Eleena used the car very very often to ridicule and hurt me. When she comes up, I tend to want to sleep and often deal with her that way. I sleep until she goes away. Instead of going out and having fun, I sleep, no matter how much the rest of me doesn't want to.

Lots of problems here, Dad. The therapist said that an abusive mother is the hardest to resolve. She said that I can't integrate until things are resolved.

Eleena undermines my confidence. Just lots of things that are bad, Daddy. She hasn't come out to the surface, and to be honest we don't know if it's another person or a part of all of us.

But she's not a child. But it's Eleena.

Fractured Mind

The therapist said that sometimes a person will create a personality to be like her mother in order to try to get her mother to care about her. It doesn't work, but that's why Eleena is in me. All this came at the end of a two-hour session that I was compelled to ask certain questions about being a woman and why I feel poisoned and stuff. So we'll be working on the mother issue.

Grandfather's here, Daddy. He just said that he'll help us deal with her and not to worry.

I really hope you're feeling better and you'll be able to help people this weekend! You'll do great!

hug ***kiss***

Lucas: Hi Daddy. Are you feeling better? I sure hope so!!

I know what the others wrote to you. Daddy, she's the person in me that calls me a whore. I don't believe it anymore. And she says I can't do good. And I get all scared and everything. She's the person we all have to overcome all the time, Daddy. I have to say no to her all the time. But, boy, if she changes, then I'll really transform! She saps any kind of confidence. If I don't have to overcome that all the time anymore, then, boy, I'd sure feel better about stuff!! I think I'm supposed to just let things unfold now.

Ian Bruch said that a way to beat her is to do well. One of the things about the Eleena in me is that she's highly critical of not only me but of others. And I thought that was a good way to say no to her. I don't want to be like her in any way, Dad. She's the dark side of me that I have to say no to a lot cause I don't want to do to other people what she wants me to do.

She doesn't wanna have anything to do with you. Don't know why.

There's a nice man your age who is coming over tomorrow to my house. He wants me to teach him how to project. Grandfather said (after I said okay to him) that I may not let him into the house and I may not touch him (something that's common when I teach projection, even though I always ask the person's permission to touch). But he's nice to me and I've met his wife and everything. But I'll obey Grandfather, Daddy.

Have a good time!

hug ***kiss***

Bruce: Greetings Lucas, Scott

I am feeling better. I am leaving right after I type this e-mail. I have confidence that between the therapist, Grandfather, God, you and me that Eleena is out numbered. Love conquers all – even Eleena.

Each one of us has part of their parent in them and part of being an adult is to decide whether you want to follow them or create your own person. You are in the process of being liberated. **GOOD ON YA!**

hug ***kiss***

Daddy/Bruce

Scott etc.: When I focus positively on other people, then the Eleena in me has no hold of me. And I give people great advise when it comes to doing something public. But I can't follow it myself because when *I* try to do something, there's the Eleena in me. I'll call her Anna Marie.

Hope you're having a good time! Bye Dad.

*** hug *** *** kiss ***

Lucas: Hi Daddy

God said for us to stay with Grandfather and to stay with him. So we're all with Grandfather now and sticking around God as he does his thing. Grandfather's holding me.

I've always known that my focus has been to help other people. God told us that that is how we've combated the Anna Marie in me and it's how we've managed to succeed to live in life. But focus on myself, and she's been stronger. So I've been doing things for others. Daddy, God told me that that was an act of self-love. Beating around the bush a little, but it was. By living my life to try to help God and help others, I've been combating the Anna Marie in me. And the act of combating the Anna Marie in me is an act of self-love. So I do love myself. So far, though, it hasn't been I guess like other people. I just haven't been able to focus on myself until this process. But, Daddy, I DO love myself!! Yay!

Boy, I sure don't know what to do, Daddy, except to just let it unfold. But bits like what God said is totally cool.

Hope you're having a good time.

hug ***kiss***

Bruce: Hi Lucas,

Be as strong as you can be. This battle will actually make you a stronger person in the long run and that is not all bad. So, maybe you can thank Eleena for making you stronger – that ought to really upset her.

Even though this is a difficult time I still have high expectations and a high level of confidence in your ability to choose. So, work it to the best of your ability, be strong, be tough and don't whine. Eleena

wants you to be weak and you need to show behaviors of strength as much as possible.

Call me after your session tomorrow.

Daddy/Bruce

Lucas: Hi Dad!

> Well, here's my morning. I lost the battle.
>
> Woke up happy and alert at 6:30 with no alarm, the way I used to wake up before all this started. Got up to go exercise and still happy. Went to bathroom. By the time I hit the bathroom, I was extremely tired. Got water and made it into the second bedroom where I exercise and lost the battle. Lay down on the bed to sleep, but the body was wrecked while the mind didn't sleep much. Nightmares. Don't want to go to the therapist. (That's a new one.) An hour later and I have a headache. Peeled myself up. Grandfather's urging me, but by now he's saying to do the stretching. I do the stretching. I feel water-logged and sick. I feel like calling the therapist and canceling. Fortunately for some reason, Peggy's coming along today to shop for a water heater. So no canceling and that helps. I'm a wreck. And it's only 8:00 a.m. I'm dead tired. I don't want to do anything.
>
> I'm scared, Daddy. I don't want to live like this.

*****

> I got the therapy time wrong and Fran called me whilst I was driving. I stopped the car and got out to talk to her. That's when Anna Marie came out. She immediately saw a different life and immediately changed. That was the fastest healing I experienced. She also integrated within just a few days. Anna Marie was 24 years old, the oldest part of all.

*****

Anna Marie: Hello. I'm sorry I've made things difficult. I did not know that I existed, which is a way to say that I had no ability to choose until now, which I suppose is a difference between the first-life and the second-life. I reject being like my mother. I can't say that I know any other way though. I'll have to work that out.

> You took some responsibility for me not coming to the surface and out. Don't. Everybody (except the therapist) thought I was a demon personality, including me. And I was just downright afraid. I was on the phone, walking around on the grass. Seeing the world for the first time by looking at the earth is not a bad way to enter.
>
> I think I'm facing what all of the others have faced: to shed a very powerful world view. This world view is not only about the Self, but

also about relationships and especially expectations grounded in fear. This world view helped us all survive. The biggest challenge I see is saying no to this world view, which has been our parent until you. As to what other world view must be adopted, I'm not sure. Everybody has had to constantly work at this.

I don't particularly like the name Anna Marie but I'll accept it. It'll be back to Deb one of these days anyway. But the name is TOO girly for me. Except for Eleena, I have no female role model at all. I do think that women don't care about me much. And we couldn't handle being a girl in the body with all that hurt that came with that. Throughout my young life, I saw Eleena care about the boys. She just did not do to Jack and David what she did to me. Being female has been a very bad thing for me. But I think people need to recognize that they and everybody else has both male and female inside, just various degrees. We were made in God's image. It doesn't make a man less a man.

My need for somebody, for my mother, to care about me has been powerfully strong. As my mother has not been able to love or feel love, neither have I. But unlike my mother, I am not mentally sick. (As strange as that sounds.) Reality is quite different once you come out! I came out, and immediately the world was different!

God tells me that you are my parent. And with the others surrounding me, I have a strong urge to call you Dad. Will that be okay? I really do need to relax about that. It's really very strange to me.

I do not want to be who I've always been: like my mother Eleena. I would like to be a kind person I think. I don't know what I'm doing, but I just came out. I just woke up.

Well, I'd better get going. Have to take the dogs to the kennel, then pack up and leave.

take care and thank you,

*****

All parts integrated. I do not know why the parts of me integrate when they do. I thought I would have a wonderful kind of knowing and feel a great change, but that did not happen. All I know is one day I could identify the specific parts and the next day I could not find them. I did not experience any kind of knowing that I was healed. Neither was it a feeling of loss. It just was.

*****

Fran's Notes: *She recognizes the people who helped her loved her. She's changing on the inside. More self worth. She sees other's kindness and giving was a sign of love. Her body feels more energy. Debra acknowledges that she is now a girl and feeling her body. She went* *bike riding for the first time yesterday. She feels nausea suddenly. We'll explore this and the anger.*

Deb: Hi Dad!

There you are getting sand between your toes. Cool!

I'm okay. I don't FEEL stuck at this age, but instead I feel changes going on. I guess I'm just supposed to live and experience and practice. Yesterday I felt I could just barely touch my body, like I'm almost there. Gosh, hope you know what I mean. My friend wanted me to help him out in the basement of somebody's house, fixing stuff. Turns out that he is deathly afraid of snakes! So I'm laughing and telling him I'll hold his hand and I'm looking for the snake that he saw and doing the work while he's standing clear across the basement. He's bemoaning the fact that he'll never live it down. Of course I didn't find the snake. Snakes aren't stupid. They don't stick around.

Chapter Five
Subconscious Level 4: James (12) Wakes Up

Darkness is the absence of light. It does not seem to be an entity unto itself, but connects to light. Without light, darkness would not be.

If a person looks at himself or herself deeply enough and with honestly and integrity, I think he or she will find a darkness within. We seem to have a darkness within our psyche, a hungry, frightening darkness. It is not pretty. But within our psyche, our darkness yearns for substance. Darkness wants some kind of direction. And that is why we all need to place something into the darkness within us. Not light or anything that generates or holds light. Light causes darkness to diminish. What we place within the dark reaches of our mind or soul is what we choose to place within the dark reaches of our mind or soul. What we place has no light. It is, indeed, the dark side of the psyche.

Darkness WANTS. I think the strong urge for darkness to want may be why my second-life parents focused on my very strong urge to get and do whatever I want. Without the discipline of tempering want, I could not accurately discern the want of darkness that would lead me to get and do unhealthy things.

I do not think that darkness is evil. Neither is it good. It just is. And because darkness connects to light, I think the quality of darkness within a person reflects the quality of light within a person. If light shines brightly, the darkness residing within can be controlled because the choices a person makes to help his or her light shine brightly diminishes the power that darkness has in its yearning for substance. If the light within a person is corrupted and dimmed, then the darkness can and will become strong enough to overwhelm that person. Because the quality of darkness reflects the quality of light, if the choices a person makes corrupts light, then the choices a person makes to fill darkness will also be corrupted.

The choices my first-life parents made corrupted much of their light. The dark substance within their psyche, being corrupted, justified their actions. Their own choices diminished their light and grew their darkness to the point of creating illusion. I think illusion brings evil into the world.

But I don't really know. My thoughts about darkness is speculation.

I think God loves my first-life parents as much as he (or she) loves you and me. God's light does not diminish. Indeed, it is the Creator's light within my parents as within all, and while their choices corrupted that light, it was still within them. Their choices severely corrupted their psyche and their soul, and that was a terrible act they did upon themselves. But God was there to help them heal if they wanted it, or more accurately if they could want it. Perhaps one purpose we all may have is to help the Creator heal – to weaken corruption – despite or perhaps because of our own wounds. But throughout my parents' lives, the Creator is and was there to heal and comfort and nurture them with an understanding I cannot comprehend. And now that they have passed, they are surrounded and immersed in Love. My prayer is that they choose to heal.

My therapist often told me that she was proud of the choices I made. She was not only talking about my life choices, but the choices of my psyche. Because of the long severity of my trauma, I should have been a psychopath or a sociopath, a killer. But that did not happen. Mrs. Waters thinks my turning point was when I was around fourteen years old. I was in a library looking through books when I came across a book about the Holocaust. For the first time in my life, I hated. Waves of hate hit my psyche because I knew people would hurt others that badly and I could empathize with the Holocaust victims. Mrs. Waters thinks that the key to my mental health is in my tendency to empathize with other people in pain.

It did not stop me from hurting other people. I wondered why my father found hurting me to be so pleasurable, so I beat up people once in a while. My mother also hurt other people with her ridicule. She and I would sit in a public place and as strangers walked by, my mother debased them just loud enough for them to hear. Nobody confronted her but just walked on. With her, sometimes I practiced the art of ridicule. It felt like poison to me.

I was confused. My mother ridiculed me in public and in private all the time, even during my adulthood. But in my child's reasoning I thought that was the right thing to do because I deserved it and her ridicule was true. But how did strangers deserve to be hurt? I (as Philip) could not reconcile any ridicule toward other people. My mother's corruption helped me say no to ridicule towards other people. Ken thought it extraordinary that a child did not mimic a parent's actions toward others. But the only way I could reconcile this dilemma was to embrace their hurt and accept my own hatred of myself. My parents' actions were for me alone and that was the only way it made sense to me. Because this helped form my foundation very deeply within my psyche, stuck in my trauma, my child's reasoning carried into adulthood.

James resided within the darkness of my psyche or soul. Somehow I made the choice to put him there. Perhaps I made the choice to allow God to put him there. It was like James was in a placental sac. He held the rage and violence that my darkness held, the violence I wanted to inflict upon myself and everyone else. But he could not act. I chose to place James within my own darkness in such a way that he was unable to gain control over my psyche. My choice for developing my light was mainly one of empathy with others' pain. When it was time for James to wake up, another part of me cut his prison open, his bag, and he awakened. The image was of James' placental sac being cut open and liquid fell out as well as James. Fear of himself caused him to delay entering the known world.

When he entered the waking world, James was, indeed, a psychopath. But he looked at Mrs. Waters and light took over and he did not want to hurt her or anyone else. Empathy must be mighty powerful! Just as every single one of us has a darkness within, so do we have light.

*****

Fran's Notes: James came out today. He has intense anger. When he was out he felt embarrassed that he needed to be touched. I explained that he has a common human need. He needs to get rid of anger.

James: Hi. I'm James and I'm 12. And that's not lying, like Scott did.

I know everything, but can't say I believe everything. The therapist says it's all true and it's come out of the body as well and the body doesn't lie. She named me James today cause that's her brother's name and she said he's a good guy.

I've been carrying the anger and I've been too friggin' scared to come out. Figured I'd kill somebody, like me. It took a long time for me to come out today with her, and then it took even longer for me to let any of the anger out. I knew it had to come out through the body, and finally figured out a way. You can't tell anybody, though, cause it's the most embarrassing thing any of us have ever done. I couldn't tell her what I was gonna do and she was a little concerned but she said that she trusted me. So finally I got up enough spunk and swallowed my pride and did what I've always wanted. I sat down in front of her and put my head on her chair. She touched me! She patted my head and rubbed my back and said that physical touch, good physical touch, was a good thing and a needed thing. And she said that I just needed to be comforted. She said that I probably haven't ever had this before and I said no, especially not from a woman. So a hunk of my anger went out into the blanket that she covered herself with cause I cried. But you can't tell anybody I cried, okay?

Bye.

(Later. Bruce was out of town.)

James: Hey. The therapist knows if there's more by looking at the body it turns out. The only thing I know for sure are the headaches when there's a person at the surface and when it's really strong the body feels nauseous. She even knows who's out by looking at the body. Don't know how she does that, but she does. And I don't know what of the body she sees, but she does. Anyway, knowing that has helped me accept all this crap.

I think a hunk of me was in the Adult. She's not around anymore, and whatever pieces of her Jesus kept is in Deb now. She was pretty upset knowing that most of her was gonna die, sorta. But, crap, if it was up to her, we'd be on the couch watching TV and eating ice cream all the time and that would be all. She wasn't well really. But none of us blame her at all cause she was the product of the first-life ya know. I'm still kinda angry about that though, that she had to go. Doesn't seem fair, since the rest of us weren't healthy either really. I guess that God kept the kids cause maybe kids can be reformed. Oh, God just said that the best of the Adult stayed, and that was a huge hunk. Oh, and he just said now that what was lost really was her identity, her oneness. He says nothing's lost really and he says that we'll all lose our identities the same way when we merge and we'll become one identity. Okay. I guess it's something I have to experience to understand.

I'm pretty mixed up I guess. A hunk of me is like the monster and another hunk of me is pretty revolted about that. Man, if Damon was in me, I'd wanna have sex, violent sex. I wanna hurt people and get off by hurting people. I wanna see what it's like to get off and sodomizing somebody. This body can't, I know. But, man, another hunk of me doesn't wanna do anything like that. I don't wanna hurt anybody. So I guess it's a good thing that Damon isn't around. God just said right now that the more I release my anger, the more I can become my true self.

There's this huge Indian standing beside me. He just reminded me that I'm 12.

Gotta go.

(Later)

James: This Grandfather keeps taking me by the ear to get me to do stuff! Crap! Okay, so I didn't get up in time to exercise. I'll do it later. Geez. I'll do it just as soon as I quit helping Roger. Grandfather says if I don't just as soon as I get home again I'll get my ear pulled again, all the way upstairs and into the exercise room. He's mean. Dang it! I'm goin!!

Hey did you realize just how much emailing you really helped everybody with this process? Totally! Helped totally! Helped get the poison out. Kinda like vomiting. Picture it, dude. Oh geez, this big Indian

Okay, exercising done. He says he's Grandfather. My Grandfather. Period. He says I'm colorful and I'll colorful myself right into the woodshed. Yeah, I know what he means.

Okay, showered. Man, Grandfather's demanding. I'm not used to this at all, you know? I've always felt like nobody cared, you know? That no matter what, I was on my own. But Grandfather's on my case and I guess I'm getting to like it. You know, not having to worry and having somebody bigger than me, you know? Grandfather says you're here too for the same reason. It's like maybe I'll be able to stand on my own a different way than what I've been doing. The others say I have to obey. I'd rather fight.

Okay, signing off.

Deb: Dad, I've got some bad news. At least it might be bad news. Last Thursday I told the therapist that I don't think I ever grew past age 14. I did intellectually and spiritually and mentally, but not psychologically. And that it doesn't have anything to do with maturity. Cause I did mature to a degree in the first-life. But I didn't grow past my age now. She agreed. I told her that I didn't have a clue how to grow older. But she said that it'll happen, and she'll help it happen, but I gotta resolve these issues first, and that's what's keeping me at this age. Issues mean anyone else in me and then working through their issues. And also the feelings, the hurtful or ill feelings, I have about stuff, and the stuff I've gotten wrong. And the positive changes and experiences that's going on too. And learning how to live a disciplined life and I think having that engrained in me. You know, being raised.

She said that it can't be forced, but I'll grow. I have the idea that it'll just be more slowly than before. Well, that's what's been going on anyway! The changes have been slower, but they're still there! I do know that I've never felt like I fit in anywhere.

What little of Damon was in me, God pulled out. I think cause part of James identifies with the monster. And he's gotta work on his anger and let that out and gone in order to release the monster in him. Gee, Daddy, I dated a grand total of four times in my first-life, and all of it was a bad experience. I couldn't even kiss without feeling bad.

Well, gotta go. I'm sorry about the bad news, that my growing will go more slowly. I think. I've been wrong before!! Maybe once it starts, it'll go fast!!

hug ***kiss***

Bruce: Greetings,

> **No bad news about your age. You are in a process and the process has a sequence of things that need to happen in order to create a healthy merge. You are doing fine.**
>
> ***hug*** ***kiss***
>
> **Dad/Bruce**

James: Hi. Grandfather's nice to me, man. He puts his arm around me and wrestles with me. He's stern sometimes. But I'll behave. I'll obey and everything. I don't wanna hurt anybody anyway. I know it's my spirit he's touching instead of my body. But he ain't no monster and he don't want to hurt me. He says the woodshed if I don't work on my anger today and I believe him. But I can tell that even that's caring. I'll fight anybody who tries to hurt me. He says that's okay, but how I fight is important. He says I got stuff to learn.

He don't have to pull on my ear to get me to do stuff anymore. I'm supposed to obey you, too. I won't obey you, though, if you're gonna hurt me. The others say you won't, but I've never trusted it yet. Sorry. A big hunk of me says that you've never done anything that would wreck any kind of trust. Another hunk is still tied to the first-life though. I'd say that if you don't want me, that is care about me, like you do the others, then I'd say I don't blame you at all. I've never trusted anyone. But the therapist was nice and Grandfather's cool. So I trust them. You've just been out of town and you got a right to live your own life. Okay, I choose to trust you until you hurt me, my insides. How's that?

Bruce: James,

You are a part of a whole. What you do or don't do impacts the others. So, you have to give an extra effort at first until you trust me, Grandfather, God and Fran. There are authority figures in your life now that care about you. These authority figures will do things to help guide you. You on the other hand, have a propensity to want to do what you want when you want without regard for others. So, at times the authority figure administers a punishment that gets your attention, sets a boundary for you and lets you know we care. Punishment isn't about hurting someone, as much as it is about setting a boundary for a person so that they will grow in productive ways. You are capable of doing great things. "Not trying" is not one of them.

Dad/Bruce

James: Hi Dad --

Turns out the same thing doesn't work all the time, that is, the punching bag didn't quite work. I'd feel it, but I think I was trying to feel it. Doesn't work. Tried the bag twice. So I tried what the therapist told me about and that worked a little. Then I tried writing, and that worked a little.

I have a hunk of the old adult in me, Dad. I seem to be disconnected from the others, and that hunk of me is in denial. I don't seem to have the memories that the others have. Maybe writing will help. I don't know. I do know that the therapist has techniques to help with that. I'm nearly panicked about this! Having a hunk of the old adult, and a hunk of the monster in me sucks.

I'm having problems with both short term and long-term memory (and that's cause I'm disconnected). But I do have a big desire to be out and figuring out about life and stuff. And I just can't suppress my anger, or the hunk of the monster in me. Otherwise, it'll all go back in and that's what must not happen.

What I do remember is the great relief I felt when I left the monsters. I could do what I want when I want. Sound familiar? Ha! I do believe that's the core of why I have that tendency. I think the no regard for others connected to it comes from the need to survive.

So I've been good really. Do I get a hug and kiss from you too when I'm good?

Bruce: Greetings James,

Healing is a process that takes time. You have anger but no memories may be a good thing until you deal with the anger. So keep trying different techniques to deal with the anger issue and allow Fran to help you. Perhaps when you merge you will then have some memories of the first-life.

hug ***kiss***

Dad/Bruce

Fran's Notes: She made considerable progress on working through her anger and reframing her cognitive distortions. We'll continue to work on her anger.

Deb: The therapist said that she'd much rather help children who are DID so they don't have to go through the adult life like we did. Jack Jones suggested that we take a little ball to squeeze to help get out the anger during the trip. We'll do that, too.

I just can't stay at 14, Dad, I just can't! To tell you the truth, living really is pretty scary to me and I'm trying hard to be responsible and everything.

James doesn't have the driving skills that I do, so I have to drive all the time too which means I gotta be out then.

James: Hi Dad!

I've been having tornado nightmares and I had one last night even before I went to sleep. A tornado swirling around and around with the monster and Eleena, Jack, David, grocery bags, barns, pulleys, rope and all sorts of things caught in it. It began as one tornado, and often it splits off into several. I've had these dreams all my life periodically until recently.

Well, until Scott, and then they came up again when I came out.

I know my story now, Dad. It came last night.

Eleena left sometimes. She usually took David and sometimes David and Jack with her. She'd either stay with a friend in town or visit her parents. She left me. *I was born when the monster hanged me. He was drunk and he took me to the barn and knotted the rope and put it around my neck and lifted me up. So I woke up kicking and I kicked him in the face and he let go of the rope and I fell and then got the rope off my neck and ran and hid. I was 12.*

When Eleena left, he'd get drunk, but he always always cared about what people thought so he never went out. But he wanted a drinking buddy and I think that first time I didn't go along with him. But I did from then on but I was smart and I was careful. He'd force me to drink sometimes, and I'd get pretty sick sometimes, but most of the time I just became him. I was like him and acted like him. I've felt like I was like the monster since I woke up recently, you know. But then when he got mean drunk, I'd run and hide, easy to do on a farm. I felt sick most of the time but I figured that if I didn't drink too much then I'd be okay. He smoked cigars, too, and got me to smoke with him.

I REALLY hate Eleena. I'll never understand why she would leave me behind. He never had sex with me, but I wasn't out all the time either, just when he got drunk. He expected me to take care of him when she was gone. We all have remembered one time she left for two months cause that's when she left behind David and Jack too. He'd woo her back.

I hope I'll really make you proud of me someday. We all do. Thank you Dad. You've seen me through a really hard time. Thank you Dad!

hug ### ### kiss

*** hug *** *** kiss ***

Bruce: James/Deb I am fine and so are you. The center is going through a transition. We have been busy with that and I have been spending a lot of time the past few days networking with labyrinth people trying to put together a ballpark figure of how much an outdoor labyrinth would cost for the center. You are in good hands. I have read your e-mails and all the information seemed positive. So, enjoy and relax.

hug ***kiss***

Dad\Bruce

James: Hi Dad!

I knew that my process wouldn't exactly be on hold while I'm gone, but I guess I didn't expect it to be this hard or strong I mean.

We were on a sleeper coach last night and I slept okay. My chair wasn't with anybody, and I was the last on the bus, so I was alone. I woke up in the middle of the night and Jesus came and talked to me and Grandfather and I had a vision. Grandfather was with me throughout all of this. God said that I must separate myself from Eleena, and there was this long cord that tied me to Eleena. We were pretty much not separated, so the others experienced the same thing, Dad. Anyway, Grandfather said that I must walk away from Eleena, so he and me did that. But I kept looking back cause I didn't want to walk away from her.

Jesus came and cut the cord between me and Eleena. Eleena's cord tried to reconnect to mine, but couldn't. I cried through this, Dad, and I'm trying not to cry now cause I'm in public. I asked if she was gonna be okay and Jesus said yes and I asked if she was gonna be happy and Jesus said that yes she will after she learns some stuff. All this time, Grandfather was right next to me and getting me to walk away from her. Jesus told me to turn around and look, so I did and right with Eleena were two angels and she was smiling and stuff, so I knew that she was in good hands.

Oh gee. I'm crying, so I gotta stop for a minute. Anyway, God said that I'm having problems knowing love cause of Eleena. I told God that there's a reason why she is the way she is so that's why I couldn't just leave her, you know? And then I asked if anybody is gonna love me and God said look ahead. So I did and there was you and everybody who really do love me. God said that I need to turn my attention to the people who love me and no longer need love from Eleena who just can't. So I gotta keep walking away from Eleena and toward what's real. But the cord is cut, Dad. And it feels strange.

Anyway, that's what's going on. Boy, this sure is hard.

Gotta go, Dad! People are coming around.

hug kiss

(stupid keyboard!)

James and Deb: Hi Dad

Last night Grandfather told me to get to bed and he wanted to talk to me. I started to cry cause I thought I was in trouble cause I know I've been acting my age sometimes. He said, 'What did I tell you about the negative?' So I wasn't in trouble or anything but I felt like I was.

Grandfather said that I've been doing okay. And sometimes I really do really good with people with trying to comfort them. Um, making them feel good when I feel like they don't really but they should. Grandfather said just a couple of times I did the opposite and to watch that. He told me to never say anything that would hurt anybody. He said for me to focus on the other people and help them feel like they have worth. He said that when I do that like I did sometimes that that was good. He said that he's not saying I haven't been doing any of that. But for me to focus on that more with people so it can help me create that habit and to grow that way. That's it.

Have a great day, Dad! Love you.

Hug kiss

Bruce: James and Deb,

Sounds like you are having some good learning experiences. Cutting the cord with Eleena was a very important step for her as well as for you. It was necessary if you ever hope to have a healthy relationship with her in the future. But, she has many things to learn and to be confronted with. Time will tell if she is able to make the right choices towards her own healing. Angels are a good sign.

Helping other people and being kind to other people are great lessons. Watching our language is a discipline, one that we need to practice all the time. Carpenters say measure twice before you cut, humans should say think twice before you speak.

Enjoy!

Hug kiss

Dad/Bruce

James: Hi Dad

How come you and Grandfather are in sync?

It's good for me to know that there might BE a future with Eleena. I'm not supposed to even worry about her any more. Yeah, the angels are really really good. I want her to heal, but I don't think she can in this life.

Grandfather said I HAVE to work on anger when I get back home.

Okay, Dad. Gotta go.

hug kiss

Bruce: The lessons just keep coming and you keep growin'.

James: Boy, you sure got that right, Dad! Man, with all the stuff I gotta do and remember, my life sure isn't too simple any more! Grandfather's holding me. It's tough. I know you and Grandfather love me. I wish I could get it right, right now!

I learnt today that it's not so much Grandfather being with me as it is me being with Grandfather. I had to stick close. Strange having a parent around. I see you and Grandfather as being pretty much connected, Dad. That's okay I think. Two parents, and when one says something I know the other will back him up. But especially today I guess, I had to stick around Grandfather.

love ya, Dad!

hug kiss

James: Hi Dad

I think I'm understanding stuff, Dad, more and more. I know that you're not Grandfather, but because you're a parent team, it feels like whatever he does, you do. I know that you and Grandfather love me in a special way. I want you and Grandfather and God to be proud of me.

Ever since my reliving, I really haven't had the strong desire to drink, Dad. I don't want to drink, Dad. I don't want to create an illusion. I REALLY don't want to be like the monster! I guess I'd much rather honor you, Grandfather, and God. But I think I see why you strongly say no to drinking, Dad. It creates an illusion, and illusions aren't of God. And it can do really bad things to your body and your mind. And I figure that if I can say no last night, which I did, and sometimes I was kinda embarrassed about it but I don't really care about that, then I can say no anywhere. Last night was a huge test for me, Dad.

How's that?

hug kiss

Bruce: James,

I am proud of the choices you made and of who you are becoming. There may be a benefit to a 4-ounce glass of wine but people generally do not stop there. And therein lies the problem. And as you observed people become different, some in happy, laughing ways, some in arrogant or depressing ways. But it isn't good for them nor for the people around them and they know that deep inside. Maybe that is why they continue to push others into drinking with them so they are not alone in the illusion, fantasy, depression or whatever expression it turns out to be.

You are doing good but get more rest if you can.

hug ***kiss***

Dad/Bruce

James: Gee, Dad, you kinda made me cry and everything! Thanks for being proud of me! Wow!

Fractured Mind

I CAN just not go to dinner with anybody. But I really like the people and they like me and I don't wanna blow that.

I've drunk coke sometimes cause sometimes water isn't around and I've had ice cream, but with Grandfather's permission. And if I try to nag Grandfather I've discovered that I get into trouble, so I don't do that too much any more. Grandfather says that if I have a coke or Pepsi, then no ice cream that day. And vice versa. And asking to try to get around that gets me into trouble. We'd rather you and Grandfather be proud and happy with us than anything.

Well, gotta go I guess. I'll try to get more rest. Thank you Dad!

Okay. Gotta go. Love ya!

hug kiss

James: This hotel is right next to the Pacific Ocean! Cool! I took off my shoes and socks and let the water run over my feet, Dad. So I got to step into the Pacific Ocean at the southern hemisphere! There's no swimming here cause the ocean is too violent. Boy, it really looks cool.

Dad, Grandfather doesn't tell me what to do all the time. Not anymore. He lays down rules like the coke-ice cream rule that's just for this trip and he says that I won't continue that once I'm home. But I made a really bad choice yesterday, Daddy, and it scared me, I mean the consequences did, but I did okay. I took a horse and buggy ride and the man took me through the downtown. Then he stopped and said he wanted more money to take me back. So I got off and walked back to the hotel. Cause I was mad and I didn't want to give him more money. I remembered the name of the hotel but not the address. But I remembered what I saw on the ride. I overshot the turn to the hotel a little and got a little lost, but I asked a nice old man where the hotel was and I was about two blocks away from it. So I got back okay.

I'm sure grateful I had access to a computer during this trip, Dad. I know you didn't get a break from me, but you didn't say not to write, so I didn't worry about it. But writing to you has always helped us with this process, you know. And what you say to me has always been important too.

Thank you, Dad!

hug kiss

Bruce: James,

Grandfather is providing an opportunity for you to experience a little independence so you can see how you would do in the choices you make. And when you make choices how you will assess them as to whether the choice is good or bad. Horse and buggy ride is fun.

The man was trying to take advantage of you and you didn't go for it. Not a bad choice as long as you felt safe. I am sure the buggy driver was disappointed.

Safe travels.

Hug kiss

Dad/Bruce

James and Deb: Got another confusion though. Before, Grandfather would say yes or no. Now a lot of the time he's saying 'I'd rather you ___'. Like I asked the other day, 'Can I have a hot dog?' and Grandfather said 'I'd rather you had a hamburger.' So I had a hamburger. Now I asked if I could go to the casino and Grandfather said that he'd rather I watched the ocean, but if I want to go, to just take $20 and leave the rest of your money at the hotel in the safe. So I've got enough pesos for lunch and a $20 bill in my pocket. But why doesn't Grandfather just say yes or no anymore? Am I older? I don't get it. I accept it, Dad, for sure, but I don't get it and it's making me feel kind of insecure.

Bruce: Get use to it. This is what being an adult is all about; making decisions, being accountable, using wisdom, assessing situations.

James: Oh, so when Grandfather says for me to take $20, which I did and took a long time to lose, but don't take any more, that's guidance, right? So Grandfather's teaching me wisdom and how to assess situations, right? You do that, too, I think. The only difference is, is that Grandfather's here all the time. But, Dad, I can't be an adult yet cause Grandfather says I gotta stay with him all the time. But maybe you're saying that I'm growing and not there yet. Right? But I'm learning.

Anyway, thanks, Dad!

James: Hi Dad!

Grandfather told me to quit worrying about how old I am and trying to be an adult. He said it'll come, and it's a learning experience. He also said that I'm still accountable to you and him, so don't go getting any ideas! He said I'm growing and to just let it happen. He said for me to keep trying.

I get it now, that I have to change the way I think from "I want" to making decisions based on wisdom and smarts. Boy, that's a huge change in a way for me to think, Dad. Oops, Grandfather said for me to get to bed, NOW! Bye Dad!

Gotta go. Bye!

Bruce: James,

Going to Michigan for one or two days tomorrow. Will not have e-mail. Glad you are home safe.

Dad/Bruce

*****

James did not integrate for over a year. During his time, he worked on releasing anger and accepting life as it is.

Section Three: Ritual Rape

Sometimes when a person dissociates, a part will experience similar violence as another part. Some people will dissociate every time they experience trauma resulting in perhaps hundreds of parts. Dissociation becomes the way to handle violence and hurt; dissociation itself becomes the usual coping mechanism. Little Debra and Laura had similar experiences as an infant and small child. They shared the life experiences of being out, but Little Debra was psychologically stronger. Little Debra did not seem to dissociate to form Laura and vise versa. While I guess once in a while, I do not really know which part was born into this world as they both seemed to live together without knowing each other or each other's experiences. Perhaps the trauma was not difficult enough for my infant mind to fracture. I do not know. I know that infants can and do dissociate however, but my case is not clear.

I think Laura resided lower in my subconscious than Little Debra because she experienced the first evil generated by a satanic rite. Satanic rites or rituals seem to be a different kind of violence that results in a trauma connected to a person's deep psyche. This first satanic rite dissociated Laura into several parts that ended up residing even lower in my subconscious.

Chapter Six

Subconscious Level 5: Laura (4) Wakes Up

Sometimes I ask, "What kind of a God would let adults traumatize children?" "WHY DID YOU LET THIS HAPPEN TO ME?" So I'm tempted to be angry with God or walk away. I want to blame God for not doing something to help when it happened, not just now after the fact, but when I was so utterly defenseless. As strange as this sounds, pondering that renews my relationship with God. It's okay to get mad and yell. God is God. So I metaphorically run full speed into a brick wall that is God's patience a few times and eventually give up.

Ultimately, the question itself is infantile. LIFE IS. Bad things happen to good people because LIFE IS. Everybody has a story to tell. Everybody has experienced pain and has suffered. Each and every story needs to be honored. Not judged and certainly not compared. Life is.

What kind of beings would we be if nothing hurtful happened to us?

God does not test us. God, our Creator, does not give us life lessons and there isn't a divine reason for everything. God does not kill people or harm creation. God does not want us to suffer or starve or live in a world of fear. But we do. Living in this world, we live in a strangely complex web of action, reaction, thoughts and relationships. Life is. And what we do about it makes all the difference between health and despair.

The thing is, God did let this happen to me, but God did not stand idly by. God was there when it happened, not just now after the fact, but when I was so utterly defenseless. God was there. God protected me. And now God is crafting this series of events to heal me. Because God protected me back then, I am able to heal now. We are beloved. You are beloved.

What kind of beings would we be if nothing hurtful happened to us?

*****

James: Hi Dad --

Dad, this process sure didn't quit any. There's another one of us. Dad, none of us knew that this would be so very complex and everything.

Anyway, she's 3 or 4 and we named her Laura. I don't know if she'll have the skills to type or anything, but I think she can talk to you through me, Dad, if you want her to. She's very afraid, Daddy. And I mean really really afraid. She came with nightmares and that's all she has is nightmares. Grandfather's got her, but all she wants to do is run away and hide. So she's giving Grandfather a workout. I'm trying to tell her that Grandfather's okay and she believes me, so she's coming around. Dad, she's so very afraid. Oh gee, Daddy, she's so scared! Her nightmares are full of monsters in the air.

I love you, Dad! Thanks for being there and in the middle of stuff! Thank you for being our parent!!

*** hug *** *** kiss ***

Bruce: James, Give Laura time to feel secure. She will be fine.

hug ***kiss***

Dad/Bruce

Fran's Notes: Laura, new state, is out and is 3 to 4 years old. She was so scared. I gave her art supplies to draw. She drew herself very little and Eleena and Walter Amundson angry standing over her. She shook with fear. She drew a face of angry mommy mouth and scrubbed over the face – "tornadoes – that's what I see." She drew a tornado in black. She drew the house and groceries and put more tornadoes of different sizes in them. She drew a stick figure of her brother Jack and a big tornado. She drew Walter Amundson's eyes that represented both of them. We'll continue to process this at the next appointment.

James: Hi Dad!

Laura came out with the therapist yesterday. She drew how she felt. Gee, Dad, we found out that Laura's left-handed!! She knows some things. She knows that you're Daddy and that you won't hurt her. She knows about the process. She knows that Grandfather is okay and that he's pretty stubborn about what he wants her to do, and she knows that he feels good. She's pretty surprised that the body is so big.

We think she was able to come out cause of the cutting of the cord with Eleena and cause things are stable now and everything. She can't type or write. She says hi to you, Dad. It's hard for her to understand about the second-life, but I think the goal is to get her to not be afraid anymore and she's seeing different parents now as opposed to the first ones. I'm helping her as much as I can. So she won't get confused and scared more, it's me and not both me and Deb doing that. I'm thinking that she holds the primal fear. But we discovered that she has her own story. If there's a reliving for her, Dad, I'm pretty concerned for her about that.

*** hug *** *** kiss ***

Bruce: Greetings Deb and James,

James, Laura will be fine as she goes through her process. You just keep reassuring her along the way. AND it is back to the routine – exercise, eating right, chores – the party is over and now it is back to reality!! Sounds like you had a good trip but now you need to focus

on credit card debt and establishing the discipline of making regular deposits in the savings account.

hug ***kiss***

Dad/Bruce

*****

Laura woke up before the other parts of me were able to see her. As Laura, I woke up as an infant. Grandfather held me and I felt safe. I saw his smile and the love in his eyes. So I grew older before the others knew Laura. After the others knew about her, the Laura part of me was too young to type for a very long time. Once she grew to about four years old, her relivings and memories came back. She became very afraid of everyone. James carried the brunt of her relivings when it came to communicating via email.

Sometime after my biological father lost his land, we moved to California. When I was three or four years old, my mother divorced him. There are some questions as to whether or not she was in touch with Walter Amundson before the divorce, but they became involved with each other during that time. I found out that my mother had kept in touch with his parents all through her marriage with my biological father. She and Walter Amundson were together during their high school years. She told me that he showed up on her doorstep one day after she told his parents her marriage would not last.

*****

James: I really didn't want to tell you, but Grandfather says I have to. He's got me by the ear!! Dang it!! He says I HAVE to deal with my anger and it hasn't been happening.

Grandfather told me to tell you that I'm a smart mouth today and rude to him and disobedient. I told him that if he wants you to know something to tell you himself.

I'll straighten up. I'm sorry, Dad.

I tried to get into Laura's mind, but couldn't help her with her secret. It just isn't coming easily. Something happened, Dad, and we don't know what it is. She spends most of her time on Grandfather's lap and in his arms, sleeping too.

Boy, me, Lucas, and Anna Marie came from the subconscious, but Laura's even deeper. Trying to help her is like reaching into a dark hole but my arm isn't long enough. But something's at the bottom.

The only thing we know that came out with the therapist is that Eleena took her outside and left her alone, that a lot of times Laura was hungry and messed herself and nobody came for a long time in baby time, that

Eleena would get mad at her for crying and put her in a closet, and that Eleena explored her genitals, the inside of her, more out of curiosity we think than malice. The therapist told her that mothers don't do that. Mothers respect the body of her children. And that Eleena was sick. Knowing Eleena, she saw Laura as an inconvenience and did what she did because of that. But the drawings included the monster too. So I don't know what's going on. Laura got pretty scared just drawing pictures.

Well, anyway, I gotta go exercise and behave better. I guess I'm hoping that you won't punish me more. At least that's what *I'm* scared about.

Bye Dad. Have a great day!

Bruce: James,

Here is the deal. First, you will apologize to Grandfather for each time you showed disrespect. Second, you cannot be out until Sunday morning - 9 am. Third, when you come out on Sunday you will apologize to Grandfather again and tell him what you have learned in the last 2 1/2 days. Then you will write to me and tell me what you have learned. If you haven't learned anything then you will go back into your room until you do.

Now, go apologize, with sincerity, to Grandfather and then go to your room.

Dad/Bruce

James: Yes Dad. I apologized to Grandfather for disobeying and being rude and angry at him and now I'm off to my room. I don't think I'll make it to my room until I quit crying though, Daddy. But that'll be soon.

Deb: Hi Dad -

I think I'm older and I think that all of us (except Damon, James, and Laura) are merging. I feel this because the identities are fading. Before you (BC?!), it felt like an accordion - in and out, in and out. I told the therapist that I'm not supposed to think negatively, especially when I don't know what's going on. She said that that takes practice, and every time it happens, to think of a stop sign, to image that, to stop.

The Credit Union let me create two more savings accounts. One is called "True" meaning that's the one I don't touch. The other one is called "Car." I was thinking about the Car to save for a new car, but maybe I should put the insurance in there too, or should I ask for another account?

Changing a way of thinking from "I Want" to "Responsible Choices" sure is a challenge!! James has noticed that every single time he goes the way of I Want, he gets into trouble. I think that God just isn't gonna let up until the mindset changes completely to Responsible Choices. I take it that's what you do and that's what growing up means. Right?

Well, gotta go. Bye!

*** hug *** *** kiss ***

Bruce: Deb, I set up a car account and an insurance account for auto insurance. Added to that is a vacation account, a Christmas account, furnishings account, clothing account, eye account (for eye exam and glasses), and medical (co-payments and costs that medical insurance doesn't cover). I figure out how much I spent in each category last year and divide by 12 and that is how much I place in each account per month. This way I already have the money to spend before I purchase.

Deb: Okay. So I'm thinking:

True (don't touch) Car CarInsurance Trips Furnishings Clothing Eye Medical Escrow (already there)

What's furnishings? Furniture?

My mortgage payment is taken out automatically.

Bruce: Furnishings - furniture, lamps, tables, kitchen stuff, towels curtains, etc. Just figure out how much you spent last year, divide by 12 and put that amount in the account per month.

Deb: Hi Dad! This morning I had a dream and at the end I thought that I was supposed to die and I was in water and went under. Two angels grabbed hold of me and lifted me out of the water and I woke up being carried by two angels. They took me to God. God told James to come out of his room and come to him. So he did, and me and James stood in front of God.

God told us that he didn't want us to die, but to live. And that he wants us for something special. He told James that James is responsible for the anger and that he has to work on it, even though it's very painful to do that.

God told us to not be scared when we connect to the body. He said it will be intense, new, and like a dam breaking.

God told us to not be too frightened about what happened to Laura. We all have to go through Laura's reliving. But God told us to not allow what happened to Laura to turn us. Kill us. I can't explain this any better, Dad. God told us to not be too scared and to not act on how we feel.

God then told us both to behave ourselves. And he told James to go back to his room and he did. That's it.

I had questions about Laura even before this, Dad. And I know I'm stupid about some things, and I never did babysit any. I understand that exploring a baby is wrong, but I guess I'm thinking that it's okay to put a baby outside and leave her. Don't parents do that? A 3 year old and younger? And babies cry a lot, so isn't it okay for a parent to just let the baby cry? And if a parent is like totally frustrated, isn't it okay to lock a baby in a closet? That way, the baby is safe I think. The thing is, is that this stuff came out of Laura when with the therapist. But is Laura just complaining about stuff that's normal? It isn't that I don't have compassion, Dad, it's just that I don't know. I mean, there seems to be a huge difference between being tortured and being alone outside on the grass.

Bruce: Deb,

Consider a baby and think about your questions. You should be able to come up with the appropriate answers.

Deb: Dad, Laura's ME (although I'm more separated from her than anyone else), and I've never been afraid of the outside as far as I know. I've never been around babies. I think you want me to say that what Eleena did was wrong, but I just don't see it.

Bruce: Think. What have you observed in nature and in town? IF you haven't observed in town start observing and find the answer. Interview a parent of a baby.

Deb: Oh. Coming in and out of town I pass Moyle Pond where geese come to raise their kids. I've seen them protecting their kids and their kids follow them. When they eat, a parent always has his or her head up to stand guard. I've also seen a parent teach the kids how to fly. They're on the water and the parent is in front and the kids mimic the wing movements.

So, Eleena put me in danger? She didn't protect me. She didn't feed me when I was hungry too good. She didn't teach me anything. But mainly she didn't protect me. Right?

There's some things in life that I've been too embarrassed about to reveal just how stupid I am about some things. No interview. I don't need to be laughed at.

So I'm good with the protection thing.

Bruce: You might be embarrassed but you might also be surprised about how little parents know.

Protection, holding and comforting, teaching and when older – your

favorite - discipline.

Deb: "and when older – your favorite - discipline."

I burst out laughing at this one Dad!!!!

Points taken with the rest of it. (I'll ask the therapist.)

I've been dreaming about what you wrote about babies. I know I wasn't protected. I think I was comforted by my maternal grandmother a couple of times before I could walk, but she lived far away. And I had a nanny for a few months after I was born named Jeanie, and she's the first face I remember. I don't think I was ever comforted in the physical except for that. But I've certainly been comforted in the spiritual, in this second-life. You let me put my head on your chest and hold your hand. I velcroed myself around Grandfather plenty of times! Especially when I was Scott. And now Grandfather has Laura and he's comforting her all the time.

I just can't believe how separated I am from Laura. There's something about hands. And physical pain. And an image of this huge penis. Laura doesn't know what that is, but I do. I'm wondering if she is the key to my disconnect from my body and my life-long fear of sex, which as you know I'm trying to get over. Sixteen year olds have sex, Dad.

Have a great weekend, Dad! *** hug *** *** kiss ***

Bruce: Deb, Yes, sixteen year olds are having sex but that doesn't make them smart or right. Sixteen year olds also have babies, sixteen year olds also get dumped by boys right after they have sex. Sixteen year olds are not emotionally mature enough to handle sex.

Deb: Okay Dad on the exercise and the sex.

Fran's Notes: Laura was out and continued to tell her story. She said Eleena wanted her to die. "She put me to die and put me outside with the big dog. I was hungry a lot and I messed myself. She be mad. She put me up. She be mad cause I cried and if I messed myself. She picked me up by my arms and put me in this place and it was dark. A closet." I helped her process all the feelings, dirty, sad, etc.

James: What I Thought About and Learnt About Whilst In My Room

By James D. C

I've seen on TV and movies that teenagers can be angry, rude, and disrespectful to their parents and anybody else really. I thought that it was okay for me to be that way, well a part of me did, even though my alive parent taught me it wasn't when I (we) was younger. And I thought that I could get away with it as long as I didn't do it in front of my alive parent. I thought that it was okay for me to do be that way. I didn't want my alive parent to find out, but Grandfather made me tell a little.

I learnt that what it is on TV and movies is an illusion. Kids with good parents get hammered for being rude, disrespectful, and angry toward other people. And they don't HAVE to do that, be rude I mean.

When I had to tell my alive parent by email, I didn't really care and I was angry that I had to. And then my dead parent grounded me and I thought that was it, and it wasn't all that much really. But when I called my alive parent and found out that he'd hammered me for it, I was ashamed, I think cause I actually talked to him and talking makes everything close up and more real, unlike emailing. But I found myself ashamed of what I'd been doing with Grandfather the past two days and I remembered that I was supposed to honor my parent, Grandfather, and God. And doing that didn't.

When I'm rude and disrespectful, I tell everybody that I don't care about them. I don't think that kids think a lot about gratitude toward their parents, and I don't think I'm different in that respect. But being rude and disrespectful says I have ingratitude. And I don't want to say that at all. I know that deep inside of me I have a lot of gratitude, but being normal, I don't think about it much. But I know I do.

When I don't tell my alive parent about the stuff I know I'm doing wrong cause I don't want to get hammered, that's when I'm lying to my alive parent. And if I lie, then my alive parent can't trust me any, and I don't want that at all. But this is the only time I lied and thinking about this made me think about it and I don't want my alive parent to not trust me.

I think that when I'm bad, then I get hammered. And that's just about the only time my alive parent looks at me. Even when he's teaching me, it sounds like he's mad cause he just responds, and it's usually about something he doesn't like. I'm not complaining cause that's the way it is and this essay is real stuff, that's all. And I know that my alive parent has too much on his plate, so he doesn't have time to do anything except respond, and I have a whole lot of gratitude for whatever time he gives me cause he doesn't have to cause he's not my real dad. The therapist told me that not every parent is affectionate, even with healthy families. She also told me that affection doesn't make a kid dependent. I think maybe this paragraph sounds like a complaint, but it really isn't. It is what it is and I have lots of gratitude for anything at all. And I thought about this, too. I can't have any expectations and I shouldn't have any expectations.

My alive parent cares enough about me to hammer me. And I'm really really blessed for that! And really really grateful!! And I thought about that, too.

I figured out that just about every time I do what I want, I mean when the motive is "I Want", I get into trouble. I think that God and my parents want me to think different and to think in terms of responsible choices. The whole history of the first-life after leaving the Amundsons has been "I Want". But all that means is that I gotta work at thinking different. And I have to quit giving in to the "I Want".

Grandfather started saying stuff like, "I'd rather you ___" so I thought that I could do what I want and when Grandfather said no, I got angry and disrespectful cause I thought that it was okay now to do that.

I want my parents to be proud of me, but it seems to me to be a pretty futile want, as I don't think they ever will really. And it's my fault cause I keep screwing up. My alive parent says I'm self-absorbed and I don't like that label cause he means that to be really negative about me, but I've been thinking about that too. And I think he's right that I'm self-absorbed and that's who I really am. And cause that's who I really am deep down, I can't change that so I might as well not feel bad about it but just accept that's who I am. But God says that I'm supposed to be self-absorbed so I can heal, so I'm really screwed up about that.

That's it. Can I stay out of my room, Daddy?

Bruce: Yep. I like the line that states "my alive parent thinks enough of me to hammer me." Thanks for the essay. I learned some things about your perspective.

Dad\Bruce

James: Hi Dad -

Laura says "hi Daddy".

It's like her stuff is going through me and I'm getting more and more in despair and stuff. It feels like I'm standing in an open field and screaming and nobody hears me. Dr. Jones says that people just can't reference what I'm going though and what I've been through because they just haven't experienced it. I told him that the monster hanged me, he hanged me, and I keep reliving it and I don't know what to do about that. Do you care that the monster hanged me, Dad, or did I just deserve it? I feel pretty mixed up now. Was I supposed to let it happen and die?

Ian Bruch said that he thinks that Laura being put outside and left alone, and being put in the closet, and being ignored is the reason why we ALL have this unending feeling of not being wanted. I asked Dr. Jones about that, and he agreed. He said that that message was very clear to me at the earliest age, and that people are imprinted from birth about things. Maybe God will turn that around, but I don't know. Maybe there's hope though cause we're being imprinted again by you, God, and Grandfather.

I do know that there's something else, something very very bad with

Laura. We have tornado dreams now every night. And I cry myself to sleep. I try to live like normal and everything, but it's hard.

Dad, do you care about me? Do you want me around? Am I too much of a burden? Do you care that he hanged me? Should I just go away? I'm just scared all the time.

Bruce: James,

You never deserve to be hanged. You did nothing wrong. Keep in mind that you are safe now, even if you are scared. Scary imprints, like Laura's and yours need time to heal but they also need to be acknowledged and that is what you are doing. You are acknowledging the imprints so you can see where they came from and understand them better and then you are reminded that those imprints come from a different life and that this life that you have now is for healing, becoming stronger, to find out that you are cared about and that there are no monsters like Walter Amundson around you anymore. So, you are in good shape but you have some more difficult things to deal with first - like getting rid of the tornado dreams. You will be fine in the long run. Hang in there!

hug ***kiss***

Dad/Bruce

*****

Up until now, I thought Laura's reliving was her being neglected, so I did not understand the warnings. Yet before, during, and afterwards I felt my mind "bend." That's the only way I can describe it. My mind bent and it hurt a great deal. I was afraid that my mind would break and I believed that if it did I would no longer be sane. But it bent and did not break.

When my mother got together with Walter Amundson, they became involved with witchcraft. Eleena told me that when I was four years old she had friends in the apartment complex who were Wiccans. Eleena told me that Wiccans were good witches, but it seems to me that these people who claimed to be Wiccans were not good. Or Eleena made it up that they were Wiccans.

Laura's reliving is incomplete. She dissociated right after the barbed wire, but later in this healing process revealed the entirety of this event. Deeper in the subconscious were other dissociated parts who experienced this same satanic ritual rape.

During early chronological childhood, Laura and Little Debra lived side-by-side because Laura dissociated when Eleena hurt her earlier than the satanic ritual rape. At the end of the rape violence, Laura went to sleep and did not wake until this healing process. The next day, Little

Debra behaved differently, even though Little Debra did not know what happened to her because of the dissociation. Throughout the years, Eleena described her past with me.

*****

Deb: Hi Dad.

God told us not too long ago to NOT act on how we feel after we find out what happened to Laura. We know almost all of it now, Dad, if not all of it. We won't act.

We've sorta seen Grandfather get upset before, but today he cried, Dad. Grandfather just cried. Laura told the therapist at the end of it all that she didn't feel anything, but she went kind of catatonic with Grandfather. She went that way at the end of the therapy, and James came out, and the therapist didn't know what happened although she knew that something happened and we were pretty confused so we didn't tell her cause we didn't know what happened. Grandfather just held her and cried, Dad. She just went limp in his arms and stares. Michel came to help me and James and James is with Grandfather now. Michel is an archangel friend we've known for about 20 years now, who takes care of animals. Two angels came and took Laura from Grandfather and they have her now. We think she'll be okay, but she just isn't responding to anything, Dad. Can't be in better hands than angels, though, huh. And Laura hasn't gone completely through the reliving yet!

You already know that Eleena explored her, left her outside, didn't care for her, and locked her in a closet. We're talking infant to 3 or 4 years old.

There was a time when Eleena and the monster got together, and the time frame for all of this is right, cause Eleena told us where we were living and when a long time ago. Eleena also got involved with the occult. She's admitted to being involved with Wiccans. Wiccan are supposed to be good, so I doubt this was true. She got involved with a group of people who were interested in the occult, and we think eventually the monster was a part of it, if not from the beginning.

Between 3 and 4 years old, they did ritual stuff once in a while. Somebody took Laura out of her crib or wherever she was at and placed her face up on a table with a red cloth over it. There were maybe 4 or more people. All of her clothes were off. They took red yarn and tied her to the table, around her neck, her arms, and her legs. Her legs were apart. They took barbed wire and tied her to the table with that around her chest, her stomach and her vagina area. They put a ball of wire inside her a little ways. Then they pressed in the barbed wire and slapped Laura all over to make her red. She had to be red. After she was all red, they took out the ball, untied her, and then placed her face down on the table. They tied her to the table with the red yarn. Legs apart. Then they slapped her body until that was all red too. Then they inserted something into her rectum that was hot. She doesn't know what. She knows that it burns, but so did getting raped, so we don't know if the thing itself was hot or it hurt her like burning.

They laughed a lot through this. They did it so that Laura would be transformed, would change. They said that they had to do it to make Laura right. Laura was a girl, so they had to make her right, to cleanse her, they said.

The time frame is right, so we're pretty sure that this is when Little Debra took all of her dolls and put them in the closet and never played with them again. And she rode her tricycle in circles, and later did the same with a bicycle. It comforted me. And we think this happened after the first ritual happened. Nobody knew why Little Debra did this until now, not even Little Debra. But Little Debra wouldn't have known about Laura, and it was Laura who took this.

Something happened to make Eleena not be involved with this anymore. She told us that the occult scares her.

Maybe this is the source of all of us being separated from our body.

The only good thing about my first-life is that (1) I didn't die. and (2) they didn't permanently maim my body.

The therapist told us that it's important that children be touched with caring. She said before Laura came out today that just leaving a baby outside alone and ignoring that baby would dissociate the baby. James burst into tears at that, lying on the couch with his face buried. The therapist came over and rubbed his back. The only other time anybody who's alive has touched me right as a kid, besides my grandmother once in a while, has been Ian Bruch, who comforted me physically the right way a couple of times, and Ken a few times. But James told the therapist that touching us feels wrong, sometimes just hurts, that it feels weird. The therapist told us that that's because we weren't touched right. Sometimes I like to be hugged, but mostly I don't.

Anyway, that's the big step forward.

I'm pretty pissed off. I had to keep it together to get home and made it okay. On my way home, I left a phone message with the therapist that I'll do anything she needs to help other people like me. And if that means signing some kind of release, I'll sign it. Next week, she's going to San Diego to train people. And a couple of weeks later, she's going someplace else to train people. I just need to help as much as I can, Dad, if she needs me to. Daddy, I just don't care who knows anymore.

Love ya!

*** hug *** *** kiss ***

James: Hi Daddy!

We're pretty sure that Eleena, the monster, and the other people were drinking when they did the ritual with Laura. So it wasn't a serious occult ritual. When Eleena protests too much or makes something out to be okay over and over again, we know there's guilt in there. But I'm pretty sure it was the occult instead of Wiccan, which we admittedly don't know much about, because Eleena stopped hurting Laura this way, and something scared her enough to stop. And Eleena told us that the occult scares her. The thing is, Dad, is that Laura didn't feel anything, and the therapist is concerned about that. We think that when she separated from the body, that she went kinda catatonic like she did the other day. And we think that this is what scared Eleena.

Gee, God just told me that working on the anger will make the first-life fade.

Well, gotta go, Daddy! Hope you had a good time!

*** hug *** *** kiss ***

Fran's Notes: Laura feels ashamed. She hurts right now. She still has tornado dreams. Feels like a tornado is coming right from her stomach. "Feels like poison."

*****

I did not know this at this time of the healing process, but this traumatic event lasted a great deal longer. And worse. The other parts involved went deeper into my subconscious than Laura did.

Unfortunately, this event did not stop my parents from becoming more deeply involved with the occult later on. I think that Little Debra's reaction to this trauma is what really scared my mother, not the event itself. Afterwards, I put all my dolls in a closet and never played with them again. I also rode my tricycle around the enclosed apartment complex yard, around and around. My mother told me that people in the complex asked her what was wrong with me. I suspect she became afraid that people would find out what she and the others did.

*****

Bruce: Greetings Deb/James,

We are back from Chicago.

You have been through a lot these past days with Laura. I am glad she is doing better. It was difficult to read what she went through especially just having spent time with my granddaughter.

I am glad you went to the Woodlands Rally to be with people. I am also glad you are willing to help Fran.

Might I suggest you start praying about what your little group is going to do this year. Since you have this relationship with God that is terrific and I am happy about that closeness but you may inquire if there is a direction for you with this group for the year.

Take good care.

hug ***kiss***

Dad/Bruce

James: Hi Daddy!

Took a huge step forward last night. You see, the rest of us have been in denial about what happened to Laura. Couldn't help it, Daddy. But we reread that vision we had 20 years ago and it's a really pretty meadow with a road cut right through it, with a ditch and barbed wire fence on both sides.

We know symbolism enough to recognize what the barbed wire cutting us off from going into the pretty meadow means. And we've had a lifetime recurring dream about barbed wire for as long as we remember. And we had it again last night/this morning.

No more denial! We're all very very upset. We're feeling what we're supposed to in order to go forward, Dad. So I'm not supposed to push it down. When we go into denial, then things get stalled. We did that with Scott too. And that didn't last either. It's just that the two monsters did so much Daddy!! It's like unreal how much they did!

We scream, Daddy, when we have a reliving. The pain and the horror of it and everything makes us scream.

On the way back from conference, I thought about a couple of good times I had with Eleena. So I called her and she talked to me a lot about what she's doing and everything. I'm glad I called her, Daddy, because I couldn't now again. But I still don't have that the connection to her that I had before Jesus cut the cord between me and her. So I can leave her alone again just fine.

Gotta go. Bye!

*** hug *** *** kiss ***

Bruce: James, Recognizing denial is a big step. Good for all of you!!

hug ***kiss***

Dad/Bruce

Deb: Hi Dad --

James came out right after we went to bed to work on the anger. He had no idea what would happen. He moved right into Laura's reliving of the ritual abuse. You know what that was. Then all of a sudden he had a reliving of his own.

This did not happen in the barn, but in the living room. Eleena was gone. The monster beat him and then choked him with one hand, saying how easy he can kill him and laughing. The monster made a game of it, choking, then letting go, over and over. The monster then kicked James over and over while James was on the floor. Then he pulled down his pants and ended with sodomy.

James thought that he wasn't raped, and now he knows that he was as violated as the rest of us. I can't tell you just how much in despair he is. He's with Grandfather.

But Grandfather came and ended it. He took James and immediately we all fell dead asleep.

We were blessed with no physical screaming throughout any of this. There was simply a wall.

Have a great day, Dad!

*** hug *** *** kiss ***

Bruce: Deb and James,

I would think you feeling tired is quite natural after what you went through. This is why you need to take care of yourself and get extra rest. IT is the rest and eating right that will help your immune system fight off sickness.

Grandfather is compassionate with you and helps you set limits when you are on the edge emotionally. Thank you Grandfather.

Have a great weekend. Enjoy the beauty of the early fall.

Hug ***kiss***

Dad/Bruce

James: Hi Dad -- Report: I feel so poisoned and despair that I couldn't do the anger for quite a while. I felt seriously cold, so I went and took a really hot bath. Doing that connects to my subconscious or something, always has, and I felt stuff come up to the surface. The sodomy's so demeaning, Dad. What came up was some revelation, but it was barely there. It was that I'm supposed to make him happy and if I didn't then he'd kill me (which isn't news). I'm not a person. And making him happy means that I'm supposed to not have control and he's supposed to hurt me and then I'm supposed to be demeaned like not a person. And I'd better make other people happy, you know, like anybody, cause if I don't then I'll get thrown away and die. And the two are connected, Dad, and that was the revelation. So people are supposed to hurt me and then demean me cause if I don't let them then I'll get thrown away and die. When that came up, I threw up some. I called Dr. Jones and he told me to do the Wii. I guess it took somebody to tell me because I did it and I threw up some again and felt lots better. And then I cooked and ate right for the first time in a long time, and that made me feel better too. I went to bed and cried and fell asleep.

Sometimes I think I'm not gonna make it, Dad. I've got ALL the anger and despair in me.

Me and Deb are trying to not email so much. But I miss you.

*** hug *** *** kiss ***

Bruce: Greetings James,

This is a very heavy experience and revelation. Now you need to begin to reinforce to yourself that you no longer need people to hurt you and that no one here desires to hurt you. You also need to try to reflect on that fact that no one has hurt you physically and no one that cares about you has demeaned you. You are a person of worth just as you are and you always have been. You were unfortunately connected to someone who took that from you but now is the time to reclaim you worth. You are a person of worth who people love and care about. I imagine that turning this around will take time and Fran's help but now that you have the revelation you can begin to dismiss it as an untruth. You are not an object anymore. You are a gifted person. AND you are going to make it!

Dad/Bruce

James: Hi Dad!

Driving downstate, two angels came to me, Dad, and I had a choice, a really hard choice. I didn't have much time to think about it, Dad. And I had to choose for all of us. Either stay or die. I chose to stick around though. Nobody around here wants me to die, I know that. But now I have to really face it. I have to face it all. It feels like I'm full of vomit, Daddy. But I'm determined to get that crap OUT OF ME!!! I want to be happy. I want to be healthy. And if it means going through hell, then I will. So I will. I know that you and Grandfather and God will continue to help me.

Grandfather's here, but I feel like I want to stand up on my own. I know I can't do that all the time. But I want to.

I love you, Dad. You and Grandfather are good parents!

*** hug *** *** kiss ***

Bruce: Hi James,

When you have the stomach flu a lot of times you feel like vomiting. Sometimes you feel real bad and sometimes you may feel like you will never get over it – but you do. And most times, after you have vomited you feel relief. So, go ahead and vomit out the bad stuff and find some relief. One step at a time and you will be fine. Jesus says, "Let not your heart be troubled nor let it be afraid." Your heart/soul will be cleansed when the anger is gone. You are not alone.

My reflection was with God when I said that when you deal with your anger and it is all gone your self-image will improve and your connectedness will increase. But just as it takes time to dispel the anger so too does it take time to fill the gap. But it will happen. I believe this is a life long process for most people – myself included. Perhaps the anger for most people is not as intense as yours, but nevertheless everyone has anger issues.

hug ***kiss***

Dad/Bruce

James: kiss kiss kiss kiss kiss kiss kiss kiss kiss kiss Thank you, Dad!

Debra Bruch

Chapter Seven

Subconscious Level 6: John (14 - 20) and Ephrin (14) Wake Up

Both John and Ephrin woke without warning. John is connected to James and it seems to me he helped James be contained within my subconscious. I even think John may have put him there!

A person living in despair, at any age, needs some kind of hope in order to remain mentally healthy. Perhaps it does not matter if that hope is real or not. I am very grateful for the John part of me that kept hope going, not only for James but also for the rest of me.

*****

John: Greeting's Dad!

It's about TIME James vomited me out!! I'm NOT the anger. That's in James and that's an emotion. He still holds it. I'm a GREAT facilitator!! My task is to reach down James' throat and help him by pulling the vomit out!! (Nice picture, huh? Ha! Ha!) James' task is still his to do.

I know everything. I have a lot of energy. I'm optimistic (about time, huh?). Poor kid's been in despair forever it seems. I love you with a passion. I love Grandfather with a passion. I love God with a passion. I do believe that I'm the nurturing part of this person-as-whole that the therapist has been wanting to tap into. And James thought HE was buried deep! :)

I won't give you any trouble. I'm in my 20s, so I'm older. I laugh a lot. I feel joy. The task is tough, but I'll uphold everybody. The body's very tired, so we slept in today. We have to leave by 7:30 because we have a therapist's appointment this MORNING! At 10 to noon. Love to talk to you, perhaps after we return? I'll make sure we exercise after we return, bowflex exercise.

The body's sick, but it's because James has been vomiting up some anger the best he could. God told us to get ready for the body to be pretty sick because toxins will be released during this getting-rid-of-anger activity. If I remember right, we need to drink lots and lots of water.

Well, gotta go. I reckon I'm evidence that James worked on his anger last night! Ha! Ha!

*** hug *** *** kiss ***

(Yes, you get THAT from a total stranger!!!) :)

Fran's Notes: John, a new one, appeared. John's purpose is to help James with his anger and he's the optimist. James felt suicidal and John helps him. John entered the session giving me a hug. James feels more despair than rage.

James: Hi Daddy! Report: I fell asleep at the therapist's office yesterday and slept with Grandfather until now. I feel better.

*** hug *** *** kiss ***

Bruce: Good, you have been through a lot and the rest did you good.

hug ***kiss***

John: Hi Dad!

I helped James with his anger. He cried to sleep.

Deb is sooooo frustrated!

Ephrin is getting really young. And he's really confused. He came out not knowing anything, including the date. He thought the first-life was yesterday. He's scared and he wants to know if he can write to you, too, and if you'll hurt him.

I'm okay. I'm getting younger too. I'm in my teens right now. Boy, it's difficult to act older when you're not!!! I feel like I lost something! Oh well. It'll work out!

love ya, Dad!

*** hug *** *** kiss ***

James: Hi Daddy!

I still feel sick inside. John is helping me by shoving his hand into me and pulling crap out. I feel like I'm vomiting all the time when he does that. But most of the time I'm with Grandfather.

But I don't feel so in despair and stuff. We should know how much money the sewer hookup should cost by this weekend. Hopefully we'll pay for it then. If there's money left over, we plan to call the therapist for an extra session next week. If she's available. Maybe not, cause she's going to New York to train people. But we don't remember when. So I don't know if that will work out.

But I'm okay. Hope you are too!

*** hug *** *** kiss ***

Bruce: Deb, James, and John. James, keep working on your anger and you will be relieved in the burdens in time. This is an ugly business but in the end you will be liberated.

John, Getting younger is something I cannot imagine. I only know about getting older. Keep working with James and maybe all of this will lead to a bundle experience.

hugs ***Kisses***

Ephrin: Hi Dad --

I grew younger and right now I'm 14 years old. Something happened this morning.

Right before we did the bowflex, we went onto the bed and held Frodo. Laura had another re-living then. *She was an infant and she saw these hands, these big hands and they were blurry. But they hit her over and over. And she heard shouting, loud voices, but didn't understand what they said. And then the hands turned into tornadoes. She cried and cried and just got hit and hit.*

During the bowflex, James was out and the anger and grief of Laura's reliving came to him. He cried a whole lot, but didn't stop with the bowflex. It felt like an angel came and touched the body and we could feel something about the body. Nobody knows what. So James like processed the anger and everything.

Then I finally came out. Daddy, the therapist said that I'm not the monster and that I didn't do these things. But I feel really really bad, and guilty. I know I thought that I was supposed to do these things and I wanted to do these things, but Laura's reliving just made me sick. I don't want to hurt anybody. But I don't know how to do anything. I don't know what to do with myself at all. I feel like I'm the monster, but I know I didn't do anything really. Why would somebody hit a baby, Dad?

Dad, I don't know what to do. I've got to do something, but I don't know what.

*****

Unlike most of the dissociated parts waking up, Ephrin did not know where he was or the year. During the trauma, he tried to be like Walter Amundson. When he woke, he thought he was as much a monster as my stepfather. It didn't help for the other parts to also see him as a monster. Our therapist said no, and that it is typical for a part or more to closely identify with an abusive parent. The reasons are twofold. One reason is because the child longs for the parent to care, to love, and the child hopes that being like the parent would create that bond. The other reason ties to survival. Being like the parent may decrease the parent's need to be abusive by identifying with the child.

Once Ephrin realized he was not a monster, he had no role. His complaints about not knowing what to do tied to his confusion. Slowly, he became a fierce protector for the rest of the parts out at the time, especially for Laura. He was sickened by her reliving. It's a miracle that I cared at all!

*****

Fran's Notes: Ephrin made a huge shift but said he still gets off on violence. There was a major breakthrough as the Monster dissociative state emerged and was reframed into a peacemaker who helped James release his despair. This one is working now with the others as they share information with him.

James: Hi Daddy -- Did the anger work yesterday and today it just happened by accident. Grandfather said that I don't HAVE to do any more today, but he still wants me to do the aerobics and to get into the habit of doing that. Okay.

I really AM feeling better, Dad. And I can tell now that I feel better after I do the anger stuff.

Hope you're having a great time!

*** hug *** *** kiss ***

John: Hi Dad!

I'm 14 now. Dad, I REALLY don't know why I grew younger. Ephrin did too. But it is what it is. I don't even know if that's done with or not!! What a ride!

*****

Growing younger is not only strange, it's frustrating! I suspect both John and Ephrin woke up older than they actually were as a way to survive. Ready to fight if necessary. Once they discovered it was safe, they became their correct age and were able to heal. At the time, though, I was not only frustrated, I was ashamed of growing younger.

During this time after a therapy session, John and Bruce would talk over the phone. They both enjoyed it as John was very optimistic and had a sense of humor. Thank heavens for that!

*****

Laura: Hi Daddy! Can I come out? I can type now. See?

Bruce: Laura, You are out if you are typing!!

Laura: oh yeah!

Fran's Notes: James talked about wanting the monster's love and thought it was acceptable. Even when he was tortured – sodomized – monster got off on it. When he feels like throwing up, it's like cords – red and blue representing monster and Eleena – coming out of his mouth and angels cutting them out. Overall he feels better but at the time it hurts.

Deb is discovering herself and sex is okay. She still can't see she's worthy. She sees that it will come – connection with the body. She's holding her body to blame. She'll make a list of negative messages and get them reframed.

Bruce: James, John, Ephrin, Laura, Deb,

Hi. Ephrin, relax about why you are here. Just go with the flow and observe everything that is going on around you. You are a wonderful person and you are about to discover some things about yourself. The purpose for each of you is to heal the body, take care of the body, to work at being successful as a teacher and scholar, and to heal emotionally so that you can merge - bundle etc.

Laura, no I do not want you to be invisible. I want you to live well and for you not to be afraid. You are wonderful also. So hugs and kisses to you.

James keep working on your anger. You are making great progress.

John, keep helping James.

You are all doing well. A few slip-ups now and again but that is normal for all of us.

hug ***kiss***

Dad/Bruce

Everybody: Wow! THANKS DAD!!!

-- Ephrin, James, and John

Thank you Daddy! Yay!

-- Laura

Thanks, Dad!

-- Deb

*** hugs *** *** kisses ***

James: Hi Dad!

Something happened today that I want to tell you about, Dad!

We got up and started to bowflex. We've all been very reluctant to do Monday's and Thursday's because that's when the exercising targets our middle of the body. Now I know why!!

Fractured Mind

Right away, the body broke an adhesion. We know our middle is full of them because the doctor told us so when he took out the gall bladder. Anyway, I was exercising and really strong emotions came up. I couldn't help it, Daddy. The two monsters were in my face, I mean I could SEE them, and I cried and cried and told them to get the fuck out of me, you fuckers. I think it's okay to cuss when things are like this, as long as I don't cuss in front of anybody. Okay, Dad? Anyway, I said, "You hurt me so much! Just so much!" It felt like I was throwing up but nothing came up. But I could like "see" this stuff like cords come out of my mouth. And that's when two angels came and they'd cut the cords once they came out so that that part of the cords wouldn't go back into my mouth. I said thank you to them, but it seems like angels don't talk to us but are always just focused on what they're doing. I know the sickness is in my middle of my body.

But I was in like despair, you know? I said, "This is the only thing I know. I don't know anything else." cause I don't know what'll replace it and I'm scared. That's when Grandfather came and said that I do. I know this second-life. Just let it go. And then I said, "I gotta trust. I gotta trust." I still don't really know but I gotta trust. All this while I was actually doing the exercising, the cords were vomiting out of my mouth, I'm crying, and the angels are working. I still wanna cry all the time. But then I remembered what you told me to do when I couldn't stop crying before. So I tried to take deep breaths until I could and I settled down.

Grandfather said this morning that I didn't have to work on anger any more today. But to play with the Wii. To have fun with it, and do the archery and stuff that isn't a workout really if I wanted to. He said that I COULD do the exercise stuff on there if I wanted to, but I've had enough high emotions for today.

So now I know what I REALLY have to target on to get this sickness out. I'm really glad it happened, but I sure do wish that healing and everything didn't hurt so bad and that I didn't feel all this despair so much, but I just can't help it when they hurt me like they did. Boy, it sure is in my face. Will it ever end?

Okay, I'll go now.

*** hug *** *** kiss ***

Bruce: Greetings All,

> **James, you are making progress in this difficult business of healing. You will need to trust those around you - Grandfather, God, myself, angels. The observation that some or all of you are afraid of being thrown away but each person that cares for you doesn't throw you away is a good reflection to remember - especially when you have**

doubt. Cutting the cords is a great image of liberation, of freeing you from the 1st life to allow you to trust in the second-life. I know it isn't a pleasant experience but it is symbolically the death of the first-life, cord by cord, and the resurrection of Dr. Bruch & company in the second-life. It is a work in progress and as hard as it may seem should be celebrated. You are all courageous. Keep up the good and difficult work and you will arrive at a good place.

I saw Ian Bruch at the Home Coming and we visited for a few minutes. It was good to talk with him.

You all are doing great and don't worry the exercise will come as a good habit eventually. It is actually good for you in many ways. It was the activity that started this and it seems to be an activity that keeps stimulating healing - though it is unpleasant.

hugs ***Kisses***

Dad/Bruce

James: Hi Daddy --

I've been having nightmares at night and last night was a really bad one. We're in the present and went to visit Walter and Eleena Amundson who were still together. We had a good time and they were nice to me and everything. He invited me to a ball where I could meet the president. And then I thought, "Wow. Maybe I can forgive them and everything will be okay." But I had to get a gown, a really nice one cause I don't have any. And where they lived was in a mall so I wanted to go into the mall to buy a dress. But they wanted me to take my car to the other side of the mall instead of walking there. But I thought that was silly and didn't want to.

Next thing I know, Eleena has to leave and she looks at me real funny like. She leaves. I have one piece of underwear left and it's girl's underwear but it's not little and nice but it's WAY too big for me and ugly. But I have to put it on. Walter Amundson enters my room and sees it on and laughs at me. That's when I know I have to do laundry so I can have clean and different underwear. So I try to do laundry and I have lots of problems with it. Walter Amundson gets all aroused and wants to stick his thing up my butt. That's when I know that they were both just playing me. And nothing's changed.

Then all of a sudden I was at World Conference and we were in session. Steve called me to stand so I did and I was really embarrassed cause it was in front of just everybody. He told me that God was well pleased with me. He told me that I belonged to the church, to the people of the church. I didn't understand it. He said that I was accountable to the church. This clip ran about three times. Then I woke up.

I still want the monsters to love me. I know I want them to love me and I feel really desperate about it. I don't know where I belong. I don't know who I belong to.

When I woke up, Daddy, I cried and cried. I woke up crying. And I felt really sick and wanted to vomit. But I knew and know that I'm not physically sick like the flu or anything. I woke up being seven years old, too. I'm back older now I think, or close to it. But I couldn't do anything, Dad. I got up to exercise and all I did was to hold Frodo and cry. And then I like vomited more stuff out and out and out and out. And the angels did their thing with it.

Thanks Dad.

*** hug *** *** kiss ***

Bruce: James,

All of these experiences are giving you things to ponder and process. Why you still want the affection/love of Eleena and Walter Amundson is something for Fran to work with. I haven't a clue at this time to the answer to your yearning. I would focus on the part of the dream that Steve was in especially the message. Allow this message to soak into your being - over and over. You can ponder the accountability part but each member is accountable to the church.

If you get a chance try to get some extra rest today and eat well. This is tough stuff but you are doing great.

hug ***kiss***

Dad/Bruce

James: Gee, I think I know what Fran would say. I think she'll say that children want their parents to love them. I guess one of my tasks is to accept, really accept, that they don't and it doesn't matter. And to do that, I'll focus on what the Steve in my dream said, like you told me to, over and over. And to trust that you and Grandfather and other people love me too. And to focus on that over and over. How's that? Yeah, I wanna go home and go to bed!!

*** hug ***

Laura: Hi Daddy

I'm sitting on your lap with my head against your chest.

So, a secret, okay?

I'm really scared of being hungry. And even when I'm not hungry I gotta eat a lot so that I won't get hungry later on.

Is that secret okay Daddy?

So I gotta get what I want like last weekend cause we weren't home or anything and that's the only food I could find. And none of us knows what to eat when we're in a gas station store. And I gotta get something to have in the car cause I'm not at home and I'm scared and everything.

I got lots of secrets, Daddy. Is that okay? Can I tell you my secrets? I think I can do it if I got my head on your chest and you're holding me and stuff.

*** hug *** *** kiss ***

Bruce: Laura, I am glad you are sitting on my lap with your head on my chest.

You are going to have to get over being scared about being hungry because that fear causes you to eat the wrong foods that hurt the body. You are fed on a regular basis so do not buy all the candy and junk food. IF you need help in this I can put you in your room at the times that you travel and are away from home. It is up to you. This may be hard for you to do and going to your room may be a better option until you get older. But, the bottom line is you can not do things that hurt the body because that is hurting yourself and others and hurting yourself and others does not honor God, Grandfather or me.

hug ***kiss***

Dad/Bruce

Bruce: Deb, James, John, Ephrin, Laura,

I am traveling tomorrow and will not have my computer so I will catch up with you all on Monday. Keep eating right, exercising and doing good stuff. OH, and James - work on the anger - your holding up the works!! I know it is hard but get on with it!!! You will be fine.

hug ***kiss***

Dad/Bruce

Laura: Hi Daddy!

I got my head on your chest and I'll tell you another secret I think. I'm afraid of people. Okay, John says for me to say that I don't feel too secure and stuff.

Bye Daddy.

*** hug *** *** kiss ***

Fractured Mind

Bruce: Laura, no more chocolate cake for a while. Between your chocolate cake and John's mountain dew and candy bars the body is suffering.

IT will take time for you not to be afraid of people.

hug ***kiss***

Dad/ Bruce

Laura: John didn't do the mountain dew and candy, Daddy. I did. I'm sorry.

Bruce: Laura, I appreciate your honesty. It is a good quality to be truthful. As I have said before, you are responsible, as is each of you, to the body. Your eating habits are harmful to the body - chocolate cake, Mountain Dew, and candy bars. So, I want you to go to your room for today and tomorrow and think about your responsibility to the body. When you come out of your room Thursday morning you can tell me what you have learned and what your goals are for eating better.

Dad/Bruce

Laura: Gee, no, Daddy. Please? I don't wanna go to my room!

Bruce: GO!

James: Hi Dad! I told Laura that she can't get out of it, so quit trying. She's in her room now. She's more anxious about the essay than anything! Hey, welcome to MY world!! :)

John: There's something else with Laura, and we don't know what.

Deb: Dad! I'm bleeding again! As much as I know I'm being healed, I just HATE this process sometimes. I'm sorry, but I do sometimes!! Something's coming down, I think with Laura. Dad, can I put my head on your chest too?

Bruce: Yep!!

Laura: Don't get mad, Daddy, okay? I'll go right back into my room!

I had a reliving this morning and stuff. *He put his thing inside of me on his lap and stuff. But I cried, Daddy, I cried cause it hurt and I'm not supposed to cry and stuff. But he said that he had to punish me and everything cause I'm bad and stuff. And I gotta not cry or tell or anything. He put his thing in my mouth and it went down my throat and it hurt and I couldn't breathe and I got really really scared. I went to sleep in the first-life, Daddy. Cause I cried and stuff.*

Okay, I'm going back to my room now Daddy. I just had to tell you though. Grandfather's here.

Bruce: Laura, I am sorry for your experience but it seems that this process is the path to healing. I want you to know that it is OK to cry now, to tell now, and that you are not bad, you are not a bad person. You are a good person with lots of potential. You do not have to live that lie anymore.

I am glad that Grandfather is with you and I hope you can rest this afternoon.

hug ***kiss***

Dad/Bruce

John: Hi Dad!

Yeah, we're all upset from Laura's reliving, which is good I think because it just tells us that we're getting connected pretty good.

Don't think the others will write today. Everybody's focused on Laura.

Grandfather's been with Laura in her room. He even brought her some toys to play with while in her room. I know it's spiritual stuff, but it is what it is!

Bruce: John, Thanks for the report. I hope all of you have a calm afternoon.

Laura: What I Learnt Whilst in My Room

An Essay by Laura C

My responsibility to the body is to eat good. I was bad when I got a bunch of stuff bad to eat when the body wasn't feeling bad. Eating bad makes the body feel bad. Except when the body needs to feel better, but eating bad makes the body feel better a little and then the body feels bad. I don't know how to make the body feel better when we're in the car and stuff. So I eat bad cause I know it makes the body feel better, but then the body feels bad a whole lot later. So I don't know what to get at the gas store when the body feels bad to make the body feel better, so I get stuff that's bad. So my goal is to ask Daddy to tell us what to get, really, when the body feels bad when we're in the car. We get as much sleep as we can and we exercise and stuff and the body still feels sleepy when we drive and stuff and I don't know what else to get except bad stuff cause bad stuff wakes up the body and stuff and I don't know what else is in the gas store that isn't bad and will wake up the body so we can drive and stuff. But my other goal is to not eat bad when the body doesn't feel bad and I think maybe I can eat grapes and stuff.

Bruce: Good essay Laura.

Try taking vegetables with you when you travel and eat carrots, celery, or some raw vegetable and see if that keeps you awake. Sugar only keeps you awake for a short time before you begin to feel bad.

hug ***kiss***

Dad/Bruce

John: Yesterday, Laura asked Grandfather that if she was good if she could die now. He said no. In spite of that, I think we love ourselves now. We all were pretty messed up because of Laura's reliving. Felt like crying just all the time and did once we got home. James didn't dare to try to work on the anger because it was just too strong yesterday and he got pretty scared of it.

All we want to do is go to sleep. Can't though.

Laura: Hi Daddy

Daddy, I don't LIKE vegetables. They're ucky. And I wanna be normal and stuff. So I got a root beer. John's gonna tell you anyway. I see people get stuff like that all the time and I wanna be normal.

Gee, I guess that having a Daddy is normal too, huh? And getting raised is normal too, huh? But Daddy, I see people get stuff like root beer just all the time and I really really really wanna be normal and stuff and I don't like vegetables.

The first-life's in my face, Daddy, and I'm thinking I deserve it and I'm bad anyway, but you said I wasn't bad. Okay, I'm not bad so why do I hurt? Why do my insides still hurt if I don't deserve it?

Can I hug and kiss you anyway even though I got a root beer and wanna be normal and stuff?

*** hug *** *** kiss ***

Bruce: Laura,

Part of raising children is having them eat vegetables. So I am strongly suggesting you try. This is normal, very normal for children not to like vegetables so you are normal and I am a normal parent. So here is the deal – You eat vegetables and you can have a root beer once in a while. Like when you go to therapy. If you do not eat vegetables, some everyday, no root beer. This is very normal.

hug ***kiss***

Dad/Bruce

Laura: Okay Daddy.

> yucky veggies

Laura: Hi Daddy!

> Does V8 count as a veggie? Can I get other stuff at the gas store when we travel? Like chips? Can I have a candy bar going and another one coming? Can I have cashews? When we get sleepy when driving, what can I get at the gas store that will wake me up?
>
> Bye Daddy!
>
> *** hug *** *** kiss ***
>
> P.S. I've been good.

Bruce: Laura,

> **Yes, V8 juice can count. Chips do not wake you up – sorry. Candy bars are out. Cashews - roasted, peanuts, almonds are OK.**
>
> *****hug*** ***kiss*****
>
> **Dad/Bruce**

Laura: NO WAY!! Really? No CHIPS????? When we travel. We don't get them into the house hardly ever!! Gee, Daddy, that's so harsh!!!

> Um, I think I'm six or seven.... now .... wow .... I'm getting old.

Bruce: Yeah, I really feel bad that I am not allowing you to eat worthless food.

Laura: And that would be sarcasm. I think we all take after you on that, Daddy!

> No chips. Boooooooo :(

Ephrin: Hiya Dad!

> Do you like me too? I think I'm to look at the world in terms of need, and to honor you, God, and Grandfather means to me to seek justice for other people. I grew up thinking that I needed to be a monster in order to survive so that the monster will love me. He doesn't love me. To tell you the truth, I'm not sure anybody does, or should. I really want to be loved though. I'm just not sure anybody can.

Bruce: Ephrin,

> **And why not? We all love you Ephrin!**
>
> *****hug*** ***kiss*****

Dad/Bruce

Ephrin: Because I used to be like the monster, Dad. I used to be like him.

But I'll hear you anyway. Okay?

Bruce: The key word is "used." You are a new creature (person) in Christ now!!

Laura: The others don't want me to write or anything, but I think it's okay for you to not want me and stuff. Fran said that everybody wants what she called the ideal, I mean that's normal with any people and everything, but she said most people don't get that with parents. But does that mean you don't wanna teach me anything anymore or tell you stuff? Does that mean that I can do stuff and I don't get sent to my room and stuff?

Bruce: Laura, I still will teach you and listen to you AND no it doesn't mean that you can do stuff and won't get sent to your room if it is inappropriate stuff.

Dad/Bruce

Laura: rats .... :)

*****

During this time, a part of me finally admitted that makeup and cleansers were things we just could not understand, mainly because the number of choices in a store were overwhelming and I didn't know what I was looking for. I did know how to apply makeup due to my profession, but did not understand the kinds of street makeup. So a friend taught me about makeup and cleansers. Admitting my ignorance was a significant step toward healing. I wanted to be more normal and try to explore myself as a woman. But to do that, I had to let go of my survival mode enough to admit my ignorance and seek help. Any drop of my survival mode meant that I became vulnerable to ridicule. I had to trust my friend.

*****

Laura: Hi Daddy!

Do you still love me, Daddy? I'm six years old. Do you love a six year old? I'm not five anymore.

God talked to us this morning while we were doing the bowflex stuff. He talked to James mostly, but all of us and stuff. James is getting the anger stuff out, but nothing's replacing it and we feel more and more empty and stuff. God said that the next step is replacing stuff. James asked God if that was his task to do and God said no. I think it might be mine, but I don't know yet or anything. But God said that James doesn't have too much yet to do and stuff. But we feel empty, really empty and we're in despair and everything and it feels like nothing's changed at all. God told us, too, that when this process stuff is over, he's not done with us. He said he's got stuff in store for us. It's really really hard to be empty and not feel bad, Daddy. Just all the time now. We feel really really lonely and stuff. We all think you're really really mad and disgusted with us and stuff and don't wanna have anything to do with us anymore, but I think that's cause we're empty or almost.

We don't sleep good and the body needed to be awake during dinner. So I got a mountain dew, Daddy. I drank about an inch, and I'm not telling fibs or anything about that. I wanted just enough to wake up more. So I ordered both mountain dew and water. But once I felt the body wake up, I quit drinking it, and I drank that inch of it really slow so I'd know.

Last night it got to be about 3:30 and Deb put in this tape that helps us know how to relax and stuff. It's like hypnosis stuff to help a person lose weight. We fell asleep during it and woke up about 6:30 this morning.

I know I'm a bad girl, Daddy, and I'm sorry I'm not a better girl and stuff and I don't get smiles cause I don't deserve anything at all like that and you're here to help us if we're good but it's hard to be good all the time. Would it be better for you if I was a boy? Do you want us to go away and leave you alone now? Grandfather says that email makes you seem like stone, but that's email. So we're pretty confused and stuff.

Okay, I better go and stuff. Bye.

*** hug *** *** kiss ***

Bruce: Hi Laura, Even though you are six now I still love you.

It is difficult to be empty, kind of makes you feel really flat but you will get filled up again with good stuff; that is the way it works. So be patient and you will see that the empty feeling will go away pretty soon.

You are a child learning how to grow up. When we learn how to grow up we make mistakes and sometimes do things that are wrong. This does not mean that you are a bad person, just a normal child.

I am happy that you are a girl and no I do not want you to go away. E-mail is not the best way to communicate, especially on a personal level, but that is what we have so we will make the best of it!

hug ***kiss***

Dad/Bruce/The Stone

James: Do you still love me too, Daddy? -- James

I'll settle for like. Do you still like me too, Dad? -- Ephrin

I hope you still love me though, Dad. Do you? -- John

Do you love me at all, even though I'm on the verge of seventeen? -- Deb

Bruce: Where does all this insecurity come from? Is the insecurity due to the emptiness that you are feeling? Yes, I still care/love each of you.

Dad/Bruce

Deb: From being more and more empty. It's creating a lot of despair. But like you say, be patient. Really, there's nothing in us almost. And it's terribly frightening. There's no good stuff either - it's a true nothing. We ALL want to come and put our head on your chest, Dr. Stone, but too scared to ask. We know that perceptions are skewed.

Bruce: Dr. Stone's chest is available. Lean in.

Dad/Bruce

Everybody: Thanks Dad/Daddy. We think the real molding will take place with Laura. She's different.

Have a good weekend, Dad!

Man, we love you....

*** hugs *** *** kisses ***

-- The Gang

James: God told me that we can't watch TV except for news in the evenings until I do my anger thing for one hour. Every day. From now on.

THIS JUST SUCKS ROCKS!!!!!

Bruce: Get over it and get it done!

James: OKAY DAD OKAY

Deb: Hi Dad --

God wants Laura to change her name to Debra. Something's coming down. Everybody's scared.

From all of us: *** hugs *** *** kisses ***

Bruce: Dear Gang,

If God is asking and there is change in the air, who do you think is in charge of the change? Could it be God? "Let not your heart be troubled, nor let it be afraid."

hugs ***kisses***

Dad/Bruce

Debra/Laura: Hi Daddy!

Daddy, are you gonna raise me even though I'm six? Can you remember me even though I have to change my name to Debra?

I don't understand the body, Daddy. We ate right and stuff and the body then just had to had to have something but I couldn't figure out what it wanted and stuff. And it was so strong and I gave into it and had sherbet and even toast cause the sherbet didn't do it.

The others are going blank, Daddy. Like The Adult did. Except maybe Ephrin. But he's already kinda blank but not completely you know. And he's already changed as a person and everything. The others are losing themselves. They feel like they're dying.

I sure don't know how this is gonna work. I'm not scared too much though.

I gotta go and do the exercise stuff. It's legs today. Bye Daddy. You won't forget me, right? Are you gonna raise me? Can you remember me and remember that I'm not The Adult or Deb and stuff?

*** hug *** *** kiss ***

Bruce: Debra/ Laura,

I will not forget you and I am here to help raise you. You will have to trust in God right now and trust that God is very active in the process of you being here, changing your name, and the others are going blank. Maybe you are merging and my hope is that this is a positive action that is happening now.

hugs ***kisses***

Daddy/Bruce

John: Hi Dad!

We feel like an accordion right now. The only thing that I can figure is that all but Laura have some unhealthy patterns like throwing away. I guess the bottom line is that you have to lose yourself to find yourself. We're going blank, which means that we don't know who we are and we don't have opinions about anything and we don't have much emotion at all. Maybe this is the way to change perceptions and world views. I don't know. But we all think all of this is positive. For instance, we know that The Adult - or whatever parts of her God kept - is in Deb, but we can't identify them or her at all as separate from Deb. There's no self-identity. But Deb is also losing herself in all of this! Ephrin seems to be standing alone.

Can you hear Grandfather, Dad? I don't know why at all, but Grandfather's been talking to Jesus and God a lot. And there's some things Laura's gotta connect with you about while Grandfather takes the little stuff. For instance, this morning, Laura thought about how cruel people are and how people kill other people. And she cried a lot. But Grandfather came and took her and showed her all the people who are good people. And he showed her how many people are cruel and kill, and there's lots more good people than bad people. She's learning this, Dad, and this is something that I can't even accept because of the first-life. So I'm becoming lost while she isn't. Because Laura can learn and accept while the rest of us can't. Except maybe Ephrin.

Ephrin is pretty blank himself and he's losing himself like the rest of us, but he doesn't have as far to go and unlike the rest of us, he doesn't seem to be losing his self-identity. I'm thinking that he'll be protecting Laura and doing the work stuff like Deb does now, and driving. But he won't be the focus of your teaching or learning. Just Laura. That's what SEEMS to be coming down now.

Can you handle just one of us, Dad? Can you help fill her up with the good stuff? Even though she's six right now?

Have a good day, Dad!

*** hug *** *** kiss ***

Bruce: HI John,

Yes, I will help Laura/Debra. IT appears that things keep changing so we will take this one day at a time. Something is happening but I cannot tell what because I have no knowledge of the process. Maybe Fran can help with this. Do you see Fran tomorrow?

Dad/Bruce

John: Yeah, we see Fran tomorrow. Should we call after or not? (Depends on your busy-ness, Dad!)

I CAN tell you that, according to Fran, the process is different for everybody. I really do think that in this case, God's in control. And we know that it's not good enough for God for us to merely integrate. (Yay!) :)

James: Hi Daddy!

Yeah, I've been doing the anger stuff and I feel better now. I did it last night. Laura's starting to take over. It's not her fault, Daddy, she's just finding that she's like OUT!!

We all thank you for being so flexible. Things are happening inside of us, Daddy.

*** hug *** *** kiss ***

Bruce: I am running errands tomorrow and packing for my trip to New Mexico on Friday. Call the cell phone.

Step by step, day by day, the process is moving forward. We just do not know where we are going to land. But, God is with us so – no worries!!

Dad/Bruce

Debra/Laura: Hi Daddy!

God wanted me to change my name, Daddy.

I was with Grandfather when God told me to come to him. So I did and I kissed him and stuff and he made me sit on his lap. And I asked if he was God and if he'd sit still cause he was busy changing and everything. So he laughed at me and changed into a big old dragon but I wasn't afraid and I told him so. And then he changed into a mouse and then a rabbit and I just wanted to cuddle him as a rabbit you know. So he changed into a man. And that was fun, Daddy.

So I was on his lap but I said that I didn't like sitting on laps, and God told me that nobody will ever ever hurt me like that again so it's okay to sit on laps and stuff. God said that nobody will ever put anything inside of the body that I don't want them to. And if I want them to when I'm older, then that'll be okay and it won't hurt and it won't hurt my insides too. So I said okay.

God told me that I had a Task. You know, a job like James had. God told me that my job was to get the bad stuff out of the body. He said that you can't do that for me or Grandfather or even him. But he'll help you know. He said that the body remembers the bad stuff and holds it in and everything. Gee, that's what the therapist said too. But God said that it's my job to make the body well.

He said that I'm not supposed to eat stuff like shakes and candy bars and stuff. But I told God that I liked it. But he said that there's lots and lots of things that people like that aren't good for them. Like a lot of money and power. And he said that I had to exercise too, but that can be fun and stuff. God wants me to have fun and to work and play and read and do the computer and stuff. God said that I like the outdoors. But I told God that I didn't like bugs, so God told me to eat garlic cause bugs don't like garlic. So I said okay.

God told me to just experience life and stuff. But I had a job to do and I had to do it. He said that he gave me parents to help me learn and remember. He told me that it's like the big people hold my hand while I walk down a path and when I let go and go down another path instead, they come and get me and put me back on the path and help me learn to be on the right path. Then he got really really serious, Daddy, and told me that you'll discipline me if I need to learn and to remember. And he said that Grandfather and he will too. I'm not too happy about this part, Daddy. And God said that there's ways like TV that will be taken away to help me learn and remember and I didn't like that. But it's really really really important I guess. I reminded God that I really like pop and chips and candy and stuff and he said that he knows but I gotta learn and do my Task.

Then God got even MORE serious! God told me to never ever hurt people, ever. So I have to think about stuff. He said that it includes people who want to hurt me. I can't hurt them, either. I asked him about the people who want to hurt me, and he told me that he'll make sure that they can't hurt me until I'm grown up cause then I'll know how to make them not hurt me without me hurting them. So I'm not supposed to worry about that.

I asked God why he's doing this to me and he said that he loves me, but I said no, really, why are you doing this? Gee, Daddy, God got all dark and rumbly and said that he didn't like what they did to me, he didn't like it at all. And he doesn't like what some people do at all. He told me to leave those people up to him and to not hurt them. But he's got people down here who can hear him enough to help people who are hurt by other people. And the people who are helping me and who have helped me in the past are those kind of people who can hear him pretty good and want to be people who help other people. I asked God just now if I can send this email to those people too, and he said yes except for the therapist but to print this out for her and give it to her the next time.

Then God reminded me of what Grandfather showed me, that's there's lots and lots more people who are good than people who are bad. And that made me happy and stuff. So I got off of his lap and ran to Grandfather but God called me back to him so I did.

He told me to grow and to just live life and not worry about anything or if people can see me. He said that he'll continue to make it so that the people he doesn't want to see me won't. And he'll make it so I can act older when I have to and everything. But otherwise, just be myself and live and experience life and stuff.

I looked at God really serious, Daddy, right to his face and stuff. And I asked him if he'll bless you this weekend with your stuff. I sorta think that God laughed cause I was so serious and stuff, but he said yes, he would. God laughs at me a lot, Daddy. And sometimes I don't like it but God said that learning to be humble is a good thing. Geez. But I just laughed right back at him!

I asked God how long it's gonna take for the others to get into me and he told me to not worry about that but just look at life and have fun and do my Task and I said okay.

I guess I gotta tell the truth and say that I got kinda bored being that long with God, Daddy, and I wanted to get up and go. So God kissed me and stuff and I kissed him too, Daddy, and he let me go. You know, I got stuff to do! Like write this email. And laundry and dishes and stuff. I don't mind doing that stuff. Makes me feel important and everything. But I'm supposed to play, too! Yay!

And I want to say thank you to you and Grandfather and everybody else who can hear God to help me and stuff. Wow! Thanks!

Okay, bye! *** hug *** *** kiss ***

-- Debra, who used to be Laura

Bruce: Debra,

Good for you on the chores and homework. I cannot tell you when you will get older. We will all wait and see together.

hugs ***kiss***

Dad/Bruce

James: Hi Dad

I'm still around. God wants me to continue to do the Wii. I guess I feel unhappy cause there's nothing and I'm fading and nothing's changed or anything and I just have a big empty inside of me. Are we bad, Dad? Are we turning into a bad person?

Bruce: James,

There is nothing "bad" about you or any of you. Remember this, that you are loved and cared for. You have had issues with anger that weren't your fault. The anger was a burden that you carried and now you are dealing with it. So, know that I respect you for all that you have been through and all that you have carried upon yourself and within yourself. You are a brave soul, you are God's beloved child.

hug ***kiss***

Dad/Bruce

John: Hi Dad!

Several times we asked our therapist if all this is true, even though when the reliving happened we screamed. She said yes, that the body doesn't lie and she can tell from the body. Boy, that's true. The body actually releases things, Dad. In my case, I'd belch. I just thank God it wasn't farts!!! Headaches, nose bleeds, bleeding down there in BOTH places, hair loss. All sorts of things.

I know that Walter and Eleena Amundson were very careful and concerned about appearances to the neighbors. They never took me to a doctor except for vaccinations, and the one time I fell off of a horse and broke my arm. But they SEEMED to be okay people to everybody around them. I do know one time at church at Bedison after I left, Marge took me to the church and it was all a surprise to Walter and Eleena too as well as to me. I had hinted that things were wrong about them and this was after I had left. I think Marge took me there to reconcile with them. Plus, I was scared about living on my own and had a taste of living on the street, and begged to come back but he got really angry at me, got in the car and drove off with me crying and running after them. He didn't know it (and I didn't until after), but two men witnessed it all and all of a sudden people saw the situation somewhat for what it was. I guess people have to witness something for themselves to believe that evil is around. But meantime, the kids are hurting. It turns out that the Amundsons had told people that when I left I hurt them deeply. I'm very glad he didn't take me back though. But at least I KNEW what life was with them and I couldn't figure out much of anything when I was on my own.

Then there came the time when Walter Amundson went to the university and lied about me. I'm pretty sure he wanted me back as his farm hand by then. The result of THAT was all of a sudden I was required to go to counseling and the chair of my department made me accountable to him, so people started seeing me a little. I asked them once if they'd help me get a student loan and Walter Amundson said no, that it wasn't anybody's business how much money he made. I honestly don't know how I managed to get an education. It was semester by semester, I'll tell you!! But I got pretty upset about the Missouri thing and Ian Bruch's reaction to it.

*** hug *** *** kiss ***

Ephrin: Hi Dad!

It's 3:00 a.m. and we've been awake since 1:30 so why not talk to you, eh?

Grandfather told me to tell you, okay asked he says, that all of us had to process our reliving and the first-life to change. Except Debra/Laura.

Yeah, she had to relive and process, but that's not it for her. She's supposed to live this second-life.

Grandfather says it isn't the growth that leads to experience, but experience that leads to her growth. I don't get it but he says you will.

Say, Dad, if you ever want to give the kid a Christmas present, call her up and read her a bedtime story, even if it's during the day. She keeps seeing it in movies and none of us have ever experienced that and she wants to. We all told her to not hold her breath - and meant it. You give us enough.

See ya, Dad!

*** hug *** *** kiss ***

Bruce: Greetings Ephrin,

I am glad you are around and helping Debra/Laura. Thanks for the tip about the bedtime story.

I hope you have a good day.

hug ***kiss***

Dad/Bruce

John: Hi Dad!

Let's see. Lots to say. I'm fading fast right now. Man, I can FEEL myself break up into pieces. I'll be the first to go into Debra though. Most of me anyway. Man, I can hardly THINK!! I'm not bundling into Deb first, but going right into pieces and then into Debra.

Grandfather says that me going into her won't make her older. The experience of life will. When I say that Grandfather says, he's asking me to tell you, you know. Grandfather's talked a lot with God and Jesus.

Grandfather says the Force is strong in this one. Ha. He's feeling like Yoda today, Dad! He's talking about Debra. He's also talking about her willfulness.

Grandfather says that one reason the rest of us are going is so that Debra can communicate things herself. He said that other people reading a person's mind isn't usual, and Debra needs to be usual. Debra's now saying Good, maybe nobody will tell on her anymore. Ah, but there's the lie factor!! Kid angst abounds at the moment.

Debra thinks that if she kisses you really fast and a whole lot then maybe she won't get disciplined. Worked with Grandfather once. And Grandfather's now saying that he's only human. Um, actually Grandfather, you're only spirit. hahahaha!

With you not being at e-home for a while, Dad, this might be my swan song. Oh. Okay. God says that when Debra looks at the world around her without her being completely the center, that'll be me. Wow! God just said that it'll happen sooner in her than in most children, well, maybe God's saying stronger I can't tell, and that's one way she's special and truly God's. Wow! Oh, okay, he's also saying that her age will be what it is and she'll tell you and you'll tell her and he'll tell her and he'll tell you. (Got that?) (I think in other words, God's gonna tell you and her and when she doesn't know or isn't sure you know.) That's new, Dad. We've always just guessed.

We were watching a commercial the other day. A parent was holding a new child and the narrator was saying that parents look at a child and see a wonder, or some such thing as that. And Debra cried a little and said mine didn't. God said that her second ones do, and Grandfather held her and said yep.

When in pieces, God's filtering all of us before going into Debra.

Debra's supposed to do aerobics in the afternoons, Dad, as well as the bowflex in the mornings. This is according to God. But God says that the afternoon stuff could be a variety of activities, not just the Wii. She needs to find what's fun for her. God wants her to have fun and be physically active after work, not just mentally active on the computer. She's supposed to actually quit focusing on the computer work all the time but STOP and have fun physically and THEN go back to it, and God says she's gonna need help doing that, but he says it's really important. Boy, that'll be hard, Dad. Really really hard. The stopping the mental stuff I mean and getting into the lifestyle of having physical fun.

Well, I'd better sign off. If I can't physically write you tomorrow, Dad, your last day e-home for Thanksgiving, I guess I'll see you later in a different way. I don't think I'll be here, or James, by next Monday. As you do the labyrinth, know I'm thinking of you.

I love you, Dad. Thank you for my life. See ya later. See ya soon.

*** BIG HUG *** *** HUGE KISS ***

Bruce: Greetings John,

>You are a stabilizing force in the life of the gang. I have greatly appreciated your presence in the midst of all the challenges that everyone has courageously faced. As you integrate into Debra piece by piece I think your stability will be one of the gifts to her being; this is a huge gift in a world of chaos, anxiety, and fear.

>I look forward to Debra growing up and becoming what God envisions for her. One thing for sure, she will be abundantly gifted

and will more than likely have a variety of pathways that she can follow - personally and professionally. God's guidance will be extremely helpful as will the presence of Grandfather.

Most children will know the boundaries of the parent more than once in the growing up years. And just when the child thinks he/she is too old for the hammer to drop - SUPRISE!! She will learn.

May the force be with you as you transition into the next phase.

God has blessed you in these days and God will continue to bless each of you in the days ahead - trust in Him.

HUG ***KISS*** ***LOVE***

Dad/Bruce

James: Hi Daddy!

> Well, I'm fading fast too. God says that my anger work is over and any anger felt will be normal stuff, even if it's about the first-life. I think there was a lot of poison in the anger that came out Daddy.
>
> I'm sorry I hurt you sometimes Daddy. Gee, maybe if I can quit crying I can type and stuff.
>
> Unlike John, I don't know when I'll be going into Debra. Oh gee, Grandfather just said watch out for the teenage years! Grandfather's all happy and stuff. I'm not. Feels like I'm going away or dying.
>
> I'm glad you scared me into not drinking and that I had a reliving right in the middle of the jungle of South America. I think that Debra's in for some unusual and cool experiences like that. Well, not a reliving but you know what I mean I hope.
>
> Well, Grandfather told Debra that something's in store that's good for her this Thanksgiving. Maybe me and John leaving is it. That'll be okay. I guess I'll see you again when Debra's a teenager, huh?
>
> You're not going anywhere, are you Daddy?
>
> Well, I'd better go. Bye Dad! I love you.
>
> *** hug hug hug *** *** kiss kiss kiss ***

Bruce: James, I am not going anywhere. I haven't gone anywhere for 10 years now. But this last year has been challenging and we are all seeing positive results. So, we have been blessed.

> **Fading is just part of the process. It is not the end, it is blending the parts to create the best possible individual who is gifted and able to love (but no sex yet :>))**
>
> **Have a Happy Thanksgiving. God's continued blessings.**

hug ***kiss*** ***love***

Dad/Bruce

Ephrin: Hi Dad!

Grandfather says he's got your back. You're the quarterback and he's the receiver. (Geez. Football metaphors now?) :)

Wish you could see and hear him, Dad. He's this tall, dark haired man who laughs a lot, is stern sometimes and feels great when he hugs you. He's got these big hands that will hold a face very gently. He held Debra when she was a little infant with those hands, too, Dad, and he says he held her when she had her relivings. He wishes you could have experienced holding her but knows all about realities, although he also says that if you work at it you might be able to hold her spirit if you wanted to. He says to pay attention to your dreams. He says that it's important that Debra experience the living so she can know a balance between the temporal and the spiritual. He says that unlike most kids, her earliest experiences were with the spiritual, before she could read or write and couldn't make contact with you. Ha! He just said that despite his big hands, she's a real handful!!

I'll do my best, Dad. I'm not sure I'll be able to talk to her. I guess I'll find out! But I know the experience of living must be hers.

What you said to John was totally cool and he hasn't quit crying since!!

Thanks Dad. I love you too, you know. See ya later and have a great Thanksgiving!

*** hug *** *** kiss ***

(Later)

Hi Dad --

Happy Thanksgiving.

I'm feeling more low than I expected. Do you realize that you ignore me most of the time I write? Sometimes I feel like I'm being punished for being a little more independent than the others, but probably the reality is that you're tired or something and it doesn't really have anything to do with me. At least I can't figure out what I write wrong.

Anyway, I'll be here for Debra, as best I can.

Today we just got hit with a $600 car problem. And then on top of that, we need 4 new tires. I don't see how we can save anytime soon.

take care

*** hug *** *** kiss ***

Bruce: Perk up Ephrin,

You are loved and cared about. You bring an important role to this setting and you are now the stable one for Debra, so, lots of responsibility in the days remaining.

The car issues are exactly why you need to have a savings account with money in it. We will figure out a way to get there. Do you have a monthly budget on paper? The monthly items such as utilities, food, gas, phone etc. If you don't spend some time and map one out. This will be an important learning experience for Debra for now and the immediate future – and stuff :>)

Have a Happy Thanksgiving.

hug ***kiss***

Dad/Bruce

Ephrin: Thank you, Dad. I think the money might be something to do between now and Christmas, hopefully before Deb is gone, but maybe that Deb will be gone is something nobody needs to worry about. I know that Deb has tried to do that a couple of months ago -- and failed. Thank you, Dad!

*****

Whenever parts blended together, we had plenty of time to prepare. But sometimes it seemed to me to be too long a time. Ephrin stayed with Debra/Laura longer than the other parts. Of course, I thought this was the end of it but I was wrong. The parts blending into Debra/Laura and allowing her to grow and experience living for a while seemed to give me a time to rest and gather myself together. (Get it?) Heh. I had no idea at this time that the process would get more painful.

*****

Chapter Eight
Debra/Laura Grows

For about a year, Debra/Laura took the time to grow and step-by-step aged to about sixteen. This part of me became Deb. The other parts blended into her.

During this time, imagery became more and more significant and meaningful. For me, imagery seems to communicate and reveal an understanding and an emotional life beyond words. The imagery did not happen in the Other Realm, but in my own psyche. I did not deliberately cause it; the imagery just came.

*****

Deb: I called you and told you about my dream, Dad! But it's better than that even!! I dreamt again!! But it was more like a vision, Dad.

I was in the meadow and Grandfather was there. I was running and happy and everything. I turned and looked back and away from us were these really dark storm clouds. Not on the horizon but closer. There was lightening and fire in the clouds. Beneath the clouds was the land and the land was gray and dead. I realized that that's where I lived all my life. I looked at this beautiful place and asked Grandfather if this is heaven but he said it was my second-life.

Grandfather asked me if it's time for me to put on the armor and I said that it's time now for me to turn my back on the first-life and live. So Grandfather put the armor on me. It's like a force field, Dad.

I turned back to the storm clouds and said "You can't get me!!" That's when demons came out of the clouds and came straight for me. They threw bricks and pulleys and ropes and wire and boots at me, but mostly bricks. But it all just bounced off of me and didn't hurt me at all.

I then saw the earth swallow the bricks and things once they bounced off of me. I asked why the earth did that and Grandfather said that I belong to the earth, wherever I may be.

The demons gave up and went back to the storm clouds. I then saw God and went to him. I thanked him and I asked him why he did all this for me. He laughed and told me he loved me. He held me a little and kissed me and stuff. I asked why Grandfather did all he's done for me and God said that Grandfather loves me. So I asked God why you've done all you've done for me and God said that you love me. I then asked God why all the others who've been supporting me did that, and God said that they love me.

I asked God if I was gonna grow old now and he just laughed and said for me to not worry about that.

I went back to Grandfather and we stood there together with his arm around me and looked at the first-life. That's when I woke up.

Bruce: Deb, Good vision/dream and for once the demons can't touch you. I hope these kind of dreams continue for you and that your confidence in the second-life grows. Keep resting, drinking lots of water and eating correctly. Have a great day.

hug ***kiss***

Dad/Bruce

Deb: Had a different dream last night, not as rosy as the other one. The dream was Grandfather didn't seem right and I said he wasn't Grandfather. Then he turned into a huge demon and made the first-life storm descend upon me. It was like a sand storm. Movie magic!! I laid on the ground face down and just let it surround me and come down on me. But, Dad, it didn't bother me! I just laid there and let it come and waited until it went back to where it was supposed to be. I woke up with it on me but it just didn't and couldn't affect me.

Boy, Grandfather's got a hold of me so I really CAN'T go back to the first-life. I really want to because this second-life is really confusing to me and in this second-life I'm 13 and I feel bad about that because I think I'm supposed to be old but I'm just not.

I have antibiotics now and I'm supposed to take 2000 mg a day of that for the next 10 days. But, Daddy, I can honestly say that I did the best I knew how to do about being sick. Hope you have a good day!!

*** hug *** *** kiss ***

Bruce: When you have an infection you need to go to the clinic early on and get the antibiotics that you need. We talked about that earlier when you were first not feeling well but you didn't want to go. So the longer you wait the more time it takes to get over the illness. When you are well you may want to get in touch with a naturopath to work on strengthening your immune system. With all that you have gone through emotionally, physically etc. I would guess your immune system is in a weakened state. Your eating habits have improved a lot and that has helped you. Good on ya for your discipline in that arena and the exercise arena. Do not exercise until you feel better and the medicine has begun to work (48 hours) and make sure you take your medicine every day until you finish them all . Keep up with the fluids and rest.

Dr. Stone :>)

*****

Walter Amundson died during this time and before he passed I found myself embroiled in a relationship with him. It was amazing since all of my adult life I had no relationship with him at all.

*****

Deb: My brother left a message on my answering machine to tell me that the monster, Walter Amundson, is dying, in hospice, and won't last long. So I called the monster.

It was a short conversation. He said that he believed in God. And he told me a story about not too long ago when he was having a CT scan and he wasn't supposed to move. But his face itched something awful and he prayed to God to help him and the itch went away immediately. He felt the love of God then. Do I believe it too? Yes, I do. And I believe that God loves him, although there's still a part of me that wished God didn't. But I also know that God isn't happy at all with what he did with me. Maybe he turned his life around; I don't know. It doesn't matter. Not to me in the long run.

He said he's ready to go and that he's not scared. That he's ready to face God. He said there's no purpose in life for him any more. I told him that I was calling to say goodbye. The nicest thing he said to me was that he hoped that good things will happen to me for the rest of my life. Maybe that was an apology; I don't know.

I do know that I was kind. I didn't press anything, and I did what you said. I listened. It was obvious at the end that he didn't want to say anything else.

My anger's pretty high right now. My grief, not for him but for my own loss of life and feeling the horror and pain that he caused me, is high, too. I'm glad I did it. Now I have to process this and get over it, get some closure.

I'm sorry he's dying, but he's been made comfortable and there's people around him. I think it's right and good that a person is at peace with God when he dies. The usual attitudes and understandings by people not dying concerning life and living are out the window I think when you're confronted with real death.

The monster will be gone soon. I think that God will make him accountable.

Bruce: Deb, You just went through a significant emotional experience. Emotional experiences can influence your immune system so if you are feeling worse than yesterday be kind to yourself today. Keep the fluids flowing, rest if you can, and process your experience with tenderness for yourself and I am sensing some kind of empathy for

Amundson from you in his latter hours of life. Elisabeth Kubler-Ross, MD who is an expert in death and dying says that when you die and face God you will be asked two questions: How much love were you able to give and receive? How much service did you render? Then you will relive your life and all the good things you did you shall relive and that will be your heaven and all the bad things that you did you shall relive and that will be your hell. We all have a similar journey ahead of us in the presence of Love.

Have a good day.

hug ***kiss***

Dad/Bruce

Deb: Daddy! God just told me that I've influenced people in heaven as well as people on earth!! I don't know how, but that's what he said!! Man, I gotta relax. Going home NOW!!!

I'm tied to the monster, Dad, like I was with David, until he dies. So I'm also tied to the first-life. Once I realized that then I could handle things better, although I really wish I wasn't. I could see the cord to me and the monster. Sometimes spirituality even sucks!! :) So the first-life is in my face and I just have to bull in the china shop through it!

Gotta go! Love ya Dad!

*** hug *** *** kiss ***

*****

Several times throughout the healing process, I tried to deny that any of the trauma happened. I wanted my first-life parents to love me and I wanted to look upon them as caring people. I wanted to say I just made it all up. I asked my therapist several times if this really happened and she would always say yes. The body doesn't lie and she observed my body during our sessions. And yet I desperately tried to say nothing happened. But I could not reconcile the unending nightmares, fear, sense of worthless, my body reacting to therapy, and everything else by pretending nothing happened. It felt like I was releasing poison from my body and more likely than not I felt physically ill.

When I was able to accept the corruption of my parents, I was often angry, especially when I began to change from thinking it was my fault to recognizing I did not deserve any of it. The anger was not like James' anger, but steadier and not directed at anyone except my parents and the loss of my life. I did, indeed, lose significant life experiences: a companion and children.

*****

Bruce: Deb, Anger, anger, anger is such a dangerous emotion, and very hard to control at times. You have been fortunate I would agree. Do you feel like the victim all the time? Your anger seems to be that of the victim. No quick fix except to change your perspective and choose not to be the victim but to be the beloved. What does that mean? It means to look at yourself as the beloved child of God that you are. This challenges you to connect to love, the type that God gives you and that you have had from God since your creation. It may be a bit of a stretch at this point but if you are going to win battles it will not be through anger, it will be through love.

hug ***kiss***

Deb: Is junior mints okay? Cause I had some at the movie yesterday. I didn't have any sherbet this weekend.

Bruce: Let me help you think the junior mint issue through: What is the ingredients of Junior Mints? Does it equal candy? IS it the equivalent of a candy bar? What are your answers to this health quiz?

Deb: My Answer to Junior Mints Quiz:

The ingredients of Junior Mints are chocolate, mint stuff, and sugar. Therefore, Junior Mints is candy. Therefore it is bad for the body. I like Junior Mints. Therefore, I like what's bad for the body. I have to care more for the body than candy though. I therefore don't like Junior Mints because it's bad for the body and I only like good things for the body. Even though it's totally boring.

Bruce: This was a wonderfully boring answer I just read. You can like junior mints if you wish, but eating them is a different story. How about once a month at the movies just to keep your taste buds happy but not to over indulge for the body's sake.

One of the responsibilities for gaining health is developing new tastes for healthier food. You have done this well but you need to keep working at it by adding new dinner items, lunch items and breakfast foods. Being on break is a good time to try new things. Think about it.

*****

I would like to say my relationship with my stepfather ended when he died, but it did not. I certainly wanted it to. But the trauma was so ingrained within me that I could not just let go no matter how hard I tried. I had to continue healing for it to end.

My stepfather's death led to an amazing spiritual journey with God. As usual, I was scared out of my mind. I knew that something was going to happen but I did not know what that would be.

*****

Deb: The monster's dead, Dad. Walter Amundson is dead now.

Bruce: I hope you find peace.

Deb: Hi Dad!

Well, I'd like to say that seeing the spiritual world has its disadvantages, but I'm not sure that's entirely right.

I tried to get God mad at me yesterday so that I wouldn't go through what I knew was coming down but it didn't work. I drove through KFC and then drove through Dairy Queen and got a small milk shake. Well, THAT gave me a tummy ache for about an hour and I didn't even drink it all. Ugh. Then I tried staying up way past my bedtime thinking maybe I'd fall asleep before God could get me. I also tried getting all upset because the first-life has been in my face this week. I've BEEN pretty upset this week BECAUSE the horror has been in my friggin' face, (it turns out because the monster died) but couldn't get it going yesterday. So nothing worked.

God just ignored all this and grabbed a hold of me and pulled me to him. My spirit is 14 years old. God held me standing up against his front whilst he held me with his arm across my upper chest. He didn't let go.

Pray for Grandfather, will you? He was there and he's pretty upset about what he saw. Although there's angels helping him out. Grandfather's KNOWN about this, but it was the first time he actually saw it.

So I'm there standing up against God and Grandfather's there and some angels. Then Walter Amundson comes in there and he's being HELD by two angels. He looks like he's back in his early 40s. Grandfather's in his later 40s, by the way. And I'm 14, so Walter Amundson recognized me right away.

And he started hollering. He was pretty scared. And then through this, it was like he wanted to kill me, but couldn't get away from the angels. I felt pretty safe though, and my emotions were pretty steady. Mostly he yelled that he didn't do anything and that I'm lying.

So God showed some stuff he did. It was like watching a movie. I never knew some stuff, of course, because I was just too scared and too much in pain and in shock, of course. So for me, this filled in some stuff.

Walter Amundson didn't want to see it. But, man, one time God became the God in stories and used his voice to tell him to look at it. Boy, that woke me up pretty good!

I've always wondered how Eleena got the barbed wire when I was 4 years old. He brought it. He and Eleena were friends, she says her best friend, before they got married. Well, he lived on farms mostly, and so did I once they got married. My biological father always claimed that Eleena committed adultery and that's why they got divorced and she did and it was with Walter Amundson. It turns out that it was his idea to tie me to a table with barbed wire when I was 4. They weren't married yet. So they and their friends had a good time with me.

So I watched this movie with him and God and Grandfather and a bunch of angels. Boy, I just didn't know what he did while I was in pain until now.

He always seemed to be angry when he brought me into the barn. He said something about Eleena won't give him sex so he'll have the next best thing.

So he made me take off my clothes in the barn and he then would string me up either around my ankles or my wrists. And he'd play with me like that whilst he masturbated. So I watched the different things he did to me and mostly he'd masturbate and swing me back and forth and try to get his semen on me, but it was a game.

When I was naked and tied to a post with a bag over my head, he just stood there and looked at me. Then he'd stand over me and masturbate. Sometimes he peed on me after. I was usually lying down on the ground with something stuck up me. Sometimes, though, he'd put his hand in me and explore or spread my legs with a tool whilst he masturbated with his other hand.

It always ended with the sodomy though. I didn't know that men could do it twice like that, I mean get it up twice. There was some time in between, but I guess I was pretty surprised and still am.

After he put the bricks on me, he'd masturbate too, and usually tried to hit my face but missed a lot.

Sometimes when I was strung up, he'd use a tool like a shovel or a pitchfork to swing me. Sometimes he'd take a board and hit me to see what I'd do.

It was pretty strange watching it.

When Nils was born, after the sodomy, I didn't want to get up off of the floor. He kicked me and I just didn't respond and he shook me.

When he raped me when I was really young, he was just exploring, but it looked like he was actually exploring himself.

When he raped me after I grew up some, he was different though. He said he wanted to make it up to me and love me and make me feel better. He told me he was sorry and he wanted to show just how much he loved me and just how sorry he really was. No wonder I thought that was really love.

I saw the time he drowned me after raping me and I died for a little while when I was almost 6. Eleena came in and asked him what happened and he told her that I slipped and hit my head or something and he found me in the water. But I came back, you know, and he asked Eleena if they should take me to the hospital and she said no, that I'll be fine. Turns out this happened soon after they married.

When he beat me and kicked me in the field, he was just really angry about something I did. It ended with sodomy though. But it was my fault and that's why I got my ribs broken. When I say it was my fault, I mean it was because of something I did wrong that made him mad. So the beatings really were punishment for stuff I did wrong.

I saw my body. It was hurt and bruised. My wrists and ankles were hurt, too. Then I realized that it was summer! I never went anywhere when it was summer, I mean off the farm, hardly ever. When I was just tied to a post, I was colder, and it wasn't summer. I know I tried hard to get bad enough grades to go to summer school but I didn't make it most of the time.

All though this, he said he never did any of it. So it's not over yet. I don't know if I'll be part of it anymore or not. But I'm okay. I'm not even emotional, so this really wasn't like a reliving for me.

Afterwards, God asked me if I understood a little better why he did it. I said I think so, that he did it because he could. God didn't say that I was right or anything though. Then God brought me back.

I slept pretty good, but I'm still pretty tired.

I'm okay. Honest. Somehow, it gave me some peace. But the monster's pretty mad. I'm not so afraid of him though, but I am a little bit.

Sooo, gotta get going. Hope you have a great day, Dad, and that you have an even better weekend doing good stuff!

*** hug *** *** kiss ***

Deb: God took me again last night and Grandfather was okay. But I asked God if Grandfather could come over and God told me that he gives Grandfather personal attention too so for me to not worry that Grandfather's not right with him too this time. So Grandfather stood a ways away.

So Walter Amundson came in with angels again and he was different. Wasn't angry. He was just scared. But he wouldn't admit to what he did to me.

God asked me if I could forgive him. I told God that I didn't think I knew how. God asked me if I understood why he did what he did. Same question as yesterday. I said no. He told me to look.

So in the movie I saw his life. I knew some of it already, but I don't know how I knew. He was a very lonely kid, a boy with 4 sisters. But he was lonely! Wow, his mother was a bully and she treated his dad terrible. They lived on the farm and he was expected to do stuff. And he was always expected to take care of his sisters. His dad was nice though, but couldn't or didn't stand up for himself to her. His mom was mean. I saw bits of him with other boys and how he thought of girls. But it was like he was acting, like he was confused. It was like he was supposed to think of girls as objects and the other boys made him. He felt totally unloved all his life I think because of his mean mother. I saw bits of him with other women and how nice he was until he got them alone and he was mean. He was really really frustrated with his work and didn't get what he really wanted.

God then turned me around and made me look at him. He asked me if I understood why he did what he did. I couldn't lie, Daddy! I said that even though I saw a bunch of his life, I just couldn't know because I can't really know what goes on. God was really gentle then when he said that people can't judge - not anybody - not the people who hurt them - not the people who hurt other people or cats and things.

God asked me again if I could forgive him. But I said I didn't know how. He told me that the key to forgiveness is to see his humanity, his humanness. So he showed me the movie again and then some of the movie of what he did with me again, but not all.

God asked me what did I see. I really had to think about it. God said for me to put it together and asked me again if I understood why he did what he did. I guess I kinda understood. He did to me because of himself. What he did to me he did to himself. Way deep down inside of him that he didn't even see. And the way he did to himself was to hurt me. And he hated himself. But he corrupted himself with sex. Gee, Daddy, he never saw me at all. It wasn't about me at all. He hated himself so much that he hurt himself by hurting me.

God then asked me if I can see his humanness and I said yes. God then asked me if I could forgive him. I told God that a part of me doesn't want to, but yes. God told me to not call him a monster anymore then. To not label him a monster any more.

God turned me around then and Walter Amundson was crying and stuff. God asked him if he did these things to me. And Walter Amundson said yes, all of it. God then asked me what I wanted done with him. I said that I wanted God to heal him. God then asked Walter Amundson what he wanted. He said that he didn't want to go to hell. But God told him that it will take quite a while before he's out of hell. Does he want to be healed? And Walter Amundson said yes.

They took him away and I don't think I'll ever see him again. Maybe by the time I die he'll be healed and out of hell. But I don't think I'll see him again like this.

God turned me to face him again and kissed me and hugged me and did all the mushy stuff. He told me he was proud of me. He said, now go ahead and write the email and then go back to bed. It's 2:45 a.m. right now. So Grandfather came over and put his arm around me and brought me back.

And I'm really sleepy. Hope you drive carefully, Dad, and have a great time!

*** hug *** *** kiss ***

Bruce: It may take some time for you to process all of this but I do think this is the healing process for both of you - Amundson and you. And it seems to be some closure for you. Amundson I am sure has a lot more work to do for himself. One sad life passes on to another sad life. But you have broken the chain by all the work you are doing. Have a good weekend.

hug ***kiss***

Dad/Bruce

Deb: Hi Dad.

Demons are trying to get to me again. They morph in and out of people I know. I see my parents and hear them telling me that nobody will ever love me, then demons come out of their noses and ears and mouths. Other people around here, too. Then it's just the demons in my face. Then back into people. They're trying to make me relive the torture again and trying to convince me that the demon I saw then was really God. What rubbish. I'm telling them that I'm grown up now and they can't hurt me anymore. I'm not scared very much, but I am annoyed. There's a part of me that tends to be scared and believe them, but that part of me is pretty small. Pesky demons. Whatever I'm doing and whatever path I'm going down, they sure don't want me to. Yeah, yeah, yeah, I'm worthless, I'm nobody, I'm nothing, I'm a whore, all that crap is in my face again. Grandfather's here, but I've told him I can handle this. But if they wear me down, he's here. Boy, they sure are persistent! They even placed me back into the center of my pain! Yeah, like THAT's gonna work. Been there, and angels cleaned it up. Sorry, didn't feel the pain. Demons are idiots.

*** hug *** *** kiss ***

*****

I had yet to realize that when I experience demons, it's because other parts of me are moving to the surface. Most if not all of the parts of me seem to carry the negative images of myself that is connected to the first-life. All these parts are stuck in the trauma, and see their relationship with the world through the lens of fear. They try to seem frightening in order to defend themselves.

*****

Deb: I've been having nightmares a lot lately. Last night, and then this morning when Grandfather helped, put it together.

I'm 17 years old in the dream. My parents were Walter and Eleena Amundson and they took me to one of their parties. I was dressed up like a woman going to the prom, really pretty. But I left the party without them knowing and went to a place like a round pool with water. Very rich looking, and older women were there. A man did something to make the water red and hot. I looked at my watch and it was after 11:00 p.m. and got myself back home, but then remembered that I was supposed to be at the party. Eleena called me on the phone and I lied to her and told her that I got sick and came home, but realized that she was in the car and driving and I had to change clothes fast. I didn't make it when parents and some men came in. I told them that I'd fallen asleep. Everybody left except Walter Amundson and he did his "routine" of sodomy, rape, and in my mouth with me. I woke up.

I guess I still need to work.

*** hug *** *** kiss ***

Bruce: Deb,

You can work with Fran to overcome it AND YOU WILL! You are older but obviously there is more work to do. So do not be anxious about this just be matter-of-fact and get the work done. Take care.

Fran's Notes: We explored if there is a part(s) that is connected with "Demons." "I do know there is a part of me that really hates me but I thought it was normal. I'm not supposed to be alive. I do know Walter Amundson beat the shit out of me." She had her hands in her pocket and she was <u>feeling muscles moving – the trigger</u>. Leg muscles moving. Legs are tight. She got a severe nose bleed as we were talking about them. She recognizes that she can't ignore the body and even *though it's hard for her to know there is another part, she is beginning to accept it.*

Deb: Bad news here. There's another one of me that's surfacing, and pretty violently too. The therapist says this isn't unusual. Ended up with a massive nose bleed in front of her today. I've been "seeing" this one as the demons. Maybe it's not such bad news as it's a part of my healing. I'm just so disappointed that I'm not normal yet, you know, integrated completely like normal people are. The therapist said that I have to remember that I was significantly hurt by these people and it takes time for all the stuff to come up and out. Boy, I'm not looking forward to another reliving or dealing with a willful kid. The only thing I really know at this point is that he's a he, a little demon, and very young. The therapist said that he is hurting an awful lot himself. Anyway, there it is.

Okay. The therapist also pointed out that he's probably very very hurt and that's basically why he is who he is. Anyway, it'll be what it'll be and he'll be who he'll be. You take care too.

(Later)

Deb: Hi Dad.

I saw him last night. His name is Billy and he's 7 years old. He's taken on the meanness of both Eleena and Walter Amundson. He'll try to hurt your feelings. Really, Dad. He's a great manipulator of people's feelings. He's sabotaged in the past, even though he was in the subconscious. But he IS 7 and the more he comes to the surface, the more he wants to run around and kick horses in the ribs like he saw Walter Amundson do, and our body too.

His purpose during the first-life was to block the physical pain. He put Scott almost asleep and Philip too during the hurt. I don't know, but I suspect that he may have actually taken the hardest part of the physical pain so that the others wouldn't feel it. Wouldn't the body feel it really? I don't know. His connection to the body is pretty unique I think.

I DO know that Scott saw a demon smile at him when he was being tortured. I guess that was Billy with a combination of the monster's pleasure and taking the hardest part of the torture. I don't get it myself.

This means that when Scott walked into the middle of the physical pain with Damon and Grandfather, the angels were dealing with Billy to get his essence out of the body. Perhaps so he could be healed as well as Scott.

But his relationship with the world is pretty sick as it's what the monsters taught us. That's how he's survived. And that's what makes sense to him. He's terribly sad and unhappy.

He can't come out yet as he's not totally conscious. I'm trying to keep things together.

Grandfather's big plan is to kiss him. Well, I question that approach, but I certainly trust Grandfather. Maybe because Billy has never known kindness, just hurt.

He wants to make people, the whole world, hurt like we were and like he does. A different kind of anger than James'. Follows the monster's world view and the monster's actions. I'm a little scared of him. Geez, what a little terror!

I'll keep things together here the best I can, Dad. I don't think I can keep him from coming out once he gets strong enough and closer to the surface, but I'll do my best to deal with it.

*** hug *** *** kiss ***

Bruce: Deb,

I think Grandfather has the right idea. I cannot think of anything that would disarm Billy more than a kiss – as well as initially confuse him. The other idea that comes to me as I read your e-mail is calling upon the angels daily to be with you. They are with you everyday anyway but for you to call on them is the act of raising your consciousness and awareness of their presence. If Billy becomes unpleasant call on the angels in his presence and see what happens. My experience says that there are archangels in your presence now who are working with you even though you are not conscious of them. So invite the angels to be with you every morning for the day and every evening before going to bed. TRUST. God has never, never let you down or deserted you and will not now. Keep moving forward; keep your focus on the good. For comfort you may try pray to the Holy Mother and feel and experience the feminine side of Deity. My prayers are with you.

Deb: Okay Dad. Thank you!

Billy doesn't want to come out. Grandfather can't catch him when Billy's in just the spirit state, and he doesn't want Grandfather to catch him. He's nearly put together by now, but is running around like a bat out of hell. For some reason, God and the angels are just watching. Amused, but doing nothing. To me anyway, this is good as I can't be out when Billy's out.

(Later)

Deb: No change on Billy. OH, he just said "Hi Daddy." He's too scared to let anybody touch him. Nobody's trying right now. He's not the little terror that he was and he doesn't really want to hurt horses anymore. I think.

He won't come out, thinking that Grandfather will catch him then. I guess I don't really blame him, Dad. The only touch he's ever known has hurt.

He thinks you'll punish him no matter what. I've told him that that's what you do but you guide too. He says he doesn't care. He just doesn't want punishment. He's at least fully aware of everything. Anyway, that's what's going on in this corner.

Bottom line, Billy is scared.

Section Four: Releasing Trauma from the Body

Deeper levels in my subconscious revealed just how severely I had dissociated from my body. Throughout my life, I experienced a strange mix of physical pain and no pain. If a person touched my body, I felt physical pain. On the other hand, often I did not feel pain if the pain was generated by something like fire. I could touch a candle flame on my hand and not feel it. I felt the everyday kind of pain like biting my lip or stepping on a nail. I always felt pain in the right side of my chest.

I became numb to pain during my formative years when my first-life parents hurt me. For instance, I became numb when my parents hit me, or the torture. I thought the part of me experiencing torture just gave up caring. Wrong! When this section of my subconscious awakened, I realized that I did feel physical pain from trauma throughout my formative years. But I dissociated from my body and parts of me took the physical pain, again so I could live my life.

Trauma physically resides in the body as little crystals. The crystals "froze" the muscle surrounding them. The crystals are so small that the rest of the body compensates. To reconnect my psyche to my body, my body had to release these trauma crystals. When they released, the miniscule muscle was freed, and just like any other muscle works after a time of stasis, it was very sore. Also, the crystals are toxic, so releasing meant expelling toxins from my body. The action lowered my immune system. I was physically ill during the years my body expelled toxins.

Releasing toxins from the body also released more emotions associated with the trauma that created the toxins. This led to more parts awakening from subconscious levels. It also led to more distinct imagery indicating change.

Chapter Nine
Subconscious Level 7: Billy (7) Wakes Up

The trauma formed my very core, but my association with Ian Bruch and others gave me a way to sense my be-ing. I am fortunate to have loved others, according to my abilities to love. I have been able to define my love for others in terms of justice and need. Violence of any kind toward other people and creation sickens me. Perhaps I can thank my trauma for that. I empathize very strongly with those who experience suffering, hunger, loneliness, and pain. Furthermore, I try to do something about it. I discovered that my giftedness (what I do well and took responsibility to develop what I do well) is very public and I am more or less comfortable responding to need in a public forum. Nevertheless, I don't know most people who come across my public giftedness and they don't know me. I feel safer that way. Nearly all of the time, I do not know if I meet anyone's need, and if I'm told or hear or read that I have, then I am unable to comprehend the impact of my gifts on them.

I KNOW people love me. They say they do quite a lot now. But for the life of me I just can't comprehend it. I accept it but I do not understand it or why a person would want to love me. I'm not supposed to say that. But sometimes I get a little tired of people who care about me scold me for saying it. The bottom line, though, is I accept the knowledge that people love me but I am unable to comprehend it.

During a church reunion we had an event, and sitting in the back of the audience were our church leader (a woman) and another woman next to her. Our church leader was holding the other woman in a very nurturing way with her arm around her whilst the other woman was leaning against her. I entered from the back and saw them. It seemed to me that our church leader was taking action to express love, that is, deep caring, for the woman. I did not envy the other woman but I strongly yearned to be held and touched, and I wanted our church leader to do that with me. At that time, I also thought that I did not deserve to be held and touched – that it was for others but not me. I have tried very hard, but I do not remember my first-life parents touching me without physically hurting me.

On the other hand, I did not want people to touch me. It did not help that throughout life my trauma caused a person physically touching me hurt me. Even hugs hurt me. When Billy awakened I discovered why and the relationship between the trauma and my body.

*****

Billy: Hi Daddy

Fractured Mind

It's me, Billy. Grandfather promised to not touch me if I came out. Touching hurts. I think you're gonna punish me, but I think that I'll just run away.

My hands hurt all the time, but Deb says it might be the medication for the eye. But Deb says it just might be me.

I'm 7 and I think you're mean. I think everybody's mean and I think I'm supposed to be mean too. So I think you're gonna be mean to me. So I think I gotta be mean first.

Deb didn't know what I'd be like when I came out. Me neither. But I gotta be mean cause that's what people do. Deb says you're not mean, but, gee, people hurt me and that's what makes them mean. Deb says I'm tied to the first-life. I think Deb oughta just shut up and leave me alone and quit butting in. She thinks she's all grown up but she isn't.

It's 4:30 a.m. and can't sleep. I don't like being out. I'm wondering what's gonna hurt next. My hands hurt and I got a tummy ache.

I gotta be mean, Daddy, I just gotta. I just can't take being hurt without me being mean, you know?

I guess my secrets are that I wanna be hugged and kissed and stories read to and loved and stuff, but that just isn't gonna happen, you know? Nobody cares about my secrets. Touching hurts. Everything's big, Daddy, just big. And it's just me, you know? Deb says she wants to protect me but she can't, you know? Cause when I'm out she's not and when she's out I'm not.

I'm sorry I gotta be mean, Daddy. I guess you don't like me now. I deserve getting hurt.

Bye Daddy.

Bruce: Billy, There are people, like Grandfather, Deb, and me who are nice people and will be nice to you. But you do not trust us yet so we will give you more time to see that we will not hurt you. Someone was mean to you and you desire to be mean to others? That someone that was mean to you is not around any more and all that is around you is nice. So give yourself some time to realize that no one will hurt you that is present to you now.

Deb: Some time this morning, Grandfather finally grabbed hold of Billy. He wasn't out at the time like he was this morning. But Billy let his guard down, thinking, I think, that Grandfather wouldn't touch him after I came out and he went in. But Grandfather grabbed him. He kissed him and hugged him, but then something else happened. I can't say that Billy's in his room, although it seems close. But he's now having to sit or lay down and Grandfather's right with him. I think it's like a time out. When I was in my room, Dad, I was alone. Billy isn't alone because Grandfather's right there. Billy's crying. He thinks everybody's just mean. He says that Grandfather's a jailer. Won't let him up or leave him alone. Ha! BUT since that happened, I've felt better. Hope you're having a good time.

*** hug *** *** kiss ***

Deb: Hi Dad!

Well, Billy's corralled by Grandfather and he's like tethered to him. Last night Grandfather gave him some toys. So Billy's on the floor playing with trucks and things. He's not crying. Grandfather seemed to know that I didn't understand any of this. He told me that Billy's entire world has been pain and he hasn't experienced anything else. I have my toys that I played with when I was little and I thought maybe Billy could come out and play with them and Grandfather said that would be okay, but Billy can't email and he can come out just to play with toys. We'll see about that tonight.

Anyway, things are okay here now. Grandfather asked Billy how he knew that what he wanted was hugs, kisses, and stories and he said he didn't know. Strange. It's like Billy knows everything, but doesn't really understand anything.

He's only 7 and only God knows why. He just has no concept of kindness. Grandfather kisses him and it just doesn't compute with him. He just can't conceive anything other than fear and pain. It's not within his experience. I don't think there's a reliving for him. He seems to be the tie that took it all. My joints don't hurt as much, so maybe it was a virus. Or Billy settling down.

Fran's Notes: Billy came out and looked at my legos and held the alligator and squeezed a ball. I gave him a fish to squeeze and he didn't want to hurt the fish and said he hurt animals. He began to pound his head. He thinks he's bad. Billy said he can't tell if there are others still inside that are unknown. Billy can't tell but he said there might be a baby. Deb returned with a severe headache.

Deb: Hi Dad! Well, Billy came out to Fran today. I couldn't tell everything that went on. But later Fran told me that he's a sweetheart. No anger. No cussing. Nothing like that. He hit himself and she had to get up and stop him. Fran told me that he was respectful. I asked if he was mentally ill, and she said no, that he's been terribly hurt. Apparently he was very scared at first and cried a lot. But settled down. Yay! Billy says that she also told him that Daddys punish out of love not meanness and that's what they do so kids will grow up good. And that he needs to respect you.

See ya!

Billy: Okay Daddy. Stuff has changed in my life since I wrote. I don't want to be mean anymore and I didn't want to squeeze the blow fish toy but later when I told Deb about what I did when I was out with the woman, Deb told me that blow fish blow themselves up and stuff and I don't hurt the blowfish if I squeeze him. I know everything, you know. Deb says that I didn't go to sleep during any of the first-life. But boy I sure do feel bad. Okay. I sure am scared.

Billy: Deb doesn't know what I do when I'm out you know and I'm out now so I think I have a solution to a really really big problem. She thinks that if I'm too bad that you'll throw me away and when she thought that, I got really really scared and I cried and sucked my thumb again but then I got thinking and I have a solution. So when I'm bad cause Deb gets mad at me and I know I'm bad I know I'm supposed to get hammered see. And there's gotta be consequences see. But I don't want you to throw me away so I think that I can give MYSELF consequences see? And I can hammer MYSELF! So when I'm bad and stuff I'll hit my face with a board and that'll really really hurt. Okay? And THAT way, you don't have to raise me and stuff. And I think that if you don't have to raise me then you won't throw me away. Okay? How's THAT for a deal, huh?

I'll tell you a secret, okay Daddy? I know what the monster did Daddy. And I know that the others went through a reliving. But my secret is that I'm going through the reliving all the time now but the difference is that I don't scream. But I'm reliving everything the monster did to all the pieces of Deb and it's happening over and over again and it's all of it one after the other. And that's my secret. But I'll tell you another secret, Daddy. Getting thrown away is worse than what the monster did Daddy. It hurts more I mean than all this pain and that's why I'm really really scared now. So if I just hit my face with a board when I'm bad will that make everything okay?

Bruce: Hitting yourself in the face with a board is not a good idea. There are three possible persons who may hammer you: God, Grandfather and me. So, you do not need to hammer yourself because that is a self-destructive behavior.

Sorry you are going through the reliving. No one will throw you away.

Deb: Hi Dad!

Hope you had enough breaks!

Well, I (we) became suicidal again last night but I was able to step back from it and look at what's going on. Fran's comment that it's a part of the healing process really took me by surprise. I honestly thought she'd put me away.

I looked at how I really felt, and it was the old and usual emotional crap: whore, trash, nobody loves me, throwing away, I'm not supposed to be here. The strongest one was a feeling of absolute worthlessness. Dad, this is stuff I haven't been able to get over. It got better, but it's crashed all around me now.

THEN I looked at Billy as best I could. Dad, he was seriously reliving and scared stiff. I realized that it was at its worse in the evening when there's no real distractions. The kid was totally traumatized. Grandfather's there but he can't help because Billy can't see/feel him. Billy can't break from the reliving.

Fran said that once we deal with Billy I'll feel better. Dad, I'm so emotionally tied to Billy! I should say my overwhelming negative emotions are tied to Billy's trauma. I've known that I haven't been ABLE to choose how I feel and it's been really frustrating. At one point (or more), I lashed out at God when I was younger and feeling rotten and told him that I've gone through this process and nothing's changed! Man, Dad, now I know why. Last time I was there, Fran said that Billy needs to be nurtured, but I honestly don't know what that means really. She said that he was hurt very badly and I see this little 7 year old kid and, frankly, it's not fair that it's in him and I can't take it from him to me and I can't do a thing about his reliving.

So I lay there having all these emotions and suicidal thoughts and reflecting and figuring stuff out and refusing to move to hurt myself. (Not being able to "naturally" bleed to death has helped.) And now I'm fine again.

This is hell.

You have a great day, Dad! Thanks!

*** hug *** *** kiss ***

*****

A significant turning point in my healing was being able to physically feel Fran rubbing my back. Her touch did not hurt. I think my growing trust in Fran and her compassion throughout my healing sessions helped me considerably.

*****

***Fran's Notes:** Billy came out. He looked at the fish toy with spikes and Billy wished he had spikes and could be made bigger. Monster wanted him to die and he had to protect everybody. Billy put James in the bubble because Billy could tell that James wanted to kill people. Billy said he always saw demons but Deb figured it was the pain. He laid* down on the floor next to where I was sitting and I rubbed his shoulder. He said it was the first time he felt anyone touch him that way. I asked him to remember this good touch and replace the bad touch. Deb returned and was a bit disoriented. She didn't recall what occurred and I explained it to her.

Billy: I'm fine. Better than fine! I have spikes now like a blowfish and spikes protect me, you know! AND Fran rubbed my back, my real back. I knew that Grandfather does that sometimes but I never felt it in real life before Daddy. Gee, I can't quit remembering what it was like for her to rub my back and stuff!! Grandfather's really happy that I got a nice thing done to me and stuff. Wow, I can still feel it!!! She was talking to me too but I couldn't hear her and I couldn't concentrate AT ALL cause she was actually TOUCHING me Daddy and IT DIDN'T HURT!!! Grandfather says that I need some real experiences that's for MY age from real nice people and he doesn't like it when most of my experiences are from people who are mean.

Deb kinda falls asleep when I'm out, Daddy, and has to take some time to wake up to herself again. I think I'm connected really deep in Deb Daddy. Boy, when Deb got into the car to go home, she just couldn't drive yet and boy she had a LOT of pain in her right side. Do you think maybe Fran will read to me Daddy? Will you maybe? Just once? Maybe I haven't, but *I* think I've been good!

okay, BYE!

h k

Bruce: Greetings Deb and Billy,

I am very busy for the next few days going to Florida. I will be back hopefully Wednesday. I will not have access to e-mail so do not think I am ignoring you. I will catch up Wednesday or Thursday. Hang in there.

Deb: Hi Dad

Ian Bruch has tuned me into a book called *The Emotion Code*. The author says the very same thing that Fran does: that emotions are stored in the body, except he says trapped. And this guy tells us how to release those emotions. He writes kind of like Scott Peck did. I'll be following his technique so maybe I can rid myself of these negative emotions that relate to the first-life. I'll tell Fran about it though. I'm just trying to help myself.

I don't feel any better Dad. It's after 2:00 a.m. here and once again I can't sleep. Maybe sleeping pills.

Okay. Thanks Dad.

*** hug *** *** kiss ***

Bruce: Deb,

The Emotion Code **sounds like a good book for you. I also believe that emotions are stored in the various parts of our body so I think you are on the right track.**

I hope you can get some rest. I would say NO to sleeping pills. Take care.

*****

I find it amazing how something will come at the right time to help me heal, and in this case it was *The Emotion Code*. Through this technique, I was able to release seriously negative emotions trapped in both my subconscious and my body. I was able to open doors for floods of release later on.

But that is how God seems to work. Or as Joseph Campbell would say, the universe. When a person walks the path uniquely meant for him or her, opportunities and people come along. I think of it all in terms of potential. When a person strives for potential, however that is defined by the person, doors simply open. We were not meant to hurt others to get what we want, but to walk the path the universe has for us. We were meant to experience life. As I go through this healing process, I have realized that experiencing life means to perceive, enjoy and protect all that The Creator has made. And that includes other people.

Billy talked to Bruce the next morning and asked him if I was an adult yet. He said nope.

*****

Deb: Hi Dad -

The doctor said this flu lasts at least 2 weeks and it's rampant in this area and I've got it. It hits the trachea. He gave me antibiotics for a sinus infection. Bummer.

Sooo, I'm not an adult yet, huh? Well, *I* thought I was!

Have a good day, Dad!

*** hug *** *** kiss ***

Bruce: You have always thought you were older than you really are. Typical teenage stuff.

Deb: Parents are so .... so .... grrr .... :)

Bruce: That is correct. Feel better!

Fractured Mind

Billy: Hi Daddy

We do everything you tell us to do and boy we sure do feel sick anyway. Even the cough syrup doesn't stop the cough. The doctor gave us that. Do you think maybe we're supposed to die now? I mean, first there was the nose bleed and now this and stuff. Deb says no but I'm sure wondering.

I don't have much reliving and stuff, at least not when I've been sick. Daddy, will you read to me? I keep seeing it on TV and in movies Daddy. I've been good I think. Really really. I just wanna be normal.

I guess I better tell you a secret. I think people are mean to me because I'm bad. I know it's my fault cause I told the others bad stuff but I didn't know life then Daddy and I wasn't really awake.

We didn't tell you, but the angels came to us the other night. The mean people got to us too much and we were pretty scared and anxious and stuff. The angels fixed that.

okay bye.

h k

Bruce: Billy,

No you are not suppose to die – not for a loooooong time.

I am glad the angles helped out in your time of need.

Fran's Notes: Billy was unhappy last night because of Deb's pain. Billy said people are like poison to him and are so mean. I talked to him about his new job of releasing pain and being connected to the body in a healthy way. He said his upper teeth hurt. Billy said they are hungry and eating too much. We talked about him starving when young. I explained that the monsters did these things not because of Billy. We worked on his hunger. He liked to be a ninja – imagined wrapping his legs around the rope upside down and then releasing himself. She began to burp. We processed this body therapy. Deb said the pain wasn't as bad and her wrists – delayed reaction – as well as her shoulders and arms. I encouraged her to do this exercise at home.

Billy: Hey, Dad, here's a conversation between Grandfather and Deb when Deb wanted to go see the movie Jackass.

Grandfather: You can go. (to the movie)

Deb: Can I have a mountain dew?

Grandfather: No. I let you go to the movie. Don't push it.

Deb: I'm 17.

Grandfather: Uh-huh.

hahahahaha! Deb hasn't had a mountain dew in weeks and weeks. I wanted some candy but Grandfather said no, we've already had that this month at the movies. Deb barely got chores done this weekend too!

Say, a man on TV said that everybody farts and when a fart smells, then you're not eating right and when they don't smell, you are eating right. Guess what Daddy? My farts don't smell! Cool, huh?

Daddy, I'm hungry all the time. I can't eat enough and I don't know why and stuff. Maybe I gotta tell the therapist, huh? We go there today, so I can I guess. We eat right and stuff, Daddy, but I'm so HUNGRY!!! Grandfather won't let me have candy and stuff like that Daddy. And Deb is like ALWAYS doing what Grandfather wants. Cause if I want candy and stuff, she does too. So when that happens and we're in the store and stuff and Deb like can't handle it, Grandfather steps in and she just follows Grandfather. Grandfather's not mad at me or anything and he doesn't even scold me and stuff. But, MAN, I'm so hungry all the time! And I REALLY want the bad stuff.

Grandfather says I gotta not hold the pain back anymore, Daddy. Is that okay? I feel kinda guilty and stuff cause the body sure does hurt like all over!

Daddy, the monster hurt me a whole whole lot. I'm not really scared anymore cause he's not around and stuff. But it's like I'm still living it Daddy cause I can feel it!

I'm a ninja Daddy! Did you know that? When I was with Fran last Thursday she had me figure out how to get out of the ropes and I held my hands up like I was hanging and stuff. So I told her I was a ninja and went upside down and wrapped my legs around the ropes and I could get the ropes off. So that happened and she had me stand and stretch and stuff and that hurt my right side too much but Fran forgot about that. So I'm a ninja and that's really cool Daddy.

Boy, now things are really strange without the dogs. We got everything done for the winter and now there's nothing else to do. Before, we'd come home and work on the computer and take the dogs someplace. Deb says we gotta enter a new life now and now's the time to really figure out how to have fun cause Grandfather doesn't want us to work on the computer until it's dark. So it's gotta be physical. She says the job right now is to release trapped emotions. Daddy, I sure do miss my dogs Daddy. And I still cry. Is that okay?

okay bye

h k

Billy: Hi Daddy. I think I worked something out in my sleep. Okay?

In the first-life, I always wanted to be hugged and always felt guilty about that. Eleena, she's my real mother, never wanted me to hug her from the front or anything. So I'd try to hug her from the back. I call it a backwards hug. So I'd go up to her from the back and hug her and she always got mad. She never hugged me or anything you know. And I'd try it with the monster but he'd hit me. I don't know why I tried it so much Daddy. I just wanted to be touched that didn't hurt. And now Eleena wants to be hugged all the time and Deb will do that. But I really don't understand any of it Daddy. All I know is that I feel really empty inside knowing that I wasn't supposed to want to be hugged and stuff. And even in the second-life somebody hugging me would hurt. And I don't know why about that either.

But Grandfather says that God gave me to you and him for a little while so I can have normal kid stuff that won't make me feel so hungry empty so I can grow up healthy instead of this. That's what he says. The only normal kid stuff that *I* know besides being punished is to be hugged and a story read to. And a kiss, but the monster made me kiss him good night every night so that's kinda gross you know. Even after he hurt me kinda bad you know. So maybe now I can go home and do the release of emotion thing tonight so maybe I won't feel so empty, huh? You want me to tell you about that Dad after I try to do it?

okay bye

h k

Bruce: Billy,

Sure I want you to tell me about it. It is good to share it with Grandfather and me. And when we hug you, as you already know, it doesn't hurt.

hug ***kiss***

Or secret code: h k

Billy: YEAH DAD -- SECRET CODE!!! COOOOLLLLL! Okay, I'll go home and try emotion release stuff. Thank you!!!!!!!

Fran's Notes: Billy is so traumatized and sees ropes, pulleys, and feels the abuse. He's a sweet kid. When Billy is out, Deb is gone. Deb said it feels more like an echo when Billy's out. Deb is asserting herself more this morning and isn't a victim anymore.

Fran's Notes: Billy came out. He played with the alligator and puppet. He said he cries a lot. "I can see the rope, see the barn, and I can smell hay, horses. Every time I do reliving stuff, I have to be tortured. Daddy says I'm safe but I still see it. When I do the emotion stuff, I feel just like I felt when it happened the first time. I know he's not here, but there really is monsters in the world. I'm all confused." He laid down with the toys.

EMDR – *I'm safe now. I can release the pain from my body. Imagine a big hot air balloon and you're releasing the tension and pain and putting it in the hot air balloon.* "The monster is there. The monster is too big for toys." *Can you tell him he's not going to hurt you anymore?* "He's there – first-life – I feel it, I smell it." *But God is stronger than the monster and God will help you find a way to work through it.* "All I can do is face the monster. He's looking at me. I'm scared. I want to go to sleep but I can't go to sleep anymore. My side hurts. The guys here are growing bigger. It hurts." *Imagine God's there putting his hand on your side and healing it. He felt intense pain. The toys, three-headed dragon got huge and faced the monster. He cried. Deb returned. Deb's stomach is upset. Deb didn't know she had a sweet side of her with Billy.*

Billy: I just couldn't do what Fran wanted, Daddy. She uses the buzzies and it connects my brain together and stuff. And I saw the monster right in front of me and I was supposed to do something to the monster so he wouldn't hurt me but I couldn't figure it out and I couldn't make it happen. But it's right in the middle of the first-life! Then the monster started kicking me and I was just doomed cause the pain was just too much. Boy, Grandfather sure did jerk me out of there!

I've been with Grandfather until now and I slept with him, like with him holding me instead of in bed. So I feel pretty good now! I went from the smell of the barn to the smell of Grandfather. And I slept totally through the night. So I'm okay Daddy.

Have a great day Daddy and a terrific weekend!

h k

Billy: Gee whiz.

I went downstate and stuff and got administered to and stuff. The administration made the monster my size, Daddy, instead of big like you and Grandfather! Holy cow! And I had this nightmare last night and I was killing people, Daddy, or trying to. They were shooting shotguns at me and stuff and I had a gun and I tried and tried and finally I was able to shoot them. I didn't kill anybody but boy I sure did hurt them a whole lot! And I felt so bad about killing people that I put the gun to my own head and pulled the trigger and that's when I woke up. I was really really upset Daddy cause I don't want to hurt anybody much less kill them. After the morning came about and stuff, I told Jack and then even later he came to me and told me that I wasn't killing people. I was killing the fear. And I knew that was God talking through him and I felt better and the fact that Grandfather didn't seem unhappy made sense you know.

I still don't know what to do about the monster, but he's my size now and I think maybe I'll figure it out, huh? People seem to think that I oughta beat up the monster but I don't want to Daddy. Fran kinda wants me to but she didn't say that and stuff. But I think that with the monster my size and stuff that maybe he won't scare me so much I can't do anything, huh?

So I'm lots better! Hope you're okay and stuff.

okay bye

h k

Bruce: Billy,

WOW, the monster your size takes some of the fear out of the picture. You do not have to hurt the monster and I like the idea from Jack that you are not killing people – you are killing fear. Good stuff!!

Keep working at it!!

H K

Billy: I got my head on your chest, Daddy. I think I got courage now to face the monster. I don't know what to do yet, but he's little like me you know. So I feel like there's a big stage I'm gonna enter, even if it IS by myself! I asked Grandfather if when all these bad feelings leave me if I'm gonna disappear, you know, like die. That I'll lose ME. He said no, that the only thing I'll lose is all this fear and bad feelings and I'll feel lots happier. Boy, God sure is something else, isn't he Dad? I sure don't know why I had to be administered to for God to make the monster my size. But he did and boy am I sure glad! I sure was scared Daddy.

Thank you!

okay bye

h k

Billy: Daddy, I figured out something this morning. And I think it's important.

Grandfather came back and I ran to him and stuff and he picked me up and stuff. I asked him where'd he been and he said that he's got other family too. I asked how his wife was and he said fine. But he's got 5 kids and grandkids too. And when he told me about his own kids I got really sad Daddy. And I got down.

But Grandfather wouldn't let me go, Daddy. He knelt down so I could look at him straight and he said that I was his child but the child of his heart and the child of his spirit. Not his physical child. But me and Deb are just as much a part of him as his other kids. And I knew that, Daddy. I knew that me and Deb really ARE a part of you and Grandfather now.

And what I figured out was that how I feel when I hear about physical family stuff isn't because of what I didn't have or don't have, but how it's connected so much to how bad the physical family hurt me Daddy. I can't even make an adopted connection because Walter Amundson adopted me Daddy. My sadness about all of that has always been connected to just how much they hurt me and I just want the hurt to go away Daddy. And when I hear about family and kids it's like BAM, right to the first-life and the sadness I have about it.

And I think it's been really hard for me and Deb to separate you and Grandfather away from that first-life. I know I've always expected you to hurt me. But that was because you're physical. But NOW things are different Daddy. Me and Deb really are a part of who you are and Grandfather is and that part is with your heart and your spirit.

My heart wall is now 8 feet deep, so it's not as deep now. I released one trapped emotion this weekend. Deb tried to find The Golden Compass cause I wanted it cause of animals talking to people and stuff but she couldn't. I think she'll get it from Amazon. That's cool. Hope you're okay and stuff.

okay bye

h k

Bruce: Deb and Billy,

> **I have been distant a little recently and over the past couple of months. All my trips to Florida were not fun. So, emotionally I haven't had a lot to give to you.**

Billy: Oh GEEZ! I'll be good, Daddy. I didn't really wanna cuss and be bad anyway. But I'll be good and stuff so you don't have to worry about ME and stuff!

I love you lots and lots!

okay bye

h k (the CODE)

Bruce: I appreciate your understanding very much.

> H K (secret code)

Billy: My heart wall is now less than a foot deep! Still there though. I released despair again last night. I should say God helped me release it. I thought maybe my heart wall was gone but nope! I thought that cause my back feels better. That's right at the bottom of my shoulder blades. Above that is still torn up, but that part feels better. I think it'll be well after the heart wall is gone. God just told me to focus on parts of my body to release emotions instead of the other way around. And to stick with that part of the body until it's healed. Then go on to the next. Okay.

Boy, God sure does love you lots and lots. I do too, but God really really really does. I hope you have a really good day, Daddy, and you'll do good stuff!

okay bye

h k

Bruce: Hi Billy,

God really, really, loves you as well. Have a good weekend.

h k

Billy: Hey, guess what Dad! My heart wall is gone! I released the feeling of being unworthy last night and waited until this morning to find out cause there's this delay you know. The pain in my back in that one spot is gone. And my fingers and wrists feel better. I think I'd better concentrate on my wrists Daddy cause they hurt, especially the right one, but my right side of the whole body is worse than my left side.

Deb discovered body butter. It's thicker than lotion but it goes into the skin lots faster! So it's supposed to be like all over the body. Um, was that a report? If it was, you can just close your eyes Dad! Anyway she did the sticky feet this morning with the body butter and it wasn't so sticky cause body butter isn't as sticky as lotion Daddy.

Deb wants you to know that I have blond hair. Well, I do. The body had blond hair when it was a little kid. Blond hair and green eyes. Eyes have always been green. The monster thought they were blue - I don't think he could see me too good Dad. There's some brown in my eyes Daddy but boy they sure get a really deep green! Yep, dark green. I just looked at them in the mirror.

You know, my subconscious tells me what emotions I'm releasing Daddy. I don't tell me that myself you know.

Do you still love me like Grandfather does or am I just toast now?

okay bye

h k

Bruce: Not toast.

Billy: Daddy, I did what God said to do. I focused on a part of my body to release an emotion out of it. So I focused on my right wrist. And just as soon as I connected, I felt this really sharp pain in my right wrist. And I'm right back in the first-life Daddy and I could feel my wrist bones like pull apart and stuff. And it really hurt tonight. I didn't scream or anything but I've been crying ever since and stuff. Can I write you when it's like this? If I promise not to write you about anything else, will you care about this stuff and you can focus on this stuff or something? Is this okay? Can I put my head on your chest when it's really scary and hurt like this does? So maybe you won't feel bad cause of me? I don't - oh gee, Daddy, Grandfather wants me to come to bed and stuff and God's pulling me away. okay bye

h k

Billy: Hi Daddy!

Boy, I think I fell asleep before I got into bed last night! This morning, God put me on his lap and talked to me. He said he was really proud of me for taking the physical trauma. But it has to come out again from me, not Deb, and Deb should try to stop taking it. She just wants to take it on instead of me, Daddy, cause it hurts so much. But God said that I HAVE to connect to the first-life and to relive the physical trauma in order to get it out. He said when that happens then the pain I feel IS the trauma. It's like opening up a wound in order to get the puss out. And the puss is the trapped emotion. But God said too that he's here and Grandfather and the angels too. I whispered that those angels don't say anything and God whispered back that he knew that. God said that he wanted me to have fun and run and jump and when this is over I'll be able to do that.

I got the feeling that if the angels spoke to me, I'd be dead!! Like overwhelmed and stuff!

I asked God why Grandfather loved me and Deb so much. God said that I am precious. I told God that I didn't like that word cause Eleena says that about her stuff. God said that she looks at things and says that but you are not. I said yeah. God said that I am an innocent and so is Deb and we are pure of heart. Geez. I don't get it.

I asked God too if you resent us sometimes and God said that you are my parent. And Deb's. In other words, no answer! God said that Grandfather is also my parent and knows that what he's doing for me is helping him. He said that Fran is right that people have junk, or issues and stuff. People don't drop that when they graduate from earth and I'm helping Grandfather with his just by being and going through all of this. So by Grandfather helping me, I'm healing him. Cool! God said that me and Deb must always respect you, and me and Deb must always have gratitude that you raised us and raising us in this second-life. Gee, that's easy Daddy! God said that Grandfather sees stuff now though too that he couldn't see before and he's really happy about that. And even though people still have their junk when they graduate, there's lots of stuff that's released when that happens. I asked God if when people don't learn what they're supposed to when they're here if they have to take the class over again and God said yep, sometimes.

Well, that's it Daddy! I'll just have to keep focusing on my right wrist and opening it up until all the puss is out. And then the next spot. At least it's not all at once! I don't think I'd be able to do it all at once Daddy. I think I'd pass out. Um, actually, I think I DID pass out sometimes in the first-life! The body did but I didn't cause I was just too deep.

Hope you have a good day today! okay bye

h k

Bruce: OK Billy,

You are brave. You are good. You are innocent. You are loved. You may place your head on my chest anytime you feel the need. You may write to me when you need to as well. Oh, and I do not resent you, nor Deb, at all. So, keep up the good work because I want to see the day you can run and jump with glee and are free.

h k

Deb: Hi Dad!

I had a HUGE dream last night that felt to me that changes were made. It's long though. Sorry.

Location was like in the projects, the alleyways and backs of buildings. It was me and other girls against a bunch of boys. The boys captured one girl and I sent another to get her but she didn't return. I went and saw that the boys had boxed up both girls in one very small box, about 6 x 6 inches. I snuck in and stole the box. But another girl who was on the boy's side fought with me. Eventually I got the upper hand and expressed my love for her. That turned her around. The box was like stretching out saran wrap and it was difficult but the other girl and I got the girls out of the box. Then the rest of the girls came, and they were various ages and I put the youngest on my back to piggy-back. I expressed my love for them, too, and all of a sudden, all of them went into me.

Billy came. I asked him what was going on, and he said that I'm picking up the pieces now. That's when the boys came to fight. I expressed my love to them, too, and they all went into me. I asked Billy if that was it, and he said no, there's some in a mountain.

So we went to the mountain and a bunch of boys were trying unsuccessfully to get gold out of the mountain. They'd already mined it but couldn't get it out. I grew into a giant and pulled the gold out of the mountain. So the boys were happy. I expressed my love to them and they all went into me.

Billy could tell that I wanted the gold, but he reminded me that God told me that I don't really have to worry about money, just be responsible. Billy said I should give it to them. I looked up, and there were people on the horizon. I said okay, and spread out the gold and left. I thought that that was it for the gold, but Billy said no, that God wants me to keep mining for the rest of my life. I said okay.

I asked Billy if that was it and he said no. There's work. So we went to the building where I work and there were some people there who were unhappy and scared. Older people, men and women and they were in various parts of the building and we had to search for them. I expressed my love to them and they all went into me.

Not done yet. We went into a conference room and on the conference table were briefcases. I opened up each briefcase and pulled out another person. I expressed my love to them and they all went into me.

Billy said "Look at the body!" And I looked at my body and there's these demons with their tails stuck in me, where the pain points are. They look like wriggling black worms but their tails are stuck in me. I remembered then when Scott, Damon, and Grandfather went into the center of me and the angels cleaned them out! Well, they're almost out! Billy said that he's got stuff to do! Then I woke up.

I can't say HOW I expressed my love. I just felt love I think and they knew it. Anyway, I think this was pretty important. I don't know why.

take care,

*** hug *** *** kiss ***

Bruce: There is a phrase in your sharing of your dream that caught my attention: I shared love with them and they came into me (this isn't exact but you get the idea). I thought about the blending, coming together of all your parts to make you whole and the source of that empowerment is God's love.

Deb: Hi Dad

Billy got the last of the emotions out of the right wrist last night. When he started, there was a sharp pain in the wrist. It's good to know that

Fractured Mind

that's the trauma. Then he did the magnet thing. There's always a delay, so after we'd gone to bed, I could see the body with all the demon worms. (I think this is totally gross, but Billy thinks it's cool.) The one stuck to my right wrist came out and I literally jumped. Then I could see it "bleed" demons out of the hole. As all that crap came out, they turned to ash. Ugh.

Have a good day! *** hug *** *** kiss ***

Billy: Hi Daddy

Boy, me and Deb couldn't sleep too good. So we wanted to go and talk to God and he said okay. Humph. For a long time he looked like a man and we forgot that he usually like morphs, so he was morphing now. We asked please if he's stay put but he was playing with us Daddy! He changed into a man and put us on his knee and I wanted to look in his face and thank him and stuff. Deb too. But he was laughing and playing with us, so here we are on a man's knee cause he's big and I'm trying to look at him in the eye except his head is morphing. He settled down into a fish head and asked me what I wanted to say. Gooooodddddd! Then he changed into a little mouse and I got dumped but it didn't hurt or anything. God's laughing his head off. Then he changed into light, but not too bright and picked us up and took us above the earth. Man, my real heart was racing at that! He told us he knew why we wanted to come to him and we're welcome. Then he told us that there's a whole lot more than what we're concerned about day to day. Man, it was beautiful! I asked God why we're still breathing and he laughed at me again and said that we're in spirit form and I said oh yeah. He took us back Daddy, changed into a man and patted me on the butt and told me to go back to bed. So Grandfather took us from there. Like I could sleep after THAT! Cool huh?

Boy, I sure don't like doing the magnet thing. Sometimes it really hurts and sometimes it doesn't so much. Last night the emotion wasn't on the list and I asked myself if I need to know the emotion to release it and my subconscious said no. So something released. I'm working on my right fingers. I've done my right wrist and my right elbow/arm.

I've been good Daddy. Honest.

Bruce: Billy,

Pretty cool that you have that time with God!

Billy, you are a good kid - sweet, innocent and a hard worker.

H k

Billy: Daddy, we really gotta talk about this allowance thing! This is important! I'm 7, not a BABY!! How about $10 a week?

Bruce: This is important! You're 7 years old and you will receive $2 a week.

*****

By this time, Billy healed enough to begin to focus on living life. Bruce's discernment was amazing throughout all of the healing process. He knew when it was time for a part of me to turn to daily living and proceeded to teach that part to have normal living skills.

*****

Billy: HI Daddy!

I wanted to put dishes away for my chore. But Grandfather said that my chore is brushing teeth. He said that it's the body and I'm responsible for it and Deb forgets sometimes and it's hard for her to remember. So I have to brush teeth and Grandfather said that if I miss a day, no allowance.

rats

Oh well! I'm off to a movie after we do trash.

GETTING PERMISSION: Can I snow shoe and ski when I want since I can't sleep? I PROMISE that Deb will be with me. Hahahahahaha

Deb says that the pain in the right shoulder has gone from a 10 to a 5.

Angels are doing something to me but I don't know what. I think I know why.

okay bye

h k

Bruce: Billy,

I am glad you are ok and that the shoulder is getting better. Permission is permission. SO, when you want to ski and snowshoe you ask permission.

h k

Billy: Oh. Do I ask you or Grandfather? Cause if it's you then I gotta wait. But if it's Grandfather, then sometimes I don't connect too good.

Bruce: Grandfather would be the first choice because he is there and can see the circumstances.

Deb: Just for clarification, Dad, neither Billy nor I really know what it means to ask permission. We don't really understand. Big differences between first-life and second-life! Billy wants to follow the rules but there's some insecurity there!

Bruce: You ask: Grandfather, may I go out and snow shoe? It is important to wait for the answer and obey the answer.

Fran's Notes: Billy has been figuring a way out of the trauma, as well as the work with the magnet. Debra finds that she's really angry at Eleena and she robbed her of her life as well as the monster. I pointed out that her terrible attachment issues with her mom hasn't been projected or transferred negatively to others. She said, "Billy is an amazingly sweet kid. Billy was a monster because he learned that but then he came out and saw you."

Billy came out and did the buzzies. He wants help to do something that feels real to him. He said they have a big problem with what's real and not real – "people caring about us." It's hard for him to believe it and then people not want him around for Christmas. Deb called Eleena to say Merry Christmas and Eleena tried to make her feel bad because Deb doesn't tell her everything. We talked about if he told Eleena she hurt her. He said that Eleena would deny it and then hurt her more. We'll process this more.

Billy: Christmas is really really hard for me Daddy. The monsters would put up a tree and there were presents and everything. And they acted really happy and stuff. And Christmas morning I was excited and happy and everything. And we'd open presents. And then the monsters would get mean Daddy. I don't think they liked me being happy. Eleena got unhappy and mean to me. And the monster really got mean.

I don't remember being able to have my presents. They were just gone. Boy, I sure don't know why parents are so mean during Christmas Daddy but they sure are. And even today I keep having this hope that this time people will be nice to me, just like back in the first-life I had that hope and I was happy about it. But they're not. And I'm either alone or I'm with Jack and Eleena who treat me mean. But now Eleena can't go anywhere, or so she says, so maybe that's all over with now and we'll just be alone.

I don't know why but I still like Christmas. I still have that hope, you know? I guess I just never learn. It isn't really the presents, you know, that make me sad. It's the hope that just doesn't happen. Bummer.

Deb says all this is cause I'm 7 and when it comes to Christmas, I'm wounded about it all and bleeding. I think she's right about that.

Boy, I sure don't know what made me say all that! But it's how I feel. Deb says she doesn't care but I think she really does cause I do. Have a good day today Daddy!

okay bye

h k

Bruce: Billy, God says remember the poor, remember the sick, remember those who are hungry, thirsty and in prison. God doesn't advocate for people to spend lots of money on presents, He simply requests that we remember what happened in Bethlehem, the courage of Mary and Joseph and that angels came to the common people to share the good news. Movies and TV are entertainment not necessarily reality - keep that in mind.

Lots of people feel sad at Christmas for various reasons so you are not alone in your sadness. For many this will be the first Christmas without a loved one, a mother/father, wife/husband, brother/sister and even the faithful friend of their dog. Make those around you family and be grateful.

Thanks for sharing your feelings with me.

h   k

Billy: It's the last day of the year and I have lots and lots to be thankful for.

Me and Deb talked to God last night. Deb really really really wants to do stuff for God, Daddy. Me too. God said that he wants her to heal first. To finish that first. He told us to focus on the body. Last night I traced a muscle that really hurts in my right arm back to my back where it connects and that REALLY hurts and all of a sudden I was in the first-life and I just cried Dad. So I guess I got lots to do yet, huh.

Boy, it turns out that we're sleeping a lot after all, but it isn't me or depression or anything. It's cause we're sick. Not over it yet even! But feeling lots and lots better.

Is running the dishwasher Monday and Friday okay?

Fran wants us to come to a breathing workshop this Friday night Daddy. We'll do that. She and somebody else is doing it together and she says that people with trauma don't breathe right and that's a reason why we get sick with that stuff. As usual, I don't know what I'm talking about. :)

I've been good Daddy. Sad though.

Bruce: Billy,

Whatever works for your schedule is best for you in the dishwashing world. I am going to a breathing workshop on Chi Gong or Qigong sometime in the near future. It is for healing and health.

Do not worry, sadness will pass and things will be resolved.

Be happy my little one, life is really good even though your path has been difficult at times. Progress is being made, healing is taking place, people care for you and love you.

h   k

Deb: Hi Fran:

I'm pretty sure there's another one. He made himself known tonight. I woke up and it was very hot in the room. I got up and the heat was turned all the way up. I didn't do it and Billy says he didn't and he wouldn't lie about that. This guy was either formed by the trauma I felt last night or came out of my chest because of the trauma last night. My chest still hurts, not as bad as it did, but it still hurts, and it's 3:30 a.m. right now.

I'm not scared. Neither is Billy. I'm pissed off though. I'm just really tired of feeling either emotional or physical pain. And for this one, apparently I'm not awake nor Billy when he's out. I don't WANT any more and I'm wondering if I'll break.

Anyway, there it is.

Fran: Dear Debra,

I know this is hard but I have suspected this particularly since your body has continued to hurt with our interventions. Remember that this part probably has taken so much for you and I suspect the physical pain also. We will work it out and it is good to know about this one as your recovery will go much better. I am so proud of you all!! You are so motivated to get well as demonstrated by last night!

Love, Fran

Billy: Hi Daddy!

Boy oh boy it sure is rough! I got it into my head that you were gonna throw us away even though both me and Deb's been good. But Deb talked to Ian Bruch and discovered that it's cause of tomorrow and stuff and meeting with Fran and then the breath person and knowing we'll be under the bricks. My anxiety level went too high Daddy and this morning we had a really bad nose bleed and stuff. Deb made an appointment next week with the doctor to get the nose burnt up again. It took over an hour to quit bleeding. Don't feel too good right now but we'll be okay I think. Just thinking about tomorrow and I just wanna die. So will you please pray for me and stuff for tomorrow and the bricks and stuff?

Hope you're okay Daddy and that you're having a really good day. Okay bye.

h k

Bruce: Billy and Deb,

I am home with a cold today but I am OK. I will pray for you tomorrow as you go through this next breathing experience. Hopefully you will come away from this experience feeling some release. Trust God, trust Fran, and try to let go of the anxiety.

h k

Fran's Notes: A part emerged – a child – sad. She held on to the alligator. She didn't know me or Debra or Billy. Her chest hurt her. She is four years old. "Are you going to punish me?" I told her I don't punish kids. "That's what everyone does to me. You're not going to hit me? I'm not supposed to live. Am I going to stop hurting? Am I going to die? I want to die." I explained about the present day, safety, and that she deserves to be loved.

Billy: Hi Daddy!

Everything's okay here. Are you still sick? Boy, I sure hope it's not that cold flu that I had!

Yesterday was okay and it helped. Fran brought out the other one and I got to name her and stuff. She's four and I named her Alex for Alexandria but it's Alex cause she's a tomboy and stuff. She came out of ME Daddy. Fran said that it made perfect sense to her and stuff. Alex helped me take the physical pain and stuff and she does just what I do and stuff. She took the chest Daddy and took the barbed wire and the bricks. So you already know her story and she's just like me Daddy and I think she's why I was kinda a girl sometimes which was really weird. She was really really scared cause she didn't know what was going on. But now that she's out, then she's not so scared. And I'm not so scared either and neither is Deb just cause she's not so scared. Fran said that nobody was gonna hurt her and the monster is dead now and Deb can handle Eleena. Deb thinks she might not last too long cause maybe she doesn't have to like Annamarie and Lucus didn't. Don't know yet though. But, boy, I'm pretty tied to her. And boy my anxiety sure went down once Alex wasn't so scared!

Fran didn't want to wait for two weeks, so we're going back this Thursday. The breath person has told Fran how to help us, so that's really good.

The breathing helped and stuff. Anyway Dad, that's it and it's Friday and I want to play some this weekend. So everything's okay.

okay bye

love you Daddy!!! Hope you feel better soon, sooner than soon.

h k

Bruce: Billy,

Glad you had a good experience and welcome to Alex. Alexandria is a regal name - good choice Billy. Alex is a great name. Glad she came out to Fran and that things are progressing. Also glad to hear the anxiety is coming down. Nothing to fear. Have a good weekend.

H K

Chapter Ten

Subconscious Level 8: Alexandria (4) and Adama (15) Wake Up; Billy ages from 7 to 10

I do not know what caused the layers of my subconscious to wake as I went through this healing process. But imagery became more and more distinct and important as a way to understand and communicate. Progressive changes in imagery indicated changes in the structure of my subconscious, from one formed by the trauma to one responding to released trauma and experiencing life without it.

I was very careful about the imagery. It had to me mine without any kind of suggestion. Neither did I search for imagery, but just let it happen. I wanted to be healed, not to pretend to be healed.

Alex and Adama were not out very much and they both quickly integrated into Deb. Both were associated with Laura's trauma. I don't know why they did not wake when Laura woke, but I dissociated into several parts when my parents offered me as part of the first satanic-type of ritual.

*****

Fran's Notes: Alex is four years old and gets happier all the time. She held a lot of the fear she experienced all her life. Alex and Billy don't have anger.

Deb: I'm progressing pretty well. NOTHING happens by chance, and my therapist wanted me to go to a breathing workshop a week ago Friday, which I did. There was a breathing specialist in Marquette then. I went, and Fran (therapist) suggested I have a private session with her, so I did that last Thursday right after my therapy session.

What it did was to open up my chest. The trauma has kept me unable to breathe properly. And it hurt pretty much. I was able to open up the top front part, my sternum. The breathing therapist will leave town, but has told Fran what to do to help me along.

Things are physical now. I have to deal with the physical hurt that the body has kept all these years. I feel pretty good about it. My right arm and shoulder is coming along too. I can raise my arm over my head now.

Alex: hi daddy

i was gonna write an stuff cause i can now and stuff. they say your nice, billy says nice and strict! the lady yesterday said that nobodys gonna hurt me any more. the other lady was okay but i didn't come out and stuff. i feel pretty safe and stuff and billy says thats you too. i think so too unless your gonna throw me away. billy says i gotta hurt so i will feel better. thats stupid. with the breath lady the body quit breathing on its own and deb said the body wants to die. but a man was next to me that i could see and stuff and he told me to breathe on purpose. so i did. the lady said that when i was knowing the hurt i guess a long time ago the body wanted to die then and thats why. okay. can i just be with billy? is that okay? he says okay. so can I? okay.

Bruce: Alex, Welcome to the second-life where you are safe and you are with good people. Yes, it is OK to be with Billy. And keep breathing. That is important, because you are important and we need you to be with us. So we are glad you are here and everyone will help you and keep you safe.

Billy: Hi Dad!

Gee, with Alex coming out I think I bumped up to like 10, maybe older! Coooolllll!!

So for taking care of Alex and maybe taking out the trash which means picking up the house and stuff, can I have $5 a week? I like money, Dad. I like how we save, too, Dad. Just to let you know.

I think I can get the snow tube this weekend. Yay!

I think Alex should have the sticky feet as a chore. That's something girls should do instead of boys anyway. I know she's only 4 but she can type and spell and read and everything so I think she can do that if she'd just take her thumb out of her mouth.

Hope you're okay!

h k

Bruce: Billy, How do you "Maybe" take out the trash? Are you brushing your teeth twice a day? Are you doing the dishes twice a week? Thanks for taking care of Alex. 10 years old? Cool! I am feeling a lot better. Thanks.

h k

Alex: hi daddy! when i'm in bed i got angels poking me. it tickles. my feet itch too! i got grandfather now and stuff and i am with him a whole lot. i got scoobeedoo too. sometimes i get scared cause there is people and stuff. i am not a whole lot scared though. do you get scared and stuff? okay. do you kiss people like grandfather does? like regular people? and carry them around too? okay.

Bruce: Hi Alex,

I am glad the angels are tickling you and making you laugh. I get scared sometimes but not very often. I am also glad grandfather is there to hug and kiss you and snuggle with you. You can sit on my lap and put your head on my chest and talk to me if you wish.

Hug kiss

Billy: Hi Daddy.

Boy, I sure was wrong about the process getting harder cause of Alex! She lies there and Grandfather's there and angels are working on her. You know the holes made by the barbed wire? The angels are healing that up in her too. Sometimes Grandfather goes and talks to people. I don't know who. For a change we don't have to do it.

But Alex is getting happier all the time Dad. And me and Deb find that we're happier too!

I just got my nose burnt this morning. It hurts but maybe it'll stop the nosebleeds. okay bye

h k

Alex: hi daddy it's me alex. i can't put my head on your chest right now cause i gotta lie down and stuff and angels take stuff out of me. how come i can come out and see and still lie down in the other world? but is it okay? i dont know what they are doing but it makes me want to throw up like right now when i am here. my nose hurts. i think i dont want to be here right now cause my nose hurts and i want to throw up. okay?

i hug and kiss you to. grandfather taught me how. okay?

Bruce: Alex, You are Okay!! The angels are helping you and your nose will feel better tomorrow.

Hug kiss

Fran's Notes: Billy and Alex are tied to the body. Deb has quite a lot of pain.

Deb: Hi Dad. Going through a rough patch now. Billy or I just touch a place in the body and it's like "beam me up" to the first-life and I can see and feel the torture etc. Billy hasn't been helping Dad. The game is fine, but this money stuff is what he's more focused on. He starts hounding me on Friday for his allowance until he gets it. Looked for a snow tube and they're out so he got mad AT ME and I told him he was a spoiled brat who thinks he's entitled. I'm sorry. I'm really very very tired and Grandfather had me take a bath tonight and I just want to cry all the time. To be fair, he apologized to me Dad and offered to buy me dinner with his allowance. He did feel bad. My first thought was that he didn't have enough money for dinner for two. GEEZ!!! He's just so thoughtless Dad and self-absorbed. Nils without the sensitivity. Maybe that's his age and maybe he's just avoiding all this hurt that seems to be all the time, physical and emotional.

Okay, off to bed. Take care.

*** hug *** *** kiss ***

Bruce: Hi Deb, Welcome to the world of a 10 year old. In my world when a child hounds me for his allowance that puts off receiving the allowance for at least a day. If the hounding continues I would add another day. And you lost your temper with him; that is normal and he showed remorse, which is excellent. So, your relationship is fairly normal you just have to put your foot down on the hounding issue. Billy has never been punished by me yet, but this is leading to his first punishment if he doesn't change his attitude - quickly. Have a good week.

*****

The "somebody" or "other guy" is Adama coming to the surface. Very often, all the parts of me were afraid of a new part awakening. We felt the anger and desperation of the part coming to the surface and feared the person would harm other people.

*****

Fran's Notes: Billy is having difficulty moving his arm. He did breathing and raised his right arm and he was able to stretch it back. He had a sore knot on his arm and I had him breathe. I worked with him on focusing on the sore knot and his breathing and massaged his knot, his arm and the tendon and his wrist. I added relax, release, safe now. The one knot went away and the tendon eased and he was able to move his arm better.

Billy: Hi Daddy

Grandfather won't let me see the movie *The Rite* and I think that just blows.

I think that sometimes Grandfather sings the Blues: "Iiiiiiiii ain't got no booooody!" hahahahaha

I did all my chores and stuff. I feel pretty sick though Daddy. But Grandfather let me have some sherbet this last weekend. Deb says I got all the toys and stuff that I need. Skis and snowshoes and stuff. It was too cold this weekend Dad. Deb got all worried that she's getting old, or the body is, and stuff cause she thought, man, I can't take this cold.

THEN she went inside and found out it was 9 degrees and realized that it actually WAS too cold! hahahahaha

You going out of town? We gotta go to the therapist again. Maybe Fran can help with all this stuff, huh.

I got four cities now in the game. Cool, huh? The leadership gave me tools to make it like auto build and it's doing it now.

Okay, have a great day, Dad!

h k

Bruce: Billy,

I think you are being disrespectful to Grandfather and if I were you I might change my language in a hurry or you won't be playing any games for a few days. Your attitude towards Grandfather and towards Deb on Friday is unacceptable.

Billy: okay

gee whiz

*****

    Soon after Alexandria awakened, Adama did also. He woke as a fourteen year old. At this time, he had no name.

*****

Deb: Hi Dad!

Well, things have changed a little. The other person is fully formed and angels are with him. Looks like they're just there and supervising him. He's not doing anything. I don't think the angels will let him. He's very unhappy and somewhat confused.

Alex is with Grandfather and she's holding his hand. There was a time when she saw other kids playing on what looks like a jungle gym. She let go and started to run toward it, but Grandfather called her back but then let her go play. Something about needing to ask or tell before she runs off. I don't know for sure.

But after a while, Alex walked up to the guy. Grandfather told her to get away from him, but she turned around, looked at Grandfather and said, "It's okay Grandfather. He's me." That stunned Grandfather a little. I think it's difficult for him to remember that he's dealing with pieces, mainly because we're all truly separated in the spiritual form until the pieces integrate. Alex then went up to the guy and told him that he didn't hurt her, other people did. I think all this is self-love, which is new Dad. He said something like he should hurt her but Alex wasn't afraid of him at all. She just said that no, he doesn't really want to hurt anybody. He said that he has to survive and to survive means to kill so nobody will hurt him. But Alex said no that that's the first-life and now it's the second-life. He didn't understand. He can't seem to understand a life different from what he was taught when he was hurt.

And THEN my two dogs went up to Alex. Pippin wagged his tail and slowly went up to the guy and just leaned on him. He touched Pippin but didn't hurt him. All this seems new to him. I've seen Pippin minister to people in this life that way and I'm proud of him.

Both dogs then bounded over to me and I had a good time for a little. Unfortunately I was driving at the time. :)

Alex seems to accept this guy. That's more than I do. Right now I don't want to have anything to do with him. I know I'm in denial. But I'm not so sure that he'll kill Fran any more. For one thing, I don't think the angels will let him. I'm even reluctant to let anybody name him.

My body's on fire. Got a rash now in places. Same points in my body that's little balls and painful. Headache. Last week I had a nose bleed every day after it was cauterized. Sunday I had four nose bleeds. None yesterday or today. Nausea and some throwing up. Fatigue. Gad.

Anyway, that's what's going on. Hope you've dug yourself out by now!

*** hug *** *** kiss ***

*****

The trauma throughout my first-life childhood embedded poison in my body as little crystals. Tiny points within my tissue held the crystals and did not move, so when they were released the tissue holding them could again move. This resulted in a constant soreness wherever the crystals were being released as those points of tissue could move for the first time since the trauma happened.

The poison expelled different ways. Most of the time the poison came up through my skin and that resulted in a rash of itchy bumps. Waking up and seeing a necklace of bumps around my neck scared me quite a bit, but I knew it was connected to the times I was hanged. Many bumps concentrated around my ankles and wrists, but basically they were all over my body. Other ways the poison expelled were by vomiting, bleeding, pustules, and my excrement colored green.

When Billy awakened, the trauma poison began to expel, but when Alex and Adama awakened, the poison flowed out. This lasted several years but the intensity of the poison coming out of my body decreased over time. It reduced my immune system so I was rather sick all of the time, and I had a difficult time feeling well.

*****

Deb: The rash is still there but not so bad and not so itchy. Nice little necklace of bumps!

I can tell that little things have changed. I'm caring more about my body. Of course, I can't know or comprehend what I don't, so don't even know that I don't know. (Got that?) But I'm more tuned into that kind of care. Since yesterday and what happened at the therapist's, my body doesn't hurt as much. What really gets me is that this little 4 year old of me, Alex, who's busy playing in the spiritual realm knew what to do. She told Fran to just touch me where I hurt like the wrists, chest, ankles, legs. Fran thought to massage, but Alex said no, to just touch. When Fran touched me, she said that I was very hot. I didn't FEEL hot to me though, but the body was really hot. Where Fran touched me and just held her hands there, I could literally feel poison be released and go into the air. I asked Fran if she felt anything and she said no. Especially the bottoms of my feet tingled. And since then, the pain is nearly gone where she touched me. I've been in pain for weeks! I talked to Susan yesterday and she said that that's a technique by people to help heal. Man, I had no idea!! I never even heard of it! But for Alex to know, that was a miracle!

I feel a need to go through some physical self-therapy. This is truly strange!

Adama: Grandfather says that I'm supposed to live my life to honor you, him, and God. I asked him about God and he said that God is my creator and I live in the first place because of God. I question why that should be something to celebrate. But, then, this second-life is an alien world to me. I just feel like I need to hurt the mean people around me to stop them from hurting Deb.

But I won't hurt anybody. To honor you. And Grandfather. I don't get it. But like you and the lady says, it takes time I guess.

I've noticed that knowledge to me comes when I direct my thoughts toward certain things. Boy, these angels are pretty intimidating. They're about 7 to 8 feet tall and mostly light. They're both male and female in them.

Okay, Deb's coming out. See ya.

Deb: I kept having this dream. I was hiking down a trail in the woods when I'd come across this little white dog. He was sick and cold and hurting and dirty. I picked him up and told him that he's mine now and tried to help him get warm. I said, "You will be loved for the rest of your life." Night before last, the same dream, except that at the end after I said that, all of a sudden I was standing before God. And God said to me, "You will be loved for the rest of your life." Wow

Went to therapy yesterday and she did her technique, the thing that literally connects my brain together. Part of that is imaging and I saw this huge wall and boy I sure didn't know what to do about it. I knew that the wall was the right side of my chest. But I thought nothing happened. Except I didn't drive too far when I had to get to sleep, so I stopped and did that. Afterwards, the wall image came back, but it has sprung a leak. I guess the wall's a dam. So something DID happen, just a little delayed.

Tonight I can't sleep except for nightmares of being kicked. Also hung up by my wrists and being used like a punching bag. And it's always ended in sodomy. So something's about ready to break out. I'm really dreading it! Really. Not sleeping doesn't help me any.

You know, being hugged, being touched, used to hurt. Shoot, I don't remember ANY time my first-life parents touch me without them hurting me. It doesn't hurt anymore, you know. But I don't feel anything either. Fran asked me if I felt anything when SHE hugs me and I said no. I've been pretty ashamed of this.

Well, it's 4:30 a.m. now and I'd better get back to bed.

Billy: Daddy, I AIN'T GONNA do it! Screw responsibility! I hate everything and just everything and stuff.

*** goes to room, opens the door *** *** SLAMSLAMSLAMSLAM ***

Bruce: Think about what you just sent me and rewrite your e-mail in words that explain your feelings instead of a rant.

Billy: Can I put my head on your chest and stuff to do it?

Bruce: Yep!

Billy: I hurt like physically and stuff all the time Dad. Sometimes the right side of me hurts a whole lot. And when I do the exercise stuff it really hurts. The right side of me is lots weaker cause of the pain and stuff. And then there's the bumps and itch. And sometimes it isn't bumps but there's still an itch. And sometimes it just drives me crazy. They come and go but they're still coming and stuff and sometimes it's like I feel lots and lots of shame Daddy cause of where they are.

And all of it and I mean all of it makes me be in the first-life and I feel really really bad and really really sad and stuff. I can't do the magnet thing without being in the first-life. And sometimes I just can't hear Grandfather and you seem so far away Daddy. And I feel like I got too much pressure and stuff and I'll tell you people here hitting Deb sure doesn't help cause I have problems knowing the difference between the first-life and the second-life. And I feel like everything's my fault you know? And like I'm not supposed to be alive and stuff. And I feel really really alone.

So I don't wanna do this anymore and I want it to go away Daddy. And that's how I feel.

Am I in trouble now?

Bruce: Billy,

No, you are not in trouble at all. You are dealing with a lot of difficult stuff that you do not seem to have a lot of control over - i.e. the rash, the pain, being thrown back into the first-life. So, I realize this is very hard work, and that it hurts to exercise and to move around the right side. I also know that when you feel this way you can feel alone and sad.

I have felt this way as a child. I have had to learn to walk 3 or 4 times and I have gone through physical therapy that was painful to regain mobility of my arm and legs. I was not with my parents. I was in a hospital that did not allow parents on the floor. So, I did not receive any hugs and kisses from my parents. But the idea that kept me going was that I would be better than I have been and that I will be pain free, and I will not have to wear braces anymore. So, I kept working at it even though it hurt.

And you will be better, and Deb will be better when you get through all this stuff you are going through. There are brighter days ahead. So leave your head on my chest as long as you wish and I hope you feel better, less afraid, less worried, less anxious.

h   k

Billy: Hi Daddy!

I guess it's going to take a while to not be sad anymore, huh?

Is it okay that I think it's really cool that I'm going through the same kind of thing you did when you were my age? I'm not saying that I think it was good. But it's cool that it's something we share. Do you think that maybe God gave me to you partly cause of this? I think maybe so.

Gee, Dad, I'm afraid that I've leaked so badly into Deb that she can't quit crying too. Boy, despair is really nasty stuff, huh Dad?

I just don't know that I'll get better Dad. I think that maybe this will be my life.

I didn't exercise though Daddy. I just can't face stuff, you know? Am I in trouble for that now? And Deb just can't wake up these days without the caffeine so we're not doing too good. We don't sleep and when we do it's nightmares.

okay bye

Bruce: Deb and Billy, Are you seeing Fran this week? If you are in despair then you need to call Fran.

Billy: Yeah.

Fran's Notes: Last week Deb was suicidal. Billy couldn't quit crying and it leaked into her. Billy was acting up, refusing to exercise. The right side of her body flared up and her whole body felt despair. Billy was back to the first-life. Deb internalized and self-blamed for what happened as a child.

Deb: Hi Dad!

> I'm feeling better. My emotions are steady. I'm not anxious at all. What a blessing!
>
> Last night I went to bed and Grandfather kissed me good night and I just started to cry. So he sat on the bed and asked me what's wrong. I asked him if I was ever going to heal and leave the first-life behind and he said yes if I just keep working at it. He put my head on his chest and hugged me and he felt warm to me. He wears a flannel shirt Dad and I could even smell him!
>
> An angel came and stuck his hand into my chest. The same right side, except toward the center a little more. It hurt physically but not very bad really. I let myself down from Grandfather and lay still so the angel could do it easier.
>
> I've been having a constant vision of a wall that's sprung a leak, so there's water behind the wall. Well, when the angel did that, the wall totally broke and water came gushing out. It was dirty water, sometimes black like brackish, and sometimes red with my blood. With it gushing out, I saw within it all the images I know of the first-life. But coming with it, but not in the water, came images of my second-life childhood. It's still gushing.
>
> The left side of my face, like my sinuses, had a headache again and something seems to want to happen there too. It feels like something's about to break. And that hurts.
>
> I went to sleep, but my dreams weren't good. I dreamed of a man and a woman. Both were trying to kill me. She was helping him. I know they were first-life parents, even though they looked different. But I had a hand on him and was trying to kill him too and trying to get her off of me. Others came and he said that he was going to tell them that I was trying to kill him and to help him. That's when I woke up.

Sooo, things are happening. I'm having a lot of trouble breathing today. I try to take deep breaths, but so far it hasn't changed. I DID exercise this morning and it hurt, but, again, not bad. My chest hurts where the angel put his hand in. It's strange that it's a little different place than before.

Anyway, there it is. Have a great day, Dad. Drive carefully and have a good week!

hug ***kiss***

Bruce: Deb,

It sounds like there is movement in the healing process with the work of the angel and the reassurance of Grandfather. It is a looooooooooong haul but you are getting there. Just not being anxious is a terrific feeling. I hope your dreams are better tonight. Take care and have a good week.

*****

The imagery of a dam breaking from me carried into therapy. Adama experienced the imagery of seeing the silhouette of a man far away. Both the man and Adama were standing in a long valley. One end of the valley was the dam that had broken.

*****

Adama: Hi Fran.

This time, the experience didn't end when time was up. The "man" wasn't another personality, but a part of me, the consequences of the first-life. It was made out of what looked like oil, but it was poison and corruption. The wall had broken, putrid water was gushing through it, it was emptying into a valley that felt like a cemetery to me, and this black man thing was standing in the middle of the lake that was full of the first-life.

I asked him what he wanted and he said that he wanted to be loved. Then he walked toward the broken dam and the rest of the putrid water surged behind him as he walked. He walked into the valley/cemetery and told me that it was time for him to die and to go back into the earth where he belonged. He looked at me. The water then went over him, flattened out, and then went into the earth. He was gone, just gone into the earth. A part of me died today. It was like the experience of being with my dogs when they died. The grief is just BIG! I know that I'm supposed to be happy, but I just feel the loss right now. And we're all scared out of our collective mind.

But it didn't end there. I looked at where the lake used to be and that was just earth too. But things like trees started to grow. Grandfather and the others came and an angel also came and took us down into the valley where he died. Billy kept wanting Grandfather to come, but he didn't. Finally Grandfather told him that he can't go down there because what's there is me, but he can watch. The earth was dry by then and Alex played in it a little. The angel came to me and all of a sudden a flower grew out of my chest, my heart. I pulled it out and gave it to the angel. Over and over this happened and soon a bunch of flowers grew out of me. I was crying and crying (for real) and the angel put his finger on my mouth. He wanted me to just experience. But what came into my mind was, "You have to lose yourself to find yourself." The angel took the flowers and threw them up into the air and they turned into both birds and rain. When the rain hit the earth near us, it started fire. So we're all standing in the valley with an angel with it raining and surrounded by fire. And that's where it's at now.

I guess it's human nature to want to hold on to what you know. None of us knows what's going to happen and we all feel completely vulnerable and pretty scared, mainly because it's the unknown we've entered. None of us know who we are, but the stuff that's kept us from experiencing who we are is gone. The stuff that has blocked us all from the rest of the world is dead. Unfortunately, it's what we know, it's what we know. And now it's gone. We're clueless right now. But, hey, we're standing on top of it all, it's transforming, and we're about to catch fire, an angel is here, but what's not normal?!

take care,

Fran: Dear Adama,

What an amazing experience you have had and to know that flowers are coming from it is wonderful. I think what you said about death and rebirth is so true. Take care and know you are cared for deeply by many, including me!

Deb: Hi Dad!

We're all okay here. I'm having problems comprehending the Beloved book. I read it but I can't remember what I just read. So it's going to take me longer than I thought. I suspect that as this crap comes out of me that it will become easier. When I read the beginning of it, man, I felt it was really me. But after getting into it, (I'm in Taken,) I can't comprehend it. And so I'll keep trying and I'll probably read it several times eventually.

Bruce: Deb,

The idea of "taken" is that you are "chosen" by God, by Jesus to be his disciple. In the book of John 15:16 Jesus says, "you did not choose me but I chose you." Ponder that scripture and see if it speaks to you.

Deb: Okay, I can accept that I'm chosen by God. And now I remember reading that even though I'm chosen and that makes me special, nobody else has to feel bad for themselves because there's a miracle in it about God's choosing. I guess I feel I have a place. How's that? Can't quite get why me though.

Oh geez, Billy's banging on my head to come out. Bye!! Have a great day!!!

Bruce: Spend more time with the scripture. Read John 15:12-17

Deb: Okay. I'll do that just as soon as I get home. Thank you Dad.

Billy: Hi Daddy!

So did God choose me too? Can God choose two people in one body and stuff? Am I good for anything? I mean to God and stuff?

Bruce: ABSOLUTELY!! You are chosen and stuff :>) You are good!

Alex: HI DADDY! IT'S ME, ALEX. I GOTTA SHOUT CAUSE I'M OVER HERE AND YOUR OVER THERE! HAHAHAHAHA LOTS OF KIDS TO PLAY WITH HERE AND I GOT DOLLS AND EVERYTHING AND A PLAYGROUND AND ALL SORTS OF STUFF. I PLAY WITH DOLLS NOW. IS THAT OKAY??? AND I GOT FRIENDS HERE NOW AND JUST EVERYTHING!!!!

I LOVE MY DADDY AND I DRAW PICTURES WITH YOU AND GRANDFATHER HOLDING MY HANDS AND STUFF. AND THEN I DRAW PIPPIN AND FRODO TOO RIGHT BY US AND STUFF CAUSE THEY'RE HERE TOO AND THEY SOMETIMES HIT MY FACE WITH THEIR TAILS AND STUFF.

AND GRANDFATHER SAYS I GOTTA GO TO BED AT NIGHT AND STUFF AND I'M JUST NOT SCARED OF THE DARK OR WHEN IT'S LIGHT OUT ANY MORE LIKE IN THE FIRST-LIFE!! YAY!!!!!

BYE DADDY!!!

HHHHHH   KKKKKKKK

Bruce: Alex,

I am glad you have lots of friends and toys to play with. And I am really glad that you are not afraid!!

hhh kkk

Deb: Hi Dad!

Last night Susan did her long-distance reiki thing. I didn't feel anything physically but slowly my despair lifted and then Billy's did. So we've got some relief for a while. What got much worse, of course, are the itchy bumps. They popped up on my neck, LEFT arm, and tops and bottoms of my feet and ankles. Interesting, ain't it?

Have a great day!

hug ***kiss***

Bruce: Deb,

Interesting and frustrating I would imagine. The energy work (reiki) is really a mystery but it does work. I am happy for you that the despair has lifted some. Have a good day.

Fran's Notes: Billy came out and talked about his despair. He's lonely and he's supposed to learn to have fun. He dreams about getting out but there is a big wall. The wall represents laziness maybe. We'll continue to process his self-esteem.

Chapter Eleven
Subconscious Level 9: Angela (8) Wakes Up
Angela ages 8 to 13 and Billy 10 to 11

I think that, as Hamlet would say, there's more to life in heaven and earth than what lies within my philosophy. By way of my studies of The Dreaming, I have opened the possibility of other perceptions for myself. The Dreaming is the ancient Australian Aborigine's culture and spirituality. The ancient Australian Aborigine saw time as holistic. They did not differentiate between conscious and unconscious or time advancing. Past, present, and future reside in the conscious/unconscious as a non-empirical perception.

For instance, when a person looks at a tree, the person perceives the tree in natural time but also its seedling and the tree's older state. To live in the present and to experience the reality of the moment is also to experience the past and the future as part of that reality. Everything experienced in the present is also experienced in the past and future, and, conversely, everything experienced in the past and future is also experienced in the present.

It seems to me that a person's potential lies all along that continuum of holistic time. But along the continuum, potential holds different shapes on the same path. I had never experienced the relationship amongst the past, the present, the subconscious, and the body until this healing process. The trauma of the past resides within my own body as well as affecting my subconscious. The relivings brought the past violently to consciousness (and therefore to the present) and, in time, my subconscious was able to release the past not only from my subconscious but also from my body.

At this point, the past experiences of sustained trauma reveal themselves as present experiences. Releasing the trauma now through the body and the subconscious imagery forms a shape of future potential.

The understanding of self to an ultimate otherness is as diverse as there are persons. For me, to perceive the Other Realm is to perceive the invisible in and around tangible objects of the here and now AND separate from tangible objects. So sometimes the Other Realm is sitting next to me, and sometimes the parts of me reside in an Other Realm that seems to have a separate space.

*****

Deb: Hi Dad!

I yo-yo between "oh no, this is terrible" to "okay, this is terrible but it'll be okay." I'm kind of a wreck but I know it can't last. We'll see when the despair gets loose, which has to happen. Pretty sure Susan is doing her reiki thing because I itch all over now even when I'm trying to be physically silent. Physically I'm not doing too good, but I just CAN'T handle the despair AND do the physical!

Good grief Dad! I can even SEE red marks around my wrists! Okay, to be honest with you, I'm pretty scared. I'm going downstate partly so that I can be AROUND people.

I see Fran today.

Daddy, I really do feel a need to visit the Bruchs this summer. He has decided to not take the chemo anymore, and the cancer is throughout his body now. I'm aware that he'll live as long as God wants him to, but I hope you understand my need to go down. When he gets bad, I probably won't because I don't think his family would appreciate it much, and I think it needs to be about them. So now's the time I think.

Okay, I'd better go. You take care, Dad!

*** hug *** *** kiss ***

Bruce: Deb,

You go and see Ian Bruch. It is important for you and for him.

Try to keep your emotions on an even level. Being down at Park of the Pines will be good for you. Just getting away can be healthy.

In terms of the red marks I hope they improve soon.

Safe travels today.

Billy: Hi Daddy. I got a cold. I don't feel too good. Can I put my head on your chest Daddy?

I woke up about midnight and an angel was here. He started doing something to my body Daddy and right when he started I got a tummy ache. Lasted about two hours. Don't have one now though. Don't feel too good. It's cold here. I got too cold yesterday. But we got stuff to do. So that's good. Okay bye.

H. K.

Bruce: Yep, you can put your head on my chest. Hope you feel better and stay warm.

h   k

*****

During the first-life, I was punished for crying. I was punished mildly for being sick, but mostly my parents left me alone when I was sick. When I was ill it was inconvenient for them.

*****

Fran's Notes: Deb heard this voice, "Liar, Liar, Liar." Adama seems to connect that there is another part. Deb is feeling a lot of despair and anxiety. She wants to cry all the time and Billy wants to act up. Right now Deb wants to cry and feels like a victim. This voice said it's all true and that Deb deserved it.

Deb thinks this part is around 12 to 13 years old and cries all the time at night.

Deb said it came out of her body and it's Angela. She feels despair, suicidal thoughts. Angela is 7 or 8 years old. We started the buzzies and Angela came out. She would rock back and forth and appeared scared initially. I gave her a stuffed bear to hold and paper and markers to write and draw. She communicated with me after her fear that she'll die if she talks to me and she's supposed to hurt herself. I worked with her on these erroneous beliefs and helped her see that she is safe now, the monster is dead, etc. She felt much better at the end of the session. I suggested an internal play room for her and Alex to play and she was happy.

Angela: Hi Dad

I'm supposed to be out. Fran says it's okay for me to cry. But she says I don't think right and I'm afraid to cry cause I'm not supposed to but I'm supposed to now. It's hard for me to cry. I had a nightmare Dad. A boy was tortured and killed. The angels are here and I am supposed to go back to the first-life. Adama tried to protect me and say no to me coming out but Grandfather told him no.

I have to be hurt again huh? Dad can I have ice cream after every time? Can I look forward to that? I sure don't know how I know that you're my dad but I sure do. I felt Fran's hand and it was soft and when she touched me it felt good. She said that people are supposed to touch each other like that.

I'm supposed to see it like a movie and control the speed. And when the movie runs to get away so the body can quit the first-life and come in to the second-life. Image stuff to get away and to tell the monsters to stop it. Am I supposed to make it happen or is it supposed to just happen and I'm supposed to let it happen? Am I supposed to make it happen?

Do I get hug and kiss too? I think that feels good but I don't know. Okay bye.

Bruce: Angela,

A lot of your questions about movie and speed control are "Fran" questions. The "ice cream" question is a question I can answer, but the answer would be "no" for now. You may get a "treat" along the way but we will wait and see. I know you may be scared but that is normal. You will be O.K.

h   k

Angela: Dad can I cry? Is it okay for me to cry now? The monster said I couldn't cry and I know I pushed stuff down so I didn't feel enough to cry. I can almost be in the first-life but I gotta feel to do that. I know it's my job but I have Garfield here to help me not be afraid. Angels are here Dad.

H. K.

Bruce: Yes you can cry.

Deb: I know this sounds strange but there's been angels here working on my body. Day before yesterday I watched an episode of Bones and it was about a girl who was tortured by her parents and it showed up in her bones. I'm wondering if the angels are fixing some of my bones. Susan does reiki on me and says there's something about my bones and lungs. I do know that God wants me totally healed. The other night an angel put his hand inside of me around the chest area and I immediately became nauseous. Man this whole process sure is strange.

Fran's Notes: The major thing is she's having a lot of body memories and felt it today. Angela has the pain inside. With the pain, the despair comes.

Angela: Hi Dad. I'm trying to be out. Blew leaves today. But gee I danced a little. I wore earphones and listened to music while I blew leaves. I've been dreaming of dancing Dad. And I did it a little. Cool huh? Boy I sure do wish the body wasn't so sore. Okay bye.

H. K.

Bruce: Keep dancing!!

h k

Angela: Hi! I'm okay. I talked to Fran yesterday and she helped me know what to do and I did one with her and everything. Adama had an image and it's now like mine. An angel is behind me and he has his arms around me. I'm in a valley and the ground in the valley is black like burnt. It's raining and when the rain hits the earth it pops up little fires. And it hurts.

I did the reliving stuff with Fran and it was the bricks and I pushed off the bricks and told the monster that he was bad to do that to me. After, a little bit of my front of chest felt better. But me and Fran talked about how much I gotta do and it's a whole lot Dad.

But after it was over I saw the valley again and there were little patches of green grass and the rain fire wasn't falling on those places any more. So God has made it so I will know when I'm done! I will be done when all of the valley is green and no more rain fire. Cool, huh?

Fran said I gotta make it happen. I gotta concentrate and stuff. I sure wish it didn't hurt so much though. Is that okay?

Boy it sure did lightning and stuff today. Grandfather made us stop blowing leaves. Okay I better go now.

I kiss your nose with my nose!

Billy: Daddy I broke my ankle. We are okay but I'm at the clinic right now. Geez!!! !!

Not fair! You get a birthday cake and I get a plaster cast! :)

Bruce: You're right, it isn't fair. Are you going to stay at Park of the Pines?

Billy: Hi Daddy. Yeah. Just gonna veg out here.

Bruce: Billy, Be patient with your ankle because it takes time for it to get better. If you put weight on it too early you can delay the healing and it may hurt more. Take care.

h   k

*****

Back home

*****

Fran's Notes: Deb talked about her trauma. "I'm supposed to hurt. He had fun." I talked with her about his abuse and cowardliness. She shook some.

Angela came out and said angels are doing something with her body. "Straighten things out a little bit. Angels are healing the bones. I'm being healed from the inside. Things are in place more. Things are lined up when angels do this. The angels are holding me so I don't do stuff that will hurt me." I practiced with her on her physically kicking and pushing him away and she told him to get away and he stopped. We finished the strategy to deal with her trauma and I encouraged her to continue to use this visualization on her own.

Deb: Hi Dad. Just got out of therapy session. Angela came out crying. And a lot. The broken ankle reminds her of how she felt in the first-life. He broke bones Dad. She thinks that when the angels come and do stuff in the body that they're healing the parts of the bone that were broken. Just when I think the first-life can't be any worse it's worse. He kicked me too hard Dad. So Fran helped her know the difference between then and now.

Going to Canada. Hope you have a good day!

Hug. Kiss.

Bruce: Deb,

Do not over-do it on the foot would be my advice. I think you are correct in that this is a time to allow Angela to do her work; another step in the healing process.

Take care –   O, Canada –

Alex: Daddy it's me Alex and stuff. I know stuff now but its not finished. *I was bad. I wanted mommy to tell me a story cause sally said her mommy did that and I wanted that too. And mommy got mad and I know her and some people around were happy after and I hurt. I rode my tricycle round and round and I wasn't supposed to be here.* Okay. Grandfathers got me and I got my head on your chest and stuff too and maybe the nightmare will go away. Huh. Okay bye im sleepy now Daddy. bye

Deb: Hi Dad!

The reliving for Alex happened last night as you know, but couldn't break through completely.   She broke through this morning and Grandfather immediately took her. She's four.

It was the same process as Philip to Scott Dad. I (as Laura) was taking it but then I broke and went to sleep and Alex took it.

They were drunk, Eleena, Walter A., and friends, and tied me to the table with barbed wire (my reliving). So I was on the table and in a lot of pain. But then I broke and Alex came out when they put something in my mouth so I couldn't cry or scream or breathe too well. It was an apple. They were drunk and happy. They placed candles all around me and threatened to burn me alive. They didn't burn me. But the experience was traumatic to a four year old, enough to break me. They said that I'd be their sacrifice. The fear was terrible.

I've always had this morbid fear of being burned. Not fire really, just being burned. And I won't be cremated when I die and now I know why. To me, burning is the worst thing that can happen to you.

It wasn't just Alex though who rode around in circles on my tricycle. I did. Alex went to sleep again like Scott did after the torture. I was trying to feel better without knowing why. I put away the dolls forever then too. I didn't ever want to have kids. I was four years old and all of a sudden full of fear. I've been afraid ever since Dad. No wonder Alex kept Adama inside her. Man, she's strong! So it seems to be the fear that Alex is supposed to process.

But nightmares kept coming and it was Alex who wanted Eleena to read to her and she was punished for wanting that. The one thing that stands out was that I was terrified and trying to make it go away. When Sally told me that her mother read her stories I thought that it might make me feel better and it turns out I've wanted that ever since! But the nightmares drove Alex to wake up and ask Eleena to read to her and then to be punished for it.

My change of behavior though scared Eleena enough to stop doing those things to me for a while. Of course, the damage was done. But I also think it opened the window for Walter Amundson to do what he did later on. Maybe once you let evil in, it's hard to get it out.

I'm okay. So is Alex. Grandfather's got her.

Billy: Hi Daddy. I broke a tooth and went to the dentist today and that's fixed.

Got itchy bumps all over my body I think cause of Alex's reliving. Deb told Fran so she called and we will go to therapy tomorrow. We are really deep into stuff now Daddy. I mean deep in the subconscious. That's what Fran said.

Despite what it all sounds like, everything's fine and stuff. I've been good.

H. K.

Deb: Miracles are continuing!! Fran's schedule was shut closed this week and suddenly opened up. Had two sessions with her yesterday and am going again tomorrow for another two. It seems to be a critical time. This stuff is coming from the very deep subconscious.

Dad since I can move my foot up and down okay for shifting can I ride my motorcycle now?

I hope you had a great time this past week.

Hug. Kiss.

Bruce: While speaking with Billy yesterday there was noticeable pain to touch on the ankle. So, for safety reasons I would say no motorcycle riding until the pain is completely gone and the swelling is also gone - for a long period of time - 5 days.

Sorry.

Billy: I'm just vegging today. Supposed to rain and stuff. I mowed the lawn yesterday and ran over a ball. A kid next door came and helped me pick it up and also two other boys riding their bikes came over too. We all talked for a little and they couldn't see that I was in an old body Daddy. God asked me after if I had some fun and I said yeah and he said happy birthday to me Dad! So getting to talk with kids my own age was God's birthday present to me. Isn't that totally excellent? I think so.

Deb: I'm glad that I took Eleena out to dinner.

I still get itchy bumps on my body, so poison is still coming out. But overall my body doesn't hurt as much. Yay! It's six weeks today that I broke my ankle and just staying off of it like I have these past two weeks seems to have helped its healing greatly. Billy's chomping on the bit wanting to go outside and play. I see the orthopedic Wednesday.

Okay, better go. Thanks Dad!

hug ***kiss***

Billy: You haven't hugged or kissed me for weeks and weeks Daddy. I'm sad about that. Seems like I just do stuff bad all the time and you just don't want to.

Bruce: WOW! It has been weeks and weeks.

H   K

Billy: Thanks Dad! Hk hk hk hk hk hk hk hk

Chapter Twelve

Subconscious Level 10: Joshua (14) Wakes Up

I call this a healing process. Everybody needs to be psychologically healed. Whether it's from grief or violence or addiction or regret or despair or illness or physical harm or hatred, everybody needs to be psychologically healed.

Perhaps healing is a progress toward reshaping potential. Without self-identity, I do not understand my potential. Future potential lies within its present shape, but that doesn't mean I know what mine is. Potential certainly is not a developed set of giftedness or talent. Perhaps potential is clarity of one's self-awareness in relationship-awareness with all life encounters. I think each person's spirit is more aware of future potential than the psyche.

My healing seems to be a simple path. Awaken the parts of me, get them out of the trauma, and integrate. But it's not really that simple. When the blind man was healed and could see he encountered a life with which he had no experience. And so it is with all who heal. And it's frightening. I'm directed to experience, but I have been healed enough now to have little comprehension of present experiences. The only thing I do know at this point is that healing is a sacred act of transformation.

During the ritual gang rape at four years old, I dissociated into several parts. Nearly each part landed in different levels of my subconscious. Joshua was four in real life, but when he awakened, he was fourteen years old. I have a strong feeling that Joshua connects the gang rape with the violence toward Kate. Kate resided deeper in the subconscious.

*****

Fran's Notes: Deb said there is another part. Last night, she became aware. Joshua is now 14 years old. His task is to focus on the body and he feels and focuses on the points where it hurts. Angela is integrated. Deb hasn't thought or felt her. "In a way, it feels like loss or dying."

Joshua: I don't know why I came out but I came out of little Alex. I went back into Alex but when the body was asleep I came out of Alex and I can live now. Since then Grandfather told me everything. The others named me Joshua. I don't know how old I am. When I came out I did not know who Fran was or where I was. There's no anger in me. The others told me to tell you that. It's difficult for me to trust but I like the woman Fran.

Grandfather says that you and he are my parents. Seems I've had my fill of that but the others say you're different, very different. Kindness is something I've never experienced. I found Grandfather to be kind. I liked it a lot.

When I woke I experienced quite a lot of physical pain throughout my body. Strange looking body I think.

I have had what the others called a reliving. Looks like I was formed when Alex went to sleep. *I was four years old and tied to the table with barbed wire. Fire all around me. I know there were four people. They took the wire off of me. And they took the wire out of me. They also took the fire away. I was their sacrifice. One then went on top of me and I now understand that I was gang raped by two men. One was Walter Amundson. They were heavy on top of me. But they also made it so I would not make noise. So while one was doing that a woman reached under him and choked me. This lasted quite a while as they were able to do it several times. One person was my mother.*

When I came out in Fran's office I had a hard time breathing and I hurt a lot around the neck and chest. And my private parts. Then I had the rest of the pain. I know I was hanged also and bricks and ropes and being hit and kicked.

I don't understand much really. I would like to know some kindness. I would like the pain to go away. Seeing the moon gives me comfort. I don't know why. I like the comfort. I don't know at least I don't think I know much comfort from people. I would like to experience some of that I think.

I think I was a little rude to the woman Fran but I did not understand what was going on or where I was. I regret that. I know now that she was trying to help me but I could not trust. My pain overwhelms me a little. I would like for the pain to go away.

Thank you for listening. Dad.

Bruce: Joshua,

Welcome to the second-life. There is no one in the second-life that will hurt you. You are safe. As you live in the second-life your trust level will rise to a point where you will be comfortable and you will trust those around you.

No worries about Fran. She is a very understanding and patient person. Just live without fear and you will realize that you are safe.

Deb: Hi Dad!

Everything's okay. Not ready to deal with Eleena yet though. Too much on my plate. Boy, it sure was interesting today!!

Fran told me to not worry about another one coming out. It will take as long as it takes. Joshua is connected to the body memory as well as what happened to Alex when I was four years old. So things are progressing!

Thanks Dad!

I was wondering if my imagination was just making things up. That would work for me except that when Joshua came out, I had a lot of physical pain. As Fran says, the body doesn't lie. I was also feeling down because of the length of this process and wondering if and when it was going to end. I'm grieving. So God said what he said today. I guess that a child's trauma created by parents can be profound.

I have a phone appointment with Fran a week from Friday. Joshua feels a lot of pain when he's out and I find that I do too when he's out. We must be pretty close together.

Billy: The body seems to be moving into the second-life Dad. We cry a lot Dad. It's like I enter the middle of my pain like Scott did and there's Joshua waiting and he's really sad. And he takes a bit of fire off of the wall and gives it to me. And he's a little more happy and I take it out and give it to the earth. And the earth takes it and the fire turns into a little piece of grass. It's cool and soft and happy Daddy.

H. K.

Joshua: I have to constantly remind myself that I am loved. Even when I feel so alone. This second-life is quite mysterious. I grieve though. Grandfather is kind to me and tells me that everything is okay and for me to experience life and to live. I don't know why I live though.

Shakespeare says that the moon is inconstant. But throughout my collective life, the moon has been the most constant person I know. And she has been a great comfort to me. If that is God then I've been cared about.

I woke up with an understanding:

When a little girl plays with a doll, she's really exploring herself. The doll is an extension of herself. She explores herself in relation to the world around her.

After the drunken ritual sacrifice, the barbed wire, fire, and rape, I put my doll in the stroller and put her in the closet and I never played with her again. I put myself in a dark place, in a closet. I hid myself. I was fractured. My mind was fractured. I was terrified of the very people who were in control of my life. I was alone. I rode my tricycle around in circles trying to feel better because nobody was there. I was four years old and I was afraid all the time.

Fractured Mind

When I faced Grandfather after I woke up, I asked him if I was correct. He cried. That's all. Just cried. I do too. I grieve. I suspect that most people don't really understand. I think he does. He is kind to me.

I had a vision of this healing process over twenty years ago. I'd always wondered about the barbed wire that lined both sides of the road. Now I know though. That barbed wire has kept me from going out and exploring the world, the meadows. I could walk down my road just fine but that is all. I have been in the dark of a closet.

I do not know at this point whether or not I can move past the barbed wire. I do know that I dream about it. But I don't know if I am able. If I can. I grieve about that too.

But maybe I've begun to. Yesterday evening I felt my body want and like what I was eating. I realized that I CAN eat healthy now. And my body is responding to that. I know that quite a few things have changed when it comes to knowing how to live like normal people do. And I'm grateful for that.

I sure don't know if I can realize what I dream about though - and that's about walking and meeting people and I even dream about being able to exercise. My dreams are about my body simply being able to do. And not wanting to fall asleep. I dream of being able to step out of the closet in a real, physical way. I see the door is now opened. I can do it with my mind - my writing. But can I do it with my body. I guess that's the challenge. I would like to be able to live in a physical sense before I die.

Bruce: Joshua,

Patience is one word that comes to me. Another word that comes is unfolding. The healing process is an unfolding process where God works with us through others and directly to bring about healing. The fact that you have dreams and visions of what could be, would be interpreted as healthy from my perspective. The unfolding/patience elements are realizing these dreams over a period of time – one step at a time.

Joshua: Thank you. Dad, when you say comes to mind, is that God helping you to know what to do and say and to understand? Are you in touch with God with all of this?

Bruce: This is based on my experience with God over time and what I have learned.

Fran's Notes: Deb hasn't gotten Alex a doll and is repulsed by it. She thinks it's stupid. We talked about the importance for Alex to have the doll.

Billy: Hi Dad! I'm running the tractor and mowing. The big Kubota! I'm really really careful cause there's a bucket in front too. But I'm doing it Daddy and it's really fun! Cool huh? Okay bye.

H. K.

Bruce: Very cool! Be careful, very careful.

H   k

Billy: Yes Dad! Yippie! I thought you were gonna tell me to let Deb do it!! I'll be very very careful. I'm going really slow.

Deb: Hi Dad!

I'm leaving today to go home.

Got called to go to God last night and this morning. I'm on the edge between survival and choices. He said that I now can make choices and to concentrate on consistency.

He said that even when living in the regular world or doing for church or anything else I'm not alone and that I do not and must not go back to surviving. He said that he is still here and you and Grandfather are parents even when I step into the world of choices. But now I can make choices.

He said for me to focus on the body. Not only eating and exercise, but to stop hating the body. Blaming it. He told me to do things to help it and as I focus on it, I will grow to understand and to care. He said that it's necessary for me to continue to enter the first-life so the body can enter the second-life. He understands that I don't want to but it must be done.

I must not return to survival mode. He said I've been trying to do that lately. He said that experience will teach me the difference between independence/choices and independence/survival. I really don't get it Dad. Not now anyway. He told me to ask for his help with anything. He also told me to quit trying to turn my back and walk away from you and Grandfather. He said that that's survival mode and that people don't do that when they grow up. He said I had to do that in the first-life but it is not expected of me now or at any time in the future. Oh. I thought it was Dad. Man. I sure don't get this.

He also told me to just let Billy do his thing. That I'm not his parent. And if he gets into trouble I am not to deal with it as that enters me back into survival mode. He also said to quit trying to control and hurry up this process. I will integrate in time.

He also said that he's pleased with me. That's it.

Well I'd better get up and hook up and go!

Hug. Kiss.

Fran's Notes: I read a lengthy email about her distorted perception that touch is bad, even healthy non-sexual, hugs, etc. She is in constant emotional pain and physical pain. We talked about working with the body on reframing the body's response to accept appropriate touch as comforting and to change negative perceptions.

Deb: Hi Dad!

Some pretty serious stuff going on here.

I am not as unwilling to touch myself, anywhere on my body, but I still feel dirty and guilty. I'm supposed to use lotion and I try, but touching myself is very difficult, even when I have permission. Touching myself for healing is even more difficult for me. I feel guilty and sick whenever anybody touches me at all. I block any feelings of love. I don't want my body. My guilt is profound.

It isn't the relationship with others concerning touch that's the problem. It's the contemplation and the actual physical contact that brings all this up. It's the need itself. That just tells me that I've come a long way with healing. Intellectually I know it's permissible for somebody to touch me. I WANT physical touch and at the same time I feel downright ill about it.

I see Grandfather and angels. He says that I will have to lose myself and lose myself completely. I'm not doing very well really right now. The need to sleep overwhelms me. Exercising promotes these feelings and incorrect thinking. But I still believe that God will reveal a way for this, too, to be healed. It's a hard nut to crack. And right now I feel completely exposed.

So this is where I am. I'm trying to stay in touch with the spiritual realm to listen and do. It's a pretty big challenge right now though. I'm not sure what's real. I don't trust myself.

Thanks Dad!

Hug Kiss (cyber hugs and kisses help, you know, and are safe!)

Bruce: Deb,

Thanks for sharing where you are in the journey and your frustrations. I think you can measure your progress by degrees instead of big steps. And then after a period of time you can reflect on the progress by degrees and the degrees add up to big steps.

We all seem to have internal struggles that we either do not have answers for or we do not apply the discipline that can change the struggles to more positive outcomes. So, on the broader picture you are normal to have struggles but with a closer look, your struggles

are intense and related to a very complex disorder that is not the norm. But, even though you are frustrated you have made progress and I hope you weigh both - progress and struggles - so you have a somewhat objective look at where you are. I am not diminishing the rather large dynamics of your struggles at all. I have always felt that you are a person of courage to fight your way forward in your healing process. With all the anger, guilt and personal history of this disorder you have a lot of reasons to be angry and even violent but you are not. You are a kind person, a thoughtful person.

Another big step for you is the fact that your anger has all but disappeared. No more children coming forward with hot anger, cussing and not trusting anyone - ready to fight or run away. All of these behaviors seem to be greatly diminished or gone completely.

Feeling ill about physical touch is a conditioned response?? If so, is the only way to correct this response is to build a history of positive experiences that are private and safe like rubbing lotion on the body/feet so you can see that it is safe, good and can bring pleasure, relaxation, and rest.

I do not know if this is helpful at all. But I have confidence in your ability to continue the journey. You have a good support system that really likes you, loves you and acknowledges the challenges that are ahead. You will overcome all of these issues that are before you in time if you do not fall off your motorcycle. Be safe. Take care of your ankle!

Hug and kiss

Fran's Notes: Deb feels like vomiting and sick. She's suicidal as well and wants to take over the other parts. We did EMDR on her physical and emotional pain. She thought she didn't have a right to desire. I reframed that indicating she has a right to desire, to be whole and happy. She talked about suicidal thoughts of wanting to buy sleeping pills. I told her I would hospitalize her. She agreed not to do so. We worked on what to do instead. When I praised her, she felt pain. There is a pain associated with an apparent internal perpetrator. She's not sure if there is a part or if it is within her. I worked with her on reframing her negative cognitions.

*****

    I learned to take action when I had suicidal thoughts. As strange as this sounds, I'd go to a movie and that actually helped me get out of it. The day I saw Fran, I went to a movie after our session.

*****

Fran's Notes: She's questioning if there is another part inside because she feels out of sync. We continued to process her feelings.

Billy: Hi Dad!

In Chicago in the field museum waiting to see a short movie. They had a thing about horses that was really cool and I saw the history of the earth thing that was really cool. Going to the aquarium right after this.

My pee and poop is green again. And it's not even St Patty Day! It's really gross Dad even for me.

Okay it's starting. Bye!

Debra Bruch

Chapter Thirteen

Subconscious Level 11: Heather (4) Wakes Up

It seems that the deeper the therapy delves into my subconscious, the more imagery helps to communicate and move the process forward. The imagery does not relate to the Other Realm or to spirituality, but is an expression of what is happening when my subconscious becomes conscience. Imagery also indicates change, and sometimes that change happens very quickly. Because imagery is connected to a part of me (or several parts of me), it also indicates a part's need to defend himself or herself as well as experiencing an overwhelming fear. And yet the imagery also indicates my process of healing.

The part of me called Heather was so seriously traumatized that she broke my mind for a while when she awakened. For a four year old to be so utterly betrayed by her mother is something I can't even comprehend. Heather was so scared and so traumatized that it took heaven and earth to help her see this second-life.

And yet at the same time I was able to live life without publically revealing that there was anything wrong. Billy forged on for the most part as if all of this was. Just was. I thank God for him being in control.

When Heather awakened, she was too young to be able to write.

*****

Deb: Hi Dad!

Hope you're having a great time in Missouri and don't get caught in a storm!

A little over a week ago, Billy discovered that there is another person inside of us. She pretended to be Grandfather but mocked Billy and that's how he knew she wasn't Grandfather. We thought she was a he until she revealed herself.

We went to Fran last Thursday and I was pretty reluctant to proceed. But she got a hold of Billy and used her techniques. The image that came up was the same as before. We are in a meadow and an angel is holding us. We are one person though, so the angel is holding one person. Rain is falling and when it hits the ground it bursts into flame for a moment. So the ground is scorched but there's now some green grass growing. The meadow is surrounded by hills. With Fran, Billy saw a person on the hill and she decided to come down. All this time though we all thought it was another boy. But instead of a person, she was a centaur. Very pretty, very white. But little centaurs came through her body and they were nasty and wanted to bite, but the angel protected us. That's as far as we got with Fran.

But things don't stop, you know. So Thursday night/Friday morning I woke up at my usual 3:30 a.m. and I guess I was ready to proceed because I did. I woke up strongly reluctant to exercise. I just didn't understand this! There MUST be a reason, but for the life of me I couldn't get to it. I then asked God to help me and all of a sudden, Billy's vision came back. The centaur blew apart into little bits and swirled around and around. I heard her scream "Mommy! Mommy!" and there was huge dark clouds overhead and thunder and lightning. And then the hills cracked.

Then she had her reliving. *She was born during the same event as Joshua, the first satanic ritual rape. Heather is 4 years old. They took the candles away and then raped her. She felt her vagina tear and screamed "Mommy Mommy" but Mommy reached underneath the man and put her hand over her mouth. Eleena choked her. The man was angry at her screaming. She was raped repeatedly by both men and felt her body tear. I don't understand this, but her mind blew apart into little pieces. But then she saw Mommy in the Air and this personage held her. After they stopped they left her on the table, but Mommy in the Air held her and put a blanket over her. It wasn't a physical blanket, but it kept her warm. I'm not sure but I think that they left her on the table overnight. They were drunk. Having a good time anyway. I think the next day Eleena put a diaper on her because of the blood. And then put her to bed.*

So Heather is out and I can hear and see her now, but she hasn't come out into this second-life yet. She doesn't want to. She throws tantrums a lot. What's different, too, is that her spirit blows into little pieces and then come back together again. And she seems to control that. She'll let Grandfather pick her up, but she'll blow into pieces and scream. She screams about the exercising. I don't know why she's so afraid of it. That's something that Fran will help her with I think. Grandfather says she needs love. But she doesn't understand anything, although she knows what's going on completely. She came out of the body. And another thing that's strange is that she's Alex's twin, along with Adama!

As part of her reliving, she saw Jack watching on the stairs behind the banister. It's no wonder Jack doesn't remember me at all during his childhood. I'm sure it all scared the crap out of him!

All this makes me pretty upset, not that Heather is out, but more of the first-life has come into focus. It's like living a horror movie. Alex is trying to hold her hand. I'm trying to point things out nicely. But no luck so far. (I suppose that's the ultimate of self-help, huh?!) I thought of Alicia, but she didn't like that name. She says Heather is okay. So she has moments of being normal. But there's something in her that scares her, related to the body. I know it's the actual tearing that happened, the physical sensation of them raping her, that she took. But I don't know how or why she relates that to exercising. I think this is the first time I was raped. I know that Eleena was angry and annoyed and neglectful before that, but I think this was the first hard-core violence that I experienced. Man, I formed so MANY people with this event! Heather doesn't trust anybody.

Oh, hey, Michel the archangel and my long-time friend is here! He takes care of animals and he's brought an animal with him. Heather is tuning into that. I think she identifies with animals that are hurt and dying. I think she cares about animals. Michel helped Little Debra see that animals don't really die and would bring her animals a long time ago. Because of Michel, I'm able to see the spirit of an animal living when I see its dead body. They belong to the earth and most go back into the earth, but they retain their species spirit. I feel like I belong to the earth too. Well, the earth has told me that I belong to her and no matter where I stand, I belong. Man, I've got a headache!! Have I mentioned lately just how much fun this is? :)

So that's it. I guess progress is being made.

Take care. And thank you!!

hug ***kiss***

*****

Bruce was out of town for quite a while during Heather's awakening. But nothing seemed to stop and all my parts knew that he'd read the emails when he could.

*****

Fran's Notes: Billy cried. There is another one. I reassured him. Heather came out. She knows who I am but doesn't understand anything as of now. Heather is scared. She wants me to comfort her. She's reliving it over and over again. She keeps screaming "Mommy". Whenever Deb touches Heather, she blows apart. Deb feels that her mind breaks. Heather cried as she held the buzzies. I comforted her as I helped her process her trauma.

Deb: Hi Dad

It's 3:50 a.m. and I've been awake since 12:30. Another night of no sleep.

I went to Fran yesterday and Heather finally became fully awake. From that, I've gotten some relief! Heather's coming to the surface and her reliving fractured my mind a little. I see it like having surgery; you have to heal from the process of the cure. I haven't been thinking right. I'm talking about perceptions and coming to incorrect conclusions, mostly about people. I've been suicidal. Nightmares. No sleep. Fear. Headaches. I can't focus very well. I'm not experiencing dementia though. Fran said I've been what's called switching, which I haven't done before. That's when suddenly another personality will come out and I don't have control over my living. I also suddenly forget what I'm doing. Fran thought it was Heather. I thought it was me. But it happened again when I was driving home and it's Billy. But Billy isn't making it happen; it's my mind that's hurt. But I know what it is now and Billy understands better too. So together we can watch for it I think.

I think this event and feeling myself tear when they raped me when I was four years old is the origin that made me a multiple. Then a year or so later when he drowned me, it became permanent. It dissociated me from my body as well. This origin robbed me of my life and of any kind of normal adult relationship and family. I know it wasn't my fault. What I really feel is a deep sense of sadness that my mother would help them and hold me down and put her hand over my mouth to stop me from screaming. I continue to feel the fear, but that will lessen as Heather is cared for I think.

Grandfather has his hands full! He's trying to deal with me too! Not just Heather, Alex, and Billy. It's been a busy week!!!

I met the Mommy in the Air tonight!! She's an archangel like Michel! I still feel the comfort of the "blanket" too. I thanked her and thanked her and thanked her again. I'd say this was the ultimate of God being with you in times of need!! I think at that time, too, I switched my relationship from Eleena to Mommy in the Air. Maybe that's why I responded to Ian Bruch's teachings about God so easily.

I think, too, that these other two people kind of authorized Eleena and Walter Amundson to do what they did and to continue down that path. It's like they opened a door into their own souls and let evil in. I don't think that they're evil people; I think they're sick.

Well, it's now 4:30 a.m. and I'll try to get some sleep.

Thank you, Bruce, for going above and beyond anything expected! Thank you for being my second-life parent, your wisdom, your guidance, the times when you were tough, the wrestling matches with words, for disciplining me, for teaching me life skills, and the love, care and concern. I'll thank Grandfather for being my second-life parent, the affection, tough times when on the warpath, love, and guidance. I'll thank Fran for her expertise and her deep caring. I'll thank Ken, too, for being my parent, for doing the hard stuff of exploring and exposing my disorder in such a way that I could accept it, and for his caring, love, kindness, and his time. I'll thank Ken, too, for letting me as Philip enter this relationship and this process with Bruce, for giving his permission and for letting go, for loving me enough to let go and hand me over. I'll thank Susan for her listening ear, her love and acceptance, and her reiki. I'll thank Dr. Jones for deeply caring about me, for helping me keep on track with my work and social life as well as helping me remember that I have worth. I'll thank Ian Bruch for my LIFE!! For being my parent, his teachings, acceptance, his unending ear, his love, caring, and concern. I'll thank Jack for his love and caring, his acceptance, and for helping me to know what is normal. Above all, I'll thank God for not letting up, and, well, for being God.(!) I feel like I've won an Oscar! I've got a ways to go yet, but, man, it's all downhill from here!! Thank you!

And now it's 5:20. Ugh.

lots of hugs ***lots of kisses***

Billy: Hi Daddy!

Gee, since Deb's thanked you and everything, can I have a puppy now? :)

Me popping out when Deb's driving wasn't me making it happen Dad. I'd just think of something and all of a sudden out of the blue I'd be out, but it was so fast I couldn't even see what was going on before I was back in and stuff. Fran says that's switching. It's like I go through a hole in Deb's mind. Or something. Maybe it's cause her mind is weak right now. (heh heh heh)

I get to go to the county fair tomorrow Dad! Yay! God wants us to walk in the woods tomorrow or Sunday too. Gee, if I don't get my chores done. Oh. I don't get my allowance this weekend anyway.

Boy, Heather coming out sure was violent Dad. Fran thinks, too, that getting sick like we did the very next day was the poison in the body coming out, like in bulk. We think so too cause it happened again, but much much less, a couple of days ago. Hey, I just thought of afterbirth cause of Heather coming out. Cooooolllll. The only thing we didn't do though was bleed. So it wasn't bloody afterbirth.

Boy, I sure hope you had fun. Okay bye.

H k

Bruce: Greetings Billy and Deb,

We are home safe and sound. We had a very busy but good time. The Health and Spirituality workshop was very good. The theme was humor. We had a good visit with our daughter and celebrated her 23rd birthday on Tuesday by going to Omaha to see the movie *Philadelphia Story* with James Stewart and Cary Grant. She gave us a tour of the YMCA where she will be the Aquatics and Fitness Director starting September 25th. She is in training now.

Billy, sorry, no puppy, but sounds like the two of you are working on this "switching" challenge. Hopefully there is light at the end of the

tunnel; this is exciting!! I hope your days go well and that you are able to get some rest prior to school beginning Monday. Take care.

Hugs Kisses

Deb: Hi Dad!

Over twenty years ago, I was given a vision of this process. This morning the vision continued.

I was walking on a dirt road when God (the Master) came to me. On both sides of the road are barbed wire fences and beyond that are beautiful meadows. It's always been like I'm able to travel down my path okay, but I've never been able to cross the fences. In the original vision, God picked up a battered tin cup and said that I was too damaged to fix. I had to be remade. Today, God continued to walk with me down the road and we came to a tunnel. We walked through the tunnel and there was a green and beautiful meadow on the other side. The sky was full of thunder and lightning clouds and God said that's Heather and not to worry. There was no more road or fences. But on the other side of the meadow stood a man. He was in silhouette. We stopped and God said that this is my companion. Wow! I asked him if he was going to love me and God replied that he is going to love me more than I've ever experienced in my life. I asked if he was good looking and God laughed and said yes, and that God wasn't going to make Eleena's prediction my reality. He said that I was also good looking and I looked at myself and I was! He also pointed out that nobody is perfect and to be grounded in reality. I asked him then, I said, "But he won't be at somebody else's expense, right?" God said "No, he won't be at anybody's expense." He told me to be very careful though. He told me to go ahead and look for him, but do not jump in. He told me that he would make it very clear to me that he is the companion for me, so for me to keep an ear open from him about that. Then the man disappeared.

God then turned his attention to the meadow. He told me to explore, to go out and explore. I asked him if I was going to work for him anymore and he said yes, but for now to concentrate on exploring life. Then he left.

Cool, huh?

Bruce: Very cool!! AND good counsel about relationships - "Don't jump in." Have a great day Deb.

Fran's Notes: We did EMDR to get Heather out. She said the buzzies hurt her head. Always on the left side of the forehead, above the eyebrow. Equivalent of moving muscles that haven't moved in a long time, except it's brain synapse. "I don't feel too good. My tummy hurts. My head hurts. It feels like I'm bleeding out my eye. I see big clouds and lightning all the time. Side of my chest hurts. Everything is black. I feel something is coming out through my nose."

Billy: Hi Daddy

Boy, God wanted us to go all the way to the Porkies and do a day hike or two last weekend. So we did. It wasn't totally fun Dad cause my feet hurt. So I asked God if he wanted me to do this sometimes and he said he wanted me to do this a lot. Boy, he sure did talk to us a lot. He said that he wants us to become comfortable in the forest, no matter where we are. He said it doesn't have to be at the Porkies cause there's lots of logging trails too. He liked us having water with us. But he said other stuff too, like once he said that I just walked too close to the edge and not do that, so watch out for that. Told us to get other hiking shoes. Told me to pick up my feet more. I once asked him if he was Grandfather and he said no, he was God. I asked why and he said we'll see. Typical. :) I was nervous cause I didn't want to break anything or fall down cause there were roots galore.

Deb checked her email while driving yesterday Dad. She didn't read it, but she checked it.

I got all my chores done even before we went to the Porkies.

okay bye

h k

Bruce: Deb, Billy, Heather,

We are going camping for 8 days so will not be on line for the duration. I will visit with you when I return. Just wanted you to know so you would not think I was ignoring you.

Deb: Hi Dad!

Very strange nightmare, but I think it's full of what's real.

I was with a few people in a house. We knew each other, but nobody connected to real life. One guy hurt me a lot. He'd go in and out and dig his hands into the side of my chest and other places in my body. He'd take my ribs and pull and I was bleeding. He had an ax, but I got the ax away from him and destroyed all of his equipment. He then left to outside the house and I couldn't find him anywhere. Another person said to me that he's now really dangerous and will come back and try to kill me now. I said yes, he will. That's when I woke up. But I woke up in pain, especially in the side of my chest.

Better try to get back to sleep.

hug ***kiss***

Section Five: Changing Identity

My need for my first-life parents to love me affected my development. I wanted them to love me. I also wanted them to stop hurting me. In my child's mind, I tried to identify with them. Some parts of me wanted to be like them, and some parts desperately needed to try to be them.

The healing of the parts suffering from my need to be loved by parents meant they had to release their identity tied to parents. Bruce and Fran created an environment for all my parts to be more natural, to be kids. An identity of self did not happen quickly, but eventually I came to know myself. I think.

I discovered much later in the healing process that my identity is tied to both the first-life and the second-life. Identity is not a role you have during life and it is not a set of talents. Neither is it necessarily what you do, the actions you take. I think identity is a person's be-ing. Past, actions, choices, caliber of character mix together to help you gain an identity from within. What you do, then, comes from who you are. How you respond to life's challenges reflects an identity that resides within.

But perhaps identity is deeper. Perhaps identity connects who you are with the divine. You are beloved. God loves you. But how does that make any difference when you ponder who you are? Perhaps identity is also a spiritual awakening of the divine within you. Maybe that is a theme of being like a candle and not placing a bushel over the flame so others can see your light. The fire within you is the divine within you. The fire within you is both the source and the consequence of a be-ing who is beloved.

When I ponder, I realize it does not really matter how I was treated those many years ago. Healing has been needed; no doubt about that. But ultimately my journey is not tragic; neither is it superficial. It just is. My identity comes from the One who created me and the reason why I am beloved. It is up to me to discover myself, but I think I am unable to do that effectively unless I seek the divine.

Chapter Fourteen

Subconscious Level 12: Francis (16) and Joel (8) Wake Up

The deeper into my subconscious, it seemed to me that not only did imagery become more prevalent, but also the parts coming to the surface seemed more dangerous. I was seriously afraid that a part of me would harm, even kill, somebody. Perhaps the parts that seemed dangerous were indicating bravado due to fear and pain.

Francis awakened during a therapy session with Fran. He tried to make her feel badly by saying his name was the same as hers. He also tried to manipulate her, but Fran just ignored the attempt at manipulation. It so distinctly did not work that he quickly changed. In his attempt, he discovered he did not enjoy trying to hurt other people. Fran gave him the opportunity to name himself Francis for real, but he took some time to think about it.

Due to the time of the year, Bruce was out of town through much of the emails. That did not stop the parts from emailing him because we knew he would read them when he was able. The process did not stop during Bruce's absence.

*****

Fran's Notes: There is another part coming out and he doesn't know me. I asked his name. He said Fran. I laughed. He feels angry but has no memory. He feels pain. "I would like to end all of this." He had a headache on his right side. We bantered some and used humor. He cried because he couldn't control and make me feel bad. "Why don't I want to hurt anyone anymore?" I talked to him about our relationship and my understanding of what he felt and his need to model after the perpetrators to survive. He agreed to be called Frank. This was a dramatic shift and a significant part of the healing.

Francis: Fran, I think I'll be called Francis. I sure don't get why some people enjoy hurting other people cause I found out I sure don't. Strange how I thought I did. Thanks.

Fran: I really like the name Francis. See you in a couple of weeks! Thanks for letting me know you!

Francis: Hey. I'm Francis. Male. Around 14-16. I don't know.

Looks like I took some of the pain of being raped. I'm pretty angry. I came out with Fran today and I tried to hurt her feelings. Didn't work. Turns out she's been looking for me.

I learnt a few things. I found out that I don't feel too good when I try to hurt somebody. I've been hurting Deb and company all along, but I guess that's why I had to wake up into this second-life. Fran says that a person will form a piece like me to try very very hard to be like the monsters. I learnt that I really don't understand why people like hurting other people. It just didn't feel good at all. At the end, Fran said what should I be called and I said Fran cause I was trying to hurt her. Didn't work. She's okay, you know? So I'm named Francis I figure to try to honor the first person I met in this second-life who just laughed when I tried to hurt her and manipulate her.

Deb was pretty funny today. She had this dream and because she woke up in pain she knew somebody else was running around. But Fran asked her what she thought about the dream and Deb just said Oh my God there's another one and Fran just laughed. Deb said that she knew because she woke up in pain after that dream, and the pain was of the first-life. That's when I woke up to the second-life out of the first-life.

I also learnt that words are like magic. There are words that hurt and other words that heal. Same with touching. Seems like I was only touched to hurt in the first-life. But Fran says that everybody and I mean everybody needs to be touched in the healing way. And that it's not dirty, which is what I always thought. Everybody needs to have somebody put his or her arm around him or rub the back and stuff. And she says that's not only okay but normal. I always thought it was wrong. Damn. Every time I tried to touch Eleena in any kind of good way she'd hurt me. During the first-life. Now she wants hugs. I don't get it.

I still feel a need to be dangerous toward people though. Fran says I don't have to anymore because that's the survival mode. But who the hell can I trust?

Deb and company had always wondered why Philip didn't remember being hurt too much when he was raped. It's like a big jig-saw puzzle and we're putting it together a piece at a time. He remembers it feeling like burning. But I took that pain. Little Debra hurt a lot. Damn. We were just too little to take all that.

My body, now, the body now, feels like it's about to explode. I was not self-aware until now. I know I was running around and hurting the others, but I didn't know what I was doing. I didn't know that I existed, not self-aware. Heather's awake now. I think I got sucked up and out when Heather came out. I was formed in the first-life during the same event that Heather was. Damn. It's like when Heather came out, it's like she had to tear the mind to come through. And me. Except I don't think she actually did that; God did. Nothin' like pain, you know?

I know I have to ask Grandfather to do stuff. I asked if I could write this now, way past bedtime. Couldn't sleep at all. So he said yeah. I think I'm supposed to go and try to sleep again now.

See ya.

*****

The deeper in my subconscious, the more dangerous my parts seemed to me when they awakened. Several times I was afraid of what they might do. I think perhaps what I was actually feeling was their need to survive. All of my parts seemed to know very little except pain and fear. I don't think they became dangerous because they were waking up. I think every part of me was stuck in their own trauma and the feelings I had before and at the time of their awakening was their anger and their desire to stop feeling pain and fear. The deeper into my subconscious, the more acute the pain and fear.

So the parts of me "came out fighting." But just as soon as they enter my conscious state, they began to be released from the trauma they experienced over and over again throughout the whole of my life. My first-life parents are no longer around. At first when entering my conscious, they seem to be very confused, but all succeeded in perceiving their new world. Some took more time than others, but they all succeeded.

Once awakened, many of my parts recognized that they had been affecting the conscious in negative ways. And many parts took responsibility for the negativity. They all seemed to affect my conscious in similar ways: do not trust; people do not care for or love me; I do not deserve anything that feels good, etc. Letting go of the negative view of the world was harder than getting out of the trauma. Bit by bit, healing took place.

*****

Deb: Hi Dad!

I can't sleep. Grandfather said I can do this email.

The love that God has for me MUST be pure grace, because I have no idea what I've done to deserve this blessing. I know I've been reluctant, more than reluctant, but I also know that for some reason God wants me completely healed. As I reflect on all of this, it really does amaze me the people who have cared enough for me to support and sometimes drag me along.

I now have an idea of what Pippin felt when he died and was released from his physical pain. His spirit was so full of joy and he just couldn't contain himself toward me at all! I asked Grandfather if that's what it's like to die and he said yes but much more.

I know I have a ways to go. I'm not integrated. If there's somebody else there's somebody else. Meantime, I guess I still need to be remade. Billy's still growing up, Heather needs comfort, Francis needs to experience life and to understand, and I need to be patient. But I think this is a HUGE transformation. And if I experience pain again due to the first-life, then it will just be something that needs to be and the process of healing will continue. So far, though, so good.

I can't possibly thank anybody enough. Thank you! Now back to bed.

hug ***kiss***

Fran's Notes: I learned that Joel is another part that identified with Walter Amundson. Joel kicks Deb and emulates Walter in order to be loved, accepted and powerful.

Joel: Hi. Gee whiz, Francis made me come out just cause I kicked Deb in the ribs. She deserved it. That's what Walter Amundson did and he's right and stuff. Now I'm out and I don't like it. Walter Amundson is big and stuff and he's a hero cause he knew how to keep people in line and stuff. Gee whiz, Deb butts in and copies stuff to other people all the time and I don't like it. They SAY I'm supposed to write to you and Francis hits me on the head if I don't and stuff. I don't like Francis anymore. They SAY your my daddy but my daddy is Walter Amundson cause he's tough and I like him. Boy, he sure knew how to keep people in line and there wasn't any problems at all. I don't need all this lovey dovey stuff and hugs and kisses and stuff and I'm not gonna let this Grandfather kiss me or anything cause I'm tough like Walter Amundson and your not supposed to do all that stupid stuff. I'm tough and I can take everything that anybody dishes out. I don't want any affection stuff though. Heather does and she's a wimp. You have lovey dovey stuff and that makes you weak and stuff. They told me to tell you that I'm 8. So what? I'm still tougher than anybody here and Walter Amundson is my dad not you and stuff so don't try anything like kisses or hugs or anything cause I'm just too tough for all that. Your not supposed to be nice to me either cause Walter Amundson isn't and that's made me tough and I'm supposed to be tough and that's what I am. And I'm not gonna do anything you say cause I'm on my own and that's just fine cause I'm tough and I can do what I want except what Walter Amundson says I cant and stuff and then he'll hurt me but that's okay cause I can take it and stuff. And you can bet that I don't cry or anything. So no lovey dovey stuff. I gotta stay strong and be just like Walter Amundson and stuff.

Bruce: Hi Joel,

You have called Walter Amundson a "hero" because he is tough and knows how to keep people in line. Tell me, what makes a person a hero? Do you have any other heroes that you look up to?

Joel: Na, I don't know anybody else. Gee, he's big though and he's tough and stuff. And he doesn't care or anything and I think that makes a hero cause nobody can touch him really and make him sad or anything.

He's mad a lot but that's cool cause people respect him and stuff and they're afraid of him too and that makes people respect him too. Geez, I guess your the only other person I've met and stuff and I can't see you.

He hurts people too and that give him respect and stuff too. I mean, he got a whole lot of power, you know? And I want power and stuff like that.

Bruce: Joel, How many friends does he have? Heroes generally have several friends. Is Walter Amundson tough with children and not adults? I think heroes do things that help others, they are brave, they are not selfish. Heroes do not hurt children, do not hurt good people. Tell me more about Walter Amundson.

Joel: Gee I don't know how many friends he got. He don't let me see stuff like that. I have to go away. Gee Philip was living then out almost all the time and stuff and Walter Amundson didn't let him be around when other adults were around. But he laughed and stuff I heard him do that. I don't think he was mean or tough to adults. Just me. And Jack. And Mom.

Walter Amundson scares me. But that's cause he got power and I like that. I mean I gotta have power and stuff. I don't know anybody else except Mom and she isn't too nice you know. I don't know anybody who doesn't hurt me. Except teachers. I think maybe they were nice and stuff but they didn't see me too good.

Gee whiz. I didn't talk so much in my whole whole life! How come you ask me stuff?

Bruce: Joel,

I ask you stuff to try to get to know you. So, Walter Amundson scares you, Walter Amundson has hurt you, and because you have been hurt and frightened that makes Walter Amundson powerful. There is good power and bad power. Bad power is called intimidation - scaring and hurting people; good power is called empowerment - helping people do good things. What kind of power does Walter Amundson have? Good or bad? What kind of power would you like to have?

Joel: I guess Walter Amundson has bad power and stuff. Good power doesn't help me though. I mean, I like kicking Deb in the ribs cause it keeps me on top, you know? There. I just did it and she doesn't like it. But I got to live you know? Helping people do good things dont help me live and stuff. Theres mean people all the time and I gotta hurt them to stay alive

Fractured Mind

and stuff cause they hurt me. Except the others havent let me, you know? So I gotta stay alive and stuff by hurting the others here. Its what Walter Amundson did you know and I gotta do that too to stay alive and stuff. I dont explain too good. But I dont want the good power cause it doesnt keep me alive or anything.

Bruce: Take a look around you and you will not find Walter Amundson. Take a look around you and you will not find anyone hurting you. Take a look around you and you will not see anyone kicking another person, or hitting another person. You are in what is called the second-life. The first-life is where you needed to stay alive, survive, but you are in the second-life now. Take a look around and tell me what you see. Stop hurting Deb and by doing so you will exercise "good power."

Joel: But there's people hurting Deb all the time around here and they got the power and stuff! And I got to live! Boy, it sure does seem like Dad's here all the time and stuff and I just gotta I just gotta. I know I'm little I know it and stuff and I just gotta protect myself you know? I hear about love and stuff but I never did figure out what that is but I sure do want him to love me and stuff and if he's not here then I'm just screwed! Your making me cry and I dont like it!!! Stop it!!! I'll die if I cry!!!! He'll kill me if I cry!!!!!!!!!!!!!!!

Bruce: Look around, and you will not see Walter Amundson. He is gone, forever. You have nothing to fear. Look around and see who is there. You are safe, you are good and stuff.

Joel: But he cant be gone he just cant!!!! I just gotta I mean I want him and Mom to love me!! I'll kick Deb and then he'll come back and stuff. Okay. Kicking Deb and everything. Do you think he'll be proud of me? I want him to be proud of me so he cant be gone and stuff cause if hes gone then its to late and stuff. I want him to you know. love me and stuff. I sure don't feel safe and stuff.

Heather: Hi Daddy! I got the squitters!!! :(

Are you raising me too? Do you love Billy more than me? Do you love me too?

Bruce: Heather, I love Billy and you the same. I am raising you also.

Heather: Yay yay yay!!!! Thanks Daddy!!!

Joel: Do you love me to? Are you my new daddy now? Do I belong to you now?

Bruce: yep!!

Billy: Hi Daddy

It's almost midnight but I got a terrible headache and nausea and Grandfather said I could write to you and stuff.

I've been good and I got all my chores done okay. Dad, when I went down to take a pill and some Tylenol, I noticed that I left a knife on the counter. I said to Grandfather, "Oh oh, I'm gonna get disciplined now huh?" Grandfather said, "If you really want me to sure." I said, "Grandfather!" But then I got serious and I said "I do sometimes you know." And I thought I was giving up a big secret. But Grandfather said, "I know." I said, "You do?" He said, "Sure. Every child wants to be disciplined once in a while. But that's not what you really want. What you want and every child wants once in a while is to know that you don't have to survive, that there's somebody who is bigger than you so you don't have to survive. You just want to feel secure. But you've been in survival mode all your life, so you've had to learn security and that means trust too." I asked, "Am I okay?" And he said "You've got a ways to go, but yes." Grandfather says that he's got five kids and I'm number six. So he's got six kids. He said that that's for real. He said too that sometimes I ask him a question and I think yes in my head and pretend it's him but it's me, but I do pretty good hearing the no that's coming from him and I hear the no right after I say yes in my head. He said that's just cause I really want to hear a yes. He just said that that's typical with kids too, but I got more of a challenge. He's proud of me cause I question the yes and gotta be confirmed and stuff.

Heather's asleep in his arms. Joel just follows Grandfather, but at a distance. He doesn't look up anymore Dad. He feels awful lonely Dad. I think maybe Joel couldn't handle being in survival mode. He needed somebody bigger and that was Walter Amundson. Francis is asleep. And I'm getting that way too.

Okay, gotta go back to bed now.

H K

Fran's Notes: Debra realized coming here that Joel was the kid no one wanted and Deb felt not wanted all her life which comes from Joel. She has been so terribly unhappy and she recognizes it's coming from Joel.

Joel came out. His arms were crossed and he wasn't going to come out, but did. He said Deb said he kept everyone alive. He kept burping and his stomach hurt. He said he has a lot of stuff in his head. I talked about ways he can relax and have fun. He said Billy's supposed to figure out how to have fun. Joel said he's never felt safe but would want a man with a gun. Joel and I talked about his safety with me, etc. He said he is tough and if not he will die. I discussed with him about strength and about Amundson being weak and picking on children. At the end, he touched me and I gave him a handshake.

Joel: If I cry are you gonna hurt me? Can I cry now? Cause there's this Grandfather who keeps wanting me to come to him but I think I'll cry if I do. So if I cry am I gonna die. Are you gonna kill me?

Bruce: Crying is a natural thing to do when you are scared or are not feeling safe. Grandfather is VERY safe and when you go to Grandfather you can cry if you want and you will not die. AND no one will kill you or hurt you.

Joel: Okay. I'll try it. Gee Im awful scared. YOU won't hurt me or kill me huh?

Deb says I gotta wait til I get home and stuff though. I'm awful awful scared.

I couldn't go to Grandfather yet and stuff. I got too scared so I hid. This place is strange. Well I see the world now but I mean this other place. I know it's not the world and stuff but I don't know how I know. I didn't see the world world before now. I mean I did before but I think I been asleep and stuff before now. If I cry I won't be tough no more. I gotta be tough. When I'm out like this I see stuff in my head but its all blurry and stuff. And its really fast and jumps around. There's my old daddy and he's really big and stuff. And horses and pigs. There's grandmother and she's killing a chicken. When you kill a chicken does it hurt the chicken? I mean does the chicken hurt when he dies? There's lots and lots of people in the other place and that's where this Grandfather is. I can't find my old daddy and you said he's not here anymore. I see stuff in my head though when I'm like this. Are you gonna hurt me cause you're my new daddy? I think you should hurt me. That's what daddys do. Im supposed to hurt cause I gotta hurt to be tough. That's how my old daddy kept me in line so are you gonna keep me in line? I see stuff in my head and stuff now. Im scared of people here cause they hurt too. Im supposed to be scared of you so I am. The others say Grandfather's my daddy too. And you. Your in this place and hes in the other place and hes right here too. I can see him. I don't like that. I think hes watching me to see if I gotta get in line. Whos gonna protect me now cause my old daddy isn't here? How come I always wanted him to love me? Cause I sure tried and tried and I wanted him too but I sure don't know why I wanted him to. Yeah I do. I saw it on tv and other kids talked about their daddy and they liked him. And they were really really happy and I wanted to be happy too so I figured that maybe if my daddy loved me then I'll be happy and I wont be sad any more. But mommys and daddys don't love me much. Im supposed to be tough. I better go now cause Deb just came out then let me come back and stuff. She couldn't help it. No Im still out. Okay Deb got feelings too big to stay in. so I gotta go and stuff. Bye.

Bruce: Joel,

Grandfather is not like Walter Amundson. Grandfather is gentle and loving. You have nothing to be afraid of and when you are ready you can go to him. No one is keeping you in line the way Walter Amundson did and no one will. You are a good person. You are a good person so you have to get used to the fact that no one will hurt you in this life. You have to get used to the fact that God, Grandfather and I love you, just as you are, whether you are tough or not tough. Relax - go to Grandfather when you are ready and see for yourself.

Joel: I really really like what you say and stuff but how are you gonna keep me in line? your my new daddy, right? I know you didn't hurt the others cause they say so but im not them you know? So if your not gonna hurt me then how you gonna keep me in line? cause im supposed to be kept in line you know.

how come you love me? i wanted my old daddy to love me and i never felt happy. so how come you do and God and Grandfather when you dont even know me? im relaxed and stuff but i dont understand. will i feel happy someday cause you love me and stuff?

Bruce: I haven't had to keep you in line so far. You stopped kicking Deb in the ribs didn't you? Why? I think it is because you want to do the right thing. You are a good person!

Joel: Um, I didn't think of it as doing the right thing and stuff and stuff. Um, I did kick her but didn't while you were gone and stuff. While you were gone though I tried to pretend to Billy that I was Grandfather just so I could tell him what to do and make him feel bad and stuff just like my old daddy did and he told me to shut up. um, i don't think i'm a good person cause im not supposed to be you know. so are you lying and stuff to me?

Bruce: You are a good person. You are a kid so you are not going to do everything perfect. You will learn and you already are learning that hurting people is not good, it is not acceptable. You are also learning that you are loved and that there are expectations for good behavior. Children sometimes have to be disciplined when they misbehave and you will be no exception. So, I am not lying when I say you are a good person because all of us are always learning how to be better

people. Accept the fact that you are a good person and you will act differently.

Joel: I am a good person. I am a tough person. There. I just kicked Deb in the ribs. I'd be mean to people on the outside but the others won't let me and that's cause I'm little but when I grow up I can be mean and I gotta be mean to be tough and stuff. I don't care that the others around here are rolling their eyes. They better just leave me alone cause i'll beat them up if they dont watch it. They're the ones who said your my new daddy but i dont understand you at all. I want my old daddy back cause he's tough and he knows how to keep people in line. I know i know hes not here no more and you are. Being awake just sucks big rocks.

Bruce: You are a good person. But I will discipline you if you do not straighten up. You are not tough – you are afraid because all people who proclaim to be tough are scared. If you wish to find out how big I am you just keep hurting Deb but for now you said "being awake sucks big rocks" so you may not be out until Friday! And if I receive any e-mails from you before Friday I will get you on the phone and discipline you!! Do you understand?!

Joel: What a wimp!! My old daddy would take a belt or a rope and whack me with it. He'd take off my clothes and hang me upside down or right side up and stuff and hurt me! or put bricks on me or tie me up and stuff and I was tough! I AM tough! There I just kicked Deb again!!! I want my old daddy BACK!!!!!

Bruce: Gee, your old dad would take off your clothes and hang you upside down and hurt you – put bricks on you or tie you up. Tell me how you felt loved by these actions. Tell me how good it felt to receive this kind of attention. Tell how good it feels to kick Deb. Tell me how good you feel inside. Tell me!

Joel: tell me tell me tell me!!!! My old daddy will love me some day! I know it! he will he will!! He'd leave me alone when he wasn't hurting me so there! So yeah at least he saw me when he hurt me!! that's better than being ignored!!!! Im supposed to kick Deb cause im tough. so there and there and there and there!

Bruce: Love never comes to you through torture and you are not supposed to be out at all.

Joel: your a liar. im out. daddy.

Bruce: What does being loved feel like in your imagination?

Joel: Don't know. Maybe like a blanket. Don't know.

Bruce: Does the blanket feel warm or cold? Does the blanket help you feel safe?

Joel: Blanket feels warm. I never feel safe.

Bruce: What would make you feel safe? Have you ever felt safe?

Joel: A big man who will hide me and who has a gun and stuff might make me feel safe. I don't know. I never felt safe.

Fran wants Billy to play with me like for real. I guess so. Like basketball together. Am I supposed to? I never played before I mean with anything. I don't know what to do.

Bruce: It is good to have fun with another person. Billy will teach you how to play. Be patient with any game because it will take a little time to learn, but it will be fun.

Joel: I don't trust him. Can I beat him up if he tries to hurt me?

Billy: If he tries to beat me up I'm gonna beat the crap out of him.

Bruce: Joel, Do not beat Billy up. You are supposed to play together and have fun. So you are going to learn how to have some fun and Billy needs to learn how to have fun. So, take it slow, visit, and play.

Billy, Relax, learn to have fun together. Visit, and relax, have fun.

Deb: Hi Dad

I got some insight this morning about little Joel. Any kind of punishment means Daddy will try to kill him. It means he's facing death.

Joel kept me alive during the first-life. Joel kept Walter Amundson from killing me. And all he wants is for Walter Amundson to love him. Not to stop hurting him, to love him. It never occurred (occurs) to Joel that Walter Amundson will stop hurting him.

He has no idea in heaven or earth what it feels like to be loved. All he knows is that it relates to feeling happy.

Yesterday Fran asked Joel if he'd kick a dog. Joel said he'd never kick a dog and he felt bad just thinking about it. He didn't know why he would never kick a dog.

Dad, I've been wondering for some time if maybe there's something fundamentally good about me. I mean, a good that doesn't have anything to do with the first-life or even this second-life or you or Susan or Jack or

Ian Bruch or Fran or anybody else. But it's just something fundamentally good about me. That maybe I was born with it. I don't know.

Billy: Dad!!! Joel pretends to be Grandfather when I'm out! And says I can do stuff! Like I thought Grandfather said I could have a small chocolate shake and I did but then I found out it was Joel cause he laughed and everything! I didn't get in trouble or anything but I don't like it!

Joel: It's not MY fault Billy is stupid!

I like to eat. I like mountain dew and chocolate shakes and I even like what Deb makes. Me and Billy haven't played yet though cause I keep falling asleep and stuff. But we wanna play on the Wii. I still can't find my first daddy. Your my new daddy huh? I cant let anybody touch me and stuff cause im always scared that I'll die and stuff. I saw kids be held in movies and boy there sure is a part of me that really really wants that. I sure don't know why. But I know that touching hurts. It hurts a lot. But im tough though and I can take it all. I don't know why but I really really really don't think you'll hurt me like my old daddy did. Not like that. But youll still hurt me though. Nobody touches me nice. Billy says Grandfather does but im scared. I feel awful bad. Ive always felt bad and stuff. I have a tummy ache right now and stuff and I didn't even eat any candy at the movie or anything. Had a mountain dew in the morning though. I like it a lot. I sure don't feel too good and I feel alone and everything. I don't think anybody cares about me.

*****

Bruce taught elementary school music and was well-gifted working with children. As he told me, some children do not respond to a hard line like other parts of me did, so Bruce dropped it in favor of a lighter approach. Joel responded to that very well.

*****

Bruce: You may feel better if you stop drinking Mountain Dew. I know you like the taste but it is not good for the body. The only way someone has touched you in your life is to hurt you. You have never had the experience of someone holding you gently. IT may take a while but I hope you will get used to the fact that no one around you now has hurt you. Think about that each day. "No one around me has hurt me. I am safe now"

You are tough because you had to be in the past. You can be tough now if you like but you will need to give people a chance to be kind to you, nice to you. If you do you will find out that you will not be hurt like with Walter Amundson. Grandfather will be nice, kind and gentle with you. He likes to gently hold children and talk with them. Grandfather likes you very much, as do I. So, when you are ready

maybe you will give us a chance to gently touch you in ways that it will not hurt at all. And I will not discipline you in the near future and maybe not at all. If you can go to Grandfather, and continue to talk with me and play with Billy, maybe you will not feel alone. Try it.

Joel: Gee thanks for the email and stuff. I got a really big problem though. Every time I think about playing or going outside or look at Grandfather I fall asleep. I didn't with Fran and I haven't with you and stuff. I think that may be the only thing I'm supposed to have is pain you know? I don't fall asleep when I eat or anything. And I dont fall asleep when I write to you. I feel like I'm on overload. I feel bad cause I want to do stuff. And I don't mean that doing stuff is bad I mean I feel bad cause I want to. I look at Grandfather and I want to cry and I fall asleep. I gotta be tough and if I cry then I'm not tough and if I'm not tough then I'll die. You say that people don't hurt me but people here hurt Deb and they want to hurt Deb. So are you lying to me? I don't understand. I know it ain't a physical hurt. Is that what you really mean? Don't I have to stay tough so these people here won't kill her? Don't I have to stay tough to protect Deb? I'll tell you a secret. I don't really want to be tough all the time. But there isn't anybody who will protect me and I know your saying that nobody will hurt me and stuff but I'm 8 and I'm scared so I just gotta be tough. I don't know what it's like to be held and stuff. Seems like big people just hurt me. I'm falling asleep again.

Bruce: You will not die if you cry. People cry all the time and they do not die. So I think you would be OK if you decided to let yourself cry. The people who hurt Deb do not hurt her physically. They hurt her feelings. Some day you may want to go see Grandfather and let him hug you to see how it feels. A hug feels REAL GOOD!!

Joel: Do you PROMISE I won't die if I'm not tough anymore?

Ps. Thank you for answering my questions and stuff.

Pss. If I try to be like you, will you love me and stuff like for really real?

Bruce: I PROMISE you will not die if you are not tough anymore. You are a wonderful person who is growing in very good ways.

Ps. You are welcome!!

Pss. Yes, I will love you and stuff :>)

Psss. Have a good day!

Joel: Hi. I was able to sit next to Grandfather today. I looked up at him and he smiled and stuff. I looked at the ground though and at my feet and stuff. I asked him where my daddy is and he said he's my daddy now and you're

Fractured Mind

my daddy on the other side. A man came to him and when Grandfather saw him he got up and went to him and shook his hand. They talked a little and then the man told me to come to him. He asked me if I knew who he was and I said no. He said he was Jesus Christ. He then did something and he and me was like surrounded by light and it was all sparkly and stuff but it was really coming from him. He asked me what I felt and I told him I don't feel anything except it kinda felt like a blanket. He told Grandfather to give me more time. I tried not to let him but he kissed me on the forehead and showed me my bed. It wasn't a room or anything but it was a bed and stuff and there were toys and stuff right next to it. I was really tired. Grandfather told me to go to sleep so I got into bed and he like put a blanket over me and tucked me in and stuff. He touched my hair and stuff. Wow.

Bruce: Feels good doesn't it!!

Billy: Hi Dad!!!!

Gee whiz! Joel is eating and doing whatever he wants! Mountain Dew all the time and candy too. Grandfather told him no but he's doing it anyway! Joel had TWO things of candy today. Gee whiz.

Bruce: Sorry Billy, This isn't fair to you but it will get straightened out in time.

Joel: I'm all alone in the movie watching lion king. I'm crying and stuff. Are parents really caring and stuff? I'm just exploring and stuff.

The lion king just died. Are you gonna leave me too like my old daddy did? Am I SUPPOSED to be on my own?

Bruce: Yes, parents are really caring and stuff   :>)

I am not leaving you.

Joel: Am I supposed to know who I am now? Am I yours and Grandfather and God's now? Am I to learn now with you and Grandfather and God inside of me and be who I'm supposed to be? Like the lion king?

Bruce: Yes, you will learn who you are supposed to be. Right now you are Joel, a very good person who is learning a lot.

Joel: Billy says that I'm gonna get disciplined and you don't hug anymore. I can't feel the good stuff yet not even that light stuff. Except I like to eat and I like to feel wind that isn't cold. I like to get under blankets and stuff. Is that feeling good? Kicking Deb makes me feel good too but not the body. I mean I don't feel good in the body. I'm kicking Deb now! Kick. Kick. Kick. Are you lying to me? Me kicking helps me not remember the pain. Helps me be tough but you say I don't have to be tough anymore. Okay. Am I gonna feel pain the whole rest of my whole life? I guess this pain is different than what Scott had though. Gee. The body doesn't feel it unless I kick but I sure do. I got these images in my head and stuff. And I get scared and then I get scared that I'm scared. I don't know what you mean by a good person. I don't know how to play with toys. It's cool that I got them though right by my bed and stuff. Billy don't really wanna play with me cause in 8 and he's 11. But he says he will. Are parents really supposed to protect? Do they protect kids from themselves and stuff? I guess what I really wanna know is if my old daddy and mommy ever loved me. The others say that I became like him so maybe he would love me. So did he? I think that maybe he hurt me cause he loved me. Maybe I gave my old daddy a way to do stuff that he couldn't do except by me. And maybe that makes me special and tough. Gee I don't know. I guess I better stop now. I'm falling asleep now.

Billy: I'm sorry Dad. I know I shouldn't have said that to Joel. Sometimes I get so jealous.

Bruce: You are OK and thanks for your remorse.

H K

Joel: I got bumps on my right ankle and on top of my left foot. Boy they sure do itch! Guess what?! Pippin and Frodo let me hold them today. They were warm. But they were alive! Warm like a blanket but they were alive. I fall asleep when I think about Grandfather and stuff. But is that what it's supposed to feel like with people? Grandfather touches me when I'm in my bed. It don't hurt. But I just can't feel anything. Except pressure on me. Do I belong to you now? Is my old daddy gone for good? Am I supposed to call you daddy instead of him? My old daddy never ever talked to me like you do. He said I was worthless. He said lots of stuff that hurt and I wanted him to be proud of me and stuff. Pippin comes up to me too now while I'm in bed. I think he wants to sleep with me like he used to in your world. Is that okay? Deb wants to watch tv now. Am I supposed to call you daddy? Are you really really for real my daddy now?

Fran's Notes: Joel came out. He recognizes that his dad is gone. He feels sad. I talked to him about his wish to be loved by him. He doesn't understand that hurt isn't love. We talked about how his abuse was also torture. He said he's supposed to experience other people touching him but he wants to go to sleep. I told him it can be a protection to avoid death or further hurt. He said he likes to eat because it makes him feel good and he likes blankets. He said Deb's deceased dogs came to him and it felt good. I talked to him about kicking Deb and he said he kicked her because he was mad at Billy for telling Joel something mean. I asked Billy to be a nice big brother to Joel. Joel doesn't understand why I and others don't want to hang him up. I educated him on how healthy parents are supposed to be. He said, "There's a wall and I can't break through the wall." I asked him what that wall represents. He said, "I love my dad. Maybe I should not or not supposed to love him." I worked with him on how normal it is to love your dad and explained how real love is supposed to be and it isn't hurting a child or another person. He cried. I pointed out he didn't die and he could express feelings. With his permission he allowed me to touch him and comfort him. He is sorting out what a healthy relationship is and starting to decrease his defenses and reframe his negative thinking errors.

Joel: Hi! Fran touched me today and it didn't hurt any. I started to fall asleep but I didn't and then when she touched me I woke up. Will you touch me too? I have a really really hard time understanding stuff but I'm really really trying and everything. So will you touch me too? My body could feel her touch me but I couldn't inside my heart and stuff. It's like there's this wall and I just can't get through it. I knew that I loved my first daddy and I'm really sad that he's not around anymore. But I think I'm supposed to know that touching isn't supposed to hurt and hurting somebody isn't loving them and stuff. Boy I sure am screwed up. Deb says it's a change of worldview and it's really hard to do but I can do it. Fran says that my first daddy didn't love me and I guess I know that. Cause he left me alone or told me what work to do unless he was hurting me. And I wanted him to love me and stuff. So I guess I'm just now finding out what it's like to be loved and stuff. Huh? And being loved doesn't mean you gotta be tortured huh? Gee. I kinda like being out in this world.

Joel: Guess what? I got the same dream that the others got and just everything! I was standing in a meadow and it was raining and the rain turned into fire when it hit the ground and the sky was really really dark and lightning and everything and Deb and Billy and Heather were there too and stuff and this angel was holding us and stuff and the meadow was almost all grass. And then the rain quit and the clouds went away and the meadow was all green and no more black and it was really really pretty. The angel let us go then and a voice said that it was over. Its over now. I think I feel happy! Is that cause you love me and stuff? Am I healed now? Grandfather touched me when I was in bed and stuff and it didn't hurt and he felt alive to me you know. I don't really want him to pick me up cause im tough and that's for babies and everything but I hold his hand. Is that okay? Deb gave Heather a human doll yesterday and boy SHE even felt strange and stuff. Im supposed to give Heather time to be out and play with her doll so she can be healed. If people are mean to Deb can I beat them up? Gee, Grandfather felt like Pippin and Frodo did. I think you showed me a different daddy and I feel different now. I still miss my old daddy and I really did love him and stuff and Fran said that every child loves parents no matter how terrible they are. But I got new parents now who aren't so terrible you know. I think your better than the lion king daddy. Cause he went away and you said you won't. The kid lion got into trouble and his daddy talked hard to him but didn't beat him up or anything like that but then like forgave him and then taught him and stuff and I think you might be like that and stuff but I don't know. Boy I sure like being out. Fran said that kicking a person is like kicking a dog. Now I feel bad. Boy I sure didn't know that kicking Deb was like kicking a dog. Okay better quit now. Bye. And im not even falling asleep!

Bruce: Joel,

I am glad you feel happy - that is great! You are in the process of healing and doing a very good job. You do not have to be tough anymore unless you want to and you don't need to beat anyone up even if they are not very nice. No more kicking with your new understanding. When you kick Deb you are really kicking yourself because you share the same body. That may be why you do not feel very good in the body after you kick Deb.

Have a great day!

Joel: Daddy I cried tonight and can't quit too good. I let Grandfather pick me up and stuff and me against him feels good. I'm really sad that my old daddy is gone and that he never did love me and stuff. I feel alone but Grandfather is right here and so are you when I write and stuff. Deb says I'm grieving and that it's okay she says. But there's more than that you know. Loss maybe. I'm pretty scared cause I sure don't know what it's like and I'm finding out what it's like but I sure don't know what to think and stuff about it all. I keep looking for my old daddy. I keep seeing and feeling the Hurt and then I get scared cause I'm not so sure I can stay tough you know? But gee Grandfather feels good and I feel happy and sad at the same time. I got bumps all over but lots and lots on my legs and feet. Bummer. Boy it sure is late but I 'm afraid to sleep cause I dream even more than what I see when I'm awake. Now I can't go to sleep! Better go. I think Grandfather wants to put me to bed. And that's what parents do huh? Boy it sure is strange. Bye.

Joel: Boy, I sure like being out. Yesterday Deb got a little depressed and didn't wanna do anything so I told her I will so I came out and made her drive to the place we walk in the woods. Deb was out too much doing that though and I didn't like it!! Gee whiz, she shouldn't be out when I want to when it was my idea. I'm gonna kick her next time cause she deserves it. Nothins going on much though right now. Grandfather walked next to me when I was ALLOWED to come out during the walk. Sucks. He walked with Deb too. My foot hurt a little after a mile but doesn't hurt this morning so maybe its okay huh. We walked a mile and a half. Can I drive the motorcycle? Vroom vroom!!! Grandfather picked me up the other day too. I sure don't know what to do about any of that stuff. I cried some too but I don't feel like crying now. Deb says we gotta get dressed and stuff. Bye.

Joel: Gee whiz! I kicked Deb this morning twice and she STILL wouldn't get up! She didn't exercise or anything. She just said she was tired. Okay. She says okay.

I don't think im really courageous and brave and stuff. If I had a choice and stuff I wouldn't do it. *Every time and I mean every time I thought maybe he won't hurt me this time. Even when I took off my clothes I thought maybe this time he won't hurt me. When he put the ropes on my arms and stuff I knew he was. I let him and my body went kinda cold and stuff and I stood there and let him do that to me but I was cold and I couldn't move any. He talked all the time he did that and he told me I am bad and I had to be punished and stuff. He said I had to be like jesus and stuff. He said this is my comeupins. He said I had to pay for my supper. I found out when I woke up this time that the others took a whole lot of the pain. Scott I guess. I just said to myself over and over and over and over that im tough. But my mind went kinda black with it. I kinda went to sleep but even when I went to sleep I know that I really really focused and stuff on my body. I told my heart to keep going and that my body is tough. I went to another place when I became black and went to sleep. It was a nice place to and there were clouds and trees and grass and stuff. I told my heart to keep going. I got really really cold and I told myself I was flying to the sun now and getting warm. And when I felt stuff in my body like break and stuff I told it to be strong and said it was a rubber band. Sometimes I felt like my mind was breaking and tearing over and over again. Then when I thought it was over he'd stick his thing up my butt or the other place but mostly up my butt and every single time I thought maybe he won't do that this time. So Im stupid. But I told my heart to keep going. I think my mind was hurt more than anything cause I couldn't keep it from tearing. Im sorry.*

Bruce: Do not apologize because you have done nothing wrong. To me, to tell your heart to keep going and to visualize a nice place are very grown up things to do, actually very mature things for an 8 year old. Most, if not all, 8 year olds could not have done what you did. These thoughts/actions are also strong signs of courage, strength and toughness. You did very well and I am proud of you.

Hug Kiss

Bruce (dad)

Joel: Ive been feeling pretty bad all day and stuff. I was on the other side and I was just walking around and stuff and Jesus came up to me. I said that he was Jesus and he said yes he was. I just said to him, kinda just blurted it out and stuff, that I don't really know what I did back then, I mean I never thought of it before and stuff, but this morning when I was back then, I said what I did. He said, "Do you remember me?" And I said "Huh?" He said, "Do you remember me back then?" I said no. He said, "Do you remember hearing somebody telling you to breathe after you were drowned?" And I said yeah, I do! He said, "That was me." And I said really? And he said "Yes, that was me and I was there the other times too. I was with you my little one." He said that he was there and stuff when I was hurt!!! And that he helped me do what I did to say alive. He told me to tell you and stuff but I didn't want to any. But he said you'd appreciate it and stuff. He said I did what I said and stuff and reliving helps it all come to my surface. That so I don't have to relive it anymore in my feelings and stuff. Okay. I told you what he wanted me to.

Bruce: Thanks Joel for telling me. It hasn't been an easy day for you but you came through it OK. Jesus was with you in those experiences in the past and Jesus is with you now. Jesus is a special friend. I hope you rest well tonight. I think you are doing a great job in healing, although it doesn't feel very pleasant right now but in the long run you will feel much better.

hug kiss

Joel: Daddy I sure dont know why i dont trust you and stuff but i sure dont. i just feel like i gotta not believe anybody says and stuff cause if i believe anything then i'll die and everything. i always just gotta think that stuff bad is gonna happen to me cause every time i start not doing that then i get all off balance cause something always happens that hurts me. Grandfathers here and i just cant hardly see him cause i keep thinking hes gonna do something bad to me if i let him touch me too much. Gee, in the first-life and stuff we'd have Christmas, you know? And I thought maybe i can be happy and have presents like i see on tv. And at first it seemed like things are really good. But then my old daddy would get all mad and stuff and almost all of anything i got would be gone. I just dont understand any of it. I dont understand why that happened and I dont understand why when Deb is happy with something here at her work that people just take it away from her. What's the difference between the first-life and the second-life? I just don't get it and I don't know what's real and stuff.

Bruce: Be patient Joel and things will become clear to you in time. It takes time to trust people and trust is built on experiences and time. So, no worries, you are doing fine.

In the first-life you had Walter Amundson, pain, torture and you had to be extremely tough. In the second-life you have me, Grandfather, Jesus and God. You have no pain except for the reliving that you have done, and eventually you will learn there is no torture or physical abuse. But, you have people that love you and will not hurt you.

Billy: Hi Dad! My poop is brown and my pee is yellow. Life is good. :)

Bruce: Thanks for sharing!!

Billy: Hey, any time Dad!! I can mail you samples if you want!!! It'll really prove that I'm full of it!!

Joel: Do people who love you touch you right and stuff? Do they touch you like you mean something special and stuff? Do YOU hug and kiss maybe once a week? I used to have to kiss my first daddy and i sure didn't like it. are you different? Boy i sure hope so. how come your different? I guess what im really asking is cause i see stuff on tv and stuff and if you have me and stuff then it isnt just not hurting and stuff but maybe its you helping me feel good. Thats what Fran says you know. That people touch each other all the time and stuff and it right and good. It doesnt just not hurt. it like heals. And thats why when you comfort somebody the touch and words heal and stuff and feels good. i sure am not used to what that feels like but i sure did when you put your arm around me the other day. When you did that, I felt like i was being put back together.

Bruce: Well, you can sit on my lap and put your head on my chest if you want to. And when you are sad I will place my arm around your shoulders and comfort you.

HUG KISS

Dad

Joel: Wow! I feel like im this alien!! Sure am scared about it all but im tough you know and i can do it i think.

Do you REALLY comfort people? Like me? I dont think your lying or ANYTHING like that. its all just something im having trouble really really seeing. Its like my mind is bending. Maybe its supposed to break so the new and strange can come in, huh?

Deb: Hi Dad! Fran suggested I get a book: *Coping with Trauma-Related Dissociation: Skills Training for Patients and Therapists* by Suzette Boon. So I just went into Amazon and got it. It's big but maybe it's time I learnt something about my disorder huh? Costs about $37. I don't know why, but seeing books about my disorder made me feel better about it all.

Have a great day!

Deb: Hi Dad!

I had a bad nightmare last night. Very strange.

I went and visited a couple and then without saying goodbye, went on my way. Ian Bruch was staying with them too. They made all the gestures that they wanted me to stay. I turned around, though, and went back. When I returned, they wanted to talk with me. He (he's not you, Dad) said that he and his family love me and want me to stay with them. That this is now another life than before. He was genuinely saying it and I could tell that. He said that they love me and want me. So I stayed. I felt very very hungry for affection and touch that didn't hurt. And Ian Bruch was there. But he thought that I needed to learn responsibility, so when he was gone to work, I needed to pick up around the house. It started okay and I would essentially be their live-in maid. Unfortunately, though, when he was gone for work, his wife hurt me. She would take his tie and wrap it around my neck and choke me. This happened every day. I ended up just wanting to sleep, but Ian Bruch said I shouldn't do that. His wife would do things to make my life more difficult, like strew dirty clothes all over the house that I would have to pick up before I did the laundry.

Meantime, I was trying to do something for a church function, thinking that he would be happy with me. But his wife and kids found out and stopped that. All I wanted was for him to show me some affection and touch me right that felt good, like an arm around the shoulder, but he didn't. He talked about discipline and responsibility and how I needed to show gratitude toward him and his wife.

Finally, I sort of ran away. I left the house without telling anybody and left my cell phone there. I went to a movie theatre and right outside the theatre, they were selling raffle tickets for a whole lot of toys. Some girls there tried to physically block my way to the seller. I didn't understand their selfishness and anger. But I got there and I asked what they were selling, so I didn't want them. Then I changed my mind and told them yes, that I'd give the toys to an orphanage or something. The sellers took a ticket and told me to stay with them when somebody drew the winning ticket. I didn't win, but the sellers told me that I didn't have to pay for the ticket. They were really nice.

I found myself all alone except for one strange looking man. He shoved me and I deliberately stepped on his sunglasses. He then took a baseball bat and he was going to kill me. But near me was a baseball bat. I swung at him several times and missed because I didn't really want to hurt him. But he said he was going to kill me and moved in for the kill. I swung, though, and connected and must have knocked him out. But I had to kill him; otherwise, he'd come after me later and kill me. So I killed him. No blood.

I got scared of this world and went back "home." When I got there, he was angry and Ian Bruch was disappointed. He said that I was a member of the family and family don't just leave. That he'd been trying to call me for hours. He then said that I had to know the consequences and he had to punish me. His wife and kids were smiling. I knew that I still didn't know love that didn't hurt, and I still trusted him. I still had the hope that I'll know a different life than before. He hit me. That's when I woke up.

What's REALLY strange is how I can remember this dream with such detail! It's still with me. It makes me sad and I feel alone.

Joel: Debs a mess. Deb wants to be on her own and is scared. Shes scared to integrate too cause then she wont have anybody to talk to and stuff. And she'll feel alone and stuff. Im not a mess though. So I kicked her cause she's stupid.

shakes hands

Joel: Hey Dad

Sometimes I can feel my leg muscles move and stuff. I did today. And I felt myself breathe too. It was awesome. Something happened to us to yesterday. It felt like blinds being raised from our toes to our head. It kicked in that you're Dad. I sure don't know why it happened but it did. Deb feels bad about it. But it was physical and stuff. Like a garage door opening. Things got foggy. Then stuff cleared up. And it was like a switch turning on. We were standing at the kitchen counter when it happened. But it's like my first dad went away and you've been dad all my life. But it was with all of us not just me. All at once. Gee, nobody was even thinking about you and stuff! See ya.

Bruce: Joel,

No kicking. Use your words not your feet or hands. I am glad good things are happening for you. I hope this is a real good transition for you.

See Ya!

Bruce (Dad)

Joel: I gotta be on top somehow! She can't tell me what to do! So I'll tell her to go fuck herself.

Gee whiz Dad! You're not supposed to be around now anyway. I'm supposed to do what I want.

Bruce: Joel,

No kicking, no hitting, and no bad language. You live with other people and you have to be kind and considerate. IF you are not kind and considerate there could be consequences. Time to grow up a little bit and whether I am there or not you need to be on your best behavior.

Joel: Gee whiz. :(

Deb: Hi Dad!

Let's see. No breakfast on Saturday, chocolate, MacDonald's' hamburgers for lunch, peanut butter and jelly sandwich for dinner, regular breakfast on Sunday, peanut butter and jelly sandwich for lunch, donut, chocolate shake, big mac for dinner Sunday. Joel imitates Grandfather to get all this!! I didn't know that until the kid laughed. Joel seems to be the "I want" incarnate! I don't feel too good.

Bruce: Joel,

Stop eating all the junk food. You are hurting the body – your body.

Joel: I GOTTA! I just GOTTA!! I'll DIE if I don't do stuff!! HONEST!!! My first daddy isn't here so I just gotta!

Bruce: No you don't have to and you will not die. STOP eating the junk!

Deb: On reading the book on Dissociative Identity Disorder, I came across the concept that the key to knowing a person has DID is time lapse or times when a person does not know what was going on. I found myself wanting so badly to NOT be DID, that I discovered that I've been lying to myself. So my first reaction was "Not me!"

Who the heck am I kidding? There HAVE been times when I do not know what the heck people are talking about when they have a continuing conversation later on. This is not true so much now. But my friends DO tease me about just how absent-minded I am. What the kicker is, though, is that I know full well that when I was a kid, when I was at school I didn't know anything about home and when I was home I didn't know anything about school. I've been telling myself that I didn't do homework because once I got home I worked, and that's true. But the truth is, is that I didn't KNOW I had homework and I never thought about it. What I HAVE done is learn to concentrate and that I think has been the key to me being able to live in society. But to be finally honest, I can't hardly read without my focus breaking. I have serious problems listening without my focus breaking. I can watch TV (get into story) and do things visual. And what's best for concentration is when I use my hands, like typing. I am a slow learner. One moment I'll get it and later I have no clue at all. The best time to learn concentration was when I was a scenic artist because I always had an audience. What a blessing that was! So to study through school, I typed my notes right out of the book, so essentially I typed the main points from a book so I could remember. I don't remember learning anything when I was a kid. At all except once some multiplication. Most of my experiences of life and living has been of confusion and loneliness.

I don't hear voices, like hearing with my ears. The voices of the others I have always recognized as within me, and coming from within me to the outside. Not from the outside coming in. The very few times I HAVE heard voices has scared me quite a lot.

I have been trying to deny that I have DID for three years now. I can't tell you how much shame I feel that I have a mental disorder. It makes me feel inferior to just about everybody in the world. I feel labeled and I feel like a freak. I feel like I SHOULDN'T be in any kind of leadership position BECAUSE I HAVE A MENTAL DISORDER!!! I'm not seeking sympathy. I'm just being honest about the very strong shame that I feel that I have a mental disorder at all. Can I live with it? Well, apparently so since I am.

Thanks.

Bruce: Deb, You might start with not feeling sorry for yourself and get over the idea of shame. You ARE a wonderful person who is learning about a disorder. You ARE an accomplished person who has done and will continue to do good things. Be thankful for your new understandings and learn from them, apply them, be grateful and move forward. Staying in the darkness of self pity is just that – darkness. Come into the light of Christ where you will see yourself differently – a beloved child of God – you know the One who has helped you survive, grow and become the great person you are.

Billy: Daddy, Joel is pretending to be Grandfather again! This morning I thought Geez I gotta get going. Geez I gotta brush my teeth yet! And in the voice of Grandfather he said that I take such little time doing that I have plenty of time. Made me feel bad. Then I knew it wasn't Grandfather cause he never makes me feel bad! It was Joel and he did it just to be mean.

I'm doing good though. Got all my chores done. Broke my toe though. Well, I'm sitting in front of Frans building and gotta go. Sure hope you come home soon! I miss you Dad!

H. K.

Bruce: Billy,

How did you break your toe? I bet that hurt!! When Joel tries to sound like Grandfather just call Grandfather and see what happens to Joel.

H   K

Billy: Okay I'll call Grandfather!!! Geez, I had a basket of apples on the kitchen chair and the chair near the sink. Man, I turned around and whacked it really good with my foot! But Gee, Dad, maybe it helped the other problem. Don't know yet. But Deb got about 12 pie fillings all done and in the freezer!!

Joel: Hi daddy. Fran says im trying to make you mad and stuff so youll hurt me and stuff cause she says I think that's love and stuff. I don't know. I like candy and chips and mountain dew and all that stuff. Im awful afraid to go hungry. Fran asked me to name one time that I deserved being hurt and I said that sometimes I was slow and sometimes I didn't understand what my first daddy wanted and stuff. But she said that those things don't mean im supposed to get hurt and stuff. But my first daddy hugged me once! HONEST! He did!! And another time he was proud of me. Im so confused and just everything. Ill tell you a secret. I don't really want to be hurt. I just don't know nothing else. I want my old daddy back so bad cause I knew what to do and stuff. When you held me my mind bent cause I just couldn't get it and stuff. I just don't know what to do and stuff. I think I want you to put your arm around me. You said I can put my head on your chest and im really scared and I don't know why. I feel like I'm not supposed to do that. I mean to have anybody be kind to me and hold me and stuff like I see in the movies when kids are happy and so parents hold them and parents hold them when theyre scared too. Fran says that's comforting but I sure do think that's like wrong. Fran says everybody should have that but I sure don't think im supposed to. And when I think like that I cant hardly breathe and stuff. When I was hurt, it was like everything was the way its supposed to be, you know? Sometimes now, you know, some people think Deb's really good and stuff and none of us understand that. Its like its not supposed to be that way. People arent supposed to talk to me or like me and stuff you know. Are you supposed to show me a different world? I sure don't know. I wonder a lot about why im here, I mean alive and stuff. Lots and lots of times before I'd lie in bed or on the grass and wonder why I just don't give into it, you know? I don't know why I fight so hard to keep getting hurt like all that. I think im awful stubborn. I'll tell you a secret. I've always wondered what it would be like with parents who liked me and did to me like I see on tv. Im awful scared. Out of my mind scared. My mind bent when you put your arm around me. I just don't know how to survive that. My first daddy held me though you know when he had sex with me. But it didn't feel too good. Was that a lie? I mean what he did? So I lie in bed and wonder why I'm alive and stuff. And I wonder if I'll ever know what its like for somebody to care about me. You know. Me. Joel. I wonder what its like for somebody to touch me right and not be sick or hurt or make me feel like a whore. But boy I sure don't know. I mean I think every time somebody touches me theyre not supposed to, you know? Even when it's right and okay, like when you put your arm around me. I got these itchy bumps around my ankles. They went away for a long time and now theyre back. Okay bye. This Grandfather says I gotta go to bed. Okay bye.

Bruce: Joel,

Do not work too hard at figuring out everything all at once. Just know that I have never hurt you and when I held you I did not hurt you or ask you to do anything. It takes a while to trust someone and I am patient. If you sit on my lap and put your head on my chest nothing bad will happen. You can try it when you feel ready. There is nothing or no one to be scared of either, for your fears to diminish it will take time. In the meantime, you can be a big help if you eat right and are on your best behavior all the time.

Bruce (Dad)

Deb: Hi Dad!

The DID book says that I have avoidance issues. True! I'm avoiding ANYTHING happening! But it has also told me how to deal with it. One thing to do is reflection. That's good. You've already taught me that.

But I did wake up later when I heard a gunshot in my head. Jumped out of my skin! I looked and there's another one that actually looks like me for a change, holding a smoking gun pointed right at me. About 13 years old. Boy, I thought James was angry! This one's full of rage and cries all the time. I'm trying to avoid it but only because I have to work right now. Name? How about Kate. I'm trying to make light of it. Avoidance. The book says it's important that I accept these parts without judgment and try to empathize. Hard to do when she wants to kill you, and actively trying to. I am now more tired than I've ever experienced before. Nausea comes and goes. Have I mentioned just how unfun this is? :)

Take care.

hug ***kiss***

Billy: Hey, Dad, did you know that the definition of insanity is asking the same question and expecting a different answer? Well, being the insane person that I am, can I STILL get my allowance even though I didn't make the week's lunches? I did all the other chores.

h k

Bruce: You can get half your allowance. So you are only partially insane :>)

Fran's Notes: Joel is connected sensorialy to the body. He was there when Philip got beat up. "I remember Philip feeling the sky." We talked about what he thinks of me. He said, "You're weird in a good way. If I was a girl I would like to be like you except your hair. I like my hair." "I don't like the body much but I like the strength. I liked the body when I was with my dad. But Grandfather said I can get the body back." I talked with him on what he learned from his first dad and how he wants to be loved by him by being like him. I explained about how in this second-life he's not treated that way and why.

Joel: I know why you're ignoring me. It's cause you hate me. Now I got two daddy's that don't love me any. Oh well. I'm tough. It don't really matter to me none. I don't care. It's the way it's all supposed to be. I'm on my own anyway so what difference does it make.

Bruce: So, do you feel sorry for yourself??? You are not tough; you are just insecure and I would be too if I had gone through everything that you have been through. But don't play the "nobody loves me" card cause it doesn't work for me. You are not doing what you are told in terms of eating and you are hurting everyone else because you all share the same body. So, stop eating the crappy food and start doing what is right for all concerned. Now, if I didn't love you I would not tell you these things because I would not care – but I do.

Joel: Okay daddy. I didn't feel sorry for myself maybe. Maybe I just felt like you didn't want me and stuff. And I gotta talk myself into not caring cause if I don't then my heart would break you know not just my body and my mind and stuff. That's what I did in the first-life too. I'm so mixed up and stuff. You tell me not to eat the crap, you know, the really good stuff, but the body tells me to and my insides tell me to. It's like I gotta make my body bad cause they did in the first-life and that's what's supposed to happen and stuff. That's a secret and stuff.

Bruce: Okay Joel, It is time to recognize you are no longer in the first-life and that you are in the second-life. In the second-life we do things to help people, we talk to God and to Grandfather and learn, and we take care of ourselves - meaning that we exercise and we eat

the right foods. Making the body feel bad is not necessary or the correct thing to do, so please stop doing it. **The body does not crave crap, the body is like a person that wants to feel good, wants to feel happy, wants to feel valued and the way you accomplish this is by feeding the body good food, not Mountain Dew, not candy bars, not McDonalds. Work on this and see if you do not feel better. Everyone else will!!**

Joel: Is that my chore Daddy? To not eat candy and say I'm in the second-life and stuff? Can I get an allowance too?

Hi Daddy. How come I gotta do what you say? I'm not being bad or anything by asking or anything. Just wanting to know.

Okay. If I'm not tough and stuff how am I gonna stay alive and stuff? I let Grandfather pick me up for a while. I couldn't feel it to good. Bye.

Shakes hands

Bruce: Hey Joel,

I am really proud of you - good job on the eating!! You are doing fine and growing. This is terrific. Keep up the good work.

Shake Hands and then – H K

Bruce (Dad)

Fran's Notes: When Deb was asleep at night, she woke up to a gunshot firing and saw a 13 year old girl, Kate, pointing a gun at her.

Billy: Hi Dad!

Boy Deb sort of lost it today. She's been reading the book and stuff and things are more understanding. There's too many of us and Kate hasn't come totally awake yet. She thinks she's a whore Dad. And cries all the time. Nobody's being bad Daddy. But there's like no sleep. Dad the book is amazing. Time and time again they write about us. Daddy we always thought everybody lived like this. We just didn't know Dad. They know what happens at night with no sleep and stuff. They know about rooms and allowing time for everybody and acceptance and figuring out about how to heal and everything. We questioned about Grandfather but Susan said to doubt your doubt before you doubt your faith. God told Deb that the people in the book just don't understand about the spirit. They know there's an inner life and stuff. God said that he takes care of all of us and we have a special place with him like that. God has a big heart for children who have been hurt so bad to be DID. The book knows just how hard it is for us to remember stuff day by day and why and stuff. And the book is nice to us Daddy. They even say please sometimes. But Deb's about to break cause she just has to try to squish Kate down. But trying to control Kate is really hard and is taking a lot of energy. And Kate is upsetting Joel I think cause Kate is connected to Joel. Daddy it's like the parts of us like the book says have come in stages. The book says the broad people who lived in the real world come out first and that's what happened. But most of us experienced but hardly ever lived during the first-life. The book says our parts are stuck in the trauma and you're helping Joel, and Kate is still stuck and stuff. Not me though Dad. I'm not stuck anymore. The book mentions about body pain but maybe that's later. We've only read about a third so far.

Well. Better go. Hope you're okay Dad.

H. K.

Bruce: Greetings Billy, Deb, Joel,

You are on a demanding journey that takes a lot out of you at times. You are separate but also joined by the body. You are family and you will be one. You are a wonderful make-up of personalities, gifts, struggles, growth, love and spirituality. You are courageous, daring, adventuresome, seeking, compassionate, and fun. You are doing well. I am proud of you. Hang in there!

H(s) K(s)

Bruce (Dad)

Section Six: The Mother Issue

My confusion due to my mother's betrayal throughout my early life was intense. My stepfather tortured me, but my mother's betrayal hurt my psyche deeper.

I do not know why Eleena contributed to the trauma. I can only say that she was mentally ill. My therapist thinks she also dissociated due to my stepfather's emotional violence against her. I agree, but releasing the trauma associated with my mother was most difficult. Due to the combination of my mother's betrayal and my stepfather's violence, I stopped developing at age fourteen.

This level of the subconscious needed imagery to heal. The trauma's affects on my psyche could not be sufficiently understood by words. Indeed, Fran used imagery quite a lot and throughout my life I experienced quite a lot of imagery, usually in the form of nightmares. But the imagery after parts deep in my subconscious awakened demonstrated change and healing of my psyche.

Chapter Fifteen
Subconscious Level 13: Kate (13), Shaun (10), Cole (8), Joseph (38), David (7), and Baby Lynn (infant) Wake Up

My mother, Eleena, died. The emails I wrote about her during my awakenings were true without exaggeration. But she did not act toward other people, especially outside the family, the way she treated me. She continued to ridicule strangers and ostracized other family members throughout her life, but she was very nice to people she was in a position to know. Unfortunately, throughout her life she lost quite a lot of close friends I think due to her mental illness, but the last years of her life were very rewarding to her and she was able to keep significant friendships.

Eleena was a very nice person toward people and loved to help them whenever she could. Some people really loved her, even cherished her. She also gained a non-related family as her family, and that gave her the love and belonging she so desperately needed. She loved giving whenever she could and liked laughing in healthy ways.

While my mother's violence against me negatively affected my life and living, I am very grateful that other people saw her at her best.

*****

Deb: Hi Dad!

I guess with the book and what Fran's said to me, I've figured out some things about Kate.

During the course of my life, I chose to not mirror Eleena's treatment of other people. I remember time and time again that I thought it hurt people and therefore was wrong. I did, however, embrace Eleena in me concerning me. There's no way Kate could have come awake in this second-life before Heather, Laura (me), Joshua, Francis, and Joel. But the pieces of this jigsaw puzzle have come together for me so far. I've not only written about my formative years below, but afterwards also.

Kate's self-loathing connected to the body, resulting in the thoughts of physical harm and rejection, and that the body is bad and does not deserve to be touched/comforted, nurtured, or healthy:

Eleena's constant ridicule of appearance (what mother really would tell her 15 year old that she's ugly and will never get a husband?), her self-adulation of her breasts (mine were small growing up), touching of any kind of the body and other people **by me** is bad and is so bad that it is of the devil and evil, **anybody else** touching me without hurting me is so bad that it is of the devil and evil, touching to hurt the body by me and other people is good and what is deserved, her need for sexual intimacy with me later in life, her constant berating of me when I wanted and sometimes gained any kind of love or comfort, her need to demean when my body was going through puberty, her need to sexually stimulate herself by pushing intimacy on me when my body was going through puberty, her telling people that I am a homosexual and being sexually stimulated herself toward me by that prospect, making damn sure that my hair would look like crap (until I ran when she wanted to touch it), her need to physically hurt me when I was a kid, not taking me to a doctor, not caring for me physically as a young child without frustration or inconvenience or anger and not caring for me physically as an older child at all including when a normal type of cut or mishap would happen.

Kate's self-loathing connected to sense of self-worth resulting in negative thoughts of existence:

Besides the above, Eleena's not keeping men from raping me during the four-year-old event and actually helping with that, her tolerance and enabling of continued rape and torture, that she stood looking while I was seriously ill after being drowned and not helping until she knew I would live (in other words, she wanted me to die), her constant meanness toward me, her need to justify how she feels about me, her need to attach herself to my success and to who I am, her not wanting me around at all when I was a kid, her need to make me out as the enemy with other family members, her need to promote herself as a good mother to others, her playing highly manipulative games, her need to place guilt on me, HER LOATHING OF ME AS A PERSON AND BLAMING ME FOR HAVING SEX WITH HER HUSBAND ALL THROUGH MY CHILDHOOD, her constant need to be dominant over me, her need to be competitive with me, her need to give to Jack in such a way as to point out her disregard for me, her need to be friends with my friends later in life, taking away friends when I was a kid, being jealous of adults seeing me and wanting to give me attention when I was a kid, her need to have me work for her, her refusal to teach me life skills, her ridicule, her focusing on the times of my struggles to make fun of me and embarrass me and point out how stupid I am.

Kate wants Eleena to love her and she's adopted the same self-loathing toward herself as did Eleena toward her. So she's mirrored how Eleena feels toward her as how she feels toward herself.

This is not to say that Eleena didn't do anything good. I AM saying that the above was far too prevalent and constant. When Eleena decides to, she can be quite likable.

Anyway, just a couple o' things to work on.

H K

Bruce: A couple?? What type of mental illness or disorder does Eleena have because she does not demonstrate sane behavior? She seems very unstable.

I am glad you are figuring out things and that the puzzle is coming together. We will see what Kate needs and how she wants to process things.

Have a good weekend.

H K

Deb: Fran thinks she is also DID. But unlike me who chose differently and listened to people who were nice to me PLUS God in my life, she exhibited the negative stuff toward me. I've pretty much done it all to myself. If I had let my rage out, as Fran says, I'd either be a killer or cowering in a corner mute or dead. I DO know I've had all these feelings. This is why Fran was concerned that Kate would hurt herself.

She's sick, Dad, as sick as Walter Amundson. And that needs to be pitied and not condemned by me.

I've told some of this stuff about Eleena before. But, really, who would believe it? People say, Mothers love their children. Is this any worse or unbelievable than Walter Amundson torturing me? There's a real reason why I have had to be raised all over again. Dad, if Eleena gave me the love and comfort that I needed when I was hurt, maybe I wouldn't be this way. She not only enabled, but compounded the hurt for me. The good news is, is that because it was so severe, I've responded to ANYBODY who showed some caring toward me who didn't hurt me like this. It's good news because it's led to my health.

Eleena was hurt by Walter Amundson in terrible ways, Dad. She just chose to take it out on me. And I think his hurting her contributed to her own mental sickness. For instance, he would have sex with her, then afterwards pee on her. Then he wouldn't let her change the sheets or wash herself until morning. He constantly ridiculed her and called her fat. She would go shopping, and although he took that time to hurt me, he would always be angry with her for taking so long. He laughed at her because she liked to read Readers Digest. He took every opportunity to make her feel bad. I did not see him hit her. But the emotional trauma he laid onto her was severe. Couple all this with genuine narcissism and you've got Eleena. And because I do have this understanding, I will not hurt her. She took it out on me and what she did to me emotionally I did to myself.

She can be very giving. She doesn't treat other people the way she's treated me. But her need drives her expectations and eventually everybody she becomes friends with leaves her. She can also be very manipulative. She wants me to demonstrate my love for her. The problem is, is she can't accept it and demands more and the relationship is on her terms. Always, it is at my expense. And I have had to lay down the boundaries with her. Of course, all THAT happened after I was on my own and I became strong enough to do that.

And now, she sits and sleeps in a recliner. She's always been a social person so she does that, thank God. But she doesn't shower and consistently pees in her Depends on purpose so she wouldn't have to get up. She is physically ill, but has her mother's ageing genes (so do I) to the point that the doctors gather around her to try to figure out how she can have this MRSA infection for so long, take the medications that reduce her immune system, and still get better. So, yes, she's unstable and lonely and needs to be cared about. So my goal is not to confront or seek vengeance or try to feel better at her expense or lay any guilt trip on her, but to forgive. I can't do that yet, and doubt I can until I'm healed. I need to let God heal her, but that won't happen until her next life, her own second-life.

Love ya!

Joel: Hey Dad

No mountain dew or candy today.

I gotta put my head on your chest. I feel this body and stuff but my heart hurts and I feel really sad. Nobody wanted to cook today so I had a peanut butter and jelly sandwich for dinner. I sure don't know why I'm alive and stuff. Do you know why you are? I guess I like it when you touch me and hold me and stuff. Is that okay? I kinda think it's wrong and I'm bad and stuff. Am I supposed to die now? Grandfather says I gotta go to bed now. Bye.

Bruce: Joel,

Good for you on the Mountain Dew and candy.

It is not wrong when I hold you, touch you or when you place your head on my chest. AND you are NOT suppose to die.

Shake Hands

H K

Bruce (Dad)

Joel: I didn't do so good with the mountain dew today and I had a chocolate muffin too. Dad, Aunt Susan says that you don't punish us, you discipline us and the difference is that you don't do it for yourself but for us. I think that's what my first Daddy did, he punished me for himself and stuff. This makes me really really sad Dad. I mean, he didn't just not love me, you know? He hurt me cause he wanted to and he liked it.

I'm not too sure about Eleena though. I think she was driven inside to do stuff and it wasn't for me and stuff but it was to try to make herself feel better. I think that's different than my first Daddy. Dad, my mind bends when you say it's not wrong when you hold me and let me put my head on your chest. It bends. I'm glad you say it's not wrong and stuff cause everything inside me and my body too says it's really really bad. Boy, though, I guess I gotta admit that I'd much rather you squeeze me than discipline me though. The whole thing's so new. My body's bending too Dad, not just my mind. I can feel it in my body. It's like something in my body wants to come out and stuff, but it's not another person, it's the body like changing its mind. I gave in to the chocolate muffin, but, boy, talk about two different wants!!! It was like the BODY like debated and stuff and then gave into it. But when we were in the grocery store, the BODY said to do the stew stuff, not Billy or Deb or even Grandfather!!! Dad, it's like the body has to learn too and enter this second-life too. We haven't exercised for ages, partly cause of the broken toe and ankle. But mostly cause we're so very tired all the time. I do know that I get the mountain dew cause Deb panics cause the body wants to sleep and she's gotta work and stuff. So it's lots easier during the weekends to not have that. Okay. I gotta sleep some now for a little. See ya!

S H

AAANNNDDDD

H K   ew! yuk! gross!

Bruce: The second-life takes some time to get used to. It is a much better life than the first-life. I do not know but my guess is that the mind bending will decrease in time and being held, sitting on my lap, and putting your head on my chest will be normal.

It is a good sign that your body is debating about whether to eat chocolate muffins or Mountain Dew. The debate is a healthy sign and eventually you will not need Mountain Dew at all.

Hang in there.

S H

Bruce (Dad)

Joel: Hi Daddy

We learnt you might retire next year? And you might be going to Oregon? Deb says we'll still see you like we do now cause there's email. But, Dad, does it mean you won't? I mean, does you retiring mean you will quit caring about me? Does it mean you're gonna throw me away? If I'm really really good will you still care about me even after you retire? I promise I'll be good and stuff. Will you ignore me then? I'll try harder to be good. And I'll try to make myself integrate and stuff, we all will. If you go away like that does that mean you'll get me out? Like out of your whole life and stuff? Am I gonna be on my own again? I mean in survival mode? Should I get ready for you retiring and not caring about me anymore and get back into my survival mode? Should I start not caring about you and stuff so we can not care that you're throwing us away?

Bruce: Joel,

Whoa boy! Yes, I am going to retire but not until later. We are looking at Oregon. So, slow down - nobody is throwing anybody away. I am not going anywhere.

Bruce (Dad)

Billy: Can I have a dog now?

Bruce: No.

Billy: Hey, Dad, can you please be more clear? hahahaha What does NO mean?

I'm really really devastated that I can't have a dog, Dad. Not having a dog will hinder my development you know. I AM in my formative years, you know. I won't be my potential without a dog during this stage of my life. Ever.

Deb's going nuts at the moment. I reckon I am too!!

h k

Bruce: Well Billy, since you put it that way, we will have to be very patient with you as you slowly develop as a young person. Of course, this only puts off other responsibilities and privileges that kids are given that have gone through their formative years at a higher rate. But we can wait :>)

H K

Bruce (Dad)

Billy: Privileges? What privileges?

*** Grabs Dad by the knees and wrestles him to the floor. Billy the Magnificent gives Dad the ninja move and ... oops ... pleads for mercy until ... until ... Billy the Magnificent grabs Dad around the waist and voila! Dad's left leg is above his head and his arm behind his back. Dad is TOAST!!! ***

Deb: Hi Dad. Hi Fran. I've got a bunch of crying kids right now. Coming home a man swerved into my lane and I froze for a second then swerved onto the shoulder. We missed by an inch. I'm really shook up. Only Kate wishes it had happened. Dad, we almost died today!!!

Bruce: Deb, This kind of experience is traumatic. Hopefully you are home. Be kind to yourself tonight and relax. I am very thankful it did not happen as are you. Take care.

Fran: Oh Deb, I am so sorry to hear this but very relieved you were able to react in spite of freezing up. Do take care and help Kate understand there is much to live for. See you next week.

Joel: Hi Daddy. I didn't do too good today. Are you gonna discipline me and stuff? I sure hope not.

Boy, I sure got scared yesterday when we almost died and stuff.

shake hands

then jump on your lap and velcro

Bruce: Joel,

Anything you want to share about not doing too good today????

S H

JOYL&V

Bruce (Dad)

Joel: Nooooottttttt reeeeaalllllyyyyyy

Oookkaaaaayyyyy

Mountain dew chips candy.

Bruce: Bad day – make today a better one.

Deb: Hi Dad!

I'm writing and Billy's playing KOC. Haven't even gotten out of pj's!

Hope you have a great day!

H K

Bruce: You can both operate at the same time?

Deb: No. It's called switching, Dad, switching. :)

Bruce: Is that corporal punishment?

Deb: What a GREAT idea!! Besides, this isn't working very well. Soooo, can I?

Bruce: It would depend on who is out for me to reply. But overall the answer is no.

Deb: RATS!! -- Deb

Whew! -- Billy

:)

Joel: Mountain dew and chips but the chips were for lunch Daddy.

I'm okay and stuff. Can I spend tomorrow with you?

S H

Leaning up against Dad and hoping he'll put his arm around me

Bruce: My arm is around you. No more mountain dew.

Bruce (Dad)

Deb: Seems like everybody got praised at work today except me. I KNOW I do a good job but the politics are terrible here.

Bruce: It seems like it is a common trait for people, you and me, to take things personally, be hurt by other people's opinions, and thus allow them to assign to us our sense of worth. People in our culture do this all the time. IT is at the root of family arguments, the break up of relationships, the lack of resolutions where anger is involved. When will we learn?? And I am learning along with everyone else but it seems to be a lesson that needs multiple repetitions to just begin to understand the important understanding that God is the source of our value because He made us, He loves us and He wants to be with us all the time.

Good on ya! You are gifted, talented, humorous, compassionate, empathetic towards others, and kind. You are a good person!

Deb: You are wise and spiritual and a good person!! Thanks Dad!!

*****

I (the Debra writing this narrative) am Kate, sort of. All of the other parts eventually integrated into me, Kate. Right now, I find this chapter to be extremely difficult. I sense that my trauma has not yet been resolved. That is not to say that I am not healthy, just not completely healed.

Trauma relivings sometimes came in stages. Kate's first reliving emerged as nightmares over and over again until her reliving became clear.

*****

Kate: Hi. I keep waking up from nightmares that are becoming more and more clear. I don't know him really but in my dreams I know him. He comes up to me and I try to get away. He has a knife and he stabs me. I feel it enter. I fall and he's on top of me. He has a knife and he's about to kill me when I wake up. After I wake up, the right side of my chest hurts like hell. But then this morning the nightmare continued after I woke up. I talk him out of killing me. I turn him on. He rapes me. Oh dear God I'm a whore. I'm such a whore. I think this nightmare isn't over.

Fran's Notes: Kate came out. She said Joel had the undying hope of wanting to be happy and kept them alive. Joel knew the way the monster treated us and he wanted to keep us alive. Joel was the survival mode." "Joel feels the body. I don't want to feel the body. I want to kill it. It disgusts me, makes me feel ill, totally wrong." I talked with her on keeping the body safe. She said Grandfather will keep her from killing the body. She hasn't tried or will, but wants to. When she calls or thinks of herself as a whore, she said she will look at the moon and it gives her a lot of comfort. The earth has told "us many times that we belong here."

Kate: My nightmare didn't end.

It was after we moved to the farm in Missouri. Pretty sure this is when I was born.

Right now my body is dead cold.

I was 13 or 14 years old. Eleena left for a few months. I threatened to tell. I wanted something but I don't know what. But Walter Amundson got very angry and came after me with a knife. I ran outside but he caught me and cut me with the knife. Not bad though. But he had me on the ground on top of me. I sweet talked him out of killing me and I turned him on. He raped me. After he did that, he took the knife and told me to be very still and that I'd better relax. He put the knife up my vagina. I could feel it in me. He said that I was his whore and nobody else's. Just his. If I had sex with anybody else, he'll put the knife up there and cut it out. He'd cut it out. My body was changing and he hated that. He put the knife to my breasts and threatened to cut them off. He hated that my body was changing. He kicked me in the right side of my chest and left.

From then on, whenever he brought a knife, I knew what to do. If I had sex ever with anybody else he'd cut it out. I'm his whore. I can't have sex with anybody else. I just can't. He hated my body. I can't have sex with anybody else. My body is ugly.

I'm scared. I think I'm dead. I know my body isn't even though it's stone cold right now. But I think I'm dead.

Grandfather's here and he's crying and that's making me cry. I feel like I'm gonna throw up now.

Grandfather's telling me to go back to bed and he'll be with me.

Bruce: Kate, These are horrible nightmares and terrible memories to relive. It seems necessary to relive them in a dream or nightmare to foster healing. I hope that the intensity will diminish and eventually the memory can fade a lot more in time. To say that you have nothing to fear in the second-life may not comfort you much as you experience the nightmares because it is in the second-life that you are experiencing the nightmares. But hopefully you will, in time, feel safe enough to be at ease in your waking hours and the majority of your sleeping hours. The trauma that you have experienced doesn't go away quickly but you have people who care for you, really care for you in appropriate ways, in Grandfather, God, and me, not to mention Deb, Joel, Billy.

We will all have to affirm to you that you are not a whore, that your body is not ugly and that you are a good person. Walter Amundson, on the other hand, was a sick man – a monster. But he is not around you any more except in your nightmares. We need to create some good memories with you to overshadow the bad memories.

I hope this day goes well for you.

Kate: The others say you are Dad and you're a normal Dad and I'm not supposed to do anything with you and I don't HAVE to do anything with you cause that's the first-life. So hi Dad.

Last night Grandfather told me to go to bed and I did and he laid down right next to me and put his arm around me. I asked him if he'd wake Deb up in time to get to work okay and he said yes. He did. So I turned off the alarm cause I knew I needed to sleep. So in bed, Grandfather put his arm around me and said "You are safe." over and over again until I fell asleep.

When I'm out like this, I see images, mostly blurred and really fast.

I feel the knife inside of me. I feel him raping me. I feel the body. I feel him kicking me. I am scared cold. He cut me with the knife inside of me. He said it was my period. My period didn't really happen until I was 16.

I'm 13 years old now. Maybe 14. I hope it's okay if I don't know. My body is going cold again so maybe I'd better not be out. Wish I could just sleep. Wish I could just die.

It's good to know that this will fade. I'll try to be patient. Thank you very much for caring about me and stuff.

Bruce: Hi Kate,

This change to feeling safe and having the old memories begin to fade will take time. So, you are right in saying that you will be patient. My guess is that the fast images and remembrances are all part of your trauma. This too will fade slowly as you deal with the trauma in constructive ways with Fran and as you begin to feel safe in your daily life.

Good to hear from you again!!

Bruce (Dad)

*****

Eleena sent me a letter stating that I did not love her and she was a good mother.

*****

Deb: Boy, I just feel GREAT today! (That was sarcasm in case you missed it.) Between Eleena's letter and Kate's reliving, I'm in shock. I always thought that the monster quit raping Philip around age 13 for fear of getting him pregnant. Nope. Didn't quit I see. It's really very strange for me when another part has memories of things I don't have. I now know the source of not being able to have sex. I've WANTED it, but not able to. A morbid fear as well as disgust. There's always been this underlying something. The good news is that it kept me from going the direction that so many people with my disorder go.

Joel said no to chocolate shake yesterday. He doesn't like how he feels afterwards. So progress is being made. I walked two and a quarter miles yesterday too. The usual trails are being widened, so I walked another. This one is very wide and I discovered it was lighted for night walks! It's for snowshoeing too. That should be awesome. I'm grieving that they're widening the other trail, but, frankly, there are scores of hiking trails around here. It's just that this one is actually IN town! It's a different experience when the trail is very wide as opposed to looking like deer walks it.

Dad, I hope you're having a good day.

H K

Bruce: Deb,

There is still some things to work on. As more of the puzzle pieces fall into place you have to process more information but overall it is a good progression in your healing experience - just isn't pleasant at times.

Good on Joel! Those stomach aches really help us watch what we consume.

Kate: I slept until 5:30 so that's good but the body's still really tired. Billy got up and played the game. When I'm awake and out like this, the images just keep on, and the physical feelings. I think that Fran will tell me to image a way out of the situation, but I'm scared of that. That's what I or rather Philip did. I ran and then I fought back and I mean I fought and stuff. So he grabbed me by the hair and got a knife. I got away and ran and that's when he caught up with me outside. So I TRIED to get out of it and I made it really worse.

Do you think that maybe God didn't show that part of the movie after Walter Amundson died because nobody was ready to know about it? Cause I wasn't ready to come out?

I don't think I'll kill myself. I mean, you were awful nice and gave me a thread into this second-life. I know I'm still stuck in the trauma of the first-life, but you gave me a thread. Thank you Dad. Gave me some of Joel's unending hope.

I think maybe Deb could have ended all this process a couple of times but she didn't. A couple of times she was really sure this was all there was. I think that if she had really wanted to, God would have let her. But she always knew there was still something wrong. Once Joel came out, I couldn't stay asleep.

Eleena told Deb once that when David ran away, Walter Amundson told her to get David back. She said that for the first time in her life she stood up to him and said no. His reply was, "Well, we might as well get a divorce then." And so they did. Boy, I guess that Walter Amundson really was a coward. But I didn't count cause when I fought back I made things worse for me.

Susan talked to Deb last night and it really made me feel lots better. She's nice and everything. Man, I'm always on the verge of crying. That sucks. But she did that Reiki thing yesterday cause God asked her to. I have problems breathing and the tightness for me is right where she said she did it. Cool, huh? Man, I am so scared just all the time and I don't know why.

Well, I better go.

Thanks for being my Dad. I mean, thanks for real for real.

Bruce: Hi Kate,

> You are doing fine and making good progress. There is a great desire to live amongst each of you so I do not think anyone will kill her/himself. Besides you are loved by many and you are curious about the second-life and how it will turn out - and it will and is turning out very good!! So, relax, be patient, and let the healing process take its course.
>
> Bruce (Dad)

Deb: An interesting dialogue between Grandfather and Joel. Grandfather asked Joel if he understood now the difference about love that first dad's hurt was to him and love now. Joel said yeah and had to explain that first dad's hurting wasn't love and Joel likes cuddles a lot better now and that that's what love is. Grandfather said yes and said, "Son, there are some things you need to change." Grandfather said that what Joel's been eating has been unacceptable and now if he has to, he'll have to discipline him and did he understand what that meant. Joel said yeah and he didn't like it any.

Oh crap! Joel just kicked me!!!

Anyway, Grandfather told him to start with candy and he may not have candy until he's used to not having any. Joel said that he really likes it and stuff but Grandfather said that it's very bad for the body and Joel has to learn to respect the body.

So Joel's pretty unhappy at the moment.

Have a great day!

hug ***kiss***

Bruce: **Learning how to eat right is very important but very difficult for a young child who has a sweet taste. But it can be done and will be done.**

Billy: Hi Dad! Didn't get the chores done. Got trash out and one load of laundry. Tonight I'm fixing chicken and corn on the cob and garlic bread.

Joel hasn't had any candy since Grandfather's Big Threat so the body is feeling better. Kate is a mess.

Have a great evening Dad!

Bruce: Hi Billy,

> Busy weekend but you managed to get some things done. Now you gotta play catch up on the chores. Keep after it. Last nights' dinner sounded great!!

I hope you are having a good day.

Bruce (Dad)

Billy: Aw Dad! I gotta finish the chores? Can I wait until this weekend? Or if Deb is going away this weekend, on Thursday? Please?

Bruce: The answer has two letters....the first one is a "N". Can you guess the second letter?

Billy: **shakes head** uh-uh

Bruce: Poor effort Billy on an easy question and so I will fill in the blank for you "O" or NO.

Billy: Hi Dad

Didn't get ALL the chores done, but ALMOST done. Need to put away laundry and do dishes.

Drove through MacDonald's and had a big mac and fries. Not me. Joel.

Am I in trouble now?

Bruce: Billy, Billy, Billy,

No, you are not in trouble. Finish the chores and get your allowance. Good on ya!

Bruce (Dad)

Joel: Am I in trouble though?

Bruce: Joel,

No trouble unless you drank Mountain Dew with the McDonalds. And the answer is?

Bruce (Dad)

Joel: No, but I did earlier in the day. Oh-oh?

Bruce: Thanks for your honesty Joel. Remember, we want to stop drinking Mountain Dew because it is bad for the body. Do you like root beer?

Joel: YEAH DADDY! And I had root beer today instead too!!!!

Billy: The book says that we're inconsistent with eating because one person will want one thing and another will want another, and one might want to eat for comfort and another might not want to eat at all. Nothing like pointing out the obvious, huh? The way to be in line in the book is the same thing you've been telling us. Are you good or what? :)

Taking it easy today. On the road tomorrow.

Listening to snow sliding off the roof. Cooooolllll.

Hope you're having a great time this weekend Dad! You'll have to get a time machine to go back to the office though. Says so on your phone message thingy. Bye!

H K

Bruce: Hey Billy, A little confirmation from the book never hurts. Safe travels and I will pray for you all.

*****

As the healing went deeper into my subconscious, imagery became more and more prevalent. I think the imagery helped me understand in ways I could not otherwise. As strange as it may seem, I think the following imagery in the first paragraph connects to my life awakening and perhaps being healed.

*****

Kate: Hi Dad

Lots of things are happening to me!

I had a waking dream. I was standing outside when all around me I saw breasts and then they quickly turned into hills that rose higher and higher into mountains. Then there were volcanoes that erupted. Then blood flowed like rivers. But it wasn't bad blood, it was life blood. The mountains rose even higher and they became sharp-angled. I saw animals and death too. Then there was this orange sphere made out of orange light that sparkled and it came to me. I stood in the middle of it and it was God. He said, "You belong to me. You belong to me." Then he told me that he created me. Then he said he would show me who I am, but it would be me later. Michel was there beside me and I turned into light, but my light stayed within the orange sphere, like it wasn't time to step out. I could just barely handle this, and God told me to liberate the earth. That my ties, who I am, is tied to the earth and to liberate the earth. I couldn't take it anymore and all of a sudden I found myself in a green meadow full of flowers and butterflies.

Two times yesterday, something else happened. All of a sudden I THINK I was living in the present. I've never felt it before. But my perception changed and I looked around me and said to myself, "Look at this place." Once it was while I was driving and I was looking at the sky. The second time I was walking into my living room. It was like all of a

Fractured Mind

sudden, I'm HERE. Each time lasted only two or three seconds. Then another time I could feel my body and the feeling was the same. It was very strange. I think I've gotten close in the past when I looked at the moon. I always search out the moon, and seeing it always gave me great comfort throughout my life.

Jack got boxes of Walter Amundson's stuff! Documents and pictures. He kept everything. Jack and I both want to trace where we lived when. He kept all of his tax records since the 1940s. Deb sees it as history, like American history. There's this document that a social worker wrote when he wanted to adopt us. I was 8 when that happened and Jack was 10. It said that Jack was interested in watching television and fishing and I was interested in reading and doing school work. Jack was laughing so much I could barely understand him. So we laughed our heads off. Deb said who got the doctorate and who flunked out of college. Deb said Boy, it started early, didn't it. Jack said some things I can't repeat but we were both laughing too hard. It was later that Walter Amundson wouldn't let me read anymore. It didn't stop me though.

Jack said that he hates fishing and doesn't remember doing it. I'm wondering what Walter Amundson did to him when they went fishing. Jack also saw the document that was when our biological father signed us away. It hurt him Dad. Deb said, yeah, we both didn't have parents who cared anything for us, even our first father and Jack said yeah.

I'm doing good. I yo-yo, but I don't really see myself as a whore anymore. I'm wondering if I'm too big to sit on your lap like Joel does and if I am if I can sit next to you.

Gotta go back to bed.

H K I think.

Bruce: Kate,

I am glad you are having experiences with God and that you are understanding the past through the documents.

As far as where to sit (lap or next to me) you sit wherever you are comfortable. Sometimes I want to sit next to God and talk and sometimes even I want to sit on his lap as a child. So it is really up to you and how you feel in the moment.

Safe travels today.

H   K

Bruce (Dad)

Joel: You're the best of the best of the best, DADDY!!!!! We all think so!!!

Thankyou thankyou thankyou .... And on to infinity!!!!!!!

Lots of H and lots of K

Kate: Last evening was pretty strange. I couldn't breathe and my body went stone cold and I just wanted to cry all the time. I didn't panic. I felt the knife up in me. Gee Dad. I was totally in the first-life and my body went into shock. But it didn't wreck anything. I don't know what triggered it. I guess I just trust in this process now.

Dad, I feel like I'm too big to sit on your lap. I'm comfortable just sitting next to you. I'm hoping I can just lean up against you and you'll put your arm around me. Boy I sure needed to last night! Thanks Dad. It's good for me to know that you do that with God.

Hope you're having a great day!

H. K.

Bruce: Hi Kate,

I always have cold hands when I preach.

You can sit next to me and lean on me anytime. Like I said, whatever is comfortable for you.

H　　K

Bruce (Dad)

Joel: Hi Daddy!

This morning at the hotel I has fruit loops. I really like it Daddy. Can I have fruit loops instead of stupid raisin bran in the mornings? Please?

Hs. Ks.

Bruce: Joel,

Fruit Loops are filled with unhealthy levels of sugar. So, the answer would be no. Raisin Bran is not stupid because it has no brain. You have to eat good food for the body to have and maintain good health. That is the priority.

H　　K

Bruce (Dad)

Joel: Rats! Ooookkkkaaaaaayyyyyyy

So raisin bran and the scarecrow has something in common!! Hahahahahahaha

Bruce: Very good - Raisin Bran and scarecrow　:>)

Joel: Hi Daddy.

I had one mello yellow today but the rest was okay I guess except for the fruit loops. Dad how come it's so hard for me to remember and do stuff right? I try and stuff Daddy but I'm just in the first-life just all the time and I just gotta do what I want or I'll die and stuff. Then I know I'm in the second-life and I can say to myself no cause my second-life daddy says no cause of my body and stuff. I know I'm not being mean and rebelling or anything. I just crave bad stuff and I just can't connect to Grandfather like the others can and stuff. And then when I do connect to Grandfather he just kisses me and stuff even though I'm a bad kid. And I feel bad cause I can't not do stuff right. I'm sorry Daddy. I kinda wish I never came out and stuff cause I'm bad or I just can't be good.

Bruce: Make responsible choices every day.

Joel: I GOT TO MUCH PRESSURE ON ME AND StuFF!!!!!!

Billy: Kate just tries to just sleep and not move the body cause the body goes into shock.

*****

The body going into shock is not a memory of the first-life, but is happening at the time during the second-life.

*****

Kate: Hi Dad

Yeah Billy was right. I'm not wanting the body to move at all. I go into shock. First I can't breathe then my body gets cold and the right aide of my chest hurts and I'm totally in the first-life. Deb just read in the book that what we call reliving is termed "reactivated traumatic memories" and "you feel as though it is happening in the present." They "may include intense or overwhelming feelings, such as panic, rage, shame, loss, guilt, despair, conflicting beliefs and thoughts; physical sensations such as pain; visual images, sounds, and smells; and also behaviors, such as ... shutting down." Every time I come out it's bad Daddy. My body just hurts and shuts down. I've been sitting next to you and leaning up against you and stuff but my spirit needs to sleep too and I'm afraid to do that.

Well. Better go.

H. K.

Kate: *He hanged me. I can't breathe. If I move, I'll die. Sometimes I was made to stand on a fence in the barn or on a bale of hay. Sometimes he'd stretch me out on the ground. He puts a noose around my neck and the rope is through a pulley. He pulls, then lets go, pulls, then lets go. I* can't breathe. *If I move I'll die. I'm his whore. Just his and nobody else's. I don't understand what I've done. I'm nothing. I'm nobody at all. I have to be nothing. He'll kill me if I'm a person. I can't. I just can't. I don't know why I'm here.*

Bruce: Kate, First-life stuff that is very traumatic and difficult to revisit. You are not a whore, you are no one's whore, you can breathe and you can move in this life. Relax, breathe easy, rest. Call Fran if you want to talk this through.

H K

Bruce (Dad)

Fran's Notes: Deb started to fall asleep. Someone appeared and didn't know who he is, but he knew me. He's a boy. "I'm supposed to kill the body." He doesn't know where he got that idea. He thinks he's 10 years old. "I'm supposed to beat up people and punch people." Shaun was the name he gave himself. He agreed not to hurt the body. He had a headache.

Deb: Hi Dad

Another one came out in Fran's office today. Right out of Kate and right out of the right side of my chest. Name is Shaun. 10 years old. Only thing he knows is he's supposed to kill the body. Fran says that thinking is like a virus and needs to be deleted. He doesn't like to be told what to do. Not very emotional. Actually a pleasant little guy. But he's stuck in that mindset which I suspect IS his trauma but I don't really know. He does not know you. Heh heh heh.

Surprise! A bouncing baby boy! Congratulations!! Geez.

Shaun: You my DAD? No more other dad? All I know is I'm supposed to kill the body. But Fran says no. I guess my other dad is dead. Is that why your my dad now? Fran says I dont think right and stuff. The body's supposed to hurt and stuff but she says that's my first dad. I don't like having to do what you say. I did what first dad said okay and now all of a sudden I got a new dad. I'm supposed to do what dads say and stuff. I'm good at it! I been hurting the body like forever cause he said so. Fran said he didn't kill the body any and he could have but he didn't. I thought that was my job. I always did what my first dad wanted me to and I liked doing stuff and I was good at it. I could even tell what he wanted before he told me! I could drive the tractor and I could get him what he wanted even before he asked for it like nails and stuff. So I was a really good worker and stuff and I wanted to do what he wanted. I'm kinda scared though cause I dont know what you want. I did everything he wanted me to do and I wanted to. You gonna kill me if I don't do what you want when you don't tell me what you want?

Hey! Why do you want me anyway? I'm nobody. Or do you just want somebody to work for you?

I'm 10 but I'm not stupid.

Bruce: Hi Shaun,

I am your dad and I do not want you to hurt yourself or anybody. AND I do not want you to hurt the body. Sounds like you are a good worker and that you like to do quality work. That is a wonderful gift. Besides not hurting the body I do not want you to be scared because no one is going to hurt you now. The old dad isn't here any more and you will have to learn to trust me and that will take a little time. So relax, rest, do not hurt anyone, do not hurt the body, and let us begin a good relationship. How does that sound, besides weird?

Bruce (Dad)

Shaun: Gee. Okay Dad. Besides REALLY weird it sounds kinda scary but you said I don't have to BE scared. Gee I don't know what it's like to NOT be scared. So I guess it sounds like ... Um .... Okay. Curious. I'm like curious. How's that!

Bruce: Curious is good. Not having to be scared will come with trust.

Shaun: Hi Dad

I been doing what you say. Not hurting the body. I guess I have to tell you a secret though. I know I was supposed to kill the body, especially after we left the farm and stuff and I tried but I just couldn't do it good enough. So I didn't really do my job. I guess that makes me a loser with a great big L. I tried really hard to do what he wanted me to do and stuff and I'm just a disappointment. I sure do wish that people wanted me and stuff and were proud of me and stuff. But I feel pretty much alone most of the time and stuff. I don't think I'm a person.

Before I left the farm, when Jack left, my dad told me that I wouldn't last going away like that and that I should kill myself. He said that nobody's gonna love me and stuff. Ever. I feel pretty bad about myself all the time you know. He told me that nobody will ever be my dad except him so I better appreciate what I got cause there isn't anything else. I sure don't know what I'm doing being alive and everything. I really do just want the pain to go away and that's all. Now that I'm out, it's like in my throat and stuff.

Bruce: Shaun, Good on ya for doing the right things and not hurting the body. You are not on the farm anymore and you are loved by all of us. I am your Dad now and no one will hurt you anymore. So you just have to live, observe that your old "Dad" is not here anymore, observe that no one is trying to hurt you anymore, and learn to trust me. You are fine. AND you are NOT the big "L".

Bruce (Dad)

Deb: Hi Dad

Something interesting happened with Fran yesterday. Jack has documents and one said that I was interested in reading when I was eight. Fran said that she has thought for years that children like me who read seems to live life okay. That reading was a huge positive activity to help me keep sane and served as a role model for living. Cool huh?

When I was talking to Ian Bruch last night, I told him about the book about dissociation and he wanted the title. I think just doing that triggered Kate because the body went into the trauma stress, right on the phone with him! Couldn't breathe, then the body went cold, then pain in the right side of my chest. Just writing this, and she's going into it again. BUT last night because of reading the book, Kate psychologically went into a room full of stuffed animals and just cuddled with them and I tried very hard to breathe deeply and relax. So for the first time the body didn't go the full trauma mode and she was able to settle down. Dad, I move, I die. I said to her in my mind over and over again that she's safe now. Kate is now going back to her safe room and the body has the short of breath and the pain, but I'm calming down.

Take care and have a good day!

H K

Bruce: Deb,

Kate will progress one step at a time and she is showing progress. We celebrate the small steps.

I am running late and have to go but I will be out of town tomorrow all day. I am going to Michigan to give a blessing.

H   K

Bruce (Dad)

Kate: They wanted me dead. They didn't just not want me but they wanted me dead. I can't breathe. I'm trying to calm down. Joel and Shaun are feeling it too. We are together. I'm really nauseous. Christmas. *Nobody will ever want me. He said that. Eleena just watched. He put the noose around my neck and said if it was up to him I'd be dead. So it's my choice. I see* bales of hay and I'm standing on one. With the noose around my neck. He tied my hands behind my back and said it's up to me. I can die if I want to and I might as well cause nobody wants me here. He tightened up the noose and the rope and left me there. If I move I'll die. He left me standing there. I can't fall asleep cause I'll die. Eleena finally took it off of me and told me that I shouldn't make him angry like that. My parents didn't just not want me. They wanted me to be dead. Fran said that if he wanted me dead he would have killed me but he was careful not to. But I think he was just too chicken to go through with it. When he saw me he beat me up. Okay. I'm breathing easier now. I'm so alone. It was Christmas and I wanted to keep a present and he got mad and pulled my hair to get me out into the barn. Nobody wants me. I'm supposed to die. I'm supposed to kill the body. I want this pain to go away. I hate Christmas cause I'm so alone and I'm supposed to be dead but I'm not.

Okay. I'm calmer now. The body didn't go onto total shock. I just can't move too good and I'm cold but I'm breathing again. The alone is still here and it really sucks and stuff.

I can see Grandfather and I'm supposed to try to sleep now. Boy I sure don't know why I'm here. I don't know why God wants me to be alive. I don't really want to be alone anymore. Night.

Joel: Daddy! I'm scared! I can still feel the reliving last night. I know your going out of town today and stuff. I'm just scared!!! I think I'm supposed to be dead and stuff. My old mommy and daddy didn't want me Daddy and they wanted me dead Daddy. I don't understand what I did wrong and stuff but I sure made him mad and stuff. I try and try to do what he wants but I just didn't really cause I didn't make myself die and stuff. Why do they hate me Daddy? Why do they want me to die? I know I made Eleena really really mad and stuff and I wanted to make her mad and stuff cause she was mean to me all the time. But I tried really really hard to make my old daddy like me and stuff and want me and stuff. I was helpful! Oh gee. Grandfather's here and he wants me to go back to sleep. Okay. Bye.

Fran's Notes: Shaun is totally confused about this life. He doesn't feel like a person and doesn't think he will until he's healed. He wants his first dad back because he understands his dad and why he did stuff he did. "Deserved it." "He was trying to find himself." "He wanted to feel love." Shaun never hated Walter Amundson. We talked about how he could see Walter's own desire to connect in a perverse way.

Joel: Hi Daddy

I had a dream/vision. Me and Grandfather were on top of a hill with a path going down. A couple of women passed us jogging down the path. Grandfather asked me if I wanted to do that and I said yeah. He said I could and tried to help me take steps. But I couldn't Daddy! I couldn't move and stuff and I cried and stuff and Grandfather picked me up and held me. How come I can't do stuff Daddy? I woke up then. I don't want to sleep Daddy.

Okay. Better go.

H. K.

Bruce: Joel, It was a dream. You can do stuff. People have dreams all the time – some good – some not so good but the dreams do not stop people from pursuing their desires, hopes, or goals. Set you goals and go after them. Here's a goal: No more Mountain Dew. :>)

H   K

Deb: Kate is now trying to see that other people are okay toward her. This is new. She's trying to see that generally people are nice and the people we know are okay. Can't say care about her yet. I think maybe that's her job. To turn that thinking around. She didn't try or couldn't try before your visit. Your visit made you real to her.

Kate: I hate Christmas. I came out and we looked at presents in the morning. I was in my pajamas. He was mad at me and raped me cause I was in my pajamas. I saw kids do that on tv so I thought it was okay. I was wrong. I don't know what's okay.

I hate Christmas. I just feel alone. I feel like nobody cares about me. I don't know.

I sure wish the others and Grandfather would let me kill myself. I don't understand why I'm here. I'm really tired of feeling so bad all the time. I just want it to end. I just wanted to be normal. That's all. I just wanted to be like other kids. That's why I wore my pajamas. I knew what was normal on tv. I found out that parents weren't mean and stuff by talking to other kids. That's how I found out that other kids dads didn't have sex with them. So I tried to figure out how to be normal. And I watched tv for that. I thought maybe if I acted like a normal kid my parents would be normal too. I just got it all wrong.

Bruce: Kate, I loved opening presents in my pajamas when I was a kid. It is very normal and most families would practice this. You experienced abnormal parents, parents that did not know how to be parents. You didn't get it all wrong, you had it right, your first-life parents had it all wrong.

So, now you are learning that normal fathers do not have sex with their children. You feel guilty about what has happened in the past but none of what happened was your fault. It was not your fault.

You are not a bad person, you are a good person and a confused person and all of this will clear up in time and you will feel much better. Give it time.

Bruce (Dad)

Kate: Hi Dad

God made me come to him. I sure didn't want to and stuff. I was pretty scared. But he did. He made me ten. I'm TEN!!!! I thought that 13 was too young!!! He said I especially need to be rebuilt and I need to go back to when I was really born. I guess that was with the hanging Christmas day cause I was ten years old then. He said he wants me to be the "precious girl" I was meant to be and to grow. I admit that being ten makes the sex stuff not so much in my face, but I sure don't like it much. My biggest being scared is you though and you'll just say oh great, that's just great, and ignore me and stuff. I feel pretty much alone and scared cause I do not have any idea how to be a girl. God told me to explore myself and being a girl does NOT mean cleaning out the pig sty!! I really don't think God was talking about sex stuff and to tell you the truth I think that's kinda gross now. Before, to me, it was just hurt but now it's just gross. I can still feel the knife inside me though and cutting me though and stuff and I still feel really really scared and sick and if I move I'll REALLY get cut too deep and die and stuff. And man, I see the first-life just all the time, flashing in my head. But it's like God wants me to do girl stuff with my body like lotion and stuff but it's even more than that. It's like seeing the world like a girl sees the world. I don't know. All I know is what he said and sorta said, I mean said without words to my insides. My mind bends. Grandfather asked if I could maybe try to exercise and I got all panicked and stuff and I still do like right now just thinking about it. I sure don't know what to do any. I feel really really alone and now God made me ten – oh geez – and it's like I got this job but I don't really know what the job is. Hey, this is strange. God told me just now to start with holding the little bear doll Fran gave us, and to call it mine. Fuzzy. Do you know why cause I sure don't. I have a cold. I don't feel too good. Grandfather just said for me to go back to bed. Boy God sure is big. Bye.

H K

Bruce: Kate, One thing you can work on is what we call "stinking thinking." Thoughts that tell us that "nobody loves us" "I am not a good person" "I have no purpose in life". These type of thoughts you need to dismiss and replace them with thoughts like "I am a person of worth" "I am a person of great worth. God, Grandfather, my second-life dad and others love me and do not require anything from me except for me to heal and be happy." Try starting to change the "stinkin' thinkin'" and feel the love people have for you.

Hugs. Kisses

Bruce. (Dad)

Kate: Okay Daddy. Cleaning up the stinking thinking's my job!! to start I guess.

Deb plays scrabble with people. I'm trying to do my job like you said Dad. I think they like me and stuff but I don't know if they love me. How do I know if the scrabble people love me? How can anybody love me Daddy really if they don't really know me? And I think most everybody doesn't really know me. So how can I tell if they love me or not?

H. K.

Bruce: Kate,

Love is a strong emotion, feeling towards someone that develops over time. People that play games with others may like the people a lot and treat them well but may not say that they love them, whereas if it is church people that you have known for a long time they may say that they love you. I am sure the game folks really like you and will treat you very well - always. But your comment is correct: "How can people love me ... if they don't really know me?" In time people will express that they love you but for now you will have to settle for God, Jesus, Grandfather, the Bruch clan and me loving you.

Bruce (Dad)

Kate: Hi Dad

I had a dream/vision, but I told God it wasn't really from him so he made me have it again!!! I don't get any of it Dad.

I'm in the Other Realm and things look gray and foggy there. An angel came and took me away from Grandfather and carried me through a tunnel into a really colorful and pretty valley. He set me down in the middle of himself and two other angels. They didn't say a word to me. Next thing I know I'm traveling above the angels and above the earth. Somebody, I think it was God, said that I belong to the earth, anywhere and everywhere I may be, and to focus on the earth. I asked about people and he said to help people connect to each other and to the earth. Next thing I know I'm back in bed.

I know that Fran wanted to help me neurologically yesterday but I just wasn't ready for that. I'm still stuck in the trauma and I see and feel it over and over again. I'm scared, Dad. I'm scared about what God wants. I'm scared about this second-life. It's alien to me. I just want to go to sleep again!!

Okay, that's it Daddy. Hope you're having a good day.

H K

Bruce: Kate, Were you scared when you were in the beautiful valley? Were you afraid of the angels? The things that scare you about the reliving are not present in the second-life. You have every right to be afraid of the first-life and you have every right not to trust the second-life. But so far when you experience the second-life you do not quite understand it, although it doesn't hurt you like the first-life. (This is a hint about the second-life). It takes time to trust and it takes time to release the first-life but you will get there!! Keep dreamin' –

H   K

Bruce (Dad)

Joel: Hi Daddy. Do you still love me and stuff?

Bruce: Joel,

I still love you and STUFF. And no I am not throwing you away.

Bruce (Dad)

Fran's Notes: We used EMDR to process Kate, Joel, and Shaun's trauma with the hanging. She's realizing that her parents wanted her to die. She began to cry. I explained why parents abuse their children and it doesn't have to do with the child.

Kate: Hi Daddy

I think Deb and me were in this one together. Mostly me though maybe. This happened this morning.

Everything was in my face. Not just when I was with the Amundson's but it was like I was aware of the different parts of me who were mostly out and living. Like Damon who couldn't remember even where he came from when people asked him. This unending desperation for somebody to care about me and not knowing why I couldn't have friends. Men who appropriately were interested in me and me not being able to handle it and sabotaging every possibility of having a mate. This incredible loneliness. Then Ian Bruch who showed me a relationship with God that for years and years I latched onto with the hope of being accepted and somebody noticing me. Of walking at night and during the day hoping that somebody would notice me and want me around. For years even after coming here I couldn't hike or leave the apartment except for work and to shop. I did not understand why. Now the first-life is in my face but so is the impact of the first-life.

And with Ian Bruch who tethered me to him and to God. Jack Jones who cared about me being able to function in society. Then Ken who set me on a course to healing when I could come out in five parts. These five were the surface. But I thought I was merged for ten years and because of Ian Bruch I was healed emotionally enough and because of Ken I was healed psychologically enough to do the best I could do and to settle down enough to make church friends. Then you who mentored me and encouraged me to respond to God's calling in my life for others and to help me know how to do what to do. Then, finally, blowing apart to set me on this process of deep healing and your generosity. And Fran who is HERE of all places! Susan and her kindness who helps me understand and tap into my body. Grandfather who did not leave me alone through this healing And all this time not being able to choose to think I'm actually a person!

All this happened this morning and, frankly, knowing the rape and sodomy and beating and torture and ridicule with parents who not only didn't want me but wanted me dead and knowing the impact that has had on the rest of my life was just too much.

So I genuinely asked God if I could please just die. He had me look into his face and he said no. He said he didn't want me to die at this time. He said that part of my healing is to know the first-life with ALL of its ugliness. To know the impact and to understand why. He also said that I have a lot of my life to live yet and he will see to it that I will no longer be bound. He didn't blame me. He just said no. But that I will enter into an entirely new and different life because I will be different. He said that I will enter into a new phase of my life that will be wonderful and fulfilling to me. He said it will take some time for this grief to fade but it will. And he has something for me to do. I asked but he wouldn't tell me what but to just stay the course and keep doing what I need to do to heal for now. He recognized that my need is still there but he said that it will change.

God said that I will never be normal in the way I really want. I am unable to be like other people not just because of the first-life but because of HOW I'm being healed. And he said that included you and Ken and Ian Bruch and everybody else and Grandfather and Fran and the kind of influences the healing people have had and are having as part of my restructuring. He said that a part of these people are now in me. He said that he is looking forward to this summer. And for me to be comforted, that he knows my grief and my fear but to be comforted.

I guess this means I don't get to die yet, huh? :-) I admit though, I don't get much of what he said. I think I'm supposed to experience something but I sure don't know what. I guess I know more of why though.

H. K.

Bruce: Kate,

> Understanding something as complex as what you have been through takes time, time to process, time to deal with a sense of unworthiness, time to establish your worthiness, your belovedness, time to experience life anew. It takes time for fear to diminish and hope to ascend. So be patient and give the second-life a chance to grow and become a part of you. You can keep reflecting on what God has shared with you and you will understand more and more as time goes on. Trust the future to be good.
>
> H   K
>
> Bruce (Dad)

Bruce: Joel, Billy, Deb, Kate,

> In my meditations this morning as I thought of you and prayed, the thought came to me that you are all in this together. This is not a new revelation but just a reminder to each of you that what each of you experience, feel, eat - impacts the others in good or negative ways. Since each of you are at a different age each of you have different understandings about life. Kate is going through her reliving experiences, Deb is stressed, Billy is carrying responsibilities of chores, and Joel is trying to deal with the stress of others and be a kid by eating the wrong things.
>
> So, you have to pull yourselves together and do your very best each day to make life as good as you can for the sake of everyone. Each of you are safe, each of you are loved and cared for, each of you have shelter, food, and many advantages that others do not. On the other hand, each of you have had much more trauma in your lives than most other people would have in a life time. So be thankful for what you have and for each other. Do your best each day to relax and enjoy the good moments, and stick together getting through the challenging times. You are conscious that God is with you, God speaks to each of you. You are blessed, you have challenges, but overall you have been blessed in your challenges with people who have come into your lives to help, support and love you. Do not let fear get the best of you for each of you are worthy, each of you have value, each of you are good. You are bright, intelligent and caring people. You are way ahead of some folks in your understandings and your responses to life.
>
> Blessings to you this day and in all the days ahead.
>
> H   K

From Deb: Thank you Dad. This struck a chord with me. It's something to reread, study and reflect.

From Billy: Thanks Dad! It's been hard for me to want to keep up with chores lately! None of us feel too good, emotionally I mean.

From Kate: Thanks Daddy! I wish I wasn't so very sad you know. But like you said I gotta remember that I'm safe.

From Joel: Thank you Daddy! I just wanna cry just all the time and stuff!! Fear not huh? I'm kinda velcroed to Grandfather and stuff. But I gotta read this lots, what you wrote I mean.

From Shaun: Thanks Dad! I know your message was to me, too. I feel like I'm just wandering and lost. I'll do my very best Dad! I have to remember that I'm safe now even though I sure don't feel like it.

From Heather: Hi Daddy!! I love you too and stuff and lots and lots of stuff and stuff!! My doll's name is Timmy Teddy. Okay?

HHHHHH KKKKKK

Heather: DADDY!!!

Hi! Guess what? The mother Mary came and visited me. All of a sudden she was standing in front of me and just everything. She's Jesus mom you know. I didn't get stuff she said much but something about me and us and stuff and needing a mother and stuff and she will visit and stuff. Boy she felt different and stuff. Nobody expected it or anything. But we cried some but I wasn't sad or anything. Daddy she was really really nice.

Deb accidently washed Fuzzy in the washing machine but he's okay. Bye!

H. K.

Bruce: Great Heather,

I sometimes pray to God, the angels and Mother Mary and it seems to help me. So I am excited that you are beginning to have a relationship with Mother Mary. This is VERY cool.

H K

Bruce (Dad)

*****

Grandfather and Jesus talked together at this point. Grandfather put Joel in a pond at the base of a waterfall. Usually, the Other Realm is gray and misty. The tropical type waterfall and pond were in crystal color.

*****

Billy: Dear Daddy

> I talked to Aunt Susan today and stuff and I was thinking about being bad for real but now after talking to her I gotta trust you and tell you truth stuff. Okay. Here it goes.
>
> I miss you Dad. I feel bad and think you don't like me anymore. I know you love me but I miss you and getting h k. I think you're really really busy and I know it's really really important to help Kate. I miss you Daddy. I sure hope you're not too mad at me now and want to throw me away.

Bruce: Billy,

> **Change you focus from feeling lonely to serving the others and you will find purpose instead of sorrow. You have been very responsible at a young age and I am proud of you. Jesus came to be with the sick more than the healthy so give thanks to God that you're really doing very well and are not suffering from the first-life as much like some of the others. Hang in there and be aware that I am mindful of you and care for you.**
>
> **H   K**
>
> **Bruce (dad)**

Kate: Hi Dad!

> I just finished with Fran and it just so happens that she has until 3:00 open so we are staying for another session after a while.
>
> I had a reliving with Fran that came from really deep within me Dad. Walter Amundson suffocated me before and when he had sex with me. I couldn't breathe and all of a sudden my upper chest hurt. I think I blacked out all the time cause I woke up with him standing over me and peeing on my face.
>
> Fran says this is really serious stuff. I know that all of us out including Billy are really close and none of us has felt too good lately. We also think you've been wicked busy.
>
> I gotta go to sleep now. Thanks Daddy!
>
> H. K.

Fran's Notes: Joel said his head feels different and "feels kind of happy." Kate is in shock and Grandfather is helping her. We processed this experience and it seemed to be a major breakthrough for Joel.

Kate again had trouble breathing. I worked with her on being oriented using a technique to bring it within a tolerable range. She recalled and felt body sensations of being choked, unable to breathe and pain around her neck and upper chest.

Kate: When I first woke up I was 13 but God made me 10 so I can handle stuff better. Boy, he sure was right!

I want to write this really carefully. I'm pretty much at peace right now and I want to write to you the very best way that I can. Deb isn't writing this cause it didn't happen to her. It happened to me.

So I want to start off by saying just how much thankfulness I have for you all. A part of you are in us and I know that I have to be rebuilt now, but I just can't thank you except to do my very best to grow to be the kind of person you would be proud of.

Grandfather said that what I just went through is the end. And what I want to tell you is not only the reliving but the stuff surrounding it. I know that God has been in control over everything since the beginning and I think that he helped choose you to make me into a person who is maybe whole. That hasn't happened yet, but I can see that happening now. Heather, Joel, Billy, Shaun, and me have a special connection to the body that none of the others have or had. In the first-life, I was raised and hurt by two parents who were both monsters. So I hit the lottery on that, cause what's the odds really? By monsters I mean mentally sick people who never got to know me at all. Eleena, my mother, has what me and my brother, Jack, call the evil smile. I never knew why her evil smile hurt me so much until now.

I think you know about me standing with the noose around my neck afraid to move and lose my balance and die. And you know about the knife up in me and cutting. The hanging and the knife cutting happened more than once, but this last reliving happened only once, although Walter Amundson continued to strangle me when he wanted to. But I not only want to tell you the reliving, but it coming out.

Every since I woke up sometimes I couldn't breathe. But I didn't know why. I thought it was maybe cause I was afraid to move. "I move, I die." Fran, my therapist, uses what we call the buzzies, which is a particular technique that connects my brain nerves together. Last week I felt lost and unable to get the trauma of the knife cutting to stop. I was what the book calls stuck in the trauma. Fran helped me so the knife and Walter Amundson dissolved, but also Grandfather was able to carry me and put me in a pretty pond with a waterfall with Joel who's been in for a couple of weeks now. So I've been in water. Deb said that water is a conduit both to the subconscious and to the spiritual realm. Ever since I first came out, though, I couldn't stop crying. I didn't know what was wrong. When Grandfather put me into the water, he told me that it isn't over yet.

I knew there was something, but I didn't know what. I also kept falling asleep.

So yesterday in Fran's office I came out and couldn't help but cry again, but I couldn't figure out why. Fran gave me the buzzies and I got the headache we always get with the buzzies so I knew they were working. She asked me what I saw and I told her I couldn't see anything! I told her I don't know what's wrong. I started to go to sleep but I didn't cause Fran kept me awake. Then I started to not be able to breathe and that's what started stuff coming up. Fran sat next to me and touched me on my arm. She told me to look at her, to take deep breaths. She said that I was in the movie theatre with the remote so I can slow it down and stop it any time I wanted to. First I saw myself in the pond and Joel grabbed a hold of me throughout all of this so I could feel Joel with my spirit and Fran with my physical, and I looked at Fran and I was crying and not breathing too good and looking at Fran was like seeing her for the first time. She asked me if I knew who she was and where I am and I said yes and had to say where and stuff. I could see that Fran was totally concerned, and it hit me just how much she cares about me and all of this stuff. So I was able to just give myself up and trust Fran to protect me.

I still couldn't see anything of the trauma. That's different cause I always saw and heard and smelled everything like it was happening in the moment. I was on the ground, but I think it was in the house on the floor. The floors were concrete. Then I HEARD voices in the trauma event. I heard Eleena. At the time, I couldn't make it out. You see, when the relivings come, it comes in pieces just like a jigsaw puzzle and when all the pieces are there I gotta put it all together. After the voices, I saw Walter Amundson and he choked me. That's when brand new body pain came and it was pretty high on the pain scale. My upper back, my upper chest in the center, my collar bones, and my neck. Then everything went black but I could still hear and that's when I knew there was a pillow over my head and I couldn't breathe and Walter Amundson had sex with me. I'm pretty sure my body blacked out cause I woke up with Walter Amundson peeing on my face. Grandfather told me it wasn't over yet.

Lots of times when the relivings happened, it didn't just end with the end of a therapy session. It's like once the dam is broke the pieces just keep coming on God's time and that's what happened. The pieces came and I could hear what was said and stuff. After the pieces came, Grandfather told me that it was over. That this is the end of my relivings. I think that because this trauma was the last one and there isn't any more is why I feel so different. I feel empty but I feel clean. I think maybe that's why I feel at peace, cause there's no more. I'm still in the water and Joel is still hugging me.

So the trauma was, I was made to lie on the floor. I was 14 years old. Eleena said, "Kill her." I think it was Walter Amundson who first put a pillow on my face and I think he got sexed up cause of it. He took the pillow off of my face and used his hands to strangle me. I know I was fighting and just everything when this happened. But he couldn't have sex with me doing that so he told Eleena to put the pillow over my face and she did. I tried to hit and kick and I couldn't breathe. I think I blacked out cause I woke up with him peeing on my face and I knew he'd had sex with me. But then Eleena took the pillow and she laid down and told him to come on over to her and he did . He told me not to move or he'll kill me and Eleena said yeah. So I laid there on the floor and Eleena laid there right beside me and I watched him have sex with her. And Eleena looked at me in the middle of it and gave me her evil smile. After it was all over I had to clean up the mess.

It just so happened that Fran had ANOTHER two hours free that afternoon, so I stayed. Me and Fran both think that God made that happen! I asked Fran why this trauma was deeper than even the torture and she turned it around and asked me why. So I had to reflect and stuff. It had to do with Eleena. I've been saying that I'm not a person, and this event is when I lost myself as a person. I lost my identity. This went beyond feeling or emotion. This went to the psyche. This went beyond even spirit. It was as if I lost my soul, except it was more than a loss, it was a killing. Who I am was buried in this trauma. My physical body was changing and my mother and my father both hated that, for different reasons. So I separated from my body cause I hated it. I hated the change and I wasn't a girl who was growing into a woman anymore. I'd known for a very long time by then that nobody cared about me any, and this went beyond that. I knew by then, too, that my parents not only didn't want me but wanted me dead, and this went beyond that. They killed me.

And now I gotta figure out how to become alive.

*****

This single event with both mother and father stopped my psyche from developing. I developed intellectually and, due to later life healthy experiences, emotionally. But I stopped developing psychologically. Even as an "adult" I did not develop past the age of fourteen. Fran agreed. Until this healing process I was always searching for somebody to protect me. Fran told me that this kind of serious betrayal by a mother will damage a person very deeply.

*****

Bruce: Kate,

Feeling dirty is very normal for people who have been sexually abused. The question that you have stated is how do you become alive again, feel safe again, feel wanted again. Your trauma will take time for you to process with Fran and in your own mind. It will take some convincing inside yourself and some fortitude to claim that

you are a person of worth, a person who has something to offer the world. This will be your exploration and your discovery. The path should be difficult but exciting at the same time. We are all here to support you.

Okay - bye

H   K

Bruce (Dad)

Fran's Notes: Kate heard her mom laughing when Walter Amundson raped her. "This seemed to put an end to me. I'm gone. I lost myself when he did this. I lost who I am. I'm nobody." She said it is more than how she felt. "It's like there is another dimension to other people. Walk, talk, and know you're an individual. This took that away. You can walk and talk but you're no longer an individual. You belong nowhere. There is beauty in life but no beauty in you. It's like you're there, but there's this bubble. You're inside the bubble and you're isolated from life itself. You're no longer really alive. This is more than a feeling. This separated me from love and life. It separated me from being able to feel love. I was dead. He really did kill me."

Kate: You still my daddy for real for real?

Bruce: Yep.

Kate: Can I get a tattoo of a dragon?

H. K.

Bruce: Kate,

The answer to the tattoo request is "no."

H. K.

Bruce (Dad)

Kate: Aw rats.

Fran's Notes: Kate came out. She said that Walter Amundson and the trauma dissolved in our session and described the techniques to help her. She still has body pain. She feels empty but clean. She feels at peace because there is no more trauma. This did not last but she seemed better.

Deb: Hi Dad

There's another. Bummer but I guess all this is necessary. Kate just can't break out of her trauma so far. Last night I saw what I've always thought were demons in me. They're black with eyes. Turns out they're parts of me. I saw one come out of Kate. This morning he came to the surface with some violence. Like he busted out. Gave me a horrific headache. How can I know when I'm healed!?

He's 8 and for some reason he was automatically named Cole. Think of a squirrel up in a tree yelling at you and that's Cole. Unfortunately he has considerable influence on Kate and Joel. Stubborn little critter. Thinks nobody cares about him. I don't mean to be flippant. After all, he came out of the same deep subconscious that Kate did. But he's running around hitting and not hurting everybody around him. Flailing. He's panicked. Grandfather is just sitting there or moving around. Cole comes up and punches him in the arm and Grandfather is just ignoring it. But he's not ignoring Cole. Cole is running around the angels trying to goad them and that's not working either. Geez. I have such a headache!

Take care

Fran's Notes: Cole came out. He said "I know I'm bad because Kate can't move." Cole cried and feared he was going to be hurt by dad. I worked with him on his traumatic beliefs.

Cole: I know you're my daddy and stuff but NO DISCIPLINE!! I'm Cole and I'm 8 and I get to do what I want and that means no moving. No moving and stuff cause I'm supposed to die. I want holding and kisses and somebody big to crawl on and stuff. Until I get to die. I want somebody to care about me but I don't know about any daddy cause parents suck. I wanna be happy while I die. So I get to do whatever I want. No meany stuff and no frowns and no yelling and no hitting me.

Bruce: Hi Cole, The first thing you need to learn Cole is that you are not in charge of things. Second, whether you receive discipline is dependant on your behavior. Third, you are not going to die – ask the others. Somebody does care about you. In fact there are several somebody's that care about you so relax. By the way, did I mention you were not going to die, so you do not get to do whatever you want – sorry. So just relax and live, be kind to people and get along. How is that for starters!

Bruce (Dad)

Cole: Boy, this sucks total rocks!! I'm SUPPOSED to die!! That's what I'm supposed to do. I want kisses and holding and wrestling and stuff and lots and lots of holding and stuff. I'm supposed to be in charge of dying and stuff. You taking that away from me? Cause everything in me says that's what I gotta do. But I'm not mean any to anybody. And I'm not mad or frustrated or anything like that. I want kisses and holding and lots and lots of touching and stuff that feels good instead of bad. See?

If I keep Kate from exercising and Joel from eating right am I gonna get DISCIPLINED????? I can't help it, you know.

Nobody wants me and stuff. I feel bad all the time. I want hugs and kisses and good holding and somebody big who wants me.

Bruce: Let's see - you are 8 years old and you may be holding Kate back from exercising and you may be holding Joel back from eating right. If in fact you are doing these things are they the right things to do? Oh, and "I can't help it" is not an excuse or a reason for doing things. I will wait for your answer.

Bruce (Dad)

Cole: I don't care about that stuff! I know I'm bad I know and stuff! I don't wanna be hurt no more. No more. I want hugs and kisses and cuddles and you to like me instead of hate me and hurt me. Cause you Daddy.

Bruce: Answer the question.

Cole: I don't wanna get hurt no more. No more.

Bruce: No one will hurt you. Answer the question.

Cole: I wanna be kind to cause I dont wanna get hurt no more and I don't wanna feel bad no more. What question.

Bruce: READ THIS: Let's see - you are 8 years old and you may be holding Kate back from exercising and you may be holding Joel back from eating right. If in fact you are doing these things are they the right things to do? Oh, and "I can't help it" is not an excuse or a reason for doing things. I will wait for your answer. Can you find the question? It is in red. Now answer the question and show me you are willing to take some responsibility for your actions. You said you want to be kind so let's see if your answer sounds like you are a kind little boy.

Cole: It's the right thing to do for me. Don't wanna hurt or feel bad no more.

Bruce: OK Cole, I understand that you do not want to be disciplined, that you do not want to hurt or be hurt. I get that. Also get that you want to be cuddled, held and touched. I also get that you may be bothering Kate when she wants to exercise and that exercise bothers you. So think about what Fran said and try the Wii. It will be fun! And after you play with the Wii maybe you will feel a little better.

HUG!
Bruce (Dad)

Deb: Cole came out knowing everything. Unusual, but good! When it finally came down to answering the question yesterday, Dad, Cole knew what you wanted to hear. He actually thought about the dilemma. Do I lie and say what he wants and he won't be mad at me, or do I tell him what's real. He chose to tell you how he really feels. Yesterday before the Wii he thought about it too. I told him that he CAN choose now because he's awake now. When he was in Kate's subconscious, he could not choose. But now he's figuring out that he CAN choose now that he's awake, conscious. Such is the nature of this healing process! Wish it wasn't so very hard though. So I'm a little proud of the kid. (But I'm SUPPOSED to care about him!!)

Cole isn't experiencing depression; he's experiencing significant despair. It's like being in a balloon and the balloon is full of despair. There's fear too, but mostly despair. It's around him and through him. He wants what he wants because he's desperate for it. The parts of me are so close now that we feel what the others feel. Knowing the why of things is horrible. The despair is very heavy.

Annnddddd, that's what's happening! Have a great day Dad!!

H K

Cole: Hi Daddy. I did the Wii yesterday. I'm awful tired. Gotta go back to sleep. Normal sleep. Am I a good boy now?

Bruce: You are doing fine!!

Cole: No im not! daddy's suck!! I want hugs and kisses and stuff and im bad im bad cause no hugs and no kisses and no holding. i see daddys smile and hug their kids and stuff on tv but i dont get any cause im bad and i deserve to be hurt. no more wii no more moving cause im supposed to die.

Billy: Hi Dad!

Got chores done okay. Geez Dad my pee and poop is STILL green! Never had it this long before. Joints hurt pretty much and got diarrhea. But I'll tell ya I'm feeling lots better than I can remember. The despair is lifting too. Played on the Wii a little yesterday. And walked some today but the squitters kept me at bay today so we did what we could. Guess I'm telling you that we are feeling pretty good!

I'm starting to see stuff around me different. It's like it's fresh. Something to explore. Not just outside but inside too. I'm starting to get a little restless. And it's all coming from the body. I'm not so much focusing on the body Dad. The body is focusing on the world. Sensations. Vision. Smell. A pondering of activity. I'm not trying to make any of it happen. It just is. But the body still feels poisoned and I know I gotta have lots of patience.

Better go. Have a great evening!

H. K.

Cole: God told us to go back to sleep so we did. And the Mother Mary came and took me and I could feel her and stuff. Then she pointed and said look. And there you were when you were eight years old. And you were in despair just like me and you said that you had to discipline yourself to be okay. Cause all you wanted was to be hugged and kissed and cuddled cause you were feeling really really bad and the doctor didn't even look at your face but said "You're doing fine." and turned around and walked away. By then the Mother Mary was holding us both and caring about both of us cause that's what people need. Kids and everything else. Everything needs affection to live right. Cause affection maybe breaks despair maybe.

Kate: Hi Dad!

I'm having some problems breathing. My body went into shock but I was able to make myself relax. My chest hurts Daddy. I think this came about cause Eleena was in my face today, from the first-life. When is this gonna end? I feel like I'm being punished Daddy. But I don't know why except its cause I survived. Cole is not doing it. It's the first-life. I'm scared. I guess maybe I should go to bed. Still got the toxins in me. Am I whining Dad? Oh well. Wish I could talk to you. Bet it would help the pain. Night.

Bruce: Hi Kate,

I do not think you were whining, just expressing your experiences and that is important. No one is punishing you for anything. I just haven't written mostly due to fatigue. The toxins in the body always come out when there is a breakthrough which isn't pleasant but the body does feel better in the long run. So hang in there. All of this stuff will continue to get better as time goes on.

H   K

Bruce (dad)

Cole: what about me?   im thinking my second-life daddy dont want me around

Bruce: Well that is stinkin' thinkin' buddy boy. I want you around and I want you to be well and happy. So that is what I think!

H   K

Bruce (Dad)

Cole: YOU HUGGED ME AND KISSED ME!!!! WOW!! THAT'S THE FIRST TIME YOU DID THAT!!! WOW!!! CAN I SIT ON YOUR LAP AND STUFF? or is that too much?

Bruce: It is not too much just come on up here and sit on my lap!

Cole: oof oof oof climb climb oof splat. ahhhhh

Heather: Hi Daddy

> I was watching tv and a commercial stuff came up and I saw a little dog shivering and stuff and it said why do they beat me and I just came out and cried and stuff. I hurt Daddy cause that little dog hurt and stuff and I know how it feels. How come Eleena beat me Daddy? How come she hit me? I don't think anybody should be hit and beat and stuff especially dogs. It hurts Daddy. It shouldn't be part of the world I think. Can I get cuddled instead and can little dogs get cuddled instead?

Bruce: Hi Heather,

> **I have a niece named Heather. It is upsetting to see animals suffer and it is equally upsetting to see people suffer. In part, that is why we are here, to help people who do suffer and to take care of the animals and the rest of creation. So, yes you can cuddle and little dogs need cuddling also.**

H   K

Bruce (Dad)

Deb: Hi Dad!

> My reliving with the satanic ritual rape put me at 4 years old. It's always been my age that nagged at me. Eleena told me that she and my biological father separated when I was four.

> Tonight I found an envelop buried from what I had borrowed of Walter Amundson's documents. My biological father and Eleena legally separated when I was three and a half years old. The court said that they could live in all respects as single people. So she and Walter Amundson could have done it to me when I was four.

> This was important to me.

H. K.

Heather: HI DADDY!!!!

I had a terrible nightmare last night. We dreamed that somebody gave us a baby and we set it on the floor. We had three new puppies too and the puppies were set on the floor too. Then we went hiking and stuff cause we were supposed to find more puppies. And we came back into a house and did stuff. And all of a sudden I remembered about the baby and it wasn't moving and it was dead. And I looked at the baby and it was all blue and sunk in and stuff and it was horrible. You see, I forgot to feed and water the baby so she died. When I touched her face, we woke up.

It was in the middle of the night and we did some stuff and then we went back to bed. Yep, there was the image of the dead baby again Daddy!! We went right back to the nightmare and Daddy I felt really really bad, like all the good stuff was draining out of me. I know I was dreaming and stuff but it was real. Then two angels came Daddy and they stuck their hands in the baby and the baby came back to life. And all the good stuff that was draining out of me came back into me and I didn't feel bad anymore. And then God called me and I went to God Daddy and I sat on his lap. I asked him if I was supposed to play with my doll and he said no. He said that I was supposed to live and experience life stuff and I was supposed to have fun. Boy, that made me feel lots better!! He wanted to cuddle me and stuff and I said sure! I fell asleep against God. I think Grandfather took me but I don't know cause I was asleep!!! Hahahahaha But I woke up in bed Daddy.

Cool huh? I really like angels even if they ARE kinda scary! And I like God too. He's nice.

H K H K

Bruce: Hi Heather,

Well, a bad dream turned into a really good experience. That is what God can do for us, not to mention the angels. The angels are terrific also!! VERY COOL!

H K

Bruce (Dad)

*****

We did not know it at the time, but Heather's nightmare was Isaac and the satanic coven beginning to come to the surface.

*****

Billy: Hi Dad!

We are on our way downstate.

Have I mentioned recently how cool you are and stuff? :)

H. K.

I'm fine, except I feel what Deb feels. Last night though was pretty funny. I didn't want to go to bed. Grandfather told me several times to go to bed and I said okay but didn't get up off the couch cause I was playing my game. So I'm on the couch and I look over and there's this big wolf spider just standing there. Pause. Then that spider charged me!! I never got off that couch so fast in my life!!!! I went to bed.

:)

Bruce: Nothing like a little wolf spider action to get you motivated.

Always remember, your worth comes from God, not an institution.

H   K

Bruce (Dad)

Billy: Hi Dad!

I think I'm older now but I don't know my age.

I'm fine Dad. The developers have changed the game and it's better but now everybody is doing stuff to get strong.

Kate still has a panic attack whenever Grandfather talks about moving and exercise. That's what we gotta concentrate on with Fran I think.

We found out that our real grandparents visited periodically but neither Jack nor I remember them visiting at all. Deb told Jack that we were both in the survival mode. That was all we could focus on. Grandmother also wrote about us and that Walter Amundson complained that me and Jack couldn't do anything right and she noticed there was no affection in the family. Well gee whiz. She didn't give any affection either because I would have responded to that.

Gotta eat breaky. Have a great day Dad!

H. K.

Bruce: Billy,

You are making good progress in the healing department. The fact that you feel older is a sign of that. Hang in there.

H   K

Bruce (Dad)

Billy: But DAD!! How old am I? Am I too old now to get in trouble? Can I do what I want?

Have you quit raising us?

(Gee, those are the really IMPORTANT questions!!))

Bruce: Gee!! BUT BILLY!! No you cannot do whatever you want but we can talk over what you would like to do. No, I haven't quit raising you. No, I do not know how old you are but you sound older, and you sound responsible. So I would say you are older than 4. :>) Just kidding! Maybe you are a teenager ------------------Yikes!!

Bruce (Dad)

Kate: I don't want to go to therapy anymore. I don't want to deal with Fran. Nobody loves me so I don't give a shit. I just want to be left alone. I'm not gonna talk to Fran anymore. So there.

Bruce: Sorry, this isn't about just you. Your actions, thoughts, attitudes impact the others so you have a responsibility to work on the issues you need to work on for the good of yourself and everyone else. So you will be having opportunities to work with Fran and I suggest you take advantage of the opportunities.

H   K

Bruce (Dad)

Kate: I don't like you right now!

Bruce: That is OK. Maybe you will like me more later.

Fran's Notes: Kate is 9 years old and was present today. She was clear with me about her feelings. She felt at one point that I was treating her differently by not using EMDR and imagery and that I was judgmental of her. I apologized and explained that my suggestion of an exercise of having the others go for a walk might help her see that she isn't going to die if the body moves. Kate explained it is not the body moving that is the issue but the original trauma as she's living still in the first-life. I was glad she was forthright with me and indicated so. She feels distrust toward me and others and we talked about our relationship and my hesitancy to offer suggestions. As we talked, she recognized that is what we needed to do. The time between us was one of building a relationship and hopefully some trust. She understandably holds anger and suspicion of other's motivations. I felt there was some progress today in building a relationship.

I was pleased she could express herself so well. Deb returned. She said she's not one to complain. I again reassured her that I was pleased Kate felt strong and secure to tell me how she felt. Kate wants affection but is afraid of it. All of the others are trying to help Kate. Kate wants to be alone but is totally stressed.

Kate: Hi Dad

> I rode the bike again today. But it was right after I ate and got a stomach ache. Grandfather says I gotta tell you I'm not wearing the helmet. It makes me look stupid. I never cared about how I look before. So I don't wanna wear it.

Bruce: Hi Kate,

> **Wear the helmet when you ride the bike. Because I want you to wear the helmet is a way of telling you that I really care about you and about your safety.**

H   K

Bruce (Dad)

Kate: Hi Dad!

> I got an email this morning that tells of what little kids think love is. I got sad and stuff cause there just wasn't any kindness toward me in the first-life. But then I got to thinking and stuff and I thought about what love is to me.
>
> Love is telling you that I don't like you very much and you saying that's okay, that you'll just wait until I do again. And then when I want to again, you act like nothing's happened. I think that's love.

H K

Bruce: Good Morning Kate,

> **Thanks for sharing your thoughts on love. I liked them.**

H   K

Bruce (Dad)

Kate: Hi Dad!

> I can't sleep. Fran figured out that she was triggering me Dad, and that's why I haven't been very cooperative. Couldn't tell her apart from Eleena and the first-life. She didn't trigger me yesterday and we had a good talk and stuff. I let her hug me Dad. First time. We figured out why, too, me riding my bike is safe for me. I'm in the first-life when I do it Dad, believe it or not. But riding my bike in circles or patterns comforted me

in the first-life and that's what I'm really doing, just around the neighborhood and stuff. It got cold again though. Boy I sure am having trouble getting unstuck from the first-life! I'm trying though.

Everybody's okay here. The body still feels sick.

Oh gee, all of a sudden I got gut cramps. Gotta go.

H K

Joel: Hiya Daddy!

I WAS okay but Grandfather disciplined me. He told me like over a week ago that candy is forbidden.

I don't think I'll be out again the rest of my whole whole life and stuff. Maybe that way maybe I won't get it no more. Nobody likes me anyway.

H. K.

Gee whiz. Everybody else gets h. K. But not me. Oh no. No candy. No h. K. Everything just sucks rocks.

Bruce: Joel, Joel, Joel,

Your report sounds like you are having a pity party for yourself. Get over it. IF Grandfather didn't love you he would not discipline you so that you could live a better life, a healthier life. People who care about you help you learn good behavior, good habits. They help you learn and grow up to be responsible and accountable. So, people care about you and there is no need for a pity party unless you just like to feel sorry for yourself.

H   K

Bruce (Dad)

Joel: :p:p:p:p:p:p:p:p:p:p:p:p:p:p:p:p:p:p:p:p:p:p:p:p:p:p

runs and hides. Looks around corner and sees Dad

Dad's trying not to smile

runs to Dad and climbs on his lap and smashes face against Dad's chest*

I'm sick Daddy. I just wanna feel better. For real.

sneezes and gets Dad's chest all gooey

Sorry Daddy.

Fran's Notes: I talked to Kate about how I was triggering her when I encouraged her on moving. It was a reminder of control in the first-

life. Kate said she didn't trust me and I understood. We'll continue to process this.

Billy: Hi Dad

Billy here. I think I'm older Dad. 12 or 13.

H K

Deb: Something different happened too a couple of nights ago. In the spirit world we are completely separate. I went there and saw Heather. She came and jumped on me. I held her and asked what she was doing. She said she was playing with her friends and playing with dolls! She said that the others are teaching her how to play with dolls. Wow! It didn't occur to me that what we lack in healing here due to circumstances we heal there! Or rebuilt rather. And, Dad, this was the first time we've touched each other in the spirit world! Wow!!! I let her down and she ran back to play. I saw Jeanie and she's babysitting. Grandfather says hi to you.

Well. Better sign off. Have a great day.

H. K.

Bruce: Hi Deb,

Hope you are feeling better. It is a good sign that you can tell the difference between healing process and illness. Although I think what you body goes through in the healing process contributes to you not feeling well at times.

God is always at work trying to restore us to wholeness. Many times we do not see God or the angels working on our behalf. I am thankful for your awareness of this. It gives us reassurance of God's love for us and God's investment in us.

Say hi to Grandfather for me.

H   K

Bruce (Dad)

Billy: Hi Dad!

Boy, today we feel lots better. I'm tired and woke up tired but lots better.

I wanted to stay up last night. Couldn't sleep anyway, but I wanted to know if this alliance I'm in was gonna merge or not. (The vote was no.) So I didn't go to bed until 11:00. Just as soon as I got up to go to bed, Grandfather was on my back. He just wouldn't let up, so I finally burst out what's the big deal about bedtime anyway? I was in bed by then Dad and he sat down on the bed. Boy, I could almost see him for real. When he tells me stuff I don't know, it's really hard to hear him. It's like there's this wall, but I think it's cause it's something new and stuff. He said something about the body and doing what the body needs. But what came clear, finally, is that my task is to think about the body all the time. I told him I didn't really want to. I still hate my body sometimes. He told me how terrific it really is and how strong cause it survived the physical stuff and I should be grateful. Okay. So my task is to think about the body all the time and to learn to give it what it wants. Heh, Joel just said that what it wants is candy!! Hahaha Okay, what the body needs. And this is my task. Seems like I have a lot of responsibility Dad!!! I guess I don't like that much. Anyway, that's what's up.

Have a great day Dad!!

Joel: Hi Daddy!

We went to Fran today. Well she was talking to somebody. Deb or Kate. Fran got up and went over to her desk to fool with the computer stuff and I came out. She has her back to me so I turned upside down on the couch with my feet up on the back and my head down. Fran turned around and got a big surprise. I told her it was me. She said I was gonna give her a heart attack. Hahahahaha

H. K

Fran's Notes: I talked to Kate about releasing her shame as keeping it is keeping her in the first-life. I explained she didn't earn the shame. She felt shame when she did things to Eleena to make her feel bad but I explained that was a normal way for her to feel some control and to defend herself during the first-life.

Kate: Hi Dad

Ian Bruch is in hospital and Deb can't quit crying. It's just like when the dogs died. Deb is trying to help his spirit.

God loves me so much Dad! We couldn't get away until yesterday. I kept wanting to fall asleep which means that Deb was fighting sleep while driving again. We stopped and slept some but it didn't do any good. We passed Fran's building and Deb called her. Fran said that she had a cancellation until 3:00. It was about 1:15 when we called. So we turned around and had a session. I did. It really helped me a lot. Eleena's face has been in my face but now her face is a melted face. And that helps. Joel helped me a whole lot with Fran too! I see the barn and hay bales and ropes and Joel played on the ropes! Swinging on them. Fran said he's showing me that they don't have any power any more. I think Joel is healed now. He plays superman and wants to save the world. When we left Deb could drive without falling asleep. We all think that God made it happen that Fran was free and we drove by then.

Right now it's Ian Bruch dying that's important. His wife seems to think that he can stabilize and come home. But we are pretty sure that he will either die tonight or be put in hospice. Our spirit has been connected to his for days now. This has happened before so we know what the feeling means. When the anxiety lifts in us then he has passed. Meantime Deb is spirit talking to him. He has some regrets that he didn't do enough for us, but Deb is trying to turn that around because he saved us a long time ago. He wants to watch his grand kids grow and Deb is trying to assure him that he can just like Grandfather does. He is regretting that he didn't write his story like he wanted to and Deb is saying that his story is written in the lives of hundreds of people. This is going on over and over. Deb is trying to help him die Dad. We all know that we are crying for ourselves.

What a bummer. Just like when the dogs died.

We are right now sitting outside of Meijer. Crying and typing. Fran says we are bonding but not integrating yet. We are in Gaylord. Gonna go get some food and get to the park.

H. K.

Deb: Ian Bruch died.

Bruce: Hi Deb, Joel, Billy, and Kate,

I am sending my prayerful support to all of you in this time of loss for a very important man who made a big difference in your lives. May he be remembered for his service to others, for his courage to take some actions that others would not have pursued. May you be blessed with comfort and I am sure Ian is grateful for the guidance in his transition that you gave to him.

H K

Bruce (Dad)

*****

Ian Bruch's death hit me very hard. When I was Damon, I was homeless for a while. Ian Bruch was moving to Lamoni as he was transferred from Center Stake president to Lamoni Stake president. I was hitch hiking up I-35 and he picked me up. He asked me where I was going and I said "Nowhere". He asked me if I wanted to go to a church reunion for a week and I said no. He then told me that it was a free bed and free food for a week and I said yes. He hounded me all week to settle down. I finally gave in. He said that I couldn't steal anymore and I laughed at him. But he never let go of me. He taught me about Christ. I asked him why he stuck it out and he said three reasons. First he said he saw that I was socially inept. Second he saw my potential. And third God asked him to. He came to see me perform some years ago. He said he was proud of me and he was proud that I took his name. He said that whatever debt I felt I owed him I have paid for and then some. He wasn't talking financial debt. He saved my life. The best way I knew how to thank him, the only way really, was to be the kind of person he wanted me to be.

A few days after he died, I became aware of his spirit in the Other Realm. He knew about my trauma, but once he passed over he understood. He was SO angry!! Grandfather calmed him down. Since his passing, he has helped me in the Other Realm with my healing process.

*****

Kate: Hi Daddy

We are doing better with grief stuff. Ian Bruch's been talking to us today.

So the focus is on healing stuff. Gee Dad. I still see Eleena melted so that hasn't changed. The body is doing stuff. Dad, I'm getting another boil but it hasn't come to a head. Last one didn't and it went away on its own so I don't know. Got the itchy bumps on my right ankle but not my left. No green stuff coming out. My body is sore and stuff. The right side of my chest is feeling better and I think the exercise is helping that. Joel is drinking mountain dew or mello yello when he can and I don't think that helps any cause when he's doing that we're not drinking water. Water today though. I been drinking a small gator aide at night. Detox tea sometimes.

I see Eleena Daddy but today I didn't feel like I was looking at the first-life. I mean I wasn't in the second-life really but not in the first-life either. I just feel better with emotions.

I better go now. Have a great day!

H. K.

Bruce: Hi Kate,

I am sure talking with Ian Bruch helps with the grieving a lot. How wonderful for you and for Ian Bruch that you can continue a living relationship. Tell Ian hi for me.

It sounds like you are making progress with the body stuff. It just takes time to get rid of all the junk - first-life - that has left such challenging impressions, scars, wounds in your life. I am sorry for that but I am also very proud of the fact that you keep working at it diligently. It is raining hard down here this morning and probably will continue the rest of the day; but the temperature is a little warmer.

Take care and tell Joel to lay off the Mountain Dew!

H   K

Bruce (Dad)

Kate: Hi Daddy

Ian Bruch told us that what really happened was the rapture and we missed it. I thought that was funny. It was good to hear him laugh. He's pleased that we're taking our break by working here. He says hi but more. He says that what you're doing with us is sacred. I understand that Daddy cause I told Fran that Eleena and Walter Amundson did more than just hurt us. They misused something sacred and that's what God has people do who raise other people. Anyway Ian Bruch is really grateful for what you've been doing.

Rash has cleared up. But I'm working pretty hard. Right now I need to sleep a little cause the body is tired. I will go back to work in about 30 minutes. Have a great day Dad!

H. K.

Bruce: Hi Kate,

A nap is always good to have when you are working hard. I hope it is refreshing. Enjoy the Park!

I am also glad that you can talk with Ian Bruch.

H   K

Bruce (Dad)

Kate: Hi Dad!!

Boy, it was really great seeing you and being with you for a little while. Talk about a life-experience! My pee's been green again since Friday night!! So what you did with the group really made an impression!! hahahahaha We just couldn't help switching around so fast!!

We saw Fran yesterday. Our schedule's changed cause of summer stuff and she's out of town sometimes and we are too and stuff. But it's all worked out. Yesterday though the buzzies were going and I was in the middle of the first-life and stuff and Ian Bruch came into it!!! Boy, that was a surprise. Dad, he was mad, and I mean furious!! He was so very angry at Eleena and Walter Amundson. I don't think he really knew how much they hurt me Daddy until yesterday. And then he got mad at God and said that I shouldn't suffer one more minute because of what they did!! Grandfather tried to talk to him, but, Dad, he was REALLY MAD!!! And, wow, I thought the whole thing was totally cool, that he got so mad at them, you know? It told me just how much he really cares about me and just everything. It was like he was protecting me from them!!! I think he knows now why I have to go through this healing process, that there's a real and maybe a greater purpose for it all, but I don't know.

I went through it Dad but nothing really changed. Last night, though, I realized that this time around I can't get Eleena to leave me or me get out of the situation. But I'm supposed to leave her. I'm supposed to just leave her and Walter Amundson and the first-life myself. That's lots different than what the others went through. Joel tried to help me again in the midst of it all. I won't see Fran until like next month cause she's out of town, but I think it's something I gotta prepare to do.

Life is kinda mixed up right now. Billy's been forgetting to clean up dishes and stuff but he's trying to turn that around, and trying to get into a schedule that works. I think maybe this forgetfulness is part of grieving stuff.

Well, I hope you're all rested up and everything. Dad, do you still exercise in the mornings at the gym? Are you okay? You seemed kinda thin to us.

Have a great day, Dad. You're awesome!

H K

Bruce: Hi Kate,

Good to be with all of you as well. The quick change team.

I think the purpose for your healing has many elements to it and you will discover them as you move along. It is the healing that is primary for now.

Just leaving the first-life sounds good because you do not need Walter Amundson or Eleena, not now, not ever. So as much as you can – let go! And when you let go – you will be fine, you will be better.

I am not completely rested yet but I am getting there. Take care.

H   K

Bruce (Dad)

Joel: Hiiiii Daaaadddddyyyyy

Grandfather yelled at me yesterday and says I gotta tell you. He said I could have junior mints at the movie and I took peanut m&ms. I didn't have ANY mountain dew for three whole days. Gee whiz. Billy didn't get all his chores done and HE didn't get yelled at. Not fair.

Kate's walking away from the first-life little by little but I think that makes everything just hopeless. My first daddy won't ever love me then and Eleena too and stuff. Are you really really really my second-life Daddy? Can I sit on your lap and put my head on your chest and stuff or am I too bad now? I wanna be loved and stuff. But maybe you'll just ignore me and stuff and just be mad and stuff cause I'm bad. Are you like my first-life Daddy? I don't mean like monster stuff, but something real like he was. I got this big empty inside of me. I'm awful hungry.

Okay. I'll shut up now as usual.

Bruce: Hi Joel,

Good for you not having Mountain Dew for three whole days! Can you go three more days without Mt. Dew? You need to listen to Grandfather and do like he says. He loves you and cares for you. You will appreciate all this later.

Yes, you can sit on my lap and put your head on my chest and stuff. Don't worry about Walter Amundson loving you or Eleena loving you. They are not normal people, they are not kind people, they are not people who are going to teach you anything good and they are not capable of showing you love because they are not mentally well. You are a good person without their "love." So do not fret over Kate leaving the first-life behind; everything will be fine.

H K

Bruce (Dad)

Kate: Joel has been crying. Last night he told Grandfather that me leaving the first-life means he'll never be loved by Walter Amundson and Eleena and that's a loss to him I think. Guess he isn't completely healed yet.

Grandfather and Ian Bruch have been talking together and it's been driving us nuts.

I did walk in the woods again yesterday. Mosquitoes and black flies went after me. So much for mushroom hunting! I'll have to use OFF from now on I think. That works for me.

Dad, we all hope you have a wonderful day today. Your living sure has made a difference in the world, and not just cause of us.

H K

Bruce: Hi Kate,

Those flies and mosquitoes are enough to ruin anyone's walk in the woods. IT should get better later in the summer. Do not worry about Joel. He will be fine.

Thank you for the birthday wishes.

H K

Bruce (Dad)

Kate: Hi Daddy!

I walked in the woods yesterday and stuff happened. At first I was aware that Grandfather was walking with me. I told him that I can do this myself, so he left. Eleena was about 50 feet behind me. She's still melted, but there, and as I walked she did not get any further away. But I still knew I was walking away. Then in front of me about 50 feet were you and the others who love me, including Grandfather and Ian Bruch. I could see you but you guys were in a gray mist and stuff. You guys didn't get closer as I walked either. That just told me that this will take time. Joel came and walked with me. Then I was aware that all of me were walking together: me, Joel, Heather, Deb, Shaun, and Billy. We weren't merged, we were walking together.

I came to realize some things too. I don't know what I'm walking into. It's unknown, and it's kinda scary cause it's unknown. But we were okay with that. Maybe cause you guys are there.

I still feel the knife up in me and cutting me as well as the rape stuff and sodomy stuff and this unending sexual competition with Eleena throughout ALL of my first-life, and I still feel pretty bad about myself cause of all that like it was my fault. I'm not sure, but I think I want a beloved like you have with your wife. More importantly to me right now though, is that I want to BE a beloved to somebody. And I want this beloved stuff to be tied to God's plan for my future. I'm not a whore. I think, Dad, that maybe I've never been a whore. All I know is that I've never wanted somebody else's beloved. I've wanted to be loved and there's a big difference. To take away somebody's beloved is the worst thing to do to somebody and that would make me a monster. I'm not a monster, and Philip made that promise to not be a monster when he was born when the body was six.

So I think stuff is happening. Boy, it's amazing what a little exercise does, huh? :-) Thank you Dad!

Have a good day. I gotta go take a shower.

H K

Bruce: Hi Kate,

A good reflection on things (or stuff). I sense you are in a good healing mode and I celebrate that. It is never too late to find a beloved partner. I believe it will happen in time and when you are ready. You have never been a whore, you have only been the victim

of someone's violent acts and sickness. **You are growing into a wonderful person who has lots of potential for a relationship, a mature relationship. You will know when it is time. God will guide you in this.**

I am proud of your progress, your courage and your willingness to struggle at times for the greater good of your wholeness. Bravo!!

H K

Bruce (Dad)

Fran's Notes: Deb suddenly felt a sharp pain. She said, "I came out of Kate." "I'm not a part of Billy." Later he said Grandfather is holding him. He felt so embarrassed and shamed. He gave himself the name, David, because Deb was working on a sermon about King David. She has uncovered a boy who took considerable physical pain as well as the shame. She has some strategies to manage them.

Deb: Hi Dad!

We are at the PofPines now.

I had a session with Fran yesterday morning. Right in her office, another part came out. All of a sudden we didn't know who was talking to Fran! He didn't know who he was! Everybody was surprised and had to work it out. Name is David. He is 7.

Dad, I always thought that my body was in shock after the torture. I knew the sodomy afterward hurt and burned, but didn't feel that much. Maybe too the body might be in shock but it still feels it in full. Dad, David took that sodomy. Nils took it when the monster was violent and angry. David took it after the torture. When he woke up, he came right out of Kate.

He knew who Kate and Fran are but it took him a long time to know me. He knew Billy.

He cried and cried with Fran cause the butt hurt so much and she helped him. Dad, Fran said that every single client of hers who has been sexually abused that way has gone through this kind of physical and emotional pain. I said, you mean it's normal? She said yes it's normal to have this experience. She said that the body is releasing the memory of it. She said it will fade in time.

After Fran, Grandfather took David. He's got him across his lap and holding him. Ian Bruch came too and sat next to Grandfather so David could be on his lap too. That's so that they can hold him and rub his back while an angel has his hands up inside David. Just like they did inside my chest.

Fractured Mind

We told Fran that this whole thing is pretty personal. Intimate. She said I don't have to feel bad with her. That's when she told me that it's normal. David cries a lot but Grandfather is taking care of him, having him sleep when the angel doesn't have his hand up his butt. And they are holding him and rubbing his back and kissing him while the angel is doing it. Grandfather and Ian Bruch. I think that angels don't care much about modesty! The pain has diminished a little but I still hurt a lot. So I think it's working. It seems that what the angel is doing is helping the body release.

Dad, children aren't big or long enough inside to take sodomy. My muscles around it hurt too. This pain is with me almost all the time. All I can think is, is that it's supposed to, and I think it's because the angel is accelerating the process.

Grandfather says also that it is time now to get some exercise. So he had us bring the bike. Fran told David and Kate that when it's too much emotionally for them to go into a safe room while I continue to help my body. Okay.

So that is what is going on here and it's quite a lot. I'm really tired partly because of the pain. All I can really do is to do what you and Grandfather say, let things happen, and be thankful. I really am Dad.

Hope you're having a great time!

H. K.

Bruce: Hi Deb,

I am glad you are down at the P of P doing physical stuff. I hope the discomfort subsides quickly. David, as did all the other children take time to enter into the world, get their bearings and realize they are safe. David is fortunate to have a team of Grandfather, Ian Bruch, angels, and God to work on him in order that he will feel better and that all of you will feel better. Hopefully Kate is impacted by all of this in positive ways.

Take care and have fun.

H   K

Bruce (Dad)

Deb: God said after I wrote you that I will soon enter into a new life and I won't BELIEVE how great it'll be. He said he's gonna make sure it will be and everything will come around. I sure don't know why I still hurt after THAT, but I think maybe it's like grief and I'm human.

H. K.

David: Dear Daddy

> Grandfather is helping me type and stuff but I'm talking. I am 7.
>
> Thank you for being my second-life daddy. I know stuff that the others do. I have to have an angel do stuff inside of me and it don't hurt as much like before. Grandfather and Ian Bruch kisses me a whole lot and cuddle me and stuff and now sometimes I go to sleep when it happens. I don't know when the angel will stop doing that.
>
> Jesus says your my daddy now and you will never hurt me. I know that Nils took what I did but boy his was angry stuff. I'm afraid a lot. When we were in Australia God said we had too much fear and he was talking to me, but I didn't know how to stop it or how to know and stuff. I think people will hurt me if they can and I always want to be in survival cause I'm scared. I know I'm not supposed to but I'm scared all the time that somebody is gonna hurt me. I feel bad. I like Grandfather and Ian Bruch and Jesus.
>
> How do I get you to like me? Okay I better go now. Grandfather says I gotta go to bed now. Will you hug and kiss me too? Bye.

Bruce: Hi David,

> **Thanks for writing to me. I know that you are scared and that you are afraid that you will be hurt by someone but you will learn over time and through experience that no one is going to hurt you in the second-life. You will also learn that you do not need to be in the survival mode any more. These understandings will come over time. So, as best you can, relax and try to look back on each day and ask the question: Did anyone try to hurt me this day? I bet the answer will be "no". And when you have a lot of "no" answers in a row that can reassure you that you are safe and that those around you care for you and love you.**
>
> **H   K**
>
> **Bruce (Dad)**

David: That's my chore, huh Daddy? To figure out if somebody hurt me at the end of the day after Grandfather let's me? I can do that huh Daddy?

> I come out and I look around and I'm really afraid that somebody is gonna kill me. I think one of that people is gonna kill me. I think they're gonna stick something up my but and then stick a needle in me and I'll die. Or maybe hang me and stuff. The body's real big now so can I kill them before they kill me?
>
> Thank you for the H. K.
>
> H. K.

Bruce: David,

What you are feeling is very normal. Give it some time and things will get better, a lot better. But no one is going to hurt you or kill you and no one will shove anything up your butt. So relax.

H   K

Bruce (Dad)

Deb: Hi Dad.

Grandfather managed to get David back into his world. David got away and wouldn't let Grandfather or Ian Bruch touch him. David is scared out of his mind. Jesus caught him but David just screamed and kicked him and hit him. Then God took him like a tractor beam and suspended him in the air. David's been screaming that they're gonna hurt him and kill him. So David's suspended in the air and God said "Kill you? I created you." Then David said, "Now you're gonna kill me." God said "why?" and David said "Cause I'm bad bad bad so you're gonna kill me". God told him that he was good not bad and that he is beloved. David said that he didn't know what that means. God asked if he can feel love from him and he said no and why can't he feel love. God said that he can't feel something he's never experienced and he can't experience something he doesn't believe in. David got a little angry and told God that people are mean and somebody's gonna kill him so he's gotta take care of himself. God then said, "No child. You are seven years old and at the moment so is Deb and everyone else. You took care of yourself in the first-life, with my help. But now I will take care of you. I love you. I will protect you and people will protect you." David asked why God didn't protect him in the first-life if he loves him. God said that he did protect and that he protected us all our life. David said, "But you let him stick his thing up into me and they hurt me". God then said, "Does it really matter? At the time you didn't know because I protected you by separating you. You were able to live. I taught you throughout life and caused you to be able to connect with this world throughout your life so I could teach you the basics of right and wrong. I gave you a listening ear. I placed people in your path to guide you. So does it really matter that he tortured you? Does it matter now?" David said yes it matters. Its gotta matter. God then said "Yes it matters. It has made you who you are now. You have made choices in your life and that matters too. And because of all of this, it will matter in your future and you need to walk through fire. It is time for you to be remade."

All of us were in David throughout all of this and that last part didn't help the anxiety any. But trust came back.

Bruce: Deb,

Have you gotten younger all of a sudden?

H   K

Bruce (Dad)

Deb: Yes today and the past couple of days I am younger. I don't want to be here Dad. My butt hurts and I know why and Dad I'm so ashamed. I feel so ashamed. I'm around people now. I just feel nothing but shame. Can I go home?

Bruce: Why did you come? You came to help and to serve the people of the reunion. You have nothing to be ashamed of so you will have to let go of your feelings and refocus your attention on service.

H   K

Bruce (Dad)

Fran's Notes: David remembers "Walter sticking his thing up my butt and feels so bad." David said angels are as big as this room and don't talk to him. They don't have wings. They are big and powerful and intimidating. I suggested that the anal muscles relax now and particularly when angels remove the trauma. David said, "I feel like I'm going to die. Something is stuck up me and it's going to go all the way through." I suggested that he use his wisdom and creativity to gain mastery over what Walter did because he's in a different place now. He's safe. He told Walter, "I don't want you to do this to me anymore. You don't have the right to do this to me. He's just laughing: 'I can do whatever I want.' I'm telling him now that he won't do it again. It still hurts but there is something going on in my insides down there." David opened his eyes and said, "Everything is clear. I still hurt. It just takes time. I think he's out of me though." I suggested the muscles can relax.

Joel: Daddy will I ever feel safe and stuff?

Bruce: Yes.

Deb: Hi Dad

Grandfather says I gotta tell you that me and Billy have become real teenagers. And the house is a mess cause we don't pick up stuff or put it away after we take it out. I sure don't know what that has to do with being a teenager but Grandfather told me to tell you.

Bruce: It is typical teenage behavior and the response from parents is to clean up the house – now and keep it picked up and clean. If you do not then the next step are restrictions.

Deb: Restrictions? Picking up now.

Joel: Hi Daddy

I know you're busy and thinking about stuff and you'll talk to me when you can and stuff.

I'm having nightmares Daddy. There's a bunch of me and people are killing a lot of me and making me eat the parts. I'm scared all the time and stuff. Deb/Billy is staying up late all the time and stuff. Grandfather says they're real teenagers this time. So I'm glad cause I don't wanna sleep Daddy. I'm scared a whole whole lot and I don't know why and stuff.

I sure hope your not mad at me or disappointed or anything.

Okay. Better go.

H. K.

Bruce: Hi Joel,

First of all I am not mad at you or disappointed about anything. Wow, what a relief. :>)

Sorry about the nightmares. I am not sure how all that works but when one thing happens to one it seems to affect all.

Billy, is the house picked up? Everyday? Chores done?

Kate, are you walking in the woods? Exercise in the morning?

IF the answers to any of these questions is "no" then I suggest you stop staying up late and get your act together on the things you are supposed to be focused on. I look forward to a good report – today.

H   K

Bruce (Dad)

Billy: Hi Dad!

Aw rats! House is picked up. I've been doing chores Dad, but not at the right times. I'll get back to weekend chores this weekend. Not walking not exercising. I'm sorry it's not a really good report. Not a bad report, but not really a good report. Well, gee whiz, Dad, you haven't been "home" and I figured I'll straighten out in time. Oops.

Fran's working on the fear. It's huge Dad and I think that's what's making the nightmares.

H K

Bruce: Greetings,

You sound very busy in good kind of ways. Glad you are doing OK. We are doing OK also.

H   K

Bruce (Dad)

Fran's Notes: David thinks Amundson was supposed to hurt him. David thinks this way as I tried to help him see his cognitive errors, and that good men don't do those things.

*****

I dissociated when I was a baby, and Kate is now connected to the baby that came out of her level of subconscious. It seems to me that there are degrees of dissociation. We ended up calling this baby, Baby Lynn. She stayed in the Other Realm and quickly integrated.

*****

Kate: Hi Dad!

Me and Fran figured out that my fear was the Eleena poison inside of me and with a push from God and help from an angel and Grandfather and Ian Bruch, Eleena came out of my gut.

I couldn't stay awake on my way home and guess what. Right when I was going to sleep I was on the floor again right after I got raped and Eleena smothering me with the pillow and I was watching again while Eleena had sex. And she was looking at me and guess what. I got up and walked away. Just walked away. Is that just terrific or what?

Maybe I just needed to feel secure again but it's more than that I know. Thanks Dad!

H. K

Bruce: Good on ya, Kate. Step by step, experience by experience you all are getting stronger and better.

H   K

Bruce (Dad)

Kate: Hi Daddy! Everything's okay. Susan did her Reiki on me Daddy and I'm better. Not much pain in my gut. Just sore.

Love ya!!

H. K.

-- Kate

Hiya Daddy! I'm okay too! H. K. Joel

Bruce: Good to hear from both of you KATE and JOEL!!

H   K

Bruce (Dad)

Kate: Oh geez Dad! I feel what the baby feels. I can't breathe like for days! Eleena put a pillow over my face lots of times. I'm hungry all the time and I feel bad all the time. She stepped on me Dad. Fran says Eleena had no idea how to deal with babies and I think she was trying to shut me up and stuff. I feel cold and awful. I hate babies Daddy! I hate them! I see people care for babies all the time and I've seen you look at a baby with like total love. Jeanie left Daddy and nobody cared about me Daddy. I just hate them!!!

Do you still love me and stuff?

Bruce: Yes, and stuff :>)

Kate: h k h k h k h k h k h k h k

Okay, I look at this and I can't hate babies. Not really. It just isn't fair, Dad. It just isn't fair! I've seen a picture of you looking at your grandkid like that too! Do you love me like that Daddy? Does anybody really?

Bruce: Kate, Sit down, take a deep breath and plant your feet on the ground. Now, for a moment reflect on who has been around you lately and has invested a lot of time and energy in helping you. Got it? Now, reflection is hard to do when you feel sorry for yourself. Growing up requires appreciation for what you have and what surrounds you. Very few people have a relationship with God, Jesus, and the angels like you – very few. Be grateful, be humble, think of others and serve and you will be fine. Going into yourself and feeling sorry for yourself is common for people who have been through difficult life experiences but the discipline of helping to pull yourself out of your pity parties is important for your health. YOU ARE LOVED!

H   K

Bruce (Dad)

Kate: Fran told me to write this week about what I'm experiencing so that's what I'm doing.

She said that I transformed yesterday. And I think I did! I'm not finished with it yet, but things are happening.

Fran has what we call the buzzies. It connects my brain together (and gives me a headache). It puts me into a hypnotic trance or state. All of a sudden yesterday, everything went dark, like pitch black. I could tell that all of you and Grandfather and angels and the Mother Mary were there beside me. Great support!! Then I could tell that I was standing on the edge of a cliff and felt I was supposed to jump into what seemed to me to be an abyss. Man, I was scared out of my mind!!

But I jumped and I fell in the dark. While I fell I felt things peal off of me. I fell a long time. None of you came with me. But I could feel you up there. It was like I can have all the support I need, but when it comes down to it, I have to do it alone. Except I think I felt God was with me all the way. I don't think I could have jumped without God.

Then I didn't hit the bottom, but I found myself standing. It was still pitch dark. I couldn't see, but I felt like I was at the bottom of a well. And this well is as deep within me as I can get. Then I started to hurt. First my heart hurt, then my head, stomach, chest, back, shoulders, teeth, arms, legs, wrists, ankles, hands, and the feet. I was like that when a thought came into my mind that woke me up completely. I don't exactly know what it was, but it was something about .... and it's there but I can't get to it so I can't tell you.

Then, and even today, emotionally I feel like nothing. There's an echo of grief and sadness, but nothing. I'm not sure if this is peace or not, but it's nothing. My body still hurts, just as much as yesterday. I plan to take an Epson salt bath this evening and do stuff to try to make myself feel better.

I still see myself in a dark well with no light. I know it's not over.

But if I DO feel something, I think it might be hope. But I think I brought that hope down with me and that's the real reason I jumped in the first place.

The others are in me. Not integrated, at least I don't think so, but within me and we are all having the same experience, except with me the experience has a clarity that the others might not have.

Thank you! Thank you! Thank you!!

H K

Bruce: Kate,

Epson salt bath will help detox you a little. Go for it!

H   k

Bruce (Dad)

Fran's Notes: EMDR with Kate. She says that God held Baby Lynn and said, "Innocence was replaced by fear and that is an abomination to me." Then God said something to the baby that no one heard and it healed the baby. God said to look at her because the baby is Kate. God put his hands on her head and said she was a healer of the heart. God blessed Baby Lynn and put her into Kate's heart.

Kate: Hi Dad

Got bad news. I blew apart - gently this time. Having a fever did it. I have problems emotionally handling a fever anyway. Only Joel came back out. Did nothing but cry and is now velcroed to Grandfather. I knew my integration wasn't really stable yet anyway. I feel like crying too but I'm older. Don't feel too good Dad.

I've been having nightmares but not of the first-life. I was in a house during the holidays and all of my blood relatives were there. None of them wanted me to be there. I felt totally alone surrounded by these people. I started to cry to a woman but she didn't care for it. That's when I woke up. Lots of wandering around!

Right when I woke up God talked to me. He wants me to go out in the wilderness when I can to gain a sense of belonging. I belong to the earth but I need a sense of belonging. He told me too that my body will be able to handle it for several years. I'm excited about this.

Taking it easy today Dad. I hope you're having a great day!

H. K.

*****

With Fran's help, I figured out that any dreams about a house was an imagery dream about my body. The house represented my body.

*****

Bruce: Hi Kate,

I want to wish you a Merry Christmas. I imagine you have a lot of snow for Christmas. I heard that Gaylord has 19 inches and Cadillac had 9. We were in Southern Michigan yesterday and there was none by the Ohio border and a little up in Lansing.

H   K

Bruce (Dad)

Kate: Hi Dad

I'm having nightmares again. Last night it was two!! The first one: I'm with a whole lot of people I don't know. An overseer gave each of us a child around 3 years old. I found mine to be pretty annoying, but dealt with him okay. Then the overseer had all of us go into a very large room and she said that we can begin. All the people started cutting up their kids and eating them. I was really hungry too, but I watched them chop off the babies arms and legs and the kids were just screaming in pain. The overseer came up to me and told me to eat. She said that some of them go ahead and cut their throat and let them die before they start chopping them up. I couldn't do it. I picked him up and told her that I was going to adopt him, not eat him. I tried to leave, but the police wouldn't let me. I woke up.

The second one: I had my camper trailer all hitched up. All of a sudden I had another camper trailer also. This one was very small ... as long as its own door. I unhitched the big one and hitched up the little one, then I hitched the big one to the little one. All of my parts were in the big one. There didn't seem to be anybody in the little one. Some people came with machine guns and entered the big one and shot all my parts to death. The inside was all shot up and carnage but nothing went through the outside, so the outside of the big camper trailer looked normal. The phone woke me up from this one.

I'm still sick Dad. Pretty miserable.

Hope you're okay.

H K

Fran's Notes: Kate thinks if she exercises, she'll lose herself. "I don't have myself to begin with. I don't have a sense of self. I'm afraid it won't change and I'm afraid of change. I'm not supposed to be pretty. If I turn pretty, my mother will never love me." I pointed out that she doesn't love her now. She is afraid of her mom's wrath.

Kate: I'm having a really hard time with the body. There might be another person or part Dad but I don't know yet. Fran talked to me and I'm pretty distressed about it because I can't move Dad. I can't be active much. So that's my being stuck and what I'm going through right now.

Take care Dad!

H. K.

Kate: Hi Dad

Fran says I'm transforming again. It's like spikes all over my body that have to be pulled out. At first I was in a chariot and then a dragon was pulling the chariot. Then it was like the movie Snow White that scared me when I was little. Except this time it was Eleena who turned into the dragon. Scary. Then there was a tunnel hole that I found myself crawling through. That's when spikes grew from my body all over. Saw a light and got out of the tunnel. Where I was it was really pretty. The spikes hurt. An angel guy came. He wasn't a real angel but he was full of light. He was big enough and he talked to me. Said I was full of fear. He wanted to pull out the spikes but I didn't want him to. He did anyway and my body really hurt and my real body hurt and I itched on my legs and feet. I watched myself throw up greenish black stuff. I tried but I couldn't wake up completely in Fran's office. So I couldn't leave the angel guy. Then there were a lot of them and they were really one but they said it would be best to pull all of them out at one time. Whenever he pulled one out this greenish black stuff came out of my body too. I told him that I'll pull them out myself but he said he needed to be there to heal the holes. I couldn't do it right then though. At the end I realized that the angel guy was me. He was older than me but he was a man. I don't get it but he was an older me. Boy it sure wasn't fun.

Fran told me to just let my life unfold. Don't try to make things happen. Opportunities.

Long day. Hope you had a great day!

H. K.

Joseph: Greetings!!

I am Joseph and I believe I'm around 38 years old. I think I was awakened when Kate went through another transformation today with Fran.

First I want to tell you how thankful I am for you and your kindness. Thank you!!

I don't know why I'm a man. Maybe body gender is luck of the draw!! :) I'm pretty sure that I hold all of the body memory/crystals of all of the trauma. Kate now knows and will tell you that the only person who has resisted the body connection is her. I'm not putting her down at all; it's just the way it is. I've been trying to pull her out of being stuck which might have caused her conflict. Her nightmares haven't been me though, but Eleena. Actually, Eleena isn't in me at all, but in her. I am only the body holding the trauma memory/crystals; it's Kate who connects the body memories to the details of the trauma. But she can see me now and she knows that I'm here to help her with her/our body memories. By helping her I'm helping myself. But God talked quite a lot to her tonight and then Grandfather tried to help her understand. She's not there yet but I admire her trying because she tries hard and now she needs to break the fear and trust the process. My entire focus, though, is the body and helping Kate connect. Hope you don't mind an adult calling you Dad!!!! There seems to be a LOT of you, Grandfather, and Fran in me!!!

Kate called me an angel guy because she saw me just as light. Tonight she could see me through the light and realized she was looking at herself. My task is to help her connect to the body by drawing the trauma memories out of her. And by doing that I'm drawing trauma memory/crystals out of me. She looks like she's been attacked by a porcupine! Her entire body is covered with quills or shafts!! God told her tonight that this will make her pretty sick, so she knows that now is the time. The body is sick right now with nausea and diarrhea. I am not experiencing fear, just concern.

It's after 3:30 a.m. and we need to try to get some sleep!!

Hope you have a great day!!

Take care,

H K (yep, that's a K!!)

Kate: Hi Dad!

Stuff's happening with me. When Fran uses the buzzies I guess I go into a trance, hypnosis, and that's when I see the imagery and I can progress. So I transformed again in her office. I actually tried to wake up and couldn't completely for a long time. I got scared and my body itched like fire.

But I go back there when I'm like half asleep. There now is a small valley surrounded by mountains. It's really pretty there Dad. I came into it by crawling out a tunnel hole. That hole has collapsed so now I can't go back. I've wanted to. Joseph is still light but he's here. He pulls out the quills or shafts out of my body. I've learnt to focus on my real body when I'm there Dad. I can literally feel it when Joseph pulls one out. It's the size of a pin head and it literally jumps or moves. I'm really happy that it doesn't hurt when he pulls one out Dad!!! Yay!! I've realized that I shouldn't try to control this or what Joseph pulls out, but just focus on my real body until I feel something.

Yesterday he concentrated on my butt. Don't ask me why, geez, I don't know!! But I haven't been able to move much since I first got sick the week before Thanksgiving. Yesterday my butt was so sore I could hardly walk. But yesterday early evening I was able to get up. So I feel like I'm being released!! The soreness went away, so now it's just normal sore and that I think will go away too. I'm pretty sick to my stomach and gassy but so far I can handle it pretty good!!! Joseph is going slow now Dad and I guess maybe he's learnt to do this as fast as I can tolerate the effects of it. I know to drink lots of water.

God told me that once this is done my body will tell me what it wants to eat and what it doesn't like. And my body will tell me what it wants to do. I don't know what he means right now. Gee, maybe that's cause I haven't experienced it before???!!! He said that I will WANT to do what my body wants to do. He said that releasing the trauma in my body will also mean that I won't be keeping the stuff in my body and it will be a natural thing to not keep the stuff. I know, Dad, that I've always wanted to not lose anything!!! To lose anything even in the body would mean that I lose myself and I'll tell you, my survival mode said never to lose anything and that's been hugely strong. But God said that I will WANT to do what my body wants to do, and that will lead to physical health. Okay, I'll just trust all this. Grandfather had to repeat what God said to me several times to get it to sink in. It's TOTALLY against my survival mode.

I think what is happening is that when I actually feel my body move, the size of the pin head, move, that that little bit is unfreezing. Then I'm really sore when a lot of that happens. If I move that part of my body and stretch it, the soreness goes away. Well, not completely, but it mostly does. I'll know how long I'll be sore soon enough I guess!!

Eleena, in the form of a dragon, is trying to get over the mountain range at me. So far, she hasn't been able to. Ugh. She wants to stop this. And I've known she's wanted me to be her idea of ugly (which has resulted in physically unhealthy, mentally and emotionally too maybe) for a very very long time now. I guess I'd rather be healthy.

Well, better go. I hope you have a good and prosperous day Dad!! Thanks for listening!!

H K

Kate: Hi Dad!

Grandfather says I'm Deb now, not Kate. He says I'm integrated. It feels strange to not be Kate Dad. I still feel like Kate.

Dr. Oz says to have half your plate be veggies. So I started doing that and now I've been eating too much!! It just occurred to me yesterday that I don't need to eat as much of the other stuff. When it comes to meat, I've heard that the size of a deck of cards is good, so I've been doing that. My body is telling me stuff I don't really understand Dad. Seems mixed up.

I've had this image for years of a house falling down and in disrepair. I never could place it as anywhere I've lived. It's in a cornfield. But I would dream about it from time to time. I think it's ME Dad!! The image came back in my dreams and there's Walter Amundson in it. He's naked. At first I thought maybe this was another trauma or maybe a time I liked it, but nope! I go into the house and I see him and he just disappears, blows away in the wind. And now the house is being healed. Strange how the mind works, huh? So when I see the house it's a little more repaired. Maybe it's my body, huh?

Better go! I hope you have a great day, Dad!!

H K

Bruce: Greetings Deb,

Eating veggies is very important and eating fresh veggies is even more important for nutrient values. Garden salads are a staple in our household as are steamed broccoli and kale.

I am very happy for you that you are integrated. I am very proud of you for the courage and strength that you have found to move forward on the healing process. You have much to offer others who are on similar journeys. It is nice to read about an image of Walter Amundson that isn't violent nor threatening and is taken care by the wind.

Blessings,

Bruce (Dad)

*****

Kate has now switched to the name Deb.

*****

Deb: Hi Daddy

I keep physically trying to move and I keep falling asleep. I'm really frustrated. It's like Eleena in me keeps trying to come over the mountain and I'm scared. I don't want to feel bad Dad. I really really don't. I mean feel bad about myself. To feel humiliated. Geez. I've felt this way all the time and I'm scared if it. It's like I can't handle it.

I feel really bad that I fall asleep Dad. I feel Ike I'm disappointing you. And I'm really sad about that.

This afternoon my body said stew so I went to the store and got stuff. I already had some stuff. So I made stew with meat and lots of veggies. The thing is Dad is I didn't feel any resistance and I didn't fall asleep. Easy squeezy. Cool huh?

Bruce: Hi Deb,

Hope you are staying warm up there. It is 10 degrees today, up from 6 yesterday. This is great stew weather. Stew warms you up and stays with you for a while. Glad your resistance is down and your appetite is up.

H   K

Bruce (Dad)

*****

A particular sequence of imagery seemed to have gotten stuck within my psyche. I was standing in a valley with mountains all around me. A dragon (who represented my mother) came over the mountains and attacked me. The dragon tore me to shreds until I was four years old. I then had to confront the dragon, but that is where it ended. Fran suggested that I figure out a ritual where I can kill the dragon, but that never came to be. I think that this sequence was my psyche pushing something up from my subconscious and trying to transform as well as opening a door for another part of me to rise.

*****

Deb: Hi Dad

The dream happens when I'm awake too. Now the dragon comes over the mountain, tears me apart and what is left is me at 4 years old. Now I'm just standing there in front of the dragon. Me as 4 facing the dragon. Eleena. Not running away any more. And I don't feel so scared. Boy I've never been able to control imagery. Thanks Dad. Still working on a ritual. Wish I could cut myself and bleed her out.

H. K.

Deb: Hi Dad!

The daymare nightmare changed again today. Again the dragon came over the mountain and tore me apart until I was 4 years old. I'm standing there facing the dragon. What changed is that animals like a bear a deer a rabbit and stuff came and stood next to me.

When I told Peggy about it tonight I involuntarily shook. That's a good thing as it's a sign that I'm letting go and feeling safer.

Anyway that's it. So far. Have a good day.

H. K.

Deb: Hi Daddy!

Well the day/nightmare images haven't changed. Eleena as a dragon gets over the mountain range, comes and tears me apart until I'm 4 years old, instead of me running like a bat out of hell I'm standing up to her (stupid, huh?! when you think about it!), and animals then come to stand beside me, bear, wolf, deer, and rabbit. Aunt Susan thinks that's connected to American Indian stuff like the four directions. I'll have to look it up. She said it might be the influence of Grandfather, and maybe it IS Grandfather!

I think I know that it's related to the 4 year old trauma of the occult ritual/barbed wire/gang rape with Eleena putting her hand over my mouth to shut me up. That still hurts Dad.

I think maybe I've figured out a ritual sort of maybe. When I WAS that age, I had a little dog doll named Tippy. I managed to get Tippy once a long time ago. I stole him from Eleena. But my dogs tore him apart. That's when I discovered that there was another Tippy inside of Tippy. I think it was my Grandmother, who I believe DID care about me until she went nuts, who re-covered Tippy when he was worn out. I've had Tippy in pieces ever since my dogs tore him apart. For some reason, I haven't been psychologically able to sew him back together. I think maybe doing that might be a good ritual. Huh Dad?

I hope you're okay!!

H K

Bruce: Tippy sounds like he has got possibilities and you stood up to Eleena - in your dreams/nightmares you can stand up to anyone you want!! It is always a little easier when you have God's creation standing beside you with their strength, courage and wisdom.

H K

Bruce (Dad)

Deb: HIIIIIIIIIII DAAAAAAAAD!!!!

H. K.

Bruce: HIIIIIIIIIIIIIIIIIIIIIIIIIIIII

*****

The dragon image finally broke enough to change. When that happened, another image took its place, but the spiral image was a healthy image sequence of transformation. Images connect to the body in such a way that while the image is releasing toxins, so does the body. I was physically ill for a very long time.

*****

Deb: Hi Dad.

Once again I found myself saying that I'm not supposed to feel good. And I was back in the first-life when I was sick after he killed me. Then I said that's nonsense. Then I was facing the dragon again at 4 and I had a sword and I killed the dragon. Then I like flew upwards into a spiral and I spun round and round. And toxins were coming out of me. So that image is playing over and over. Doesn't hurt any.

Have a great day!

H. K.

Fran's Notes: Deb had an experience of imagery with the buzzies. She was up to her chest in quicksand. Someone pulled her feet down and she saw stars and was floating in space. Stars turned off like a lamp, pitch black. She thought she is supposed to be in a well and she's back in it.

A voice said, "Do you want to be happy?" and she said yes. She felt somebody pull down with her legs. She is back with the stars and they turned off again and she's floating in pitch black. She sees a galaxy spiral in space. Spiral means to process, an infinite circle, come out or go in, with her, she could go in a spiral and it ended. I discussed with her the symbolism of this experience. She's not panicked about it. It's a new level of processing.

Deb: My session with Fran was incredible. I walked in half-way into the mindset and started into the hypnosis without the buzzies, then with the buzzies I went in all the way. When it ended, my mind was alert but my body had to take a lot of time. Fran said that it's because I went very very deep into the subconscious.

I have a little 6 year old boy still in me who is still stuck in trauma. He runs around my body, and I'll tell you, I have pain coming and going right now!!! Holy cow!!! Says I'm not supposed to be here and I'm supposed to be sick, all of all that. Fran says that abandonment issues are the toughest to deal with, especially from Mother, and I go through this and I'll burst out the other side!!! The little boy looks like a back upside down teardrop with eyes and a mouth and I am familiar with that image and have always seen it as a demon. Fran says he's masked. So I tried to talk to him and a couple of times he stopped and listened. He wouldn't let me touch him. After Fran said about the mask, I asked him if he was batman and that got his attention and I could tell he liked that. I don't sense anger Dad, but I do sense just intense hurt and confusion. He runs around in my body. Oh man, I'm having a LOT of pain!!!

Fran said I have had fragments of "people" in me, and I've already had many come out. That is, a person isn't a developed personality like Billy was and Scott. Maybe this is one. I don't know yet. Grandfather is near him.

Something else happened too. I was SO deep into the subconscious I figured something out that made Fran really really happy!! She's been trying to figure out why I didn't turn into a murderer. Now we know. There was one point in my life, Dad, that went so deep into the subconscious that all parts of me remembered it. When I was in high school, freshman, like 14, I was browsing through books and came across one book that had pictures of the holocaust. I told Fran that I'll never forget it. I knew it happened. It was if I was there. It was my first memory of hating, and I hated the people who hurt those people. But I was also flooded with compassion for those people who were hurt so very very badly. When I said it was if I was there, Fran made the connection and realized that this is why I turned out okay. That this is the moment that defined my core as a person. And I realized that as messed up as I was, I was primed to listen to Ian Bruch a few years later. But my compassion for those people and my identification with them turned me. I've had a strong sense of justice ever since.

Fran said, too, that I've been in a cocoon with work. That although I was always in survival mode, the core of who I am has been surrounded by the structure of work. I think maybe this is why God doesn't want me to be involved with church as an employee – to step out of one cocoon into another. Fran says I need to discover my core free from all that – my identity, who I really am. She sees me backpacking too.

Well, I think I'll take my pain and try to sleep through it Dad. Have a great Maundy Thursday. It's already been a miracle for me.

H K

Fran's Notes: EMDR. Deb is very deep in her subconscious. She saw Ian Bruch. "Embrace all of this is to embrace my body. Bottom of my feet are itching. I feel so dirty, ever since I left here, stuff is coming out." She shook and moaned. A restlessness. "The box is forming a tunnel in the center of the spiral. I'm resisting this like you won't believe. Am I going to have more responsibility? It's like I'm being purified. I see myself and I'm clean. But I feel dirty." She caught her breath. "Pain, like I'm having a heart attack. I have a headache now too. So my heart released something? I still feel something in it. I'm moving toward the spiral but I'm in the box, open ended on both ends. This is worse than jumping off the cliff. More scary. God, am I going to be okay?" You'll be okay. "Spiral is getting closer. I see the center. It's like a whirlpool. I'm fighting the current. I feel a whole lot of anxiety in the moment. Stuff is coming out of my ears, eyes, nose. It's going around, around me. Will I be a new person?" Yes. "Will I see life different?" Yes. "What should I believe in?" Believe in me. "I have a distinct lack of gratitude at the moment." "I'm exiting the spiral and it's still space, darkness, but now the spiral's at my feet. My heart hurts again. I feel something is physically going over me. I don't understand it. My heart hurts. I can see the sun."

"Now I'm standing in the meadow full of flowers. I'm part of it. There are flowers all over my body. Flowers don't end. They go on top of me like I belong. I don't feel anything at all. I feel blank. My heart hurts. There's somebody there. He's standing right in front of me. He has no features. He's all light. I said who are you? He says 'I am you.' Flowers are gone. I actually look pretty good. He said, 'Are you ready?' No. 'Are you ready?' For what. 'For you and me to come together?' Will I be alone then? He said no. My heart hurts. Oh, he just laughs. I see a baby. 'Why can't you go pick it up?' he says. I said I don't know. I don't have any flowers on me anymore. This person is all light, no features or clothes. I pick up the baby. He's standing right in front of me. I'm holding the baby. Is this me? I'm feeling something. He said, 'You feel compassion for everyone else under the

sun. Why not yourself?' I'm not supposed to. 'Who says?' He says, 'Who do you see?' I look around and I don't see anybody. I don't even see Eleena. He is standing in front of me. He takes hold of the baby too and says, 'You ready?' Okay. Maybe this is something I have to do on my own." She started to cry. "The baby went to my heart. I'm Kate. My heart. He says, 'You're ready.' I said okay. This person. He's coming into me too." She woke up.

She made remarkable progress in integrating the baby, but couldn't go further with the man.

Section Seven: Coven and Satanic Rites

I will never understand a person's need to be a member of a coven and engage in satanic ritual. It explains the depth of my parents' corruption.

But the only comments I can say about this are:

What we do to others we do to ourselves.

What we do to any of creation, we do to ourselves.

Chapter Sixteen

Subconscious Level 14: Michael (6), Dawn (14), Baby Heart (infant) and Isaac (6) Wake Up

The subconscious level 14 was, indeed, the deepest subconscious level I experienced. Michael, Dawn, Baby Heart, and Isaac are all parts connected to a particular series of traumatic events.

All parts of me knew of the Big Empty, but we did not know that a part, Michael, was inside. All my life I could see the image of a black hole and in it were strong despair and loneliness. All my life I actually called it the Big Empty. I was surprised to discover Michael living within it.

The evil that I experienced was so traumatic that the relivings came in pieces that were not chronological. These series of events were scrambled and intertwined amongst the individual parts when the awakenings happened.

Is there real evil in this world? Yes.

*****

Fran's Notes: We talked about how she is at a threshold of her recovery. She and her brother talked about how they both turned out okay. They both have wondered about that. I pointed out that she has not only done okay, but she has excelled.

Deb: Hi Dad!

It took a while but things in me are happening. Last night I stayed up to watch the end of the basketball game MI/SYR so it was pretty late. But God wanted me to take a bath. I thought it wasn't God but my imagination cause I was dead tired but it was so I did.

I think what formed Michael was a series of events. Telling Helga and being called a liar and people angry, Eleena then being angry on the way home, the monster then being angry, raping me again, then telling me if I told he'll kill me, then the monster demonstrating that by killing me in the bathtub, then in bed and feeling so badly and Eleena coming in and just looking.

All parts of me have known about what I call the Big Empty forever. I've also learned to ignore it. The Big Empty is like a hole in me that is just black; empty darkness. I have discovered that that is where Michael has been living all his/my life. There's no love or kindness or security or anything else in the Big Empty. It's just a hole of darkness. And complete sadness and alone.

Last Thursday with Fran was a little strange. For the first time, the brightness from the windows and light bothered me. So she closed them and turned off the light. She gave me the buzzies and said that I asked it be turned lower. It seemed the same to me, but the setting was different, lower, than usual. Fran said that I was experiencing Michael's physiological connection.

Yesterday I got some relief from the pain. Just my upper chest, right side of my chest, and right elbow were still in pain. Still there now. Not so itchy either. Yay! While in the bathtub last night, my ankles felt very strange like the skin was moving. I realized that when he drowned me, I was kicking and he held my ankles with one hand and pushed down on my upper chest with the other. And now I see Eleena was standing in back watching him do this.

Before last night, once Michael came out of the darkness the best anybody could do was have Michael stand a ways from Grandfather and they could look at each other. Ian Bruch was there too.

Last night, God called and I was Kate again and ALL the parts of me were standing in front of God. I couldn't HEAR God very well. At the time I thought it was me not being able to but now I'm wondering if what God said was something I wasn't supposed to hear. Words are a barrier. Then we all came together again, not specifically into me, just together, except for Michael.

God called Michael to come to him and he couldn't. Michael doesn't run much but cries as he wants to go back into the darkness. God pulled him to himself anyway and sat him on his lap. I don't know what God said. God did something to Michael too, like a blanket of light surrounded Michael. Michael couldn't handle it and got away from God as soon as he could. A change came when Grandfather was able to pick up Michael. Michael was just scared and cries and wants down so he can go back into the dark. He managed to squirm away and ran toward the darkness but God shot light into it and that scared Michael even more. Then an angel would pick him up and return him to Grandfather. This happened several times. Ian Bruch tried too. First time I saw an angel actually SMILE!!! I was told to go to bed while this was happening so I did. Finally, Grandfather was able to and given permission to wrap Michael in a blanket and be in the dark so he could sleep. That's when I fell asleep.

I feel empty, sad and scared, but I think that's Michael. Soooo, things are great Dad!! (not sarcasm) Have a good day!!

H K

Fran's Notes: EMDR. She sees a little demon running around her body, looks like a tear drop. "It's like what I saw as a kid when I was being tortured. I always thought of it as a demon. It's running around my

body. Upside down tear drop." I suggested she reach out to that part that contained the worst of the desertion of mother. "For a long time he was running around me but now he's stopped. He must be listening." I indicated that he took that utter black pain of your mother's desertion. Deb felt sadness and suicidal. When I suggested that she felt better when I hugged her, it felt good. When she was going to hug him, he ran around again. I suggested she thank him. He stopped. She told him she cared about him. He doesn't believe her. I suggested she thank him and that she wants to get to know him. She was sleepy and her body was numb. She gradually came back.

Deb: Hi Dad

Boy, the process didn't quit this week! Despite all the sitting, I've been moving more than usual and I feel like I'm on the verge of getting sick but not. My body feels different like more free. And I can't understand or really explain but it's like the toxins are moving out through my skin like radiating out. I'm thinking that maybe now I CAN move without getting sick!! The moving feels different to me, like good.

The big empty isn't so dark and Michael can sit on Grandfather's lap but that's all. He doesn't speak. Grandfather can rub his back now too but I don't know if he can feel it.

I feel different. Not much pain. Shoot. I can't explain it. It's like I'm not having the usual hurt. I feel pretty happy Dad. My thinking is good. Attitude is good.

I visited Ian Bruch's grave and I didn't really feel anything. It was like looking at his marker and that's all. Like looking at my tombstone. Boy I sure don't get it.

It's been really cool being with you this week!!

H. K.

Deb: Yesterday was more difficult than I wanted. I had pain all down the right side of my body. My hair is falling out. Pain is mostly gone now. Must be the sense of loss and fear of being homeless again. Think so. God told me he'll tell me as much as it takes that that won't happen. I DID walk around yelling Fffrrreeeeddddoooommmmm! Fun.

Bottom line, Dad, I'm getting happier. I really do think it's Fran working with Michael. Looks like this will take longer than all the others, but that's the way it is.

Bruce: It doesn't sound like you are suffering too much – like I was worried :>)

Have a very good day and it sounds like Michael is making progress as I knew he would.

H K

Bruce (Dad)

Deb: I had a dream last night. All first-life people, Jack, Eleena, monster and some others were there and I was hosting them in my house. It wasn't long before my house started to fall down! I had a terrible water leak and it was wrecking the wood. I went upstairs and I wanted them to help me but they hardly did. Found a pipe and lifted it and water came flooding but I couldn't find the source. So I went back to the first floor and they did help me after I got totally frustrated and wanted them to get out. So they started to tear up the walls and the floor to find the source. All I could think of was that I needed to rebuild my house. The house wasn't this one. Pretty sure it was my body. I woke up when I saw a little person's hand and arm stick up out of the wall. I think that was Michael.

Have a good day. I'm going back to bed. I'm really tired.

H K

Deb: Michael's still with Grandfather and the angel is still blocking the way into the Big Empty. So Michael cries a lot.

Fran's Notes: Deb felt invisible as a child. She said there is a part of her that really wants to kill but she doesn't want to. I talked with her on how sadistic sexual abuse can lead to rage. She cried and felt total aloneness and total hate. I explained how a child has these feelings because of what happened. Michael came out and looked around. He was afraid. I gently gave him a stuffed dog to look at and touch. He let me put it on his leg. He then fell asleep and Deb appeared. She felt a little strange in her heart. "I don't understand it, as often as I looked at this office, it looks more alive, a little bit." This was another major breakthrough.

The next day Deb was very sleepy with EMDR as I talked with her about her resistance and influence of possibly Michael. Michael came out and glanced around. He was silent and looked around. The brightness seemed to bother his eyes. When I was going to give him a stuffed animal, he looked scared. I stayed seated. When I said bad things happened to him, he pounded his chest and hit his head and his nose. I touched his hand lightly to stop it. He then touched my hand and let me touch his hand. Then he shook all over and cried. I reassured him it was okay to feel from me the touch that's caring and not hurting.

Deb: Michael can't really feel Grandfather yet. He's just crying and wants to go home. To him that means to go back into the darkness. An angel is still blocking the way so Michael can't go back. He doesn't kick or run away Dad. He just cries and sucks his thumb. He can't feel Grandfather. Not yet. I think Michael has to learn to surrender like the rest of us has had to. He can't hear me either.

Fran's Notes: Deb EMDR. She said, "Son of a bitch. Looks like Walter Amundson walked out of the darkness." I think that was Michael masking himself. "I'm noticing that I'm having a lot of memories of how Walter treated Eleena. He's a mean son of a bitch. I'm sick of him, of it in my head. I'm not supposed to be alone, to be ill, be sad. Nobody cares. I shouldn't be here. I should die. I think I am Michael. It feels like shit." Deb fell into a sleep and then her eyes opened halfway and looked around several times. Deb returned. She said she was able to coax him out. She knew he looked around. "It was hard for me. Sometimes he looked like Walter Amundson and then him." She felt pain in her stomach. She was able to see Grandfather and Ian Bruch too at the end. This was a major breakthrough.

Deb: Hi Dad! I'm feeling lots better today.

Thanks!

Keep doing your good stuff!

H. K.

Bruce: Glad to hear that you are feeling better. Enjoy the rest of the day.

H   K

Bruce (Dad)

Michael and Deb: Michael had his reliving tonight in the middle of the night. Couldn't sleep. We're close enough that I felt it too. God. No wonder I've been suicidal all my life!!

I WAS going to write it for him but Grandfather told me to help him write.

I'm 6. Daddy dug me a grave. The first one was in the basement of the house but when we moved and stuff it was other places. He said this is where he's gonna bury me. He said it was a grave where dead people are and stuff. Daddy got mad at me and made me get into my grave. He said for me to be on my back but I never could watch and stuff. So I always lay on my stomach so I didn't watch. He took a shovel and threw the dirt on top of me. Stuff went black. But he would pull me up again. I always thought I would die but he pulled me up. He gave me the shovel and I had to get the dirt back out.

Deb: Michael is afraid of parents. But tonight Grandfather picked him up. At first Michael cried but Grandfather won't let him go, unlike the other times.

Okay. I have the rest of the night to put up a front. I felt what Michael felt and its blackness and complete loneliness. I am right now totally suicidal but I think that's Michael because I know I have to cool it and function. Writing this helps.

Have I told you recently how much I think all thus healing stuff sucks? Sarcasm will see me through. I feel God right now. Michael is asleep against Grandfather. We will be okay.

Fran's Notes: Michael came out. He sat up and looked around. He hit his head and I stopped him. I said he could draw and he cried briefly. He held his head and he indicated his head hurt him. He looked at the toys and games under my desk and I said he could look at them. He crawled over and did so. He whispered that he can read but he doesn't understand the words. Michael wanted to play a game which we did. Afterwards, I asked how he felt and he pointed to feeling sorry because I lost. I hold him I wanted him to be excited. I explained this life and had him look at his body. He said, "This is me? Grandfather wants me to be with him. I wanna go back to the big empty." I said he didn't need to anymore and it's safe with Grandfather. Michael left and Deb returned.

Deb: Hi! Boy, I sure did bounce back quick. Michael is finally asleep with Grandfather. I feel like there's a knot in my heart and gut. But I'm feeling pretty good. Like washed inside. I'm thinking maybe it's finished. Don't fall off the chair laughing, okay? :) One of these days I'm gonna call it right!

Have a great day!!!

H. K.

Bruce: Finished?? Really?? Glad you and Michael are doing better. Enjoy the rest of your travels.

Bruce (dad)

Deb: Is that sarcasm I hear? Hummmmm.

I'm sitting in Fran's waiting room.

I've been through my usual denial with Michael's reliving. He said it happened twice. And he saw only the grave in the basement, not the others. But the monster told him about the others. I saw his reliving after he had it and when it was happening during the first-life he didn't say or do anything. Didn't cry. Just did what he was told. If I know Walter

Amundson, Michael's non-response made it boring for the monster and I think that's why it was only twice. Michael still can't feel anything.

We had a dream that somebody was trying to drown us in a lake. When we woke up all of a sudden, Michael had his reliving.

I'm sick with infection in my chest. Called the doctor and I'll continue the antibiotics.

Well it's about time. Have a great day Dad!

H. K.

Fran's Notes: Michael appeared with EMDR. He cried. "I feel bad. I think I'm going to die." He doesn't want to be here and doesn't feel safe. "It was dark. They had these lights. I see candles. I couldn't move. There's a bunch of people. Daddy. Don't know for sure if Mommy is here. It's black. He's dressed in black. The others are dressed in black. I'm so bad, so bad. I'm bad. Daddy said. Nobody cares. I'm all alone with all these people. There's the stairs. I see stairs. Dark. I just want someone to hold me and read stories and rock me. They tried to break me in two. Daddy held me. Somebody else there. They took me and like pulled like that over my daddy's lap. My body bent. I was on daddy's lap. He did it over his knee. I had clothes on. They tried to break me, break my chest. I was sideways. It hurts. They tried to break. There's the grave. Black with hoods. They made these noises and stuff but I don't get it. Think Mommy's there but I can't tell. There was daddy and he was really mad. Cause I'm bad. They tied rope around me. Two of them. I went, (he made the motion of pull), pulled the ropes like that. He put me in the grave before. He was alone. He didn't have any hood on or stuff. They were trying to break me apart like in two [making singing sounds] afterwards all they have to do is put me in the grave but he didn't have to do it. I feel so bad. Can I die? I guess I see red stuff coming out of me. After they broke me it hurts. Shoulder hurts. I feel like I'm bleeding inside. I think blood is coming out of my face." I reassured him that he won't get hurt now and he's safe.

Deb returned crying. She felt very suicidal. She put a plan in place to stay at a hotel and go to a movie tonight. I'll see her in the morning.

Deb: Hi Dad

Lots of pain during my session with Fran today. Muscle spasms in the right side of my chest and back. I'm staying and having another session with her today. Then a double session next Tuesday and again next Thursday. Maybe tomorrow too. Lots of pain. I have no clue what's going on. We think it's Michael. It doesn't help that I'm sick again. Fran said she was surprised that so many of her clients had to cancel I think because they're sick. Looks like something is going around. But she said that now she knows why. God really is amazing huh? He didn't make them sick I'm sure. Just took advantage of the situation. But what do I know about miracles? I'm crying all the time today Dad. Wish I wasn't but I guess no matter what healing is bloody painful emotionally, psychologically and physically.

I'm in no shape to go home today and Fran suggested I stay here. Super 8. We've added another session tomorrow too. Another cancelled. Michael had ritual stuff and they tried the break him in two. The real source of chest and back and shoulder pain. Totally suicidal and Fran made me stay. I came up with a plan to feel better so I'm going to a movie tonight. I should be not so suicidal then. Wish I could talk to you. Michael is afraid of parents but Grandfather has got him and he's allowing it.

Fran's Notes: Michael came out. It was too bright for him to see and I closed the curtains. He said his mouth hurts and they put something in his mouth. "I don't see too good. They're doing stuff to me. They broke me. There's a bunch of people. I can't see them. Daddy, he broke me. People are mean and I don't like people. I hurt, here, my side, they're hurting me. It hurts to breathe. They're supposed to hurt me. They wanted something to happen and after it was over I was supposed to be dead in the grave but I didn't die. They were saying stuff, but I don't know what they're saying. I'm scared and I hate them." I brought up that Grandfather was nice to him. He said, "Grandfather helped me and rubbed my back and he gave me to Jesus. I don't like people. I hid in a wall. They couldn't find me. That's my secret wall. They couldn't see me. It was black and they couldn't see me or find me. They hurt me. They said they were supposed to. They wanted stuff to happen. Somebody fell into the grave, a grownup. They let go of me, said oh no. On the floor was this stuff on the floor. Candles on the floor. They put me in the middle of it. There was white stuff on the floor. I was trying to make it so they won't hurt me. Somebody fell in the grave and I took off under the stairs. They started looking for me and they were shouting. There was a hole and I went in the hole and they couldn't find me. They were so mad. I stayed there a really long time. It was really dark and really quiet. I knew where to go now." I told him that people care about him and he deserves to be treated well. I suggested he open his heart with Grandfather to feel his love.

Deb and Michael: Hi Dad!

You wicked busy?

A lot of core stuff resides in Michael. Geez, I can't believe it all!! Yesterday the buzzies didn't give me a headache for the first time that I can remember. I had pain in my right elbow but NOT my right side. I'm wondering if that is over.

Michael's more curious now and wants to come out sometimes, although he hasn't except in Fran's office.

Yesterday, Mother Mary came to us. She told Michael that she wants to be his mother. He said why and she said because she loves him. He asked why again and she just smiled and said because he is who he is. Michael didn't understand and doesn't really want a mother but asked her if he could call her mommy and she said yes. Boy, Dad, she seems like a tough person to me. But that wasn't all. She wanted me to talk to her too. She said that parts of me have accepted her, but not all of me, and would I also see her as my mother. I told her I have a mother and she said she knows, but she'd be my second-life mother. I will Dad. Boy, I guess relationships have to be formed in the spiritual world as well as in this one. And that takes time. I asked her why too, Dad, and she said that I don't know myself very well. Ian Bruch is there too.

HI... Im michael and stuff and they say youre daddy and grandfather is daddy and fran says im safe now but I wanna go home but the angel wont let me in stupid angel. I poke my arm and I can feel skin and stuff at least I think its my skin and stuff. Theres a place on my tummy that feels like frans arm so I think that's skin. Fran played a game with me. It was stupid but I was out and stuff. And now mommy says shes mommy and she says to go back to grandfather and stuff. I can type now. Yay

Boy, that happened fast!! Annndddd on that note, have a great day Dad!!

H K

Bruce: Hi Deb,

> Yes, wicked busy! I just finished 8 days of retreat with two different groups and tomorrow we leave for Kentucky. Next week the agenda is getting everything lined up to go to Oregon for a house buying trip and we will be gone until June 26th. Everything is moving quickly now and we are in full transition mode from now until the movers unload in Oregon sometime in August.

> Hi Michael, I am very proud of you that you can type and communicate so well. You will have to learn to trust the angel, grandfather, Fran and myself. The trust will come over time. In the meantime, you do not have to be afraid and there are lots of good things, fun things that you will experience in the future. I am glad you are out and I am proud of your courage to come out. Everyone loves you.

Deb, safe travels to Park of the Pines. I hope the camper is in good shape.

H K

Bruce (Dad)

Fran's Notes: Michael came out. He sees trees and it's dark. He's crying. "It hurts right here. I saw a bunch of trees and it was dark. I'm walking with people into the trees and they're all dark and I can't see." They are dressed with robe and hood. He cried. He held his side. "I hurt right here." He doesn't know what caused it. I suggested he put the buzzies on the side and angels can help. "I see people with black stuff on. They have sticks like a bunch of baseball bats." They are hurting him with it. He turned over and hid his face. "They tied me up with my hands and they lifted me up and hit me so I would go around and around." I encouraged Michael to tell them to stop it. He said, "They won't listen. I'm on the ground. I can hear them but I can't tell anymore. I don't care. They untied my hands. It doesn't matter anymore." I asked him to make a bridge from past to present. "Now I'm back up hanging on a tree. They put a rope on the tree. There's a fire under me. My arms hurt. I just hurt. I'm hanging above the fire. I figure I'm going to die. I can hear them but I don't understand anything. Everything is black to me. I can't run and hide this time. Somebody's got a book, reading in a book. I hate this. I hate everything. I hate me." He wanted to go back to the big empty. I talked to him about this life with people here that can comfort him.

Deb came back suicidal. She saw what happened. Then she didn't feel anything and she rocked back and forth. Michael was close to her. I had to reassure her that she is worthy and deserving to be love, that she has a purpose in life. She will take time to process it. She said, "He blacked out. He doesn't remember coming down. There was a big book and somebody was reading out of it. Even now I get something, they wanted something from me. They wanted something through me." I talked with her about the cult. "I'm the sacrifice. There really are powers out there."

Deb: Hi Dad

Michael had another reliving in Fran's office today. We're pretty connected emotionally. I got suicidal and have come up with a plan for tonight. I'm staying at Super 8 again. I ate dinner. At 7:15 there's a movie next door about magic that I haven't seen. Michael is shut down now and so am I. Anyway at 9:00 is a tv show I like. I'm dead tired right now. It's about 6:15 and I have the tv on.

First-life parents engaged in satanic ritual with me as their sacrifice. I know where this was at. Fairfax, West Virginia on the farm there. Had a forest joining the property.

Michael first saw the forest the trees and it was dark and he was walking with people who wore black robes and hoods. They took a rope and threw it over a tree limb and strung up Michael by his wrists. They brought baseball bats and sticks and hit Michael with them so he'd go around and around. Then they let him down. Then they strung him up again but this time lit a fire right under him. Somebody was reading out of a big book and they were saying things but Michael couldn't understand anything they said.

Then Michael didn't feel anything. Fran said that that is when he dissociated from the body. Fran said that other people have described the same experience. People suck.

Michael: Second-life daddy nobody will let me into my hole and nobody will let me make another one and stuff. I'm Michael and I just want to go away and stuff. Fran says I'll get thru this and Deb will to but I just want it to stop and stuff. Can I just go away? Fran says nobody will hurt me again but boy I sure don't believe it. She says I'm still in the first-life but I sure do feel alone and stuff. I wish people will stop hurting me. Okay bye.

Deb: Hi Dad

I woke up tonight and Grandfather was sleeping with me like he did when I was a kid. Of course Michael is here too. The dogs came over and kissed me some but Grandfather told them to go back to bed and they did. Then Mother came and picked up Michael. He asked her if she was gonna hurt him and she said no. She said he was beautiful.

That's when we were in the woods again strung up over the fire. Michael heard them say blood of the innocent and Michael saw somebody walk to him with a knife. He was already bleeding from his head and his nose but I think they were going to disembowel him.

I think that's when Eleena stopped it. One of the few times she stood up to people. She stopped it. I'd feel more grateful toward her for that except I think it shouldn't have happened in the first place.

Then Michael found himself back in Mother's arms and all of a sudden she wasn't holding Michael anymore. She was holding me. Ian Bruch was there and I saw his face. Everybody seems to be trying to get me and Michael to experience the difference between the first-life and the second-life. It's hard right now.

I feel like I've been inside of pure evil. But I feel better.

Going back to bed now. Drive carefully unless you flew to Kentucky. :)

H. K.

Fran's Notes: Deb had more memories of how the trauma ended. She emailed me the horrific end of the ritual abuse in which she was hung up on the tree and the people with hoods and robes on with knives and baseball bats. They planned to disembowel her but Eleena stopped them from killing Deb. She's not suicidal anymore, but feels on the edge. "All through this healing I feel I'm bending and the bending is a little bit more. I feel if I break ... It's really hard to understand or believe others really care about me." She needed to maintain her protection by not engaging with her mom. She felt better.

Deb: Hi Dad

I'm being flooded with sound and images. I think this changed me Dad. The evil I mean. Eleena was happy with herself. She'd get angry with me and told me she saved my life. Michael is six years old and he didn't trust her and he didn't like her and he didn't tell her anything after that. I was a rotten kid Dad and I was just sullen and quiet. I was a rotten teenager too. I liked school but I didn't like my parents. Eleena would ask me how was something and I just said okay and that's it. I had no gratitude for her at all Dad. Even when I was old I wouldn't tell her much of anything at all. Whenever I would tell her something she looked like triumphant and I couldn't stand it. I think I just knew that she didn't really care about me and there wasn't anything she could do to change that. Even when she was nice to me she couldn't change that. So she got angry with me and told me I was fat and ugly but I'm thinking it was my fault she got angry cause I was such a rotten person all this time. I don't think I ever remembered why I was so angry with her until now. I really hated how she used saving my life as a way for me to feel bad about myself. I feel really really guilty of how I treated her when I was a kid. I sure don't know how you and Grandfather and Mother Mary want me around now. Everybody's been telling me it wasn't my fault but how I treated Eleena was my fault. I'm not sure I had much of a choice though. I don't know. I'm pretty confused.

Deb: Hi Dad

You're not going to believe this but Fran had a cancellation this morning and I saw her. I'm better now. My reaction to Eleena was normal. Fran said that yesterday she was afraid that they would disembowel me but she didn't say anything. With the satanic ritual that is what happens. She's a really strong person to know all this and deals with all this with so many people Dad. And all these cancellations she's had during my crisis is nothing but God in my opinion! Fran thinks so too. It's just too weird!

Fran said that Michael is now getting what he needs. He was asleep through our session this morning so he didn't come out. Fran said she will be curious how I am physically and emotionally now.

Fran will be gone while I'm down at the park! She's going to Germany to train people. Amazing huh Dad?! What a miracle for me. You are too but you know what I mean. Well gotta get going. At last. :)

H. K.

*****

Dawn awakened at this time but did not interact except in the Other Realm. She dissociated during the satanic rite but was a small fragment.

*****

Deb: Hi Dad

It's pretty tough right now but I'll be okay. Mother has Michael again and gets him to go to sleep. Fran told me not to judge this other one that, like the others, this one is experiencing wrong thinking and identity. And we'll deal with it when I get back. She said that God and Grandfather will keep me safe.

The ol' bod is pretty sore but I'll survive. I think all that will get better in time.

Okay. Better go. Have a great day Daddy!

H. K.

Bruce: Each person takes time to work out the first-life experience and you go through everything that is connected with each experience. But in the end things work out, the process works and a little more healing takes place. Hang in there.

Michael: Hi Daddy

I'm out today and stuff. Mommy says not for too long cause I still see the woods and stuff but she says when I can see a second-life even when I see the woods and get scared and stuff that's good and stuff. I don't get it. Do I have to do what Mommy and Grandfather say all the time? Cause I still wanna go into my black home but the stupid angel is still there so I can't and stuff. I guess I feel safe out here but I'm not to sure. Boy I sure do get dizzy when I sit up and stuff goes round and round. Deb says we got a cold in our ears. Ew. We took a nap and I just woke up. Boy the pillows all dirty!!! Okay. I'm gonna walk outside a little but Grandfather says Debs gotta come out to do stuff. Okay bye. Debs not feeling to good Daddy cause she sees the woods to like I do and she wants to cry all the time. Okay bye.

Michael: Mommy said I can come out and stuff and everybody says its daddy's day and stuff so I wanna do what normal people do and say happy daddy day to you cause your my second-life daddy and stuff and you don't hurt me any. Okay? Will I ever feel any better? Will you make the bad stuff go away? Are you big like my first-life daddy and mommy? I see it and stuff. Okay. Mommy says I gotta go back to sleep now cause I don't feel good insides. I know the code now and h. K. And stuff. Is it okay to cry cause I cry and I don't want you to hurt me cause I cry. Okay? I can't help it and stuff but I don't wanna hurt any more and I don't want to keep being alive. Okay? Boy mommys pulling me back. Bye.

Deb: Hi Dad!

I've been staying up at night as a way to try to keep myself from what I felt was coming down. When will I ever learn that it doesn't work????

The other one's name is Dawn and she's 14 and it's amazing how quickly she changed once she came out. God took her and held her face in his hands and told her she isn't Eleena and her task is to know that and figure out how she isn't Eleena. She's turned into a protective part.

As soon as I went to bed last night Grandfather had us. Mother joined us. Me and Michael, who held Grandfather's hand, had to enter the Big Empty. Michael was pretty happy about it until the pain came. I'm glad this didn't happen in Fran's office because I screamed. The pain was emotional pain, not physical pain.

First, we confronted God and everything turned into color. Then it looked very Catholic all of a sudden and there was a high chair made of gold and beneath it was the entrance to the Big Empty. Everything went pretty dark, and Dawn joined us. I thought it might be like Scott's experience entering the middle of his own pain, but it really wasn't. All of a sudden, we were back in the woods in the middle of the satanic ritual, but this time it was like we were separated from it all and we saw Michael hanging over the fire, the people in robes, and the person reading from a book. Then we saw the angels who were surrounding everything, and beyond that we saw the real demons. I said that I thought things weren't in duality like that, but God said much isn't, but this is, and there's a time when it comes down to duality. God said that the angels were there when it happened, that we're seeing when it actually happened, and the angels kept these people from opening the door to let this evil in. The real demons were trying to get past the angels, but the angels were pretty stoic and just like a wall that these things couldn't get over or past. I knew then that God really DID intervene with this.

Then the fire changed into a hole. Kind of like a grave, but it wasn't big enough to be a grave. The Michael hanging over it wasn't aware, and it was like nothing had changed but what we saw had changed. But in the hole was a box, and I knew that my heart was in the box. I picked up the box and opened it and it was me Dad. As a baby. We're calling her Heart, but I'm not sure she will have the process the rest of us have had. Grandfather took her. All of us are still there and what I see hasn't gone away. I asked God how long we will be here and he said until I feel love. So that's where it's at.

Have a great day!!

H K

Bruce: Hi Deb, You are blessed with a forward motion in your healing process. I am very happy for your progressive experiences, though they may be painful, yet you are still getting closer to wholeness and the ability to feeling love and each step is worth celebrating. Good on ya and keep in mind that you are surrounded by angels and by people who love you.

H K

Bruce (Dad)

Deb: Hi Dad.

Went back to the trauma Big Empty forest, angels, demons. Grandfather still has Heart. Mother is still here too. She said she's not an angel by the way. I asked God how he could be my real father when Grandfather says I belong to him. God said that that is how he set it up. It's like people are on loan to other people who are parents and he's set it up that I belong. That's the bond. And the bond is necessary. He said too that that is also why it's so difficult for me with the trauma, especially with Eleena. It has to do with relationships and for me to heal I need to transfer the bond. He said I'm doing fine.

I looked at Heart then and felt her with Grandfather. Boy, MY heart just burned and burned!

I'm sorry I stay up to try to avoid all this but the emotional pain is pretty intense. I mean, really, to be surrounded by angels and demons and seeing Michael hanging there and grieving that my first-life parents would do this in the first place. You'd think healing and feeling love would mean I'd be in a flowery meadow with angels playing harps or something. By the way, I have yet to see a harp! And angels are pretty friggin' scary!!!

Have a good day.

H. K.

Bruce: Good morning,

I am really disappointed that you have not seen an angel with a harp – where is the music education in this arena??? Keep in mind through all the ups and downs that you ARE moving forward in the healing process – step by step – day by day. Blessings,

H K

Bruce (Dad)

Michael: Hi Daddy! Angels tickle when you touch them! Just a little. I'm in the Big Empty Daddy but its not black anymore. I hurt Daddy. I see me hanging and stuff and I remember but I'm not hanging now but my wrists hurt now. Mommy and Grandfather say hi to you. Daddy, Eleena didn't say happy birthday or anything but I can see her here in the first-life. How come she doesn't like me? Am I bad? Everybody says its not my fault and stuff but it sure is hard for me cause I see her now when it was back then. She looks like she's important. I think everybody's more important than me Daddy. We all think that way even Deb. we always have. Will I ever be important Daddy? Okay I guess I gotta go. Grandfather let Deb go though MacDonald's cause she felt so bad tonight cause we're not important when we're trying hard to make stuff nice for people here.

Bye!

H. K.

Deb: Fran said that my emotions are all those dissociated emotions being released and to let it happen and for me to honor them. She said for me to pamper myself. Whatever that means.

Cya.

Bruce: Be kind and patient with yourself. – Sorry, but very busy, will try to work in a call later next week.

H K

Bruce (Dad)

Deb: All the trauma emotions seem to be amplified, so the throwing away, worthlessness and everything else is coming out wave after wave. I'm struggling to remember I'm in the second-life. Timing is rotten. Wish I was home.

Thanks Dad. Have a great day!

H. K.

Deb: Hi Dad!

Gosh a lot happened this morning!

I was like SHOWN all the times I was hurt. It wasn't a reliving. I was watching it from a different place.

And I saw angels Dad.

I'm right now trying to understand, to sort it out, and God is telling me to write and it will become more clear.

Every time I was hurt one or more angels were there. When the monster put a knife inside of me an angel wouldn't let it cut too deep. When I was hanging upside down an angel held my head. When I was hanging by my wrists angels were holding me up. Sometimes telling me to breathe and sometimes helping me breathe. When the bricks and cement blocks were put on me angels stopped him from killing me. Always stopped him from killing me.

Angels helped Billy take the pain and angels helped heal my body after every time.

When I was hanged, an angel held me up so I didn't fall. When he put my hands in a vise, angels made him quit before they broke. When I was tied to a post angels helped me not get too cold. When he shoved a handle up my vagina, angels made it not impale me.

When he sodomized me angels made it so he didn't tear me up. When I was raped, angels made it so he didn't go in too far. When I was beaten angels covered my body as a shield.

When I was drowned angels helped me come back. When I went into shock angels covered me. When I was sick angels told me to breathe and helped me heal. When he stuck his penis in my mouth angels controlled my breathing.

And all the time when I was hurt, while I was being hurt, angels whispered to me. Telling me it will be over soon. Telling me I'll be okay.

When Eleena ridiculed people angels told me it was wrong and not do it. All the time about Eleena, angels were showing me who she was. Angels showed me how other people felt when she hurt them.

When I was hurt by Walter Amundson and Eleena, angels kept them from going too far. Angels kept them away from Baby Heart. I put my heart in a box and buried it to keep it safe. And I did it during the forest Satanic ritual.

I told God that it all fractured my mind anyway. He said that my fractured mind kept me safe.

Angels helped me listen to people who felt good to me. God said listening was a choice I made so angels could help me listen. It was my choice to surrender to you Dad and others in this healing process so I could be raised. Angels helped you.

Angels kept me from committing suicide. Grandfather did once too.

Because of the angels in my life, I was able to trust God and follow Christ once Ian Bruch taught me all that.

Then I had to ask, Dad. Why did God allow my terrible hurt to happen at all?

God says he let it happen so I could be me in Him. He says it wasn't really so I could help others although that is a real and vital consequence.

But he let it happen so I could be me. He did not make it happen. He did not want them to do what they did to me. But because they made the choices they made, God could see where it would lead and how it would forge me.

The bottom line, God let it happen so I could be happy.

I know I'm supposed to say Joy in Him but that's not it. It's a joy in me in God. It isn't that you know God through suffering either. We don't have to suffer to know God and God doesn't want us to suffer.

Happiness of the self in God happens when you can tap into your own potential. Human potential, real potential, can't be realized without God. Happiness of the self happens when potential becomes be-ing.

The happiness that God is talking about has nothing to do with status or even relationships with others and it certainly isn't in getting what you want. It's an awareness of having been created by God. It's an awareness of yourself as Creation.

And when you're aware of yourself as Creation, you see everything. It's like your spirit explodes through time and space. And when THAT happens you can tap into it as a resource. That action helps you realize your own potential. And the consequence of that is healing others and creation just by being yourself and acting because of who you are naturally, who you have become. Everybody can experience this.

The consequence of be-ing in God is happiness, maybe Nirvana.

I asked about people who die and how death hurts other people. And about people who are handicapped. And people who are hurt. God said the principles are the same but the path is different. The paths are as different as people are different, and that's infinite. But angels are with them too. He said that sometimes a person is healed here and sometimes it happens after death. But healing happens. Sometimes it takes a very long time.

God pointed out that it isn't only hurt that helps a person become a be-ing in Him. I must always remember that the most significant parts of my life have been people who have cared and have acted to help me. He showed me the angels who were there during the most hurtful times. He did that to help me heal and to know that I wasn't alone. Angels are with everyone. Especially in times of sorrow and in need.

And he showed me the angels during the worst times to help me let it go. What will remain are those times when I have experienced kindness. Once I let go the hurt, kindnesses of others will "be in my face".

That's it. Frankly, that's all I can handle in one morning!

Have a great day Daddy!

H. K.

*****

Everybody in the world experiences pain some time in life. People's life experiences need to be honored, I think because life experiences help develop the makeup of a person. The pain I experienced during my early life was very serious, but it cannot be considered tragic. Other people's pain is just as meaningful and just as serious, and, indeed, other's pain may lead to death.

God did not make my pain happen. My parents made lifestyle choices that led to a corruption of their mind and soul. For some people, pain and death are results of accidents or nature. People hurt other people and creation. Unlike accidents or nature, we make choices to hurt or kill. We also make choices to help and heal, and these choices are acts upon which I want to focus.

God did not make my pain happen, but he let it happen. That statement, "let it happen," alone is pretty immature, but to ignore my wanting God to intervene in everybody's life so we do not experience pain would be barbaric I think. If we didn't care about people, we would not jump to the "God let it happen" statement.

God told me that he let it happen because he wanted me to be happy. This reason is in no way universal. What God does (or doesn't do) and how he helps (or seemingly doesn't help) other people is completely unique to the individual person. Everybody's path to potential is different. And the path includes the caring and happy times also.

The only thing I really know is that God was with me then as sure as God is with me now. The reason God let it happen is beyond my own sense of judgment and ethics. If God loves us, why don't he stop the pain? The only thing I know is God is God. He loves all of us in life and in death.

God let it happen, but God was there, and he helped me in very significant ways even though I did not know it at the time. God is always there. No matter what happens in life, God is there. We are not alone.

Bruce: Happy 4th of July to D&M.

H K

Bruce (Dad)

Deb: Hi Dad

This afternoon I realized that I can feel my pectoral muscles. Totally weird! That's without using my hands! Was on the inside of my skin. I've got really good posture too. It felt pretty good Dad. Like it was ME! I actually felt ME walking around! There wasn't any pain involved at all Daddy! I even FELT thin which is pretty weird but I think I was just feeling my pectoral muscles. I have no clue at all what to do about it but maybe I'm not supposed to do anything. I wasn't exercising at the time. Just walking into a store.

I have a brand new crop of itchy bumps around my ankles. The fun just never ends huh? Hahahaha

Laters!

H. K.

Bruce: Greetings Deb,

Feeling your body is a step forward, especially with no pain and no trauma. So enjoy the sensations of your pecks, good posture and thinness. :>)

We close on our house tomorrow; we are packing everyday in preparation for the move. The movers come August 1 and we move August 2. We plan to be on the road for 10 days or so. Delivery date will influence our travel but right now the movers have given us a window for delivery from August 7- 19 – so we will see.

My office is cleaned out as of today and the focus is packing up the house now.

Blessings,

H   K

Bruce (Dad)

Michael: Dear Daddy

God said I gotta get up now and stuff and tell you stuff. I'm awful sleepy but he said you would like it really. I don't know.

I'm talking to God and stuff I was then anyway but I'm still in the forest. God asked me to tell him the truth about what I wanted. So I did and stuff and it was really hard. I told him I think I belonged there in the first-life with them killing me cause I'm trying to die cause I think I should die and stuff. But I don't know how so I've just been waiting to die cause I think that's what I'm supposed to do.

God said he was gonna do something to me now. He said he was gonna put my heart back into me and I'm gonna get younger. He says now that's why he told me to tell you now instead of tomorrow. I'm six now but I'm gonna get younger with the baby heart in me and stuff.

My heart really really hurts right now Daddy. He said he was gonna take me out of there and he did. I can kinda see it all anyway and God said that was an echo of the forest and stuff, not like before. Everything's white right now and stuff. Misty and stuff.

He said I'm not supposed to die. I told him nobody cares about me and stuff. God said that back then in the first-life nobody cared about me. No person I think he meant and stuff cause I know now that angels were there and stuff and they tickle me when I touch them. They don't tickle me with their fingers and stuff but they tickle when I touch them.

So now I'm just in white blank stuff. I don't get it. Mommy's here. There's something about Dawn but I don't know what it is. But God made the forest stuff burst like apart and stuff and I can see it but not really anymore. Boy, I miss it cause I think that's where I belong whilst I die and stuff. My heart sure does hurt.

He said he's gonna bring people in who love me. To help me grow and stuff. I don't get it.

Anyway, that's it. I'm all mixed up. I don't know what I'm seeing now. I sucked my thumb. Is that okay?

Bye

H K

Bruce: Michael, you are being healed by God one step at a time. This takes time and because you are younger now you will have good memories of the second-life instead of the first - the forest. So think good thoughts and know that you are loved.

H. K.

Bruce. (Dad)

Deb: Hi Dad

Fran's out of town today so no session.

I'm tired of being a victim.

Have a great day!!

Deb: I walked in the woods!!! I did it!! I did it!! Just finished now! Eleena and Walter and first-life were still there but not like before. It's like an echo. I was able to be in the present through most of it. Yay!!!

H. K.

Michael: Hi Daddy this is michael and stuff and I have nightmares and all sorts of stuff. Grandfather's here and mommy is to and everything. Sometimes I get to pet a mouse or something daddy. I'm scared. Can't sleep and stuff. Okay bye

HHHH K

Deb: Hi Dad!

I met with Fran today and she did something she never has before. She used a marionette puppet to talk to Michael. He didn't want to come out but finally did and didn't like the puppet hanging on the file cabinet behind Fran. She took it and used it and we found Michael listening and totally focused on the puppet. It's a HUGE breakthrough as nothing has worked to get through to him yet. The thing is, is that I feel different. I can't explain it, but some real rebuilding went on. Michael is about 4 years old now and Fran told me afterwards that children can be able to listen to a puppet better than to a person. So Michael is behaving his age with all this, which amazes me no end. I noticed at first that I had to coax him out and then "be" with him. But as he focused on the puppet I found I was separating myself from him in a good way of course, so he was out by himself.

Fran told him a lot that people aren't supposed to hurt children and they'd go to jail if they were caught and that he wasn't supposed to believe them because they're liars. She said other stuff but I don't remember. But we now know what will work to help the kid. Dad, the trauma is really deep.

I hope you're settling in okay in your new home. Exciting! And that you're kicking off your business okay. Totally cool!!

laters!

H K

Bruce: Hi Deb, I am glad the puppet is working for Michael and through that experience you have felt some positive change. We are moved into our home and still working at getting organized. Weather is warm during the afternoon but cools down in the evening. We are doing conference calls with our business partners back in Ohio and are beginning to share with a couple of folks out here. We should be working fairly close to full time by next week. Take care.

H. K.

Bruce. (Dad)

Fran's Notes: Michael came out. He cried when he came out. I talked to Michael about his trauma and how he didn't deserve it and the people who did it were evil and gone. Michael got sleepy and said his heart is breaking open. He left and the baby came out briefly and silently looked around. He then left and Deb returned and her heart did hurt. She said her heart feels like it's turning around. It's shifting. It hurt.

Deb: Hi Dad! Well, yesterday's result of the exercising had a time lag to it. Best way to describe it is sorrow. Same thing happened today. And stuff turned green again. But you know what? I think I can handle it. Dang, it's on the edge but I think I can handle it. Man, this is so difficult!! I keep turning to gratitude to help with the sorrow.

Have a great day.

H K

Bruce: Hi Deb, You can handle it and it is getting better. Remember this is a process and not one big step to healing. Using gratitude is wonderful and helps balance things out because every step, easy or hard, is a step forward. We will venture forth in social media fairly soon. We visited the Chamber of Commerce and senior center yesterday. Will probably join both and volunteer at the senior center.

H K

Bruce (Dad)

Fran's Notes: On her way to our appointment, Deb had a waking dream. She was hiking in the woods and comes across a naked 13 year old boy laying in the woods traumatized. She calls the police and tells him that he's safe now and not to move as she carries him out. She saw a man and his footprints. He attacks her and he falls on his knife. She had a quarter inch nylon rope and tied him up with his hands behind his back and feet tied up. He was out cold. She went back to the boy and said, "You're safe now and I'm going to get you back home." She doesn't think there is a part of her but a metaphor of me telling Michael is safe now. She checked internally to see if it is a symbolism or a part. She said it is a symbol of Michael grown up some. The man is life itself. Anybody can hurt Michael.

Michael: Hiya Dad!

I hope this finds you well and that you've been having a good time.

I've grown from 6 to 13 but I think I'm older now. I do remember the forest, the grave, the satanic ritual, and the pain and fear I felt, but they seem to be memories now. Got some agoraphobia going on but you know what? I think I can beat it. I'm hoping the healing spirit of the earth will trump the evil they tried to bring into the world. And the evil they placed on and in me.

I have my heart now, and that is Baby Heart. So my heart hurts all the time. Still have things to work on I guess. We'd kind of like to explore the world a little.

Grandfather says hi. He gives us space now but comes around to hug and kiss. I think that while struggles continue, there will come a time soon (I hope) that we can break the wall and become happy and healthy in all ways. What that means to me is that I can look at life and claim it as my own. I can use my giftedness to help God according to what I want to do, and trust in God to open opportunities and take care of things.

Deb thought the other day that during the winter we'll be safe in the house here. God said right then and there that he didn't want us to be safe. He wanted us to go out into the world and take risks. Nobody will hurt us anymore. That was a pretty big surprise.

I'll let you go! Have a great day!

H K

Fran's Notes: I asked if Michael had any experience in the woods with the satanic cult. Michael came out sleepy when I asked him. He said, "I'm in the woods. I don't understand anything what they're doing, the chanting, the fire, the knife. They did it to a dog. They killed him, cut out his heart. They ate it, like raw, I don't understand. It's just me, what they were going to do to me, cut out my heart, treat me like they did to the dog." Michael was strung up and they didn't try to get him to kill the dog. "Then they moved me over to the fire. My side hurt. They hurt me and then they let me down and put me over the fire after they killed the dog. They had a hole and put the dog in the hole."

Michael: Baby Heart is in me so it's her/my reliving. She was tied around her chest too tight. Can I say I feel no malice by Eleena about this? I think she was securing her and did not know what she was doing. Anyway, my image that is happening over and over now is me untying the cloth. I've never breathed so easily as now! I can breathe!

H. K.

Deb: Hi Dad!

I think Michael is as old as I am now and it's hard to tell us apart now. I have no idea how old I am except 17+.

Fractured Mind

Last night or this morning I had a terrible dream. I killed a woman who was tied up. Sawed through her head in slices until she died. Then I ate some of her head, deep fried. Tasted like chicken. (It's okay, you can laugh if you want to.) Her name was Heather, who was a part of me. I woke up when I wondered if I should eat a person. I feel pretty sick about it.

I drove this afternoon trying to get to the woods trails and nearly fell asleep at the wheel though. I didn't but that was a bummer. It didn't stop me.

So I walked in the woods this afternoon. When I started, ahead was blackness, like a pillar of darkness. It tried to scare me, but it was Walter Amundson (again) and he got really big, although he stayed a black pillar. I stood there and told him he was a coward and come on over to me and I'll beat him up. (Not QUITE those words, but you know.) I was angry. He backed off. Then a pillar of light came down and BLASTED the dark. So I continued to walk and this white pillar stayed ahead of me instead of Walter Amundson. Once the dark pillar tried to take over but the white one blasted him again. Then I saw like these tentacles from the white pillar reach out to me so I stopped again. I could hear it when it touched me and it said "I want you to heal." I sure hope if I'm gonna see this stuff that it's the white pillar and Walter Amundson won't be around anymore.

I think I'm gonna be okay Dad.

H K

Fran's Notes: Deb had a memory more of the woods trauma and it was a baby that was murdered, not a dog. She went to a park and she knew that it wasn't a dog strung up and it was instead a baby. "It was unblocked. I realize it was the baby that was buried and not me. I felt my mind bend. I don't recall the baby was alive when it happened." She got the visceral image. "They actually strung he baby up. It was out in the forest. Somebody held the baby while someone cut her open. It wasn't an infant. It was an older baby." She prayed for the baby while in the woods. Yesterday she had a horrific stomach ache and couldn't eat. "Somebody made me eat a piece of the heart. Later when I had my wits about me I asked God if this was real and he said 'Yes.' Then he showed the toddler to me. Deb told her she was sorry they killed her. The toddler said, 'It's okay. I like it here.'"

She said, "As I sat there in the car, I saw the dog again and the dog morphed into a baby and my mind bent. That's how I knew it was real."

Deb: Hi. It's 3:00 a.m. and I'm having a nightmare again. I came across a deer who was strung up by his antlers but still barely alive. The man was wanting to cut out his heart whilst it was still beating. I got to the deer first and with a knife cut his carotid artery and he died.... Then the dream switched to me being strung up in the forest. A man came to me with a knife to cut out my heart whilst it was still beating. I woke up. But I woke up angry and told him to go screw himself. Okay, I was scared too and I still am.

Geez, no wonder I've been afraid to walk in the woods.

Earlier tonight, God came and touched my head and said he was proud of me. I asked him why and he just smiled. Then mother came and did that too. I don't have a clue why. I fell asleep with that. Maybe they'll come and help me sleep again.

Night. Hope you're okay.

H K

Deb/Michael: Hi again. Went back to bed and Grandfather was there. BAM! The same nightmare, except this time the trees were tornadoes. Some of them were. I'm strung up and instead of waking up, he cut out my heart. After he pulled out my heart, my heart turned into a baby and then I was a baby. He put me in a wooden box and buried me. I didn't know that I was gonna die. Everything was dark and I couldn't see anything. I actually felt pretty good and secure in the dark. Maybe that's the beginning of the big empty.

My chest hurts and I have a stomachache. Gad, I itch all over!

Okay, now that I've processed this, going back to bed again.

H K again

Deb: Hi Dad --

I've been avoiding telling you this mainly because my mind bends and it hurts when it does that. And it's really horrible. As I sat down to write this, my body has grown cold. But God has told me to tell you so here it goes. You've heard some of this before and I need to tell you from first to last.

As you know, there were two satanic rites that I was forced to be a part of. The first one was in the basement of the house where there was a hole by a wall. Somebody fell in the hole and somebody had just untied me so I ran and hid in a hole in the wall.

The second one was in a clearing the woods. There's another part of me who saw this, I mean all of this second one. They had dug a hole near the trees. There was a fire. In the middle though there was some kind of pattern and people surrounded the pattern. Somebody had a book she read from and they chanted. There was a toddler baby there strung up by her wrists over the fire. I wasn't hug up at first but tied up and lying on the ground, including my legs being tied up. They took a baseball bat and hit her until she went round and round. Then they did it the other way. She didn't cry anymore but she was still alive. They said she was still alive but somebody said she was dead. They took her down, put her in the middle of the pattern and somebody with a knife cut her open and took out her heart. They cut pieces of the heart and ate most of it raw. They forced me to eat a bite too. Then they dug a hole in the middle of the pattern, put the rest of her heart into a box and put it into the hole. They threw her body into the hole by the trees. I think her name was Heather.

Then it was my turn. They strung me up by my wrists over the fire and hit me with baseball bats. I went in circles one way and then the other. They didn't hit my head though so I was definitely alive. They took me down and laid me in the middle of the pattern over the heart. A man came with a knife and Eleena stopped it. She dragged me through the pattern and my dad picked me up, pretty mad.

My mind transferred the baby as a dog, but when the other part came out I knew it was a baby. I'll admit that most of my life I've hated babies, that is until maybe 10 years ago when I was healed enough. But I love dogs. I think that some of that hate toward babies was jealousy because they got love that I didn't. But I think it was also this event and my attempt to block it.

This other part is six years old and we don't know his name.

I walked in the woods today and came to a clearing and saw this part of my first-life. It didn't scare me. I just got really cold.

H K

*****

The part that awakened was Isaac. There was significant leaking between Isaac and Deb (all the other parts of me) that connected to this trauma. Isaac was only six years old, but was so close to Deb that his mind was older than six! Also, Isaac and Michael were so close that their trauma became one after Isaac awakened.

Michael was not able to handle the trauma of the baby killing. Isaac dissociated at that time and held the memory.

The people in the forest tied up and hung something by the limb of a tree. My mind translated what I saw hanging as a dog, which might explain why I care and identify with dogs so much. But in the process of my awakenings I knew it was a baby. She was naked. They took a baseball bat and hit the baby until she swung on the rope one way, and then hit her so she swung the other way. By then she was silent.

They took her down and placed her in the center of the pattern. I then saw them cut out her heart, slice it, and each ate a piece. I was forced to eat a piece also. They placed the rest of her heart into a box and buried it in the center of the pattern. In my dissociation, I put my heart (Baby Heart) into a box and buried it. I think that when this dissociation happened, I completely separated myself from an ability to love or feel love. But I don't really know. They threw the baby's body into the pit.

When the baby was killed, I saw two angels take her spirit, comfort her, and the baby was not hurt or afraid anymore, but calm.

*****

Fran's Notes: Isaac is the part that experienced the baby being killed and his memory is pure and clear. Isaac is aware of me but not out. He came from Michael. Now Isaac is out and cried that he couldn't help the baby. His head hurt and he threw up. He wanted to die all his life. "When they buried the baby's heart, they buried me too." Isaac doesn't feel his body, except his head and legs some.

Isaac: I saw something else tonight. I was back there in the forest and saw it again. But this time I saw the angels surrounding everything and I saw the demons trying to get in and the angels wouldn't let them in.

While I was lying on the ground, I saw the baby Heather's spirit and angels came down to her and they held her. She wasn't scared anymore. They took her up with them, but one came to me. I wanted the angel to take me too, please take me too, and he talked to me. He whispered to me. He said I had to stay. He told me to remember. He told me to tell. He said that one day I'll be able to tell. And he told me to tell people that some people can try to bring evil into the world but no matter what, it seems they won't do it. Not completely. He told me to tell them that no matter what happens in life, angels are there with them. He said that we are not alone. He kissed me then and told me to go to sleep. After a while I was able to do that. He stayed with me until I did.

Isaac: Hi Dad

I know there were angels there. But I don't understand why knowing that doesn't diminish my trauma any. My mind still bends and my body gets cold and numb. I don't feel too good.

H K

Bruce: Isaac, Tell me about yourself.

Bruce (Dad)

Isaac: Okay. After Fran tomorrow. Hurts being out.

Isaac: Hi Dad

There's not a whole lot to say. I was six when I woke up in this second-life. Deb says I was like catatonic. All I know is when I woke up I was in the forest and then I just saw white and couldn't talk and stuff or move.

Then in Fran's office I woke up more and I could see and stuff but it really hurt my head to come out so that lasted about a minute. Deb tried to tell Fran what I was seeing but Deb didn't understand everything and got stuff wrong cause she couldn't get past the block. But then I came out totally and Deb/Michael was able to tell my reliving.

My head still hurts when I come out but it isn't as bad.

I'm older than six now. But I don't know how old I am.

I don't know what I'm doing. I'm supposed to tell but I think I'm doing that. I know everything about the second-life. I know about you but I don't know you though. But I think that's okay. I got enough stuff that hurts about the forest and seeing them kill the baby and not being able to do anything and me being next and getting hit by a baseball bat and seeing them eat her heart and burying it and wanting to be dead all my life. I don't do anything wrong for you to punish anyway. I ain't angry. Just scared out of my mind. My mind still bends and that hurts.

That's it.

H K

Fran's Notes: Deb drove in the woods, a tree lined road and she felt comfortable. She walked a path. She also walked the woods on her way home last appointment. "It was the first time I smelled the forest. Oh my God, it really did smell like perfume. I looked around and said, 'What is this?'"

Isaac came out. He said that when he woke up, Deb went into the woods and God talked to them and said how proud he was of them. "That's when I woke up. It was at that time, that Walter Amundson came as a black pillar and a white pillar came and took care of the black pillar. Deb stood up to Walter Amundson." It was at that time that Isaac woke up.

Isaac: Hi Dad -

Hope you're okay.

God talked to me a lot last night. He talked to me about what I saw too Dad. He said it's very very serious. Everybody who was there is dead now, passed you know, except Eleena. He said that she will be held accountable. He said that to kill his precious creation is unacceptable and they are now being held accountable for that. I said that she didn't actually kill the baby and he said that doesn't matter. She was there and participated and corrupted herself with very serious evil. I told him I ate a piece of her heart too and he said that I am a victim in all this and an innocent. He told me that they wouldn't let my parents attend any more because she saved me and wrecked the pattern on the ground when she dragged me over it.

There's more stuff but I don't remember. I went back to bed and both Mother and Jesus came but I don't remember what Jesus said either. I got kissed!! Then Grandfather let the dogs come up and they kissed me lots too. When Grandfather told them to go on to bed they jumped down but Pippin turned around and jumped back up and gave me one last kiss. Then he went to bed. Grandfather slept with me last night.

I think I'm still traumatized and stuff.

Okay, gotta get trash out. Cya!!

H K

Section Eight: New Family

Before I finished *Fractured Mind*, I gained a family! To this day, I do not understand how or why it happened; it just happened. I thought throughout my life that I would never have a family who wanted me and did not hurt me. My family now not only does not hurt me, but nurtures me very much.

Until the healing process, any physical touch hurt me. But God timed this right so that touch did not hurt. I've learned the importance of physical touch because my family's touch has healed me in a way I can't explain. Their touch has made me whole. It seems to me that Grandfather's affection and spiritual touch in the Other Realm prepared me to be able to be physically touched. God gave me a family that will never hurt me.

Isaac was awake when I gained a family. It was important to me that they know of my dissociation and my healing and they took it wonderfully in stride. Their touch helped Isaac tremendously to be healed and blended. And they helped me become more integrated.

Chapter Seventeen
Patrick (4), Timmy (3), Shannon (13) and Kale (14) Wake Up

It amazes me that my family did not know me very well when they "adopted" me as their little sister. They say it is a "God thing" and I also think it is God working in my life. And God working in their lives as well. They gave me a key to the house. Unlike any other close encounter with the people God placed in my life, my family includes me with the rest of their family, their grown children, grandchildren, brothers and sisters, and to my unending gratitude, they also have accepted me as part of their family.

Patrick, Timmy, Shannon, and Kale woke up after I gained a family. They seemed to me to be residual parts belonging to the lowest subconscious level, fourteen. Kale was the very last part of me to wake up. She did not communicate to Bruce or Fran, mainly because she did not seem to need to. They all seemed to be very small fragments with Kale being the most formed. She took the blood and pain of Kate being cut and during her awakening, she physically hurt inside. Kale had to process not deserving to be cut and the relationship between Kate being cut and the baby being cut open. I think the horror of killing and experiencing being cut caused Kale to reside in the very depth of my subconscious.

*****

Brenda: Hi Deb,

We have 2 guest rooms and would love to have you come. I will be working on getting ready for conference during this time which will include lots of piano practicing.

Brenda

Deb: Cool! Thanks! (My first thought though was that I suppose ice cream would make up for the piano. hahahaha)

Brenda: You can eat ice cream while I practice. How's that?

Isaac: Hi Dad.

I know how old I am now. I'm 9. Deb was gonna write you this but Grandfather wanted me to so here it goes. Boy I sure don't want to.

A couple of nights ago we were all in the Other Realm, all the parts, all of us. I came out of Michael you know. Well, everybody was happy and everything and there was like this group hug and they all came together as one person. Except me. I sort of watched them all be happy. Deb came over and asked me why I didn't do it too and I said it's cause I don't deserve it or anything.

I made something that looked like a wormhole in front of me except it was black. And it got bigger and bigger. I know it was the big empty again and I wanted to go into it and just die and everything. It was like a whirlpool on its side. But an angel came and he picked me up and the big empty went smaller and smaller and went away. The angel took me over to Mother and I had to sit next to her. She put her arm around me.

That's it.

I don't know how to feel better about a little girl getting her heart cut out Dad. I see the stuff in the forest all the time even though Deb doesn't.

Do you want me around? I feel awful bad.

Okay. It's way late and everything and I have to go back to bed now.

H K Dad

Bruce: Isaac, I do want you around and I want you to feel good.

H. K.

Bruce. (Dad)

Isaac: Hi Dad.

After I went back to bed last night I found myself in the Other Realm again. I was sitting next to Mother and she was holding me pretty tight I think so I wouldn't run away. Grandfather was there. Jesus came up to me and knelt in front of me. He poked me on my chest and said, "You have a good heart." I blurted it out Dad! I just blurted it out!! I said I don't care that I have a good heart!!! I feel so guilty cause she died and I didn't and I deserve to die cause I'm bad but she was just a baby and she never did anything wrong but I'm bad and I deserve it and I deserve everything!! Jesus said no, there was nothing I could do and those people were really sick. He said there was nothing for me to feel guilty about. I don't know what else he said cause I was crying too hard. I went to sleep.

Dad, we always had this dream, all of us, but it was different scenes but the same all the time. We were with some people or somebody and bad guys came in and said they were gonna kill one of us, of all the people in the room. I couldn't handle somebody else dying so I always volunteered to die. And they always took me out and instead of killing me they tortured me. That's the dream all my life. Deb put that together last night. I mean she saw the connection and I do too. I feel guilty.

Okay. Gotta go. Bye.

H K

I just thought that maybe if I hadn't run away in the basement that she'd be okay. Jesus just now told me no, they would have done it anyway. I feel awful bad.

Bruce: Hi Isaac, it must be very hard to have a dream like that. But you are safe, and hopefully you can believe that none of what happened was your fault. Hopefully you can accept the thought that you do have a good heart, a kind heart.

H. K.

Bruce. (Dad)

Deb: (to Brenda): What's your phone number? I'm leaving tomorrow. Maybe you could put me up Saturday and a couple of days?

Brenda: HI Deb,

Come on down! What kind of ice cream works for you?

Deb (to Brenda): Can I come Sunday instead of Saturday?

Brenda: Hi Deb,

You may come whenever you like. We have mint chip and strawberry swirl ready for you. It will be great fun to visit.

My cousin (she is also my ex-sister in law) from Nevada is spending a few days with us while she waits to close on her house. I am anxious for the two of you to meet.

Deb (to Brenda): Love to meet her ...... as long as she doesn't eat all the ice cream. Lol

Fran's Notes: Michael is blended in Deb. Isaac thought the torture was the right thing to do because the baby died. They said Isaac deserved it. I discussed with him the erroneous beliefs. He said, "Jesus is right here and he just said, 'You survived. Can you live with that?'" I pointed out that he has to accept his limitations and his humanity if he is to be at peace. He said he knows how to heal people and I said he needs to heal himself now.

Isaac: Hi Dad!

Hope you're okay and everything! There's some of Deb running around in me Dad.

Dad, I'm at Brenda and Don's house and they started right away saying I'm family and this is my house. It's giving me a headache and we just can't get my mind around all that. It threw us into the first-life too. People have said we're family before and thrown us away Dad. So we're trying really hard to remember that this is the second-life and Brenda loves me. But, man, I sure can't comprehend any of that. We're really really trying to TRUST. I know all the evidence is here, but I just can't get it. Deb tried to give her money for food but she said that they didn't have their kids pay for food and rent and they won't have me do that either. So I'm just vegging out with my game and my computer and trying to not be a guest because they don't want me to. I told her about Christmas and she said to come and man I sure don't know as that's family but she said that I'm family. I don't understand Dad. I gotta protect myself, you know?

Oh well. Looks like I'm here for a few days. They really are nice Dad.

H K

*****

I was unable to comprehend their generosity or WHY they would even WANT me around as their family. But I stayed about a week and left to return home.

*****

Deb (to Brenda): Hi! I got to Mary's house okay and ten minutes later we were on our way to Charlotte church. Time for me to repent of all my ice cream sins whilst with you! Hahahaha

Thank you two for the healing time and your outrageous kindness toward me!

Brenda: We love you.

Bruce: Hi Deb,

Are you still down south? Just finished a retreat at Powell Butte, OR on Friday morning and entered into another working retreat Friday evening through Sunday night with the Spiritual Formation team. I am leaving for St. Louis Sunday morning to facilitate another retreat Sunday night through Wednesday noon.

When I served the church in West Virginia and Southern Ohio, God told me to let the people love you and then you can love them. This will continue your journey towards wholeness. This comes to my mind when I read about your experience with Don and Brenda.

Blessings, H K

Bruce (Dad)

Isaac/Deb: Hi Dad!

I'm sorry it's taken so long for me to email you and stuff. Been busy with the game.

Dad, something happened to me with Brenda and Don. They had an agenda when I came over and that was to make me family. I'm trying to trust that and let them define what that means. But, Dad, they gave me a KEY to the house!! They said that they expect me to come home when I'm downstate and everything. And it doesn't matter if they're there or not, I have a place to stay. Brenda and I were at Sams and I found printer ink that I can't find here but I didn't have enough cash on me but did in my car. So I was gonna put it back and Brenda got really stern and told me that family means that if I need something that money isn't an issue. I told her I'll pay her back and she just said I know. I asked her a different time if I could give her money for food (I pay for food when I'm with Jack cause we go to the grocery store) and she said she didn't have her kids pay for food and she won't with me either. They're not parents Dad, but like big brother and big sister. REALLY big! Lol

I wanted administration because I've been stuck in the forest trauma so I told them. They know I'm dissociated and about you and grandfather as my parents. And I told them about the forest trauma. All this happened after they gave me the key. But after I told them I felt really good so didn't have administration. She said they were praying all through what I told them.

I think God wants me to experience real family. I guess I'm so used to you and Grandfather being pretty strange parents that having a strange family like this is just fine. But something inside me says yes to it all. But, Dad, I feel different inside. It's like my emotions, my need, is like gone or at least diminished. I find I don't even need to be on facebook so much all of a sudden. I've been thinking it'll go away but it hasn't. I feel really secure and stuff. Boy, I sure hope I don't make them hate me.

I've been having a recurring nightmare that I got physically fit and went to Jack's for Christmas, which is what I'm planning to do and then go over to the Kelney's. But Eleena was there and she took a kitchen knife and stabbed me several times and cut my arm. I said why and she was angry and told me as long as she can help it I'll never be pretty for a man. I get my stuff and leave and am in pain and bleeding. But I don't know what to do so I park my car under an overpass and try to sleep but can't cause I'm hurting and bleeding. I don't go to Kelney's cause I don't want to bother them and I don't want to bleed on their floor. But they call and tell me to get over there. I have no idea where the hospital is. So I'm really really scared because I think I have too many problems to be family. Then I wake up. It's the exact same dream every night, several times a night.

Pretty sure Michael's blended.

You home yet? Hope you had a great time!

H K

Deb (to Brenda): Hi Brenda and Don!

Thanks for the nice time.

Dad said to let people love me and then I can love them. Hope so!!! I can still feel your arm around me and I like that!!!

Does family mean I'm supposed to tell you that I got home okay? You didn't say so I'm not sure. Sorry I don't know things like this. If you'd rather I not tell you just let me know. You're awesome!!

H K hug, kiss --- that's code that me and Dad use so I figure it's good for you too.

Brenda: Hi Deb,

Family does mean that you tell us when you get home from a long trip. I thought about you this am when I got up and I was going to check on you. I am so glad you enjoyed your visit with us. I hope you were able to sleep well when you got to a familiar place. Don got your room here all ready for your next trip. It may sound strange, but it felt good just having you in the house even when I was not in the room with you.

H K back,

Deb (to Brenda): It's hard to trust all this. God also said he's given me you to experience some kind of family so I'm not losing everything but gaining. I admit I'm awful scared because I don't understand it. I think I'm supposed to trust and let you guys define it. I still dream about making narrative videos so maybe I'll be able to serve people that way.

Have fun this weekend! You'll do great!

H K

Brenda: Thanks for your prayers.

Bruce: Greetings Isaac and Deb,

I got home late last night from St. Louis area. I experienced a good, but intense retreat so I am tired. Your experience with the Kelneys sounds healing and that your trust level is rising - all good, better than "good" it is "great"!! The nasty nightmare might be released if you do some positive affirmation that states: "I release Eleena and her negative energy and welcome and receive the abundant love of God through the Kelney family." When you say this, stand up with your feet shoulder length apart and your two hands up shoulder

height close to your shoulders. When you say "I release Eleena and her negative energy" with your palms outward, push that thought away and exhale at the same time. With the rest of the affirmation make your arms as an embrace and pull them to you inhaling the love of God and the Kelney family - and you are correct – they are big – in wonderful ways. You will have to do this several times and for 21 days consistently. Let me know if this helps. We use positive affirmations daily and they seem to work.

Blessings to you Dr. Bruch. Keep working at your wholeness and well-being. You are making progress and I am very proud of you.

H K

Bruce (Dad)

Brenda: Hi Deb,

Families stick together. We hurt for each other and we celebrate for each other. We look forward to being together, and sometimes we get on each other's nerves. But through it all we are there for each other and have each other's backs.

I hope you are enjoying your trees. I pray you are gathering strength and wisdom from them. Be in the presence of the One. Let the power of Holy Spirit speak to you and bring you peace.

H K

Isaac: Hi Daddy.

I had another reliving this morning. Whew! This happened after they killed the baby but I don't know how long after.

It was the middle of the night and my dad grabbed me by my hair and got me out of bed. I had my pajamas on. My mom got me by my arm and my dad got a gun. I didn't say anything cause I was scared and stuff. They took me outside into the woods and my dad tied my hands together. He took me by my hair again and set me in front of them. I had a hard time standing up by myself and he'd come and take me by my hair and stand me up. He kept pointing the gun at me. I know I said, Daddy please don't kill me. And Mommy please don't kill me. But he pointed the gun at me and then he got mad and hit me with the gun and then kicked me over and over. My mom came and untied my hands. I heard him say Leave it and they were gone.

But I saw angels when he pointed the gun at me Daddy. Angels.

It took me a while before I could breathe and move but I tried to get leaves on top of me and the wind helped. The forest felt pretty good. I think I slept a little. I didn't hurt much. I know now Daddy that it wasn't the forest that hurt me any but the people did. And I get the idea that the forest didn't like it any.

But, Dad, it was the hardest thing for me to do to go back into the house. I stood there for a long time looking at the house. But I was cold. My feet were really cold. So I went in and I went back to bed.

I was 6 Daddy, not 9 like I am now.

H K

*****

This was the very last reliving I had. These horrific series of events lived in the very depth of my subconscious. My parents left me outside and I have always stood on the outside looking in. No sense of belonging. No sense of self. No caring. I knew without a doubt that I was not wanted. I was an object to be used. I lived without hope.

I believe that the leadership kicked my parents out of the coven because I never experienced anything like this again. A few days after I saw them kill the baby, my stepfather dragged me out of bed in the middle of the night and he, my mother, and I went into the forest. He told Eleena to get the rifle and she did. I had a difficult time standing, but my stepfather made me stand and he tied my hands together. I pleaded with him to please don't kill me. He had the rifle pointed at me but he couldn't pull the trigger. He hit me with the rifle, I fell to the ground, and my mother untied my hands. He told her to "leave it" and they went back to the house.

I was six, maybe seven, years old and I didn't know what to do. I knew that I had done something wrong by living. I had on my pajamas and I was cold, especially my feet. I looked at the house and eventually went back to bed. I figured that my life was just this, and I was right.

*****

Bruce: Greetings and Happy New Year!! What you are experiencing feels like the next phase of your healing experience. This phase should be relatively easy compared to the first phase of each reliving. So relax and enjoy the invitation to be loved, affirmed and empowered. The blessings keep flowing and God does seem to know what He is doing.

Continued blessings,

H. K

Bruce. (Dad)

*****

My mother, Eleena, died. Jack called me on a Saturday, Sunday I left to drive to Missouri, and arrived Monday. For several weeks, I dealt with her death. She lived in an apartment complex where other people her age lived. She made friends there.

*****

Deb: I'm still up and am dead tired now. Jack called again. Reba, Eleena's friend, got a hold of him and told him that he's welcome to stay at her house while he's there. Jack then asked me where I was going to stay. I'm laughing and thoroughly disgusted at the same time. NOBODY thinks about me and boy it is SO consistent. I told him I'll pick up an air mattress on the way down and stay in Eleena's apartment.

What do I care? I HAVE a family now who cares about me!!!

Going to bed if I can sleep. I'll deal with everything tomorrow.

H K

*****

I got an air mattress and slept in my mother's apartment for a couple of weeks. I went through all of Eleena's things while Jack went through her jewelry. Eleena lived in an independent living complex and I learnt that she had a good time there and a lot of people knew her and liked her. Quite a lot of people came to me and offered their condolences. It was one of those times I needed to focus on their grief.

With the help of my mother's friend, we put on a memorial service. I think it went well.

*****

Deb: Hi! It's Thursday evening and Jack and I are done. Can't believe it's done in a week and a half with memorial service, going through all of her stuff including her storage area in the complex, selling furniture, boxing up and moving stuff into a storage unit we rented, plus dealing with the funeral guy. I'm taking Eleena's ashes home until July when Jack and I will come back to empty the storage unit and bury her. I told Jack mid-July. We got here Monday of last week, spent all day Tuesday with the funeral guy and I wrote obits for various newspapers that the funeral guy sent to.

The memorial service was Saturday evening. Jack set up a PowerPoint and music of David singing. I led it and began with scripture about the risen Christ. Then said some things but forgot about talking about family and community. My focus was on the people there. Then whilst Jack said something I changed into costume. Eleena created a character called Elvirie that she would perform. Hillbilly. So as part of the memorial I performed Elvirie Jr. I ad lib pretty well and then read one of her monologues. But that's when I remembered about family and wanted them to know that they brought out the best in Eleena and they were her family. All in character.

Then whilst Jack started them talking about Eleena I changed back into my clothes. Then I helped take over and Jack and I helped people talk about Eleena. To end it, I read Psalm 23, then everybody held hands and I said a prayer. Quite a few people there and we didn't have enough chairs so people had to stand. People here in the complex who couldn't go heard about it and thought it was great.

Afterwards people mingled and talked. There was a man there that obviously didn't like me and Jack. And he was angry toward me. I already knew that Eleena had said some bad things about me. For the memorial Jack had set out some jewelry that Eleena made which is really good. So I chose a beautiful white necklace and went up to him and his wife and gave her the necklace. She cried. He let me talk a little and I said that when she was married she was traumatized by her husband and neither she nor I could break away from that life for each other. He seemed surprised by what I did. I don't really care what he thinks about me. I just saw his anger as pain and I wanted to give something really meaningful to them to remind them of Eleena. And maybe to help with their grief. I noticed that when I talked about them being Eleena's family he nodded so that was good too.

To tell you the truth I sort of wished somebody would think of my needs and stuff but I know you care about me Dad and Brenda and Don do. Boy I sure wanted to be with them but I just couldn't. Grandfather was and is here and he'd guide me sometimes. So I think I was just simply in God's hands throughout all this.

So Jack is gone now and won't be coming back. We were alone when he was about to carry out the last box of his to his car. I stopped him and asked if he wanted to say good bye to Eleena. He said yes and I asked if he wanted me to pray and he said yes. So I put my hand on his shoulder and we said good bye to Eleena and then I prayed for Eleena and for Jack. He cried a little. We went out and ate a late dinner together in separate cars and he left for Reba's house where he's staying. He will leave to go home from there.

I've been as mature and as strong as I know how Daddy. Sometimes I tended toward the first-life and that was hard. But I told you about the really hard part. I haven't cried although I almost did when we said good bye to her tonight.

I need to be at the writers summit in two weeks so I'm staying here. I paid for another week in Eleena's apartment so I can go to movies and stuff. Then for the second week maybe with Reba. I need to spend my weekdays in the Temple library preparing for the writers thing. But boy I need to sleep too. I also need to clean the apartment here. What a mess.

I was blindsided but people in the complex needed me to help with their grief too so I did. People here are nice I think. They seem to think I'm nice so I guess they don't know me too good!

Well. Time to go to bed. Been sleeping on an air mattress and that's pretty good. Miss you!

H. K.

Fran: **Dear Deb,**

How are you doing? I hope that the service went well and you are getting support while you are there. I am sure there will be much processing. Are you heading to lower Michigan? If you would like to talk, let me know.

You are in my thoughts and prayers.

Hugs,

Deb: Hi Fran. I just now got this email from you. Thanks! Starting Feb 15 is a writers' summit here so I need to stick around here. I paid to extend one week in Eleena's apartment and the next week I'll stay with people. After the summit I'll go visit a couple in Maryville and then go to my troll home in lower Michigan.

Take care.

*****

Shannon awakened and I experienced a last bout of toxins being expelled by my body. I think that the touch of my family helped her heal as after a time I no longer felt suicidal.

*****

Deb: Hi Dad! I thought I was done expelling toxins but boy I sure was wrong! It's 3:00 am here and I've had bad dreams all night. Really bad dreams. Woke up with my gut hurting and lots of gas. Went to the bathroom and the poop was a nice emerald green! I know it's gross telling it but geez! Even when that was common it wasn't that green. The only thing I ate different today was that the ladies here gave me some sugar free cake. I felt pretty sick yesterday but today felt fine. But now I feel like hurling. I sure wish this healing process didn't hurt and make me feel sick and be so gross. Geez Dad why can't it be over? Oh well. It is what it is. I'm confused about everything and boy I sure don't know who I am. It feels like my gut is trying to get out of my body. And now my body is falling asleep again. Hope I don't hurl.

Well, needed to tell you Dad. Ugh.

I'm leaving Eleena's apartment tomorrow and staying with Reba until Friday morning.

You ever seen green poop Dad? Want me to take a picture of it before it turns back to normal?

Bruce: No

Deb: Do you still love me Dad?

Bruce: Yep.

Deb: Hi Dad!

It's 1:00 am and I can't sleep.

I can't distinguish Isaac anymore and I've waited a while to see so I think he's in me now. I don't think any of these pieces are actually integrated but blending. None have a distinct identity anymore but it feels like they're all swirling around. Me too. Boy, if I didn't know who I was before I really don't now! Talk about chaos! I yo-yo in age all over the place all the way from four to something. I don't know how old I am. I feel pretty insecure but despite that I feel okay.

I also slide in and out of the first-life slicker than snot. And that gives me grief. I just can't comprehend that I'm a person and there's some kind of worth in me. But when I'm in the first-life God seems to talk to me. But I can't understand any what he says. When I'm in despair in the first-life Grandfather holds me and kisses me and sits on the bed with me. Boy, I've not been able to see any worth in me and been trying to for so long I think maybe I never will and just accept that. I feel like I've been bashing myself against that wall and it hurts.

This family thing sure is weird. I'm thinking that Brenda and Don have GOT to be sick of me by now but they say they're not. I mean, seriously, why on earth would they want me around? God says there's a reason why he gave me to them. But boy thus whole thing sure does conflict with the rest of my life. I do like it when Brenda comforts me. I just don't understand why she'd do such a thing. It feels kinda like when my spirit would put my head on your chest, Dad, but it's physical as well as spirit stuff. Sure is strange.

My intellect is okay though. Actually, I think it's developed some lately. Maybe the blending did that. When I focus on something I can play the role just fine because my intellect stays in the second-life.

Sometimes Daddy I think my need is just too big. I admit I've always been ashamed about my need to be loved and cared about. I just don't think I deserve any of it. And I'm not supposed to have any of that. But now, at the same time, I can't deny it either. So I'm pretty insecure. And confused all the time. But I guess God might know what he's doing giving me this family thing. I still trust the process and figure God knows what he's doing even though I don't.

Well. Maybe I can get to sleep now. Have a great day!

H. K.

Deb: Hi Dad.

I'm at the writers' summit. I had lunch today with my family and a couple of other people. I told them I have a family now and some more talk. I said she cuddles me and Brenda said yeah and it doesn't hurt me. Lori was rubbing my back at the time and she said that years ago she couldn't have done that because it hurt me. I looked at her and said you knew that? And she said oh yeah. Boy, I thought I hid that really well but I guess not! Wow! I guess if God wants somebody to know then somebody will know.

Day one down. I'm doing okay. Have a good day!!

H. K.

Bruce: Hi Deb,

Got home from Phoenix last night. The retreat went well. Hated to leave the 82 degree weather.

Sounds like you are in great company. Please say hello to all.

Have a great week. I know you will contribute to this endeavor very well.

H. K.

Bruce (Dad)

Deb: Hi Dad!

Hope you're okay and your business is growing!

I'm fine. The writer's summit was awesome and I did my best.

I'm at my troll home now. Managed to get sick right away, dang it. But my family is nice about that and nobody got mad. Actually, Dad, nobody seems to be mad at me at all here. You know, angry all the time with me. So family here in this second-life is lots different than the first-life. Boy, they're really nice to me Dad!! I discovered that how I reacted to them was exactly the way every piece of me reacted to Grandfather!! At first I was scared of them. But just like Grandfather, they didn't quit being nice. And now I'm not scared of them but I went to Brenda when I was sick. Like for real!!

I yo yo up and down in age but I'm trying to not care about that anymore. I think my foundation is now being built again with this family thing. So this experience of family is healing me. We went on a road trip (to Gladstone no less!) last weekend and it was really strange how I felt when I'm not a tag-along but part of the family. So I'm getting closer all the time Daddy. The thing, too, is that I can FEEL myself changing!! I think I'm becoming a person. I feel like I'm becoming a person. I can't explain it really. I don't connect to the first-life now like I used to when I was scared.

I saw Fran after the writer's thing and before I came down here. She's a little worried about me not feeling any worth. It sure is awesome how God wants me healed and is doing things to make that happen!

God talked to me when I was at Gladstone. Told me that he will open opportunities for me just like he did with the writer's summit. And I'll be able to recognize them when they come around. Told me to write my healing book because it will stand as a witness of the living Christ. I asked him why the Kelney's and he said that they are a righteous family, are gifted with love, and want to. He said to go ahead and do the little videos and get to nature when I can. And he told me to just experience family here as it's the way family is supposed to be.

Well, that's the news. My family is awesome and I'm healing. And I'm fine.

H K

Deb: Hi Dad!

Hope you're doing well and your business is on fire!

I'm doing great! Living in the land of giants and when I wake up I come upstairs and they say they hear the pitter-patter of little feet. hahahaha I'm healing here Dad. It's like I've got this great big wound, a rip right down the middle of me, and it's slowly growing together. Every time they touch me, like holding me or a hug, my lifetime anxiety goes down. It's just like me putting my head on your chest or Grandfather rubbing my back except it's physical now. I think that Fran paved the way for me to be able to do that physically. I can, but I don't think I can do it with other people though. I don't want to do it with other people Dad, you know, friends. It's like I let myself become vulnerable when they touch me but it's like the opposite of being hurt by touching me. I can hug friends better though now but that's not real intimate like now. When Brenda or Don touch me, it feels like when my mommy in the air put a spirit blanket over me when I was four in the first-life. It's really warm and feels really good and healing.

It's slow, but I'm turning my insides, transforming I think. Thinking I'm a whore or worthless doesn't hold the credibility it did before. I still do and I get afraid sometimes but it doesn't last very long. I want to think I'm worth being loved but boy that's a really tough one. I think, Dad, that I may have been rebelling even about this healing process because it's been so painful but mostly because I haven't been able to believe I should or deserve to be healed. But I have a family now and everything they do tells me I do deserve it and I am loved. I keep thinking I should give them money or something, beyond what I think is my fair share like paying for groceries once in a while, but Grandfather says no to that. I know you and Grandfather have been telling me that I deserve being loved but it seems to me that the touch part of it all has finally driven it home. When they touch me, the kid in me is pretty much out, so it's really rebuilding my foundation.

Sometimes I go into the first-life but they're doing some tough love and not so tough love on me. Gee, Dad, I really don't know how to thank you and Grandfather and Fran and Brenda and Don. I don't think I really can. And I think that sucks rocks because I really want to thank you.

Well, better go. Take care Daddy!!

H K

Fran's Notes: Deb doesn't comprehend family and questions if they want her because nobody else did. Brenda comforts her when she's in the first-life. She had tornado nightmares. All parts were involved and she started to separate. She got through it. She said she's in chaos all the time. She doesn't know what age she is or who she is. She thinks she's switching but then she said she's blended. Her age changes. The parts are going around and around and blending. She knows when she's not thinking right because she feels bad. All the different feelings come up. She is doing very well.

Deb: Hi Dad!

I'm busy transforming. Man, it takes a lot of energy and I noticed that when I take a step forward it really wipes me out. I'm going up and down in age but I've quit worrying about that.

It's like all the ingredients are here and they are being put in the pot. I think it's the physical touch that's doing it and being safe about it. What a wondrous act of generosity Brenda and Don are giving!

A couple of days ago God asked me if I'm ready for the new life that's coming soon. I told him I was pretty scared and he said I adapt pretty well. I asked him to define soon. He laughed at me and said it'll happen sooner than I think. He also said to stay here as long as I need. Sometimes I think it's time for me to leave but I also think that's my fear trying to run away. But NOW I have a sense of anticipation. Totally cool.

I asked if I should continue with the book and he said yes. Again he said it will be a witness of the living Christ. I'm at the point that I'm skipping over a lot of the you raising me Dad. I just think I need to keep the focus on the weaving of God in this, especially through you.

This morning I woke up then went back to bed. Once in bed I went into the first-life a little. I tried to call myself a whore and the word NOT kept getting plugged in there. That jerked me back into the second-life and I TRIED to say I'm a whore and just couldn't do it. Wow! I went back upstairs and told Brenda to thank her and she said Good. And that my monsters are not welcome here. Isn't that cool?!

So that's what's going on! Miss ya Dad! Grandfather is here but not all the time. Have a great day!

H. K.

Bruce: Hi Deb,

I keep thinking God has placed people in your journey of healing at the right time. When I think back to our fairly intense emails with each child, your connection to Fran, all the struggles you've had. All the work we did together and now the big blessing of Brenda and Don with the family, the hugs, the acceptance. Progress, progress, progress, blessings, blessings, blessings.

You are a courageous individual who still has work to do, ministry to offer. The journey continues in positive ways.

Blessings to you.

H K

Bruce (Dad)

Deb: Hi Dad! The book is coming along just fine. Keep doing good stuff!!

h k

*****

Killing for whatever reason is horrific. People deliberately killed an innocent baby so they could gain some kind of power. They responded to the most dangerous of illusions and nearly opened a pathway for significant evil to enter this world. It will take quite a lot of experiences of the second-life for me to completely heal from their acts.

My parents and others chose to open a most vulnerable crack in their psyche. They allowed themselves to be corrupted. For my stepfather to continue a lifestyle of violence against a child evidences just how deeply he allowed himself to be corrupted.

I was six years old, and the killing ritual planted deep fear and distrust within my psyche. I do not like to be in crowds. Even at such a young age, I could not believe that the baby deserved to be killed. And to this day, I wish it was me instead of her. Throughout my first-life, I believed that I deserved to be hurt and killed. Now I know I did not deserve any of it. And yet, they killed a baby in a most horrific way instead of me.

So I lived. I survived. I don't really know how I survived but I survived.

Despite the evil acts that some people do, I truly think the good people, the kind people, outweigh those who choose evil. All of my life I ran into good people, be it teachers during the early years to members of my church during the adult years. My experiences with good people helped me stay mentally healthy. Ultimately, the kind acts people do really do trump the evil acts people do. And, to me, that is what is real and that is what is important.

It's our choice.

Epilogue

This has been an amazing journey of pain and joy and healing and wonder. I am now integrated and do not see my therapist much anymore. I do keep in touch with her though.

Although I cannot quite yet comprehend family, I'm far more at ease with my family than I ever thought I would ever experience. Neither can I comprehend physical comfort from a living person. But I watch videos from time to time and see animals needing and receiving comfort from caring people, and that is helping me slowly understand and accept that comfort is something all need. Also, my family helps me experience healthy physical comfort.

Bruce is still Dad, and while we hardly ever email anymore, we do talk on the phone once in a while. He's proud of me. I am still in touch with the Other Realm just as clearly as I did during the healing process. Grandfather is still here in the Other Realm. So are my dogs.

I became aware of my mother after her death and I hope she will be able to be healed somehow. I am strongly aware that she no longer gets away with anything concerning her past actions with me. She is being made accountable, but I also am aware that she is surrounded by love.

I struggled with forgiveness. I am unable or unwilling to voice my forgiveness, but I have come to understand that my wish for my first-life parents to be healed was an act of forgiveness. That is all that I can handle and I believe God does not expect more.

I feel very much at peace for the first time in my life. I look forward to living; life is an adventure! I continue to need healing, and it is very slow, but I can perceive the wounds closing. Part of my life adventure will be to continue to heal by connecting to the earth and allowing the earth to surround me and comfort me like a blanket. I do not know how long it will take, but the horror is over and I am now left with hope.

I know with certainty that everybody can have a close and personal relationship with God. Life throws us some pretty awful curves once in a while, but God really does not want his creation to suffer. I can answer why he let it happen to me, but I cannot answer that for anyone else. That's a path we all walk. And it's a path God walks with us.

God let my parents hurt me partly because he loved them. My first-life parents had their free will, and every moment they hurt me, God was there for them. Were they able to perceive their own corruption and see the acts of inhumanity they chose to inflict upon others and turn themselves to right relationships, God would have accepted them with a love and relief I cannot comprehend. Every moment they hurt me, God was there, waiting for his beloved to stop, just stop. Had my parents been able to see, I think the measure of kindness would have matched the measure of their corruption in a way that could not have been without the choices they made. And that was God's hope for them. But they did not see.

God also let my parents hurt me so I can achieve my own potential. His act of Love during my formative years flys against my cultural and religious expectations of who God is. But I strongly think that God let it happen so I could be the person I am now, not an object, but a human being. By God allowing them to hurt me, I am able to comprehend this kind of violence people inflict upon others. And by understanding this kind of violence, I not only stand with others experiencing similar violence, I am able to comprehend God's awesome goodness and light in a balanced way. God was with me as I was being hurt and he protected me throughout my life. Furthermore, angels corrected my body during this healing process. When I was being hurt, God not only made sure I was not maimed or killed, but fractured my mind so I could live successfully in society. God placed people in my life journey to help me. And then he directed my healing. He did it because he loves me. He did it as an act of justice.

Without a doubt, everyone is beloved by God. If with humility and expectation you seek God within yourself and you seek him working in your life, you will find your Creator. Whether at any time in your journey, when your life is full of happiness and wonder, or painful, difficult, lonely, confusing, fearful, even experiencing death, seek and you will find your Creator, in whatever form or expression unique to you. Once you connect, you will experience a life full of wonder, excitement, risk, and comfort. My hope is you will know transformation, tying together your potential and the Divine.

You are not alone.

Fractured Mind
About the Author

Debra Bruch is a retired Associate Professor of Theatre at Michigan Technological University. She received her B.S.Ed. degree in Theatre and Speech from Northwest Missouri State University, her M.A. degree in Theatre from the University of Missouri – Kansas City, and her Ph.D. degree in Theatre from the University of Missouri – Columbia.

Debra is an ordained minister in the Community of Christ. She holds a Masters degree in Religion.

Dr. Bruch was active in the Association for Theatre in Higher Education, the national theatre association for the academe, especially with the Religion and Theatre Focus Group. She was on R&T's executive council for several years, was conference planner, and chair/focus group representative. Through ATHE, she founded and was the general editor for the peer-reviewed journal, *The Journal of Religion and Theatre*, from 2002 to January 2006. She is interested in the relationship between Australian culture and Australian drama, and has published and presented papers exploring Australian Aboriginal drama. By invitation, in January 2007, she traveled to Iran to attend the International Seminar on Religion and Drama on merit of her article about Jack Davis' *The Dreamers*. Debra also served as an adjudicator for the Kennedy Center/American College Theatre Festival for several years. She has been included in *Who's Who of America's Teachers* and *Who's Who of American Women*.

She has been writing plays since 1973. In the 1980's, some of her work such as *Times Are Changin'* and *Damon's Cage* were produced by universities. A one-act play, *A Ringing in My Ears*, was produced and then published in Bert's *Play It Again!: More One-Act Plays for Acting Students*. This play has been produced both inside and outside the United States. Other short plays such as *A Peace Portrait*, and *An Interview with Annas and Lucius* have been published. (Debra holds the copyrights.) In 1996, her monologue, *Pioneer Woman*, won a national competition and received an Equity production by Studio Z on "The Monologue Show" in Chicago. A few other notable dramas performed nationally and internationally are *Shepherd Witness* at the Mickey Gilley Theatre at Branson, MO, *A Vagabond Peace*, *Shoved*, and *Copper Country Heritage*. Debra also chaired a national playwriting competition for ATHE during the 1990's.

Dr. Bruch also has been an active director during her tenure at Michigan Technological University. She has directed such plays as *Macbeth*, *Taming of the Shrew*, *The Odd Couple*, *A Midsummer Night's Dream*, *Equus*, *A Moon for the Misbegotten*, and *The Mousetrap*. Debra also is keenly interested in peace and justice issues, and created a narrative video titled "Quest for Peace: Images in Snow" which was presented at the International Women's Conference on peace in June,

1993. Besides the rehearsal hall, Debra's teachings have been in theatre history, dramatic literature, script analysis, theatre appreciation type of courses, world cultures, and perspectives.

Other Books by Debra Bruch

Christian Drama for the Worship Service (2013)

Echoes of the Drum (2021)

Made in the USA
Middletown, DE
09 June 2022